QUEEN DOLLEY

Queen Dolley

The Life and Times of Dolley Madison

DOROTHY CLARKE WILSON

Doubleday & Company, Inc.
Garden City, New York
1987

Endpaper portrait of Dolley Madison by Gilbert Stuart courtesy of the Pennsylvania Academy of the Fine Arts.

Endpaper portrait of James Madison by Gilbert Stuart courtesy of the Colonial Williamsburg Foundation.

Library of Congress Cataloging-in-Publication Data
Wilson, Dorothy Clarke.
Queen Dolley.
1. Madison, Dolley, 1768–1849—Fiction. 2. Madison
James, 1751–1836—Fiction. 3. United States—History-
1801–1809—Fiction. I. Title.
PS3545.I6235Q44 1987 813'.52
ISBN 0-385-19762-4
Library of Congress Catalog Card Number: 86-8862

CONTENTS

Acknowledgments

The author wishes to make special acknowledgment to the following:

The University of Maine Library and its Interlibrary Service for providing invaluable resource materials and cooperating in the project in every possible way.

The curators of the James Madison Museum in Orange, Virginia; the Scotchtown Museum of Scotchtown, Virginia; and of the Octagon House, Washington, D.C., for providing materials and firsthand information.

Mr. Donald F. X. Finn, Executive Director of the United States Constitutional Bicentennial, for helpful correspondence and many resource suggestions.

A college classmate, Dr. Lewis E. Walton, and his wife Anne for acting as hosts and guides during a tour of sites in Virginia related to Madison history.

Dr. Edward Schriver of the Department of History of the University of Maine for his critical reading of the manuscript and valuable suggestions.

QUEEN DOLLEY

PART ONE

Scotchtown
(1778 – 1783)

1

It was gone. She could not believe it at first. Surely the string must have slipped to one side, away from the cleft between her small firm breasts. Putting her hand under the white kerchief folded about her neck, she ran swift fingers over the bodice of her gray muslin frock, even probing into the hollows beneath shoulder blades. Nothing. No bulging of a hard metal object. She felt all along the sides of the straight plain dress covering her thin body from throat to ankles, even looked under her feet dangling from the hard bench, in case it might have fallen when she sat down. No, it was gone, her most precious possession. The string, tied so carefully by Mother Amy that morning, must have come loose.

"Thee, Dolley Payne, where are thy ears? Out listening to bird songs? And thy eyes? Certainly not fixed on thy spelling words. Thrice have I spoken."

"I—I—" Miserably the child tried to focus her anxious gaze on the kindly but accusing features of Teacher John. "I'm sorry, sir."

"Very well. I will repeat. Friend Dolley, spell 'uncle' for me."

"U—u-n—" She still saw his disapproving gaze through a haze of misery. "U-n-k-l-e," she finished lamely.

"No, Friend Dolley, thee is not thinking. Thy mind is faraway. After school we will have a little time of Meeting together."

Oh no! Not stay in school, not today, when she could hardly wait to hunt along the path—! The rest of the session seemed endless. To make it worse, the readings for the day from the Book of Discipline were about sins of luxury and vanity. And when Teacher John read from the writings of George Fox, the founder of their Quaker faith, it seemed to Dolley that his long lean finger was pointing straight at her.

"Keep out of the vain fashions of the world; let not your eyes, and minds, and spirits run after every fashion. . . . Therefore, keep in all modesty and plainness."

School was over at last, and the pupils, curbing their suppressed energy while still in sight of Teacher John, filed out, casting smug or commiserating glances at the unfortunate Dolley. Suddenly she was glad she had to stay. Walking home through the woods with her older brothers, Walter and William Temple, usually called just Temple, how could she have searched properly for the lost treasure? Now another fear assailed her. Suppose one of them found it lying on the path, opened the bag, showed its contents to Mama!

"I'll wait for thee outside." Walter, always the more protective of the two boys, stopped by her bench.

"Oh no," she whispered back, "thee must not. Thy chores—Papa would be angry. I'll be quite all right."

Relieved, she saw him follow Temple, hoping they would be too full of vigor to watch the path closely. That had been her downfall this morning. She had let them inveigle her into playing tag, hiding from one another among the trees, breaking the rules laid down for Quaker pupils, one of which insisted "that in coming to School and returning home every one shall behave with Decency and Sobriety." If she had walked soberly as she should have, the string might not have come loose.

"Now, Friend Dolley, we will have our time of Meeting."

"Yes sir." She looked up obediently, expecting a lecture on paying proper attention, then, perhaps, the writing of a maxim on her slate a hundred times, as the teacher in her previous school had often made them do. But, no. Teacher John had other ideas.

"Let us follow the direction of our founder George Fox, who admonished us, 'Be still, allow that of God within thee to guide thy thought.'"

Dolley's heart sank. Oh dear! It was going to be like First Day Meeting, the service on Sunday, when they sat on these same hard benches and spent such a long time in silence, letting the Inner Light drive away the darkness of vain thoughts. She always failed somehow. Just when she began to feel all warm and glowing inside, as if there were another Presence, the bench would become unbearably hard or she would itch and try desperately not to scratch or her dangling feet would go to sleep.

Sighing, dutifully she tried to sit very still and shut out all sinful thoughts. It would be easier, she felt, to feel the light inside you if you were outdoors with the sunshine all around. But a shaft of it was slanting through the window, and she fixed her eyes on it. When it touched the bare floor it shone on the residue of dust raised by departing feet and filled it with flecks of gold, like—like bits of bright particles in a shining jewel.

No use. The sinful thoughts were back along with the desolate sense of loss, and she was reliving the events that had brought her the priceless treasure.

It was the summer before, when she had just turned ten on May 20, 1778. The family were about to move from their house on Little Bird Creek to Scotchtown, the plantation that Papa had rented and had recently belonged to Mama's cousin Patrick Henry. Before moving, Papa wanted to visit his mother and stepfather in Goochland, and to Dolley's delight he was going to take her and her older brothers with him. Mama refused to go. No! The Paynes, members of the Established Church, had been shocked when their John had insisted on marrying a Quaker, horrified when he had become a staunch convert to the faith, and there had been little intercourse between the families. Molly Coles Payne was as proud of her Welsh and Irish forebears as the Paynes were of their Scottish ancestry, even though John's mother, who had been Anna Fleming, claimed descent from the Earl of Wigton, and Molly had no intention of going where she was not wanted.

"See that thy head is not turned," she admonished her eager daughter. "Thee will be seeing frills and furbelows, and thee knows vanity is a sin. Thee, Dolley child, never forget, promise me thee will never forget"—suddenly she spoke with an earnestness that approached severity—"there is nothing—no *thing,* that is—in this world worth caring about."

Dolley found her intensity almost frightening. "I—I promise."

If she had visited Grandmother Payne's house before, she had forgotten it. She gazed wide-eyed at the multiplicity of *things*—carpets on the floors, sparkling glass and silver on the dining table, embroidered sheets as soft as a lamb's coat on the bed she slept in. But it was the clothes that fascinated her most. Papa's stepfather, John, wore a crimson waistcoat and braided jacket, silver buckles on his shoes, and a feather on his tricorne, a startling contrast with Papa's sober blacks and grays and round flat Quaker hat. And Grandmother Payne . . . Dolley gazed at her succession of gowns with open-eyed wonder—a rose-colored velvet, silks as blue as wild lupine or as green as new grass in springtime, and, oh, so soft and smooth to the touch! Then one day Grandmother was wearing plain gray, not coarse and dull like her own dress but smooth and shiny, and, pinned to her breast, the most lovely object she had ever seen, a golden butterfly with bits of bright color in its wings.

"Oh!" She couldn't help it, she had to reach up and touch it. "How beautiful!"

"You like it, child?" Grandmother smiled. Then her long white fingers were unpinning the brooch and fastening it to the front of Dolley's white kerchief. "There! It *is* pretty. It makes that drab dress of yours look almost passable. It's yours, my dear. I give it to you."

Dolley gasped. "B—but thee—I mean you—mustn't!"

"And why not, I'd like to know. Don't worry about its value. It's only a cheap little trinket. Come, look at yourself in the glass." She guided the child to a mirror. "There! With some pink flowers around that plain bonnet to match your cheeks, you'd be—well, not unattractive."

Dolley looked. They had no mirrors at home, since Quakers believed them things of vanity. She saw a delicate oval little face with piquant if not perfect features, a radiantly fair complexion, widely set-apart blue eyes, black curls peeping out from the demure Quaker bonnet. Yet her eyes lingered, not on the face but on the shining golden bauble.

"B—but I can't wear it," she mourned. "Papa would see."

Grandmother unpinned it, lifted the kerchief, and fastened it to the dress beneath. "There, child. Your father need not see it. But you'll know it's there."

And there it stayed, precious, touchable through the linen. She could even slip her fingers underneath and feel it. But what to do with it when she got home? She dared tell no one but Mother Amy, her beloved black mammy.

"Dar, chile, Ah knows what to do. Ah'll make yo a li'l bag and—"

"Well, Friend Dolley, has thee banished from thy mind all idle and evil thoughts? Has that of God within thee spoken? Will thee be more attentive now to thy duties?"

Startled out of her reminiscences, Dolley stammered, "Y—Yes. Oh —yes, sir!" Surely now he would let her go.

"Ah then, perhaps thee is ready to recite. Suppose thee spell for me the word thee failed on before. Spell 'uncle.' "

Dolley floundered. "U—n—u-n—u-n-k-l-e."

Teacher John was like his predecessor, after all. She had to write the word "uncle" on her slate a hundred times. Was it because of the hopeless frustration of that interminable exercise that for all her life thereafter, in all the letters she would write, she would always spell the word "unkle"?

It was over at last. She went to her hook on the wall, took down her sunbonnet, and pulled it over her curls. It was not an easy process, for now that spring had come Mama each morning sewed a piece of muslin across its front to shield the lower part of her face from the sun's hot rays. She drew on the long white gloves that Mama insisted she wear to keep the rays from darkening her hands and arms.

Teacher John shook his head, smiling wryly. "And we try to teach our children to beware of vanity," he muttered under his breath. Aloud he said cheerfully, "Goodbye, Friend Dolley. Thee is late and must go straight home."

"Yes, sir. Goodbye, sir."

She tripped along the path sedately until she reached the woods, afraid he might be watching. Then she began hunting, more and more frantically. Surely it would be in plain sight if she had lost it along the path, unless her brothers had picked it up. The other children would have taken other paths than the one leading to Scotchtown. But—all those sallies while playing tag among the trees! How could she remember each one? Now she was being punished for her sins, two of them, breaking the rule of coming to school with decency and sobriety and yielding her soul unto vanity.

Once she saw a glint of gold in the pine needles. Yes, and it had wings and little flecks of bright color. Heart lurching with relief and joy, she was reaching for it when it flew away. A real butterfly, not a make-believe one! She watched it breathlessly, more entranced by its beauty than sick with disappointment. Why, she wondered suddenly, could God make such a golden-lovely thing and then forbid his "Children of Light" to wear gay and bright colors?

Mama was waiting for her, looking more sorrowful than stern. So she had been disobedient and idle and had to stay after school. Mama snipped the threads holding the protective mask in place and helped her remove the long white gloves.

"Thee, Dolley," she said reproachfully, "thee must go quickly now and perform thy daily stint of sewing. Thee is more than an hour late."

"Yes, Mama." At least the boys had not found it, or Mama would have known. Better to lose it forever than to have the whole family know about her sin.

Molly Payne looked after her daughter with a terrible yearning. She had appeared so small and vulnerable in her staid little gray gown and Quaker bonnet, and—had she seen distress and appeal in the blue eyes? Sometimes she longed to just take the child in her arms and laugh and dance and forget all the warnings of sin in the Book of Discipline, the way simple, ignorant Mother Amy was able to do. Often, it seemed, the slave knew her daughter better than she did herself. But—she sighed—of course one could not encourage idleness or levity or disobedience. Folding the muslin mask and white gloves and putting them away for morning, she felt a momentary unease. Could she herself possibly be guilty of vanity? But—the child had such a soft and delicate and clear complexion, like wood anemones or dogwood blossoms! She could not let it be ruined by too much sun.

Patiently, mechanically, Dolley finished her stint. Now at least she could yield to the strain of long pent-up emotion. Finding Mother Amy in her loft chamber out in the slave quarters, she flung herself into the welcoming arms. "I lost it!" she sobbed. "I looked everywhere, and it's gone. The string came loose."

"Dar, dar, chile, Ah knows how yo' feels. But it ain't wuth cryin' ovah. Heah, let Mammy wipe yo' eyes. Dey's brighter an' prettier'n any ol' jool."

"But thee doesn't understand. I was wicked. I was being punished for my sin, for yielding unto vanity."

"Nonsense! De God Ah knows ain't like dat." Taking the child on her lap, Mother Amy rocked her back and forth as she had done since the baby was put in her arms over ten years ago. "An' yo' ain't wicked, chile. Don' let nobody tell yo' it's wicked to want a bit of prettiness. Ah knows bettah."

Dolley continued to cry her heart out against the ample bosom, until, as always, she found comfort in the warm black enveloping arms.

2

The move to Scotchtown had produced varied reactions from John Payne's family.

"Back to Eden!" exclaimed Papa devoutly, comparing its 960 broad acres with the scant 250 of his farm ten miles away near Hanover Court House.

"Jolly good!" exulted Walter, eyeing the miles of bridle paths for riding, the enticing woods for roaming and hunting.

"A Noah's ark!" The huge hip-roofed house, a hundred feet long and fifty wide, reminded William Temple of a picture he had seen of a long high rectangular shape with many windows.

"A barn!" worried Mama, faced once again with the task of making eight big bare rooms plus the great hall on the main floor and the numerous compartments of the bricked basement look and seem like home.

For it was not the first time the Payne family had moved here. Returning in 1769 from a three-year residence at the New Garden Quaker settlement in Guilford County, North Carolina, where William Temple and Dolley had been born, they had lived for two brief years on this big tobacco plantation known as Scotchtown, once a grant of some seven thousand acres, its house and surrounding buildings erected about 1732 by a Scotsman named Chiswell. Then with the breaking up of the plantation and the sale of the remaining acres in 1771 to Mary's cousin, Patrick Henry, John had moved his family to a farm purchased from his wife's father near her house at Coles Hill. But Dolley, of course, remembered little of this earlier sojourn. For her the big rambling house was an enticing mystery to be explored.

"It's a castle!" she marveled.

"Castle! This ark?" scoffed Temple. "Thee doesn't know what a castle looks like. Castles are made of stone, not bricks and wood, and they have towers and moats and slits of windows for shooting arrows.

This does have one thing like a castle, though," he conceded. "Come. I'll show thee."

In the great hall, left of the back doorway, he raised a trapdoor and, kneeling beside him, Dolley peered into a deep dark recess, exuding smells of dank residue and mustiness.

"A real dungeon!" gloated Temple, who had been listening to gossip in the slave cabins. "They say some man used to keep his wife chained in there. Suppose it was our cousin Patrick Henry?"

"Certainly not!" Mama, shocked, was quick to nip this rumor in the bud. "Cousin Patrick's wife was sick, yes. Her mind had gone, poor thing, after the birth of her sixth child, and she had to be confined, even tied up, to keep her from hurting herself. But she was in one of the nice basement rooms, with a servant to care for her, and Cousin Patrick used to visit her several times each day."

Dolley was vastly relieved. She vaguely remembered Cousin Patrick's wife, Sarah, a sweet gentle person with blond hair and a complexion like faded rose petals, who had seemed the mere shadow of her tall, dark, intensely vital husband. Cousin Patrick, the son of Grandmother Coles's sister Sarah, had owned Scotchtown and lived there from 1771 to 1778, just before Papa had rented it from Wilson Miles Cary, to whom Cousin Patrick had sold it. Dolley was even more relieved when Papa pooh-poohed the idea of prisoners being shut up in the dark brick-lined chamber.

"Dungeon, nonsense! More likely a wine cellar or a sweet potato storehouse."

But a possible dungeon, even a dark smudge on the boards of the big entrance hall which Temple darkly hinted was the bloodstain from an ancient duel could not long quench her delight in the new house. She admired the smooth shining richness of the mahogany and walnut paneling on the walls of the hall and living rooms. She went into ecstasies over the huge corner fireplaces, not so much because of their lovely warmth in winter as because of the polished black marble mantels supported by carved figures in white marble, all supposed to have come from Scotland. So keen was her delight in their beauty that years later she would remember them with fond nostalgia, even try vainly to purchase them for a far more elaborate decor. She was intrigued by the heavy black walnut doors with their eight panels. "Christian doors," Mother Amy insisted. Couldn't she see how the eight panels made the figure of a cross? Dolley reveled in the vast attic under the

high roof, ideal for playing on rainy days, even big enough to take off
her shoes in and run races with her brothers.

But best of all she loved the fascinating world outside—the flourishing English boxwood trees, one of them grown to form a perfect armchair where Cousin Patrick, it was said, used to rest; the path going
down a slope to the New Found River; the broad fields and woods and
gardens, for riding, for exploring, for planting her own little garden
plot.

Her older brothers secretly rebelled against the rigid discipline of
the Quaker household. She overheard their furtive grumblings. Why
could they not attend the dances and races and card parties as youths
of neighboring plantations did? Why must they always wear dark
plain clothes, no fancy buckles, no ribbons, no ruffles, and those round
flat Quaker hats that made strangers point and snicker? Worst of all,
why must they endure the taunts and jibes, even threats, of those who
called them British lovers, traitors, because they refused to shoulder
guns and fight for the country's freedom?

Dolley did not share their frustrations. Even her sorrow over the
loss of the treasured bauble had been short-lived. After all, golden
butterflies could be better enjoyed in joyous flight than hidden under
one's kerchief. And bright colors and silky velvety softness did not
have to be worn to give delight. As she tripped happily through the
woods on the way to school or First Day Meeting or tended the garden, she could revel in the pinks and crimsons of azaleas, rhododen-
dron, and mountain laurel, the pale yellows of St. John's wort, the
purples and blues of violets, lobelia, lupine, and bluets. She could feel
leaves and petals as smooth and soft as the silks and velvets of Grandmother Payne's gowns. Besides, as Mama had often told her, it wasn't
things that made life most enjoyable. As long as she lived, Dolley
would always be happy as long as she was surrounded by *people*.

And at Scotchtown human life abounded. It rippled and flowed
through the huge rooms and vast attic, spilled out with the rush of a
dozen young feet into gardens and fields and woods. It steamed and
hummed and pounded and clattered in the little brick buildings clus-
tered behind the big house, where Papa's thirty or so slaves cooked,
tanned, spun, wove, forged, carpentered, or went out to till the fields,
sometimes erupting into wildly un-Quaker-like songs and body
rhythms which set Dolley's foot tapping with surreptitious delight
under her long gray dress. It came riding up the hill to the impressive
walnut entrance door on horseback, in farm carts, occasionally in

elegant riding chairs or chariots, for, though Scotchtown was remote from the main thoroughfares, strangers as well as relatives and friends came visiting, curious to see this former home of famous cousin Patrick Henry. All were made welcome.

"Thee must at least dine with us," was Papa's invariable greeting. "And our home is thine for as long as thee can stay."

Dolley was vaguely aware that somewhere outside the perimeter of their simple life momentous events were taking place. A war was being fought. Sitting at the small children's table at dinner when guests were present or later in the parlor where children were permitted to be "seen but not heard," she listened to conversation that contained unfamiliar words. *Taxation. Tyranny. Continental Congress. General Washington. Valley Forge. Independence. Freedom.*

Freedom. She knew what that word meant. It was Scotchtown, with all its fields and woods to explore. It was running races with your brothers in the hope of beating them. It was getting out of school or First Day Meeting, feeling life flow into your cramped arms and legs. It was lying in the big four-poster beside your little sister, Lucy, in their small green-and-white bedroom and imagining they were in a ship sailing away, perhaps to that lovely emerald Ireland from which Great-grandfather Coles had come. Yes, and it was riding your little horse, faster and faster, the wind in your face, believing you could fly over the whole world if you wanted to—which was a feeling that once got her into trouble.

She had been racing with her two older brothers across a broad level expanse of field, and for the first time she could remember she had arrived at the designated finish in the lead. It was a heady triumph. Then, according to their custom, they were challenged to follow wherever she chose to ride. She led them in jumping all the low barriers that lay along the bridle paths—a pile of brush, a fallen tree trunk, a stone wall separating two of the fields—and the three horses took them easily. At one point the path she had chosen veered to circuit a deep gully which they had never tried to jump. Instead of turning aside as usual, in a burst of bravado she rode straight ahead, and her little mare, responding eagerly to her mood of boldness, cleared the small chasm. Walter followed easily enough, but Temple, more cautious by nature, was not so lucky. His horse landed on the slope of the gully and clambered up the side, throwing his rider in the process. Conscience-stricken, Dolley rode back. What had she done! And all because of that sudden reckless urge to be free of every obstacle! Temple was scrambling up out of the gully apparently unhurt and grinning, but Walter was both shocked and angry.

"Thee, Dolley! Has thee gone crazy? Thee might have hurt one of us or ruined a horse! Wait till Father hears!" Then, seeing her crestfallen face, he relented. "Oh, all right, I won't tell him—this time. But don't thee ever do such a thing again!"

Oh yes, she knew what *freedom* meant! But what about those other strange words?

"Mama," she broached one day when she was doing her daily stint of sewing in the Blue Room, "what's this war people talk about? Where is it? Why are they fighting?"

Molly Payne's busy fingers suddenly stilled. The two looked very much alike as they sat there, with the same bright blue eyes, lustrous pearly complexion, a few tendrils of fine silken black hair visible under the frills of their tulle caps, all a legacy of their Irish forebears. But Molly's eyes were clouded, their usual serenity disturbed by uncertainty, perhaps even fear.

"The war," she repeated, speaking slowly as if trying to assemble her thoughts. "Thee must not bother thy head with it, darling. It has nothing to do with us—we hope. As thee has been taught, we Children of Light do not believe in fighting. Even though a cause may be good. . . ." She hesitated, became silent. Then her fingers resumed their quick, skillful motions. "No, it has nothing to do with us. Now let me see thy hem on that pillow slip. Ah, child, the stitches should be much finer and more even."

It was Walter, six years her senior, who gave Dolley the explanations she sought. Freedom, yes, and independence. That was what Virginia and the other colonies were fighting for. That tyrant King George over in England had treated them like slaves, making them pay taxes they hadn't voted for, sending soldiers to collect them, yes, even massacring people up in a place called Boston. The colonies had all got together in something called a Continental Congress and written a Declaration of Independence. Remember that Thomas Jefferson whom they had seen at Uncle John Coles's house over in Albemarle County, that tall gangly man with red hair? Well, he had helped write the Declaration. And another Virginian, George Washington, was fighting the British now, only he was having a hard time, maybe even getting beaten. Last winter he had been with his army in a place called Valley Forge, and they hadn't had enough to eat or wear. But they hadn't given up. They preferred to die rather than give up their hope of freedom. Walter's eyes, blue like Dolley's, darkened. By heavens, he would like to go and join them! If only Papa . . .

"Children of Light!" he grumbled. "That isn't what a lot of people call us. Troublemakers! Traitors!"

Of course it wasn't so bad now as it was once, he conceded. In old times Quakers, as they were usually called, had had a rough time in Virginia. There had been a law forbidding any ship captain from depositing any more of them on the shores. They had been persecuted, driven out, their houses burned. Quakers hadn't been the only ones. Baptists had been persecuted, too, and others. But things were different now. In Virginia's new constitution of 1776, when it had declared itself independent, there was a declaration of rights that said people could believe and worship as they wanted to.

"Now, according to law," Walter continued glibly, "no man is compelled to support or attend any state church, nor shall he suffer because of his religious opinions or belief. We and others like us who are called dissenters are not just *tolerated*. We are declared equal with those of the Established Church, entitled to worship as we please, according to the dictates of our consciences." He had obviously memorized the words so he knew them by heart. Papa had seen to that.

Dolley, who had been listening with mounting anxiety, sighed in relief. "Then people can't really think we're troublemakers, can they?"

"Oh yes, they can," Walter retorted, darkly frowning, "and thee can't blame them. Why don't our men fight for liberty, they wonder. Why didn't Papa sign the Continental Association which agreed to stop buying things from England? Because he's a British lover, they can't help thinking. So far he's been safe—maybe because people know some of his Payne relatives are majors in the militia and his uncle Tarleton Fleming is second in command. Besides, Mama's Cousin Patrick is governor of our new state of Virginia, and everybody knows he's right enough a patriot."

"But"—Dolley stared at him in renewed anxiety—"could they do something to hurt Papa? How?"

"Well—" Walter temporized. He hadn't meant to frighten her. "They could take away his property. That's why he didn't buy Scotchtown when he would have liked to, only rented it. When people refuse to sign the Oath or fight in the Army, their property can be taken away from them."

Dolley's anxiety was short-lived, for she was naturally a happy person and the war was very faraway. Life at Scotchtown pursued its usual course with its few variations—the half-boring, half-exciting hours of First Day Meetings, when, after long intervals of silence, waiting for the Spirit to move, there would come bursts of ecstatic prayers and sermons and, in spite of the hard benches and her prickling feet, she could actually feel the warmth of that Inner Light; the monthly meetings, when the lives of all the Friends, even the children, were discussed, sins reported or confessed. Papa and Mama, John and Mary Payne, kept records of these, since they were the honored clerks, noting in clear careful script all breaches of the Discipline—gossiping, meddling, sleeping or chewing tobacco in meetings, excessive drinking, marrying "out of unity"—and recording all actions such as transfers of membership and provision for the poor.

There were frequent visits, too, to her maternal grandparents at Coles Hill on the Pamunkey River. Dolley loved the ten-mile ride in the family coach. Never did the family seem closer than when crowded into the four-wheeled vehicle with its two seats facing each other, Papa and Walter on the driver's seat, the rest of them—Mama, Temple, Dolley, Isaac, and baby Lucy (later the baby would be Anna or Mary or John)—bunched together like birds in a nest. No rooms or acres separating them, as so often at Scotchtown, or one place for men and another for women as at meetings! Even the discomfort of the back roads and wood trails, bumping over stones and ruts, slogging through mud, seemed a part of their togetherness. Dolley loved, too, the house high on Coles Hill with its wide breezy hall running through the center, its shaded veranda. But most of all she loved Grandmother Lucy Coles, with her lovely porcelain complexion, her dark sparkling eyes, the curls that escaped under the frill of her sheer white cap.

It was from Grandmother that Dolley learned about her Welsh Quaker ancestors, about Great-grandfather Isaac Winston, who had somehow managed to get into Virginia at a time when it was still a crime with severe punishment to bring in a member of the Society; who had founded a plantation here on Coles Hill and prospered; who had sired daughters as devout and determined as himself, two of whom had married Irish brothers, John and William Coles, and promptly brought their young husbands into the Faith.

"Like Mama," Dolley nodded with shrewd understanding, knowing that it was marriage to the beautiful Mary Coles that had transformed John Payne from a dutiful supporter of the Established Church into a staunch Quaker.

Not that he had yielded out of susceptibility to feminine charms in spite of the fact that his sixteen-year-old bride had been as strong-minded as she was beautiful, choosing him from among many suitors, one of whom, it was vaguely rumored, had been the already famous Thomas Jefferson. John Payne's experience of the Inner Light had been as vivid as Paul's on the road to Damascus. He had known suffering for his new faith, if not persecution. There had been estrangement from his family, though they had done their best to understand his aberration. Living on the two-hundred-acre farm John had inherited near his people, the young couple had suffered the loneliness resulting from family disapproval and separation from an active body of Friends; so in 1765 they had trekked with their two-year-old son, Walter, to the pioneer New Garden Quaker settlement in North Carolina, buying land there and becoming members of the Society. But they were Virginians by loyalty, and after four years they had taken the long journey back through the wilderness, this time with two more children, William Temple and Dolley, the latter born May 20, 1768. Not back to the isolation of their first home on Bird Creek, however. This time they had set up housekeeping on a farm given to them by Molly Payne's father, close to Coles Hill, where they had become active members of the Cedar Creek Meeting. Later, as his affairs prospered, John had moved his growing family ten miles away to the big tobacco plantation, Scotchtown.

Dolley's childhood world was for the most part a small cocoon of Quaker isolation. She attended the Quaker school three miles away with Quaker schoolmates. Her journeys from Scotchtown were to Quaker First Day or Monthly Meetings, to her Quaker grandparents, or, occasionally, to the homes of Quaker friends, like Judith Richardson and Nancy Morris, who lived near Rocky Hills. It was no wonder that to Dolley the turmoil and danger of war seemed far away and of impersonal importance. Until one day in 1779, when she was in her eleventh year. . . .

They came home from school to find an imposing vehicle in the yard, an ornate coach with a cream body and gold mountings, requiring at least four horses to draw it.

"O-o-oh!" exclaimed Temple. "Does thee see that? It must have cost a whole hundred pounds!"

The living room, huge though it was, was full to overflowing, or perhaps it was the tall figure standing before one of the black marble fireplaces which made it seem so. He dominated the scene not so much because of his height and the crimson cloak he wore over his black small-clothes but because of his voice, not loud but rich with resonance and commanding the attention of the dozen or so people gathered about him.

"So," he was saying, "the success of our cause may well depend on the courage and fortitude of the freedom lovers of Virginia and others farther south. If this butcher Tarleton continues his ravages . . ." He stopped at sight of the newcomers. "Ah! Do I see here some of the future leaders of our new free country?"

"Our children, Patrick, just home from school." Mary Payne proudly presented them. "Come, children, greet your cousin, Patrick Henry."

Dolley dutifully curtseyed, but even with her head properly lowered, she could feel the guest eyeing her approvingly. "This must be the young woman I once called a 'lovely infant' in the cradle. I can see that my first judgment was prophetic."

"I thank thee, sir," she replied politely.

So this was the famous cousin of whom Mama was so proud, though with reservations concerning his un-Quaker-like ardor for revolutionary violence. He was the son of Great-aunt Sarah, Grandmother Coles's sister, and for two years now he had been governor of the new state of Virginia. He had owned Scotchtown and lived there until his poor sick wife had finally died. Dolley curtseyed again as she was introduced to his new wife, who, Mama explained, was another cousin, Dorothea Dandridge.

"Remember?" Mama now reminded her. "Thee was named for her. Her mother was Dorothea also, and my good friend."

Curiously Dolley regarded the smiling, attractive young woman. "But my name isn't Dorothea," she felt like objecting. "Thee has always told me it is Dolley."

Dorothea . . . Dorothy . . . Dolley . . . Dolly. The choice would be a problem all her life, and not only for her, for all those who in future years would become her chroniclers. She would be called by all of these names, in fact, use more than one of them herself. But still the official records—the birth record in Guilford, North Carolina, family Bibles, real estate transfers, her will and tombstone—would all attest to one form and spelling only. *Dolley.*

Looking now at the lovely Dorothea Spotswood Dandridge Henry, daughter of one governor and now wife of another, Dolley smiled with satisfaction. She tried to be equally appreciative of Cousin Patrick's accompanying children, but the girls, Anne and Elizabeth, were too

shy to appear friendly, and the youngest, Edward, the embodiment of
his father's credo of letting his children run wild and untrained until
they were seven or eight, was soon making himself thoroughly obnoxious to his young male cousins.

"Huh! You talk like my grandmother, with your 'thee' and 'thou.'
Why don't you say 'you' like most people?" . . . "My brothers are
about your ages, but they're not farmers. They're soldiers, fighting for
freedom." "Why aren't you in the militia or General Washington's
army? Are you scared? Or won't your father let you go?"

Dolley saw Walter's face become redder and redder, his hands
clench into fists. But courtesy to guests was an unbreakable law in the
Payne household, and his anger remained bottled up inside. Temple,
more easygoing, responded good-naturedly to the taunts. "We're
Quakers, and Quakers don't believe in fighting and killing people."

The guests stayed to dinner, and Dolley, promoted now to the adult
status of eating at the family table, listened to the conversation with
mounting unease. The war, heretofore vague and remote, had suddenly become stern and possibly frightening reality. Always sensitive
to others' emotions, she could feel the heat of Walter's suppressed
anger silently smoldering. After barely tasting the first courses of
stewed fruit and soup, he let the successive servings of beef, ham, roast
fowl, and wild game, all of them his favorites, even the delectable pies
and puddings, go almost untouched. Cousin Henry, the zealot whose
hot oratorical fervor had helped fan the fires of revolution, became
now as eloquent as he had once been at the Virginia Assembly.

"You are not a British lover, Friend Payne," he said at last. "You
and I know that. I also am a Quaker of sorts. At least I am one by
birth."

"And I," returned Papa quietly, "am one by conviction."

"But I must warn you, if we win this war—and of course we must
win it, for we are in the right—you may be in real danger. Even now
your property could easily be confiscated. I confess, I can't understand
your position. For me there is only one consideration. As I expressed
it once long before our intolerable sense of grievance exploded into
violence—" Suddenly his eyes, a deep blue fringed by long lashes,
seemed to turn black, and the musical resonant voice rose in thrilling
crescendo—"But as for me, give me liberty or give me death!"

There was a long silence broken finally by Papa, speaking with quiet
but firm decisiveness. "And as for me, Friend Patrick, give me my
faith and a clear conscience or give me death."

Dolley drew a long breath. After their guest's dramatic utterance, she had felt, anything else would be an anticlimax. She had been wrong. It was like something she had read in the Bible, something about an earthquake and a fire. Yes, that was it. Cousin Patrick was both earthquake and fire. But—*after the fire a still small voice.*

Walter made his announcement almost as soon as the guests had left. "No matter what thee says, I am going to do it. I'm going to Williamsburg and join the militia. Or—or maybe I'll go north and join Washington's army. I—I'm not going to have people calling me a coward!"

That evening, as usual, they were gathered in the big living room. Cheerful fires were burning in the two corner fireplaces, their lovely black marble mantels shining in the glow of candlelight. It was just the same as always, the family all together, remote from the world, forbidden pleasures, all divergencies from the simple frugal Quaker way of living shut outside. Yet it was not the same. Somehow, Dolley knew, it would never be the same again. She waited with baited breath for Papa's reaction.

"No man is a coward," he said gently, "if he has the courage to stand for what he believes."

Walter was confused. "I—I don't know what I believe," he muttered. Then his lips tightened. "But I know what I'm going to do, and thee can't stop me."

Papa nodded. "I shall not try. Thee is almost a man, seventeen. It is thy life. Thee must live it as thee thinks best."

"I—I must?" Again Walter looked confused, like a colt suddenly finding the restraining bars removed yet loath to leave the familiar pasture. "Then I—I'd better get ready to leave—in the morning."

He was moving slowly toward the door when Molly Payne spoke. "Wait, son." He turned, obviously with relief at the temporary postponement of final action. "I've been thinking. Thee, Walter, before making thy decision, how would thee like to go to Philadelphia?"

"Philadelphia!" He repeated it almost reverently, for it was a magic word in a Quaker household, like Mecca to a Moslem, Jerusalem to a Jew. William Penn's City of Brotherly Love! What youth nurtured in the history and tradition of the Children of Light had not dreamed of going there?

Molly turned to John Payne, her blue Irish eyes very bright, her smile as beguiling as when, nearly twenty years before, it had captured the hearts of many suitors, his own included. "It would be possible, would it not, Friend husband? Our son could go? He would have friends there. Remember my old friend and cousin, Elizabeth Drinker?"

John Payne needed no persuasion. Of course. Some of the members of their Cedar Creek Meeting were about to move there, and they would be glad of Walter's company on the journey. He would make the arrangements immediately.

The leisurely life at Scotchtown quickened its pace, moved, it seemed to Dolley, with breathtaking speed. In a few days Walter was gone, and in due time a letter came from Elizabeth Drinker saying that he had arrived and was living with her family until work and lodging could be found for him. So suddenly had he left that there had been no time for the Meeting to prepare his credentials, and they were sent after him. It was all duly recorded.

"Cedar Creek, 8 mo. 11, 1779. By a report from Cedar Creek Preparative Meeting, it appears that Walter Payne has removed to Philadelphia." Certain people whose names were given, were appointed to prepare a certificate for his transfer.

The family circle was broken. The outside world had intruded with all its diversity of pleasures, politics, perils, and people, and the breach was to grow steadily wider. Dolley had been right. Things would never be the same again.

3

Scotchtown no longer seemed a snug little entity, remote, safe except for a few vague rumors and threats. Travelers stopping at the plantation told of events, not faraway to the north in places like Boston or New York or Trenton, but in Georgia, South Carolina, even on the coasts of Virginia. A British commander, Colonel Banastre Tarleton, nicknamed Bloody Tarleton or the Butcher, because he showed no mercy to the people he defeated, soldiers and civilians alike, had conquered Charleston and was moving north. It was odd, thought Dolley. Papa had an uncle of the same name, Tarleton Fleming, who was in the Virginia militia. Two Tarletons fighting against each other!

"Could this—this Butcher come here?" she wondered with a shiver.

Not likely, Temple assured her. Charleston was a long way off. Surely he would be stopped before he got far into Virginia. If that General Washington didn't send enough soldiers, there would be plenty of people here in the South who would fight for their homes and freedom. Oh yes, this Butcher would find most of the Virginians were not cowards like—like . . . Temple flushed and swallowed. Like Walter before him, he was growing restless and often, as now, his eyes kindled with rebellion. But he was more cautious than his brother, and his emotions did not easily resolve into action.

Some of the guests were shapers as well as reporters of events. One of them came in the autumn of 1779, riding not in a chariot or even in a riding chair, but on horseback. He was a small, rather insignificant-looking man, and Dolley was surprised when Papa greeted him with more than his usual cordiality to strangers.

"Our guest, James Madison," he announced to the assembled family, "is a man to whom we Quakers owe much. It was he more than any other, except perhaps Thomas Jefferson, who put into our new Virginia constitution the statute giving us religious freedom, the right to worship as our consciences dictate."

Madison, he continued, was a member of the Governor's Council of

State, and he was on his way to Williamsburg from his home over in Orange. He had consented to remain with them for dinner. Meanwhile, perhaps, he would like to look over the plantation, since he also was engaged in agriculture. Would he care to ride with some of the children?

"I would be delighted," said the guest, smiling.

Dolley was not enthusiastic at the prospect, though she had to admit this stranger was not so unattractive when he smiled. Still, her first impression prevailed. Stodgy, she had instantly catalogued him, weak-looking, and with a sallow complexion, as if he spent most of his time sitting at a desk. Short, too, not much taller than Temple, who was still in the gangly, growing stage. But of course if Papa wanted them to take him to ride . . .

It was a glorious autumn day, the air heady with scents of ripened grapes and sun-drenched grain and delectable odors drifting from the smokehouse. The dogwoods were turning their brilliant orange-red and the locusts their bright golden-yellow. It was the kind of day to be riding hard, jumping barriers, taking off your bonnet (if you were far enough away so Mama would not be looking) and letting your hair stream out behind you in the wind; not to be riding demurely with a stodgy stranger, listening to Temple dutifully giving details about this field and that, which ones were for tobacco or wheat or corn and why, what the yield of each had been, and hearing him and the stranger talk interminably about dull things like irrigation and crop rotation and the best kinds of fertilizer. Finally she could stand it no longer.

"Why don't we just take a ride?" she suggested when there came a lull in the male conversation. The guest seemed agreeable, and she led them off over the path she liked best, the one with all the barriers they had devised for jumping. All right, she told herself gleefully, let's see what this old sobersides can do when he's not hunched over a desk or writing state constitutions!

Somewhat to her disappointment he proved to be an excellent horseman, taking all the jumps with an easy precision which Temple, always a bit hesitant, never quite equaled. Presently she dropped behind her brother, letting him take the lead, as was proper. Mama, she knew, would not approve of a girl's being so forward with strangers, especially when she was only eleven years old. They continued along the path but, with the more cautious Temple leading, at a more moderate pace. Dolley adjusted to the slower rhythm, but unwillingly. She still felt like breaking loose, leaving behind these earthbound companions who could see nothing but crops and fertilizers and grain sales in this world that was bursting with motion and color. She envied the cardinal that went soaring up out of a red cedar tree, nothing to keep it from flying away up into the clouds if it wanted to.

They came to the place where the path veered off to skirt the deep cleft, and of course Temple turned aside to follow it, probably remembering his unfortunate accident. There it lay ahead, the deep gully, to Dolley's restless urge a tempting challenge. And why not? Walter was no longer here to admonish her. Who was to stop her? Certainly not this stodgy stranger. Suddenly she dug her heels into the sides of her little horse and headed straight for the yawning cleft, just as she had done once before. It was a wonderful feeling when her mount responded, taking her across with a long flying leap—only just across, however. To her surprise she found that the guest had followed her close behind—yes, and had landed skillfully with more space to spare than she had herself. A bit chastened, for there had been one frightening moment when she had seemed to hang on the edge of nothingness, she rode home docilely behind her two companions.

"Thee had a nerve!" Temple accused her later. "Suppose he had taken a tumble! What a way to treat an important guest! Papa would be angry."

"Yes," Dolley admitted meekly. "I guess I wasn't thinking. But—he didn't have to follow me. Thee was the one leading." Fortunately she knew she could depend on Temple not to tell Papa about her escapade.

Dinner promised to be a very dull affair. The guest sat stiffly and properly, the muted light making his complexion seem even more sallow in contrast with the dead black of his coat. The stark whiteness of his neckcloth did little to relieve the monotony. He and Papa talked about various things—crops, the price of tobacco, the depreciation of paper currency, the difficulties Governor Thomas Jefferson was having raising supplies for the Continental Army. Madison seemed slow and diffident about expressing his opinions. Only when he spoke of Jefferson did his gray eyes light with a gleam of enthusiasm which turned them almost blue.

A prig, thought Dolley. An old sobersides.

Then suddenly he smiled, and there came again a transformation. "You have a fine plantation, Friend Payne," he said pleasantly, "and some—shall I say—unusual children. Your son must be a great help to you. He knows your fields like the pages of a favorite book. And your daughter—!" He glanced toward Dolley with a whimsical twinkle in his eyes. "Children! A perplexing task, I should think, rearing them. Something I know nothing about. Twenty-eight years old and still unmarried! And, though I was the oldest child, my surviving brothers and sisters are all much younger. But I should think it might be a little like training a horse." He gave a deprecating little laugh. "I remember having one little mare that I was trying to break to the plow. Beautiful, lively little animal. I never succeeded. Somehow she was always just one big jump ahead!"

Dolley made a small choking sound, unnoticed in the general laughter. She hid her flushed face behind her napkin. And she had thought the guest dull, an "old sobersides" with no sense of humor!

"Well said," agreed Papa ruefully when all was quiet again. "Thee has expressed the problems of a parent exactly."

Conversation became serious again, and the two men returned to their mutual problems as planters.

"The most serious liability for the plantation owner," said Madison finally, "is slavery. We can't run our big estates without slaves, yet they are an intolerable care and expense, to say nothing of the burden on our consciences. How can we logically be fighting a war for freedom and democracy while claiming that we have the right to own other human beings?"

Papa's face lighted. Never had Dolley seen him look so radiant, not even in Meeting when he had sometimes seemed transfigured by the Inner Light.

For many years, he explained with unaccustomed frankness, Quakers of Cedar Creek and other Meetings had struggled and suffered because of their conviction that slavery was a grave sin, yet they themselves were slaves to the system. They were forbidden by Virginia law to free their slaves. And, as Friend Madison had suggested, how could they possibly run their big tobacco plantations without them? Yes, and what would happen to the slaves if they could and did free them? But he was surprised and relieved to find that some other planters, not Quakers, felt the same way.

"Oh yes," Madison assured him, "there are many of us. I could give you some names—our governor Thomas Jefferson, General Washington himself. I believe," he continued, his rather low thin voice suddenly becoming stronger, almost melodious, compelling the attention of all at the table, even baby Anna, who regarded him with wide-eyed wonder, "that slavery is incompatible with democracy. No matter how democratic in name a government may be, if slavery prevails, it must be aristocratic in fact. Power is in the hands of property, not people. All ancient governments were therefore aristocracies. Power was exercised for the most part by the rich and easy living. Let us hope it will not be so in our new country."

Madison left soon after dinner in order to get farther on his journey before dark. He was due at the Governor's Council, and it was a long ride to Williamsburg. The family all gathered to bid him Godspeed.

An unusual guest, thought Dolley, and full of surprises. Small and insignificant-looking, yes, certainly so beside Cousin Patrick. But just now, sitting straight and high on his horse, he had seemed a giant. And he had cheerfully accepted her challenge and showed it for what it was, an act of foolish weak bravado. Stiff, an old sobersides? But he had made everybody laugh at the table, and that clever joke he had made about her riding! Comparing her to an unruly horse! Talking in a low weak voice that could hardly be heard, as if he were bashful, yet when he had something important to say sounding like a Quaker filled with the vigor and heat of the Inner Light!

"A queer fellow," commented Temple.

"Yes," agreed Dolley thoughtfully, "but—sometimes not so queer."

4

The war . . . Slavery . . . As months passed life at Scotchtown seemed to resolve itself into these two issues, each moving inexorably toward some uncertain climax. Feeling against Quakers grew more pronounced, erupting at times into violence. Word came that in some place in the North members of the Society had been charged with being British sympathizers, taken to court, and sent into exile. At the Annual Meeting which Dolley and her family attended, usually for children the most festive occasion of the year, with Quakers coming from miles around and living for several glorious days in tents, services were interrupted by outraged neighbors shouting invectives and even throwing stones.

"Quaker, Quaker, troublemaker!" . . . "Traitors!" . . . "British lovers!"

The war was being fought now almost wholly in the South. A general named Cornwallis had gained victories in the Carolinas and was moving toward Virginia. Tales of the depredations of that "Butcher" Tarleton were arousing panic, causing many plantation owners to send their harvest crops west for safety, pack their valuable assets, and make ready to evacuate in case of invasion . . . yes, even get their slaves to fashion "chastity belts" to protect their women against possible molestation by Tarleton's Hessian "savages." Not Papa. He continued to plow his fields, harvest his crops, store them in the usual outhouses, and worry more about his sin in owning and exploiting blacks than about a war he could not conscientiously support.

It was Mama who decided to put some of their long-enunciated convictions into action. The family was all together on a day early in January 1781 when she made her announcement.

"I shall go to Philadelphia," she said calmly.

There was consternation. "But—I cannot possibly leave right now," objected Papa.

"Of course not. Thee has work to attend to. I shall go alone."

"But—the children—"

"Mother Amy is quite capable of caring for the children. She is almost as much their mother as I am, has been from their birth. And my firstborn is in Philadelphia. I would learn how he fares, and also, more important, what life is like in that City of Brotherly Love. I have long had the idea that we should go there. I want to leave as soon as possible."

"But—not now, my dear, thee cannot go now, not in winter. Why, it's hundreds of miles! And with the war . . . If thee must go, wait until spring!"

Mary Coles Payne was a determined person. She had proved it through the years by choosing from all her admirers this one man, marrying him at age sixteen in spite of her parents' objections, bringing him by power of example (or possibly a bit of persuasion) into the Quaker fold. So now she made her preparations, those not privately arranged already. According to the Cedar Creek records:

"On the 13th of 1st month, 1781, Mary Payne informed this meeting that she proposed in some short time a journey to Philadelphia, and requests a few lines certifying her right of membership with us."

The family saw her off, Papa trying to the last to dissuade her. She could not possibly realize the discomforts and hardships she was facing—days, weeks of travel through snow, ice, mud, almost pathless forests, fording streams, by stage, coach, ferry, nights in cold noisy "ordinaries" filled perhaps with rowdies and soldiers, not knowing what dangers of war she might encounter.

"No matter," she assured him. "I shall get there. I shall see our son. I shall find out if this Philadelphia is the Quaker paradise they say it is. Don't worry. I shall manage."

She did. Some weeks later her friend Elizabeth Drinker wrote in her journal: "1781, 2 mo., 5.—Molly Payne spent ye day, and lodged with us. She and son Walter breakfasted ye 6th." And letters from her finally arrived telling of her safe, if uncomfortable journey.

Mama returned in due time, as unwearied and buoyant as if she had been on a day's excursion to Coles Hill, more so, in fact, for she was exuberant over the discoveries made on her journey. Walter was well. He had found work and was a respected member of his Quaker Meeting. And Philadelphia was the haven she had always dreamed of. No disdain there of those who claimed to possess the Inner Light, no exile to some wilderness community! Philadelphia was the home of Quakers, where they were respected, prosperous, solid citizens of the community. And, best of all, there were no slaves! They must move there as soon as possible.

Papa agreed. But not right then. He would not sell his slaves. Who knew how some other master would treat them? And he was not allowed to free them. But the time would come. That young Madison and others down in Williamsburg were trying to change the law. They must wait. Mama assented, with reluctance. She did not enjoy waiting.

The family had other concerns that year of 1781 than the evils of slavery and the possibility of moving. The war had come into Virginia. General Cornwallis had advanced from the Carolinas and was plundering the country. He passed within a few miles of Scotchtown. Another British contingent under Tarleton, the Hunting Leopard, was burning crops, confiscating food, raiding barns and storehouses, carrying off horses or cutting the throats of those too young to be of use, attempting to destroy all that enabled the colonists to wage war. He had raided plantations along the James River, where some of Papa's Tarleton kin had their estates, in at least one case tearing the Tarleton coat of arms off the wall. Planters were moving their families into safer places. Thomas Jefferson sent his wife and daughters away from his home at Monticello.

Papa refused to yield to the prevailing hysteria. Let Tarleton and his marauders come to Scotchtown if they chose. He would not run away.

"If we refuse to fight," he said simply, "we should take the consequences."

Tarleton came. Papa and Temple were in the fields when the troop of redcoats came pouring along the road at the foot of the hill in a long undulating crimson tide. Mama stood at the door and watched them, the children gathered in a half-fascinated, half-terrified group behind her. The tide did not flow past. It came straight up the hill, led by a tall commanding figure riding a magnificent horse.

"Quick!" Mama ordered Mother Amy. "Take the children to thy cabin! Keep them there!"

"B—but—you, Missy, I can't leave you!"

"Go!" Molly Payne stamped her foot. "Quick—go!"

Obedient but reluctant, the servant herded the children toward the rear door, stopping only to cast an anxious, appealing glance over her shoulder. Once outside, eleven-year-old Isaac broke away and disappeared around the corner of the house.

"Mercy me, dat chile! Whatever shall Ah do?"

"I'll get him," Dolley assured her, starting after him. Troubled but helpless, Mother Amy hustled the two younger children, Lucy, aged three, and two-year-old Anna to her cabin behind the kitchen and warehouses.

Dolley found Isaac crouched behind a thick hedge of English boxwood. She seized him by the shoulder. "Thee, Isaac! Thee heard what Mama said. We have to go with Mother Amy."

But instead of yielding he pulled her down beside him. "Hist! Look! We can see it all from here."

Dolley peered through an opening in the glossy green leaves. "Oh!" Too paralyzed then with fear to move, she stared at the red tide flowing up the hill, the tall determined horseman in the lead. She could even see his face under the helmet, looking as if someone had carved it, not too skillfully, out of a piece of hard rock. That man Tarleton, of course. No wonder they called him a butcher, a leopard. He looked as if he could snarl.

He did now, stopping just at the foot of the steps leading up to the open door. "You there, Patrick Henry!" he shouted. "Despicable traitor! We know this is your house. Are you in there, hiding? Come out! Come out, or, by heavens, I'm coming in after you!"

Was Mama still there, standing just inside the door, as they had left her, or, as Dolley hoped desperately, had she followed Mother Amy to the cabin?

The Colonel hesitated, head raised as if listening. Sunlight flashed on his sword as he drew it from its sheath. Then, whipping his horse, he rode straight up the steps and through the doorway. Dolley could hear the dull thud of hoofs on the oak floor of the great hall. Then . . . silence . . . or was there a murmur of voices? She closed her eyes, as if to shut out the horror that might be taking place. That sword! Would there be time for Mama to cry out if—? Did the Butcher kill women as well as horses?

Time passed . . . minutes . . . hours? Then again there was a clatter of hoofs, and the rider emerged, descended the steps, shouted a command, and the red tide flowed down the hill, ebbing back along the road by which it had come.

For a while Dolley and Isaac did not move, just looked at each other in wonder. Then slowly they made their way back around the house, hardly daring to enter for fear of what they might find. Dolley's heart lurched. Mama was there, but not standing as they had left her. Had she fainted? Was she—? Then she burst out laughing, she could not help it, the relief was so great. Mama was down on her knees, wiping with something—her petticoat?—at the marks made by those horse's hoofs!

"Go get Mother Amy, children," she told them. "We must get soap and water and scrub this floor. Ugh! That awful man with his horse!"

Papa came running, his face white.

"It's all right," Mama assured him calmly, wiping the dust off her hands. "He thought Cousin Patrick still lived here. When I told him he had sold the house and was no longer here, this Colonel Tarleton or whoever he was just turned around and went away. But just look what his horse did to our floor!"

Later, when she was older and wiser, Dolley would wonder. Was that what had turned the Hunting Leopard about in his tracks, turned him into the semblance of an English gentleman? Or was it the sight of a slim woman in a sober Quaker gray gown, white cap and kerchief, standing with quiet courage in his path, unarmed and defenseless, greeting him courteously and without hostility?

That was the nearest the war came to Scotchtown. In October, General Washington and his French allies defeated Cornwallis at Yorktown, and battles ended in the South. Though the war was not over and negotiations would take many months, for all practical purposes peace had come to Virginia. And in 1782 the law was changed making it legal for owners to give letters of manumission to their slaves. Molly was triumphant. Now they could really plan. The gates of paradise had opened.

It was a lengthy procedure. Each slave must be given a paper of manumission and, if possible, a position he could fill on one of the other Quaker plantations. The horses must be sold. Possessions must be packed to be shipped by water. Though Mother Amy also was given her paper, she chose to go with them, and the cook and two housemaids would also accompany them, but as freed women, to be paid wages. Papers must be secured from the Cedar Creek Meeting.

"On the 21st of Second Month, 1783," the records read, "John Payne requests a certificate for himself and family to join themselves to Friends in Philadelphia." And the following month the certificate of removal was granted for "John and Mary Payne and their children: William Temple, Dolley, Isaac, Lucy, Anna, Mary, and John." John was an infant born that same year.

Dolley was torn between anticipation and regret. Hundreds of houses all in rows and bunched together, streets instead of little paths and lanes, places called stores where one could buy cloth for gowns and kerchiefs instead of having it spun and woven by servants, even silks and velvets such as Grandmother Payne wore! But no fields to ride over and fences to jump, worse yet, no horses to ride! No woods to ramble in and pick wildflowers and listen to birds and marvel at golden butterflies. Worst of all, no old friends. But at least she could write letters to them. She wrote one now, to Judith Richardson, near Rocky Hills.

"I cannot think I am nevermore to see thee my dear Judith." She was about to leave for Philadelphia, she went on to explain. She could not come to visit them as planned but urged them to come and visit her. "Adieu, my dear. May the smiles of Fortune be equal to thy merit."

The day came at last. The coach and six that was to take them to the place where they would meet the first stage was ready and waiting. Papa was still busy somewhere. About to climb into the coach after Mama and the children, Dolley suddenly turned and ran back into the house. She climbed the stairs and gazed into the echoing emptiness where she had played and raced and dreamed on rainy days. Downstairs she looked into the green-and-white bedroom where she and Lucy had slept, tiptoed into the blue room where she had sat beside Mama or Mother Amy learning to sew and sat quietly, seen but not heard, in the presence of guests. She ran caressing fingers over the smoothly polished black marble on one of the mantels and its intricately carved supporting fingers of white marble. Never, she thought, in any of the houses she might live in in the future could there be anything so beautiful.

"Thee, Dolley!" called Mama in her most peremptory voice.

"We are leaving," said Papa in milder tones as he stood waiting for her in the front doorway.

"Yes, Papa."

But she came reluctantly. For it was not just Scotchtown she was leaving behind. It was childhood.

PART TWO

Philadelphia
1783 – 1793

1

"July 9, 1783," Elizabeth Drinker reported in her journal, "John Payne's family came to reside in Philadelphia."

It was a new world, a new life. It was like leaving a quiet, unruffled backwater to plunge suddenly into a rushing, swirling torrent. Dolley could not believe her eyes. Over thirty thousand people, she was told, all living in such neat brick houses, so close together that there was scarcely room to walk between them! Wide-eyed and timorous, she roamed the narrow streets while her new friend, Sally Drinker, proudly pointed out the city's landmarks—the State House with its great bronze bell where the Declaration of Independence had been signed, Christ Church with its chime of bells which had cost nine hundred whole pounds, the Indian Queen Inn where rich and famous travelers stayed, William Penn's jewellike little house near the Delaware River, and, close by, the famous Treaty Elm where Penn had once stood wearing his blue sash and flat Quaker hat and made peace with the Indians.

"Even the British," Sally told her, "showed it proper respect. They placed a soldier to guard it so the troops would not cut it up for firewood."

Only at one historic spot did Dolley's admiring gaze cloud with dismay, where, at the west end of Market, on Third Street, there stood a platform high above the ground fitted with two crude instruments of torture, the whipping post and pillory.

"People come here on Saturdays, which is high market day, between ten and eleven," said Sally, "to watch the prisoners standing with their heads and arms pinioned, stripped to the waist, being beaten with lashes, their backs bleeding."

"Oh!" Dolley shivered. She would take care to stay away from this place on Saturdays, yes, and on every other day.

It was the people more than the buildings that she found intriguing. So many of them! "In my first thirty minutes in Philadelphia," she was to confess long afterward, "I saw more people than I had observed in all of my previous life."

They rode through the streets in chairs, sulkies, farm carts, elegant carriages, chariots. They gathered on their little porches in front of the high, narrow houses. They crowded about the "crier of news" on the street corners at the clanging of his bell. On market days they swarmed to the stalls in the tavern sheds where produce was brought from surrounding towns or from ships arriving from the West Indies.

But most of all Dolley enjoyed the promenades along the Commons on the shady side of Chestnut Street, where in the afternoons, it seemed, all the young people in the city gathered. It was like a big parade. She gazed in astonishment, yes, in delight, at the gay colors and bright finery—men wearing close-fitting knee breeches with silk stockings, pointed shoes with shining buckles, crimson and purple waistcoats, outer coats or capes, some with enormous silver buttons.

"The wealthier the person, the bigger the buttons," Sally explained sagely.

The women and girls were even more resplendent in gowns of silk and velvet and brocade, skirts billowing out under wide hoops like balloons, bright-colored stockings visible beneath their voluminous petticoats, huge bonnets that resembled the folded-back tops of the two-horse vehicle called a calash.

"They cannot be Quakers," Dolley commented once a little wistfully.

"No? Thee'd be surprised." Sally grinned. "Some of them are—at least they think they are. Oh, they don't belong to our Meeting. If they did, they'd be put out. We call them 'wet Quakers'!"

However, Dolley discovered, even the Meeting with which the Paynes allied themselves was far less strict than that of Cedar Creek. To her secret delight some of the women's gowns, though simple and modestly cut, were of silk, even satin, and, fingering the bright, shimmering fabrics in the stores where Sally took her, she vowed to have such a gown sometime herself, gray, of course, but as soft and smooth as the one Grandmother Payne had worn with the golden butterfly.

After staying for a short time with the Drinkers, the Paynes moved into a rented house, one of the tall narrow buildings in a connected row, two stories and an attic with a tiny porch in front, every one like every other, like the identical paper dolls Mother Amy used to cut out in a long strip. No garden, only a few scruffy trees in back. The lower story had two rooms, the one in front, like every other in the row, intended for shop or office. Until Papa should decide what kind of work to do, it remained bare and cheerless. The back room, with its whitewashed walls and sanded floor, was the family living room where they ate meals, gathered around the open fire, and entertained guests. As winter approached, it was the one warm room in the house.

On the second floor were the bedrooms and a small sitting room where they took special invited guests for afternoon tea. No fireplace here, and they shivered as they ate the crisp rusks and little cakes, sipped the fragrant brew from the familiar egg-shell china cups, all too unhappy reminders of the warmth and generous spaces of Scotchtown with its huge marble fireplaces, its big rooms, its immense attic and basement, its surrounding fields and woods and fresh air and open sky.

In the house Dolley felt stifled. Sharing one small bedroom with her three sisters, Mama and Papa and baby Philadelphia occupying the other second floor bedroom, with Mother Amy and the boys in the attic, she seemed to have barely room to breathe. No big attic to run races in and stretch one's limbs, no garden to dig in, no bridle paths to run on her horse—worse yet, no little horse! Even on the walks she took with Sally and other young friends, though leading to exciting places, she had to walk with ladylike sedateness, as careful to keep her shoulders straight as at a formal tea party, where it was not permissible to lean back in one's chair.

But the new life had its compensating relaxations. There was the hour each day when work was done and the weather was good that the women all along the street donned their best chintz frocks and freshly starched white aprons and gathered on the tiny front porch, called a "stoop" by Philadelphians, where they could chat with their friends on neighboring porches and, even under Mama's watchful eyes Dolley and her young friends could exchange glances and greetings with the young men who took this hour for walking up and down the street.

Molly Payne was not pleased to discover that discipline was less strict among the Philadelphia Quakers than in their Virginia Meeting. Reluctantly she permitted Dolley, and later Lucy, to join with other young people in attending parties, picnics, jaunts into the country. They were chaperoned of course, but both sexes were together, even paired in couples. Dolley, just turned fifteen at their arrival, blossoming into glowing and beguiling womanhood, sunny of disposition, interested in everything and everybody, was immediately welcomed into the youthful coterie connected with the Drinkers. She entered gaily into the games popular at such parties: London Bridge Is Falling Down, I Sent a Letter to My Love, Go Round and Round the Valley, Forfeits, with an object hung over one's head, while the holder demanded, "Fine or superfine?" Somehow the feather blown for selecting a partner more often than not was wafted in her direction.

"She came upon our cold hearts in Philadelphia," one of her new friends reported later, "suddenly and unexpectedly, with all the delightful influences of a summer sun from the sweet South in the month of May."

But popularity did not always nurture friendship. One day in July 1784 Dolley went with a group of young people to the Drinkers' country place at Frankford. There were eight in the party, all paired in couples, Walter with Sally Drinker, Dolley with a young Quaker named Jacob Downing. Sally evidently resented Jacob's too obvious attentions to the attractive sixteen-year-old Dolley and expressed herself in no uncertain terms.

"A squabble," Elizabeth Drinker noted in her journal.

Fortunately the rift in friendship was soon healed, for soon after Jacob Downing spoke to Henry Drinker, Sally's father, asking for her hand in marriage.

Dolley could not have cared less about the loss of a possible suitor. Though most girls at sixteen were considered of marriageable age and looking for husbands, she had no interest in romance. While the new nation was celebrating its finally assured independence, the treaty having been signed, General Washington having been greeted with huge crowds, bells, and parades on his way through Philadelphia after taking leave of his army, Dolley was exulting in her own small luxuries of freedom. Most of all she enjoyed occasional visits to Haddonfield, New Jersey, a stage and horse-ferry trip of some fifteen miles to the southeast of the city, where she was the guest of Hugh and Mary Creighton, Quakers who ran a public tavern for travelers on the way from Philadelphia to New York.

Normally Quakers did not approve of taverns, and Molly sternly frowned on visits of more lax young friends to Gray's Gardens, a pleasure resort near the city strictly forbidden to her children (hopefully Walter and Temple and Isaac as well as Dolley). But the Creightons were cousins, Mary a strict Quaker, and Dolley departed on these excursions with only mild objections and many stern injunctions.

"Thee will remember, child? Thee will always be true to thy Quaker faith?"

"Yes, yes, of course. I promise."

The care of the new baby, little Philadelphia, sickly from birth, limited Molly's oversight of the more healthy of her brood. Fortunately she was never apprised of some features of these excursions— frolicsome rides on the passing stagecoaches with the young Creighton cousins to a point from which they could easily walk home, shopping trips to Trenton with Mary Creighton when, while her cousin was buying supplies for the tavern, Dolley could wander through Green Street and Pinkerton Alley shops and gaze her fill at all the gorgeous colors and fabrics, even pretend she must choose among the forbidden luxuries for stuffs to make herself new gowns. And she was as popular there in Haddonfield as back home in Philadelphia.

"I can well remember her," one of the young people recalled much later, "as being of slight figure, possessing a delicately oval face and nose tilted like a flower, jet black hair, and blue eyes of wondrous sweetness."

It was in Haddonfield that she was exposed to one of the fiercest temptations of her youth. She soon discovered that Hugh Creighton was not a strict Friend and Mary was much more easygoing than Molly Payne had imagined. Dolley and one of the young cousins were preparing to attend a lively party one evening when the Creighton miss appeared in a very un-Quaker-like gown of sky blue silk which shimmered like a rippling pool in sunlight.

"Oh!" Dolley was almost speechless with surprise and admiration. "How—how lovely! Thee—is really—going to—wear it?"

"Of course. Why not?"

"But—we Quakers—what William Penn said! 'Let thy garments be plain and simple . . .'"

"But this is plain, all one color, and simple. Thee should see some of the ruffles and furbelows some Quakers I know wear! And thee shouldn't be wearing that old dull gray thing, not to this party. Here! I'll lend you one of mine."

Before Dolley realized what was happening, a soft silken cloud descended about her shoulders. Skillful fingers were hooking a tight bodice encasing her small rounded breasts and slender waist. She was being pulled to a mirror in which appeared a vision in glistening rose, the color of meadow beauty or mountain laurel, a stranger with sparkling eyes, pink cheeks, lips parted in unbelieving rapture.

"There! Thee must wear it tonight. It's as if it were made for thee!"

Dolley gazed at herself, an unaccustomed privilege, for there were no mirrors, invitations to vanity, in the Payne house. Her fingers fondled the soft folds, as once they had caressed the shining delicacy of Grandmother Payne's gown. She could actually wear this for a whole evening, be the stranger she saw reflected. And why not? Mama would never know. William Penn and his stern admonitions were long dead.

"Well?" Her young cousin grew impatient. "It's getting late. We ought to be going. Thee will wear the gown?"

Slowly Dolley turned from the mirror. "No. I—I'd like to, but I can't. I promised my mother . . . Unfasten it, please."

As she donned the familiar dull gray, hid her white shoulders beneath the discreet kerchief, she felt as if she were awakening from a tantalizing dream into hard reality.

In spite of all its advantages, Philadelphia was not proving the Eden that John Payne had envisioned for his family. He was soon suffering financially. Expecting the sale of his Virginia property would make possible the style of living to which they had been accustomed, the depreciated dollar and the galloping inflation following the war soon depleted his funds. He was unable now to feed his family from his own land, and prices were soaring. The rent of a modest house was three hundred dollars a year. The price of beef had risen to thirteen pence a pound, fowls to a dollar a pair. He must find some means of support. Starch! A commodity that was almost impossible to buy in the Middle Atlantic states, yet highly in demand, and could easily be extracted from corn, potatoes, wheat, and other grains not hard to obtain.

Some months after his arrival in the city he opened a small starch factory, investing all available funds in the plant and necessary equipment. They were obliged to further curtail expenses and move to an even smaller house. In 1785 they were living at 410 Third Street. John's little factory was on the lower floor, its exudations coating all the living quarters above with a powdery white film. He operated a small store on Fifth Street between Market and Arch.

Dolley cheerfully adjusted to the enforced changes, though, with nine people crowded into the second story and attic of the even smaller house, she often thought nostalgically of the many huge rooms at Scotchtown. There were other still more difficult adjustments in the offing. The former slave whom they had brought with them as a cook died. Since servants' wages had mounted to a prohibitive dollar a week, Molly, Mother Amy, and Dolley had to assume, with all other duties, the task of feeding the family. When church bells announced the arrival of produce, Dolley went with Mother Amy to the markets, taking almost as much pleasure in the rich reds and yellows and greens of fresh fruits and vegetables as in the enticing colors of French silks and velvets, haggling over prices like the poorest of thrifty housewives. She learned to cook as inexpensively as possible, tempting the family's appetites with recipes of her own ingenious concoction, some of which would long afterward bring her culinary fame.

Though many of the Philadelphia Quaker families, like the Morrises, the Shippens, and the Lloyds, were active participants in the social and political life of the city and state, the Paynes' total involvement was in the confines of their Quaker Meeting. In 1786, three years after their arrival, a certificate was issued transferring membership of "John Payne and Mary his wife, and their children, William Temple, Dorothy, Isaac, Lucy, Anna, Mary, John, and Philadelphia to the Pine Street Monthly Meeting." As always, John and Mary were active members, John a lay preacher or "Public Friend," Mary as well as he mounting the long platform when the Spirit moved, to exhort the congregation. Once she was asked by a curious outsider how the Quakers explained the Pauline scripture forbidding women to speak in the churches.

"Oh well, Friend," she replied cheerfully, "thee knows Paul was never partial to women."

Though she was now eighteen, with all the rights of a mature woman, Dolley never felt the urge to "exhort." She sat on the hard bench on the women's side of the bare house of worship, back unbending, at least more comfortable now that her feet touched the floor, and, though she often felt the warmth of the Inner Light, it was an experience to be treasured in secret rather than shared. Indeed, it was during the long periods of silence that she was most conscious of the Presence.

Oh, the sermons could be helpful enough! She liked best those of Friend Samuel Wetherill, who exhorted on First Days at the Free Quaker Meeting House at the corner of Fifth and Mulberry streets. He was as eloquent in speech as successful in his business of cloth manufacturing, though her attention kept wandering during the sermons, and instead of his devout features she kept seeing the brand he used to mark all his goods—the old Quaker lady sitting by a spinning wheel. It appeared everywhere as advertisement for his jeans, fustians, everlastings, and "coatyngs."

Membership in the new Meeting meant only one change to Dolley. New Friends. What a wonderful word to describe the communion of kindred spirits, the Society of Friends! She could not wait to learn more about them, to make some of them her intimate companions. That girl, for instance, whom she had met before Meeting, the one with the wide smiling eyes and the pert, slightly turned-up little nose. What was her name? Collins. Elizabeth, though most people seemed to call her Eliza. Certainly they would be friends.

Sitting silently on the hard bench, dutifully heedless of the surreptitious glances of youthful males on the other side of the bare room, she could not know that the kindling admiration in one pair of dark intent eyes would bring profound change to her life.

2

"I thank thee, sir, but—no, I mean never to marry."

Strange avowal for an attractive young woman in this year of 1787 when marriage was considered the only correct expectation of females! But Dolley was an unusual person. Oldest daughter in a large family suffering privation, she knew herself to be the pivot about which the household revolved. She could not envision a future when her presence in the house would not be a virtual necessity. Since the death of her baby, the sickly little Philadelphia, Mama had seemed to lose her vigorous incentive. Mother Amy was intensely loyal and efficient, but she was used to taking orders, not assuming direction. The other girls, Lucy, Anna, and Mary, were nine and under.

This was not Dolley's first proposal of marriage, nor was it the first time this particular aspirant had pressed his suit. He had been one of her coterie of young male friends and admirers ever since that First Day when the Paynes had become members of Pine Street Meeting and he had seen across the room a pair of sparklingly bright blue eyes, their merry glints belying the soberness of the demure Quaker bonnet.

John Todd was an eminently suitable possibility for marriage. He belonged to an old Quaker family who had lived for three generations in Philadelphia or its environs. His father, John Todd, Sr., was a longtime teacher in the city's most notable Friends' Academy, renowned for his ability not only as a pedant but as a flogger, a skill deemed both necessary and desirable in schoolmasters of the period. John Jr. was at this time a law student, already marked for outstanding success in his chosen profession.

Most Quakers with ambition turned to business as the most likely avenue to prosperity, some with an eye to attaining great wealth. Not young John Todd. He had a keen interest in government and in the problems besetting the infant American nation. Since he was a frequent caller in the Payne home as well as one of Dolley's youthful companions—the *only* one, if he could possibly arrange it—on walks to and from Meeting, picnics, and other recreational activities she managed to find time for, visits with her family, Dolley was suddenly plunged into an awareness of the new country's severe quandary.

The common purpose that had united the colonies in their struggle for independence, explained John Todd one evening when the family was together, had disintegrated, like pitch holding together a leaking boat. And that's exactly what they were, a ship in danger of sinking. True, they still belonged to the Confederation, and they called themselves states instead of colonies, but it was each one for itself, no interest in the common good. Jealousy was rampant. The small states were jealous of the large states, the industrial ones of the North jealous of the agricultural ones of the South, those in each group jealous of one another.

"And our government under the Articles of Confederation," he continued hopelessly, "is powerless. It cannot raise taxes to support itself, only request the states to provide the necessary funds. That's why Washington's troops were so often ragged and starving, why now they're in rebellion because they have received no pay. Government can issue paper money, yes, but look what happens to it. Down, down it goes in value, until people can say of the most worthless thing in existence, 'It isn't worth a *continental.*'"

"Ah yes, it is so true!" John Payne agreed from bitter experience. "All the wealth I brought with me from Virginia, where has it gone? A pound is worth no more than a few pence."

"Each state," John Todd worried, "is acting like a little nation. Some, like Rhode Island, are printing their own paper money. Some are even making treaties of their own with foreign governments. Look at what happened up in Massachusetts, that Shays' Rebellion! Western farmers so unequally taxed by their state government that they rose up in arms just as they had fought against far less excessive taxation by the King! I tell thee, Friend Payne, unless something is done, everything our people fought for will be lost. We will have nothing but anarchy!"

And then suddenly something *was* being done. A constitutional convention had been called to meet right there in Philadelphia, to discuss ways to strengthen the federal government. John Todd was jubilant. He had lawyer friends who were delegates, among them Gouverneur Morris and James Wilson, who were both in sympathy with his conviction that the present system must be radically changed.

Though the convention was scheduled to begin on May 14, 1787, it was the twenty-fifth, five days after Dolley's nineteenth birthday, before the delegates assembled in sufficient numbers for a quorum. Many of them were delayed by long travel, since it required up to two weeks to make the journey from New Hampshire, a good part of three from Georgia.

Philadelphia had not witnessed such an assemblage of dignitaries for years, since the Continental Congress met now in New York. Each morning people gathered outside the high wall enclosing the State House on Chestnut Street to see the delegates arrive, and, since many of them were lodged in the Indian Queen, that also became a popular rendezvous. General Washington, riding between the State House and the home of Robert Morris, where he was being entertained, was object of the most curiosity and admiration. Benjamin Franklin, back from France in time to become a delegate, was a more familiar sight in his sedan chair, the first one to be seen in America.

With her parents and some other Pine Street Quakers, Dolley had gone to tea once in Franklin's garden. At first she was sadly disillusioned. Surely this could not be the great hero she had pictured—this short stout old man sitting under a big mulberry tree in his plain Quaker clothes, white hair fringing his bald head, dimmed eyes peering through the bifocals he had himself invented. Looking at him, no one would have imagined that he had founded the City of Brotherly Love, been fêted in the courts of Europe while being ambassador to France, made a lot of scientific discoveries, including the identity of electricity in lightning! And he made them all feel as much at home as if they were members of his family. His daughter, Mrs. Bache, served them tea with three of her six children in attendance, reminding Dolley of Cousin Patrick Henry's in their lack of discipline. They seemed completely uncontrolled either by their mother or by their doting grandfather.

Dolley, keeping properly quiet and in the background, was suddenly startled to find the great man looking straight at her. "Thee there," he said with a chuckle, pointing his finger unmistakably in her direction, "I declare thee to be the most beautiful young lady in all America. I have never seen thy equal in all of Paris or London."

Dolley gasped, then, flushing, made him a curtsey. "I thank thee, sir," she replied, regaining her poise. "I have heard that the French are masters of flattery. Perhaps thee learned the art from them."

"Ha! Touché, my dear." Again the great man chuckled. "Wit as well as beauty."

"Don't let thy head be turned," admonished Mama when the visit was over. "Friend Franklin, good Quaker though he is, has the reputation of having an eye for a pretty face."

"Don't worry," Dolley assured her. "I saw how weak his eyes are getting."

John Todd was frustrated because the action of the convention was conducted behind closed doors and in secret. Delegates were not permitted to take from the room a record of proceedings or to disclose any part of the discussion to others. The meetings went on all through the summer, every day but Sunday, sometimes for seven or more hours, and through the most grueling heat. They called it the hottest summer in Philadelphia since 1750, and because of the rule of secrecy all windows had to be closed. General Washington was President of the convention. It was struggling at desperate odds to develop a plan for union that would be acceptable to the thirteen disparate states, some large, others small, some jealous of their industrial prestige, others passionately protective of their agricultural society with its dependence on slavery, but all fiercely committed to their own self-interests.

Two plans, John Todd had heard through the underground, were being hotly discussed, one called the Virginia Plan, put forward by the delegates from that state, calling for a strong federal government, the other called the New Jersey Plan, insisting that the Congress had been called for the express purpose of merely revising the Articles of Confederation.

"It's probably hopeless," John Todd lamented. "If they succeed in uniting on a plan for a strong central government, it will be a miracle. And of course Europe—England and Spain—are just waiting for us to make a mess of it, to make us virtually colonies again!"

Leading names among the delegates emerged, to be paired with increasingly familiar faces and figures—Franklin and Washington, of course, George Mason, Edmund Randolph, Alexander Hamilton, Robert Morris, John Rutledge, Charles Pinckney, and, with greater and greater frequency and emphasis, James Madison.

One day Dolley was walking with John Todd past the Indian Queen when he called her attention to a figure emerging from the entrance.

"Look! See that man there? He doesn't look like much, but they say he's the most important delegate to the convention. First to arrive and the best-prepared. Knows more about government than any other man alive. They tell me he took a seat right under the speaker's platform and makes a record of every speech and action. And when he speaks, everybody listens, even though he's no orator, in fact sometimes they can hardly hear him and have to lean close to listen. If the miracle happens, it will probably be his making more than anyone else's. They call him 'the great little Madison.' "

Dolley looked. "Yes," she said. "I remember him. He came to visit us once in Scotchtown."

"Really? Then let's go and speak to him. I've already met him. Let's see if he remembers thee."

"No!" Dolley's refusal was swift and obdurate. She remembered James Madison all too well, and she had no wish to arouse his memory of a foolish child recklessly luring him to possible disaster. She could still see the twinkle in his eye, hear his gentle jibe of droll amusement. *Children . . . like training a horse . . . always one long jump ahead!*

The convention dragged on through July and August into September. Then all at once it was over. On Monday, September 17, John Todd burst into the Payne house looking almost as jubilant as if Dolley had finally changed her mind and agreed to marry him.

"It's done! The miracle has happened. They've signed a new constitution, not a revision of the old weak Articles, but one brand-new, one that can create a solid union, *if only* . . ."

It was a huge *if,* for to become effective the new constitution had to be ratified by at least nine states. On September 20 it was laid before the old Congress meeting in New York, where it was fought, defended, debated, subjected to near dismemberment and crippling amendment, but finally, on September 28, passed, "to be submitted to a convention of Delegates chosen in each state by the people thereof." On the morning of September 29 an express rider, changing horses several times along the road, brought the news from New York to Philadelphia.

"Now," said John Todd, "we just need another miracle."

For the battle in the convention had been only the first skirmish. Now the real war began, with armies ranged on either side—Federalists, who backed the new constitution with its central government, Anti-Federalists who wanted to preserve the old loose confederation with the complete independence of the states. All through the fall and winter, the following spring and summer, the debate went on. It was probably two men who influenced the outcome more than any others, Alexander Hamilton and James Madison, who, in a series of essays called *The Federalist,* reasonably and skillfully espoused the cause of national unity. And again a miracle! One by one the state conventions met, argued stormily, but finally voted to ratify the new constitution . . . little Delaware . . . Pennsylvania . . . New Jersey . . . Georgia . . . Connecticut . . . Massachusetts . . . Maryland . . . South Carolina. Eight. Now only one to go. In Virginia, perhaps the deciding ninth, it was largely a contest between the fiery Patrick Henry, opposed, and the small, quiet, low-voiced but strangely eloquent James Madison.

The American states, he said, had stirred the admiration of the world by establishing their free government under the stress of war. How much more would they win admiration and astonishment if they should be able "peaceably, freely and satisfactorily, to establish one general government when there is such a diversity of opinions and interests, when not cemented or stimulated by any common danger!"

If Virginia held out, he continued, the United States might never have a government, but if Virginia consented, it might bring about "one of the most fortunate events that ever happened for human nature."

Though the brilliant and persuasive Patrick Henry held out to the last, on June 25, 1778, Virginia voted 89 to 79 to ratify the Constitution. But it was not the deciding state, after all. For already, on June 21, little New Hampshire had become the ninth to ratify.

"It's done!" exulted John Todd for the second time, arriving posthaste to share his excitement with the Payne family. "The miracle has happened once more!"

Philadelphia had a double celebration on July 4, 1778. Dolley awoke to the sound of church bells and cannons, the one from the steeple of Christ Church, the other from the armed ship *Rising Sun* anchored in the river off Market Street. Near the ship were ten others bearing flags with gold letters spelling out the names of the states that had ratified from New Hampshire to Georgia. All day long the flags waved in a brisk south wind.

There was a huge parade, forming at eight o'clock at the corner of South and Third streets. Dolley and Lucy were in the crowd assembled to watch on Union Green . . . seventeen thousand people, it was reported. There were five thousand in the procession—cavalry, light infantry, a herald with a trumpet proclaiming a "New aera," dragoons, industrial societies, manufacturers, craftsmen, traders, printers, masons, farmers, representatives of all the hundreds of other groups comprising the beneficiaries of the remarkable new document beginning with the statement: "We the people of the United States, in order to form a more perfect Union . . ."

"Oh!" breathed Lucy, clutching Dolley's arm at one point in the procession. "See that!"

It was a wonderful object in the display of the Marine Society, a big ship under full sail, its emblazoned name the Federal Ship *Union,* perfectly proportioned and complete, decorated with elaborate carvings, fresh with paint. It had been built and finished in less than four days, begun at eleven o'clock on Tuesday, June 30, and here now on Saturday morning, triumphant symbol of the new ship of state.

"Let's hope she doesn't founder," said John Todd, who had managed to find them in the crowd.

"Yes," said Dolley. She could not know, of course, what an important role she herself would play in its launching.

3

Dolley was interested, of course, in the momentous political changes taking place, but the new government, with General Washington unanimously elected President by the electoral college, was in New York, which seemed faraway. And personal concerns loomed larger.

Papa was not prospering in his starch business. He was a plantation squire, not a businessman like many of the well-to-do, even extremely wealthy Philadelphia Quakers. The galloping inflation was absorbing any possible profits. He was sinking deeper and deeper into debt. In spite of efforts to further economize, they became actually poor and kept moving into smaller and smaller houses, finally landing at 231 New Street. Though the older boys had gone south to seek their fortunes and Isaac was living independently, there were still four children at home, and the family was cramped in the smaller quarters.

Not even to curry favor with the non-Quakers who might have helped his business would Papa sacrifice his principles. When the Friends' Society and the Pennsylvania Society for the Abolition of Slavery drew up memorials to Congress for the promotion of the emancipation of blacks, John Payne signed the petition. Though he was in good company, with Benjamin Franklin supporting the movement, the signers endured much criticism and abuse. "What right have the Quakers," it was asked, "having refused to risk their lives or fortunes in the conflict, to try to impress their views on the government?" The action had not helped John Payne in his business.

Papa's discouragement was a dark cloud obscuring the normal happy atmosphere of the household. Only in his beloved Meeting, surrounded by Quaker friends, did he seem to derive strength and courage to face his problems.

Dolley, on the other hand, was becoming restless within the reclusive Quaker life-style. She who loved beauty and was blessed with a spirit of independence, was chafing under the rigid inhibitions of the stricter Quaker sect to which they belonged, and not only because of the lure of soft fabrics and bright colors. In 1789 a Quaker friend named Sarah Bertier was disowned by the Society for marrying "out of unity," in other words, to a man not a Quaker. Dolley was shocked, dismayed.

"But—why?" To Mama she expressed her bewilderment. "They—they're casting her out, as if she'd committed some terrible sin!"

"Thee knows why." Mama could well speak from experience. "We Friends must remain a unified body. There must be no alien spirit to break the harmony."

"But—do not the Articles teach us love and concern and charity? How then can we turn people away, tell them they don't belong?"

"My dear." Mama hesitated. "Does thee not know? I too was disowned when I married Papa. The Paynes were of the Established Church, not of our faith."

Dolley gasped. "Thee! But—how—what—"

"Thy father saw the light and became a Friend, a good one, too, as thee knows. He joined the Society, and I was reinstated."

"I—I see." But Dolley was troubled. And there were far more disturbing events to come. In that same year of 1789 Papa went bankrupt. And to her grief and astonishment the Society disowned him because he could not pay his debts. Papa, whose whole life had been spent in following the guidance of his Inner Light, who had often been moved by the Spirit to speak in the congregation, who had been respected as "Public Friend," as "Publisher of the Truth!" It was unbelievable. They called themselves Friends, yet instead of trying to help him, they had cast him out, turned away, like the priest and the Levite in the story of the Good Samaritan.

Not all of them, however. John Todd, now a practicing lawyer, became even more loyal to him and the family, handling his business affairs, what were left of them, trying to save him as much dignity and pride as possible.

But even he could do little. It was a mortal blow from which John Payne was never to recover, though he spoke no word against the Society nor did he renounce his faith. In time he was able to join a more liberal group called the Free Quakers, but he was a broken man. He spent most of his time shut away in a room on the second floor and took no part in either family or community life.

It was Molly Payne, always the stronger of the two, who took matters in hand. Under her leadership the family rallied. There were fewer of them now at home. Walter had sailed for England in 1785. Temple was still working somewhere in Virginia. They practiced even more rigid economy. Molly found that many of her friends needed the services of a seamstress, and she was able to eke out a bare living with her skillful needle. They managed to survive.

John Todd, who had been courting Dolley for some five years, never giving up hope, now pressed his suit more urgently. He wanted to take care of her in this emergency. And, he pointed out, as a member of the family he could do more to help them, for he was now beginning to prosper as a lawyer. Regretfully Dolley refused him once more. Why, she wondered, did she still not yield to this eminently suitable friend who had remained steadfastly loyal to the family when so many had turned away? Surely he was the one among her many suitors with whom she could vision spending a contented life. Was it because the prospect of a lifetime within the constricting bounds of Pine Street Meeting and the Quaker Discipline was somehow unappealing? Was she still, after all these years, hunting for an elusive golden butterfly?

At least now she had a good reason for refusing. She was needed even more at home. She also had skill with the needle, more imaginative than Mama's. Even Quaker women, increasingly less obedient to the admonition against vanity, were resorting to touches of bright colors and softer fabrics. Daringly Dolley managed to make herself a delicate gown, Quaker gray but of satin, with elbow sleeves and square neck, not cut immodestly low, of course, like the prevailing French styles. She did not wear it, for it would have hurt Papa and Mama to know that she had strayed from the narrow path into the broad thoroughfare of vanity. Instead she put it away under the dull muslins and linens in her clothes chest, to feel its soft lustrous smoothness sometimes when her fingers probed too deeply (intentionally?) into the neat piles. Just so she had once hidden away a golden butterfly under her kerchief.

One day she was putting to rights the upstairs room where John Payne spent so much of his time.

"Thee, daughter Dolley. I would talk with thee."

"Yes, Father."

John Todd, that fine young lawyer, he told her, had visited him—he sighed—as so few of their old friends did these days. He had suggested that he sought her hand in marriage.

"Yes, Father. I know."

"He is a good man, daughter, and it is time thee married. There is little I can do for thee now. I cannot command thee, of course, a woman twenty-one years old. But I can urge thee. To know thee settled and happy, it would be one of the few things left me in life. Mama and I are agreed. Please—for our sakes—?"

For their sakes, yes. Dolley was relieved and, yes, happy, once it was settled. Her parents' satisfaction, her young sisters' joyful excitement, and John Todd's blissful delight were full compensation for any uncertainty or regret. The wedding, of course, must be strictly according to rigid Quaker custom, a foretaste of the rest of her life.

Dolley was a bit apprehensive. It was a formidable prospect, having to "pass meeting." They must appear before the congregation to state their intentions several times before the marriage ceremony would be permitted. Suppose the elders, especially James Pemberton, who sat at the head of the Meeting, always stern and straight, his crossed hands resting on his gold-headed cane, had heard rumors that she was given to unseemly levity or, worst yet, vanity! She was not at all in awe of Nicholas Wain, who sat beside him, his face always illumined by a sunny smile, or of William Savery, who had such a beautiful silvery voice.

The day for the first "Passing of Meeting" came. John, with a friend from the men's meeting, entered the women's side, and, taking his intended bride by the arm, announced, first in one meeting, then in the other, that "we propose taking each other in marriage." This was repeated on three occasions. And—to their great relief—there was no objection to their "passing of meeting."

The marriage service itself, on January 7, 1790, was very simple, consisting merely of an exchange of vows. Dolley's best friend, Elizabeth Collins, and their mutual friend, Anthony Morris, were their attendants. In spite of the snowy weather there was a surprising number of guests. After the service of worship the bride and groom stood together and made their vows, taking each other's hands.

"I, John Todd, do take thee, Dolley Payne, to be my wedded wife, and promise with divine assistance to be unto thee a loving and faithful husband until death shall separate us." Solemnly Dolley repeated almost the same words.

As she sat at the table to sign the marriage certificate, she felt as if time suddenly stood still. An end—or a beginning? An end, certainly, of a gay and carefree girlhood. But that had come months before, when Papa had retreated into his twilight of despair. He was here today, would sign the certificate with the sixty or so other guests, only to go back again into his haven of solitude within four enclosing walls.

At least she had given him this small happiness and sense of satisfaction.

And of course it was a beginning . . . of what? A new year . . . a new life. Looking up into her husband's happy face, his lips tenderly smiling, his eyes alight with the fulfillment of five years' hope and devotion, she felt a surge of relief. Time started up again, moving inexorably into the future.

"Dolley Todd," she wrote firmly.

Queer, what foolish things one thought of at life's most solemn moments! What a pity on one's wedding day to be wearing this plain dull gray cambric gown and kerchief instead of something gay and bright-colored of lovely silk or satin!

4

Why, Dolley asked herself again, had she been so hesitant about accepting John Todd's proposal of marriage? It had not been entirely because of her obligation to family, for John had been as concerned about their welfare as if he had already been her husband, and eager to give them the help he could now bestow as John Payne's son-in-law. Why, then? Because marriage had seemed just another of the constricting webs which, all her life it seemed, had kept her from something—call it freedom?—for which she yearned. How stupid she had been! For never had she felt more free. John's love was no confining web. And when with the full effulgence of their second spring she felt the budding of new life within herself, her happiness was complete—almost. There was always the shadow of the lonely disillusioned man shut away in the upstairs room of her mother's house.

Dolley and John Todd lived first in a small rented house on Chestnut Street, but in November 1791 John's increasing legal practice enabled him to buy a handsome three-story brick house at Fourth and Walnut. It was to be a combination office and residence. He could not do enough, it seemed, to make her happy. He furnished the house with luxuries that defied George Fox's creed of simplicity—carpets, mahogany tables, Windsor chairs, mirrors, and, most elegant of all, one of the new sideboards on which to display her glassware and silver. He provided a horse and riding chair to take her on visits to friends. He insisted on commissioning James Peale, the popular artist, to paint a lovely miniature of her on ivory. It showed the youthful face smiling demurely from its frame of a soft tulle cap, its lacy frills gathered into ties beneath the small pointed chin, surrounded by curling tendrils of black hair which flowed over the lace kerchief draping the modest gown of Quaker gray. Of the many likenesses that would outlive her, this was the only one that revealed a childlike sweetness, an immaturity untouched by lines of sadness and harsh experience.

"But—thee shouldn't!" Dolley kept protesting. "I have far too much already. And all these things cost money. Suppose—like Papa—"

"Afraid I will go bankrupt? Nonsense, love. We are not poor, and how better could I make use of our good fortune than by spending a little on the most beautiful woman in Philadelphia?"

Their son, John Payne Todd, to be called Payne all his life, was born February 29, 1792, just seven days after the big celebration for President Washington's sixtieth birthday. Waking on the twenty-second to the sounds of bells and cannon, Dolley almost hoped they might signal another birth, but young Payne, destined for a lifetime of willful self-determination, was postponing his arrival for a more unique distinction, a birth date that would occur only once in four years. There was no physician in attendance, though Philadelphia was the center of medical progress, for such services were not yet considered a requisite for an ordinary occurrence like human birth. Mama and Mother Amy, who was an experienced midwife, were with her, and the latter, who had performed the same service for most of Mary's children, washed and oiled and blanketed and gathered the newborn to her ample breast with the same clucking joy and devotion.

Motherhood was Dolley's crowning happiness. Never, she confessed to her friend, Eliza Collins, had there been such a perfect child. It was a sentiment that was to persist through her lifetime, with unfortunate results.

One of Dolley's greatest satisfactions in this new happiness was in seeing her father's eyes light briefly at sight of this first grandchild. At least, she was soon to comfort herself, he had lived long enough to hold little Payne, his namesake, in his arms.

There was relief, as well as grief in his going. For the first time in three years they saw his face serene and untroubled. And in his death John Payne had been taken once more into the fellowship of believers that had cast him out. The funeral service was held in the Meeting House, and the room was nearly full. As if, thought Dolley, his old friends wanted to atone for an action that their Quaker consciences had not quite been able to reconcile with the promptings of the Inner Light. A pity more of them had not expressed the friendly concern when he was alive, thought Dolley, as had John Todd!

At the burial ground the plain wooden box was set down, so that, according to Quaker custom, the family could have a last look at the beloved and that the spectators might be given a "sense of mortality to reflect upon their own latter end." There were no symbols of grief, no crape, no flowers, no black mourning garments. For Molly and her children no symbols were necessary. But for all of them the profound grief was tempered with relief that the gentle, tortured spirit had gained release from its confining walls.

Molly Payne had suffered other severe tests of faith during the preceding years. All three of her older sons had one by one been disowned by the Society. Walter had gone to Virginia and then sailed for England. The reason for his defection had never been very clear. Temple had joined the United States Navy, denial of a good Quaker's abrogation of all that concerned warfare. Isaac had found work in Norfolk and the family had rejoiced in his apparent success, until rumors had come of an immoral lapse, the mere suspicion of which had caused his expulsion. Each disaster had left Molly unbowed, the only outward signs of inward struggle a tightening of the habitually smiling lips, a fading of the merry glints in the blue Irish eyes. Indeed, she held her shoulders even straighter. Now she prepared to cope with this new emergency.

"I shall take boarders," she announced firmly to the family.

They knew better than to demur. Even John Todd, who had tried vainly to give more than token financial assistance, was helpless in the face of her determination. Though she must have had the idea for some time, she had not attempted its execution during Papa's lifetime. It would have hurt him too much. His wife undertaking work unseemly for a gentlewoman—and, of all things, a tavern! She put the plan into operation immediately, moving out of the little rented house on New Street into a larger one at North Third. It was a fortunate time to embark on such a venture because the national government had moved from New York to Philadelphia, and the city was full of Congressmen and other officials eager for comfortable lodgings and, even more difficult to obtain, good food. Mother Amy's southern fried chickens, succulent roast hams, hot corn pone, puddings, pies, and batter cakes were potent attractions.

Then suddenly, another disaster. Mother Amy died. For Dolley it was like losing another parent. Her first memories were of the smiling black face bent over her cradle, the comforting bosom on which to weep out her childish hurts, the softly crooning voice whose haunting melodies had lulled her to sleep. This time there was no relief mingled with the grief of her tears. And for Molly Payne's new enterprise the death of her loyal helper spelled tragedy. She could not afford to hire another cook, wages being a whole dollar a week, and she refused to let John Todd help finance one. Though she had insisted on paying Mother Amy the small stipend she had received, against her will, since manumission, wages for servants in Philadelphia these days were prohibitive. Dolley and young Lucy gave her all the assistance possible, but Dolley had her own household to manage, together with a demanding baby son, and Lucy at fourteen was a carefree dreamy adolescent. Dolley helped also by taking twelve-year-old Anna to live with her, a service which proved a far greater joy than burden.

It was Mother Amy herself who in death solved the problem. All the years of her freedom, it developed, she had saved her small wages and in a simple will left the full amount to Molly. It came to an incredible five hundred dollars! Molly could now hire a capable cook. Her courageous enterprise was saved.

Dolley felt almost guilty in her own life of contentment and ease. A tenderly devoted husband, a baby who certainly had no equal anywhere in the world, a beautiful new house, and, not the least of her blessings, a social life of increasing satisfaction.

John was fast becoming one of the highly respected lawyers of the city, rendering service not only to Quakers but to people of all faiths and stations in life. His interest in politics involved him in close relations with officials of the new government, and, as his wife, Dolley was drawn inevitably into the social activities of the capital.

"Dolley, love," John marveled after they had attended one of Martha Washington's Friday levees, "never have I seen thee more beautifully alive. Even in thy sober Quaker gown thee outshone all those bedecked and furbelowed females. I was so proud of thee."

Alive, yes. Dolley had felt herself brimming with life. All those people! She had wanted to get to know every one of them, make them her friends. As for the Quaker gown . . . There had been other Quakers there, some from their own Pine Street Meeting. But she had been the only one in dull gray cambric. Before the next levee she took from its hiding place the satin dress she had made long ago and, half fearfully, half defiantly, donned it. It was still Quaker gray, but, oh, the soft lovely sheen of it! It would glow like jewels in the candlelight. To her relief John nodded his approval. She felt suddenly a sense of release. She was back in Mother Amy's arms, crying her heart out, hearing the black woman's comforting words. *Nonsense! De God Ah knows ain't like dat. Yo' ain't wicked, chile. Don' let nobody tell yo' it's wicked to want a bit of prettiness. Ah knows bettah.*

Martha Washington also approved. "You look beautiful tonight, my dear, all aglow with some inner light."

Inner Light! Yes, that was exactly what she had been feeling, as much as she had ever felt it in Meeting. She had a sudden sense of freedom. Religion wasn't meant to be a prison. She could love beauty and still be true to her Quaker heritage. She could even wear bright colors, perhaps a golden butterfly!

She was finding the President's wife a delightfully informal, motherly person with whom she felt friendly rapport. Two of Washington's nephews, George Steptoe Washington and Lawrence Washington, were residents of Mama's boardinghouse, as were several important Congressmen, including Aaron Burr, the brilliant fascinating senator from New York. Secretary of State Jefferson, whom Dolley remembered as an old family friend before he became minister to France, was also a frequent visitor.

The Payne parlor was often a center of political discussion, and, while John sat with the men, Dolley sometimes helped Mama and Lucy serve tea to the guests and perform other household tasks. She could not help overhearing some of the long hot arguments. There seemed to be great disagreement between Thomas Jefferson and a man called Alexander Hamilton, who was Secretary of the Treasury. They were even dividing the country into groups, one, calling itself Federalists, which believed in an all-powerful central government, the other, Anti-Federalists, or Republicans, which thought that all nondelegated powers should be reserved to the states.

John Todd took little part in the discussions, but he was an avid listener, and the threat of disunity worried him. The new nation, he maintained, was a great experiment in democracy, a government voted in by the people, for *all* the people, and if it failed it might never be tried again. He had been relieved when the first Congress had instigated the Bill of Rights, ten of them, and they had become amendments to the Constitution.

"It was that friend of thine, Madison," he told Dolley, "who made sure there would be freedom of religion in all the country, not just his own state of Virginia, where the Established Church used to be supported by the government. It's in the very first words of the first Article: 'Congress shall make no law respecting an establishment of religion, or prohibiting the free exercise thereof.' And it applies to all religious groups as well as to us Quakers. No more government support, no more interference, the absolute separation of church and state."

Her "friend Madison?" Dolley smiled. Did it make one a friend to dare a person to risk his neck? Occasionally she had seen the small, neat, black-suited figure of the Virginia Congressman walking along the street in the short block between the State House and his lodging with Mrs. Mary House at Fifth and Market streets. People called him the most important man in Congress, though he certainly did not look it, so small and insignificant! Dolley knew he had never married, though he had been engaged once, it was gossiped, to a girl named Kitty Floyd, only sixteen and half his age. The affair had been bandied about in great detail. There had been a young clergyman who had "hung around her at the harpsichord" while Madison and her father had been discussing the problems of paper money. She had finally sent him a letter of dismissal, sealed, of all things, with a piece of rye dough! Poor man! Yet Dolley could hardly blame her. He must have seemed an old man to a girl of sixteen, not much older than her own fun-loving, carefree sister Lucy, just blooming into radiant womanhood.

Watching the girl blossom suddenly into beauty, seeing the admiring eyes of some of the boarders, one in particular, exchanges of significant glances, Dolley felt growing concern.

"Has thee noticed," she asked Molly casually, "that young George Steptoe Washington and our Lucy seem rather friendly? Does it worry thee just a bit? She's at such an impressionable age—!"

Molly pooh-poohed the idea. "Lucy? Why, she's just a child, friendly with all the boarders, old and young."

"She's fourteen," Dolley reminded.

"Years yet to think of her romancing," returned Molly comfortably, "and when she does, it will be some nice Quaker boy, not one from outside. She's not one to get her head turned even by a nephew of the President."

It was one morning in the summer of 1793 that Mama came to Dolley's house. Never had Dolley seen her more distraught. Her face was pale, her gauze Quaker cap awry, black hair usually so neat, disarranged, breath coming in gasps as if she had been running.

"She's—gone. Look—a messenger just—brought it—read—"

Dolley took the piece of foolscap and read. "Dearest Mama. When thee gets this I shall be Mrs. George Steptoe Washington. We had to do it this way. Thee would never have consented. Never fear, we will be married by a respectable clergyman. George has arranged it all. We are going to Virginia, where he has a fine home ready for us, inherited from his father. I am sorry to have to do it this way, and I love you all. Lucy."

"I thought—she'd gone to the Drinkers' summer place—to spend— a few days," explained Molly, still breathless from haste and excitement. "Oh, dear, I never should have—kept a boardinghouse, where she could meet—all kinds of people—outside the faith. And I thought he was—such a good boy, the President's nephew and all—"

"He is a good boy," comforted Dolley. "And what's done is done. We'll just have to make the best of it."

"But—she's only a child," mourned Molly, "just fifteen. And he's not a day over seventeen. But, there!" she exclaimed, suddenly contrite. "I shouldn't be getting thee all stirred up, in thy delicate condition."

Dolley smiled. It would take more than an elopement, especially of a couple so obviously in love, to disturb the vigorous life near to fulfillment within her. She almost envied them. She had come to love John Todd, as well as admire and respect him as she had always done, but she sensed that there was a quality of ecstasy she had never attained in their relationship. That these—yes, these *children* had it she was sure. She had seen it in the looks they had exchanged.

Suddenly Anna ran into the room, fair face flushed, eyes so wide-open that their pale blue centers looked rimmed with white. "A chariot!" she announced excitedly. "I think it's the President's. And it's stopped right in front of the house!"

Dolley moved to the window as fast as her cumbersome body would allow. Yes, it was the President's chariot, a familiar sight on Philadelphia streets with its cream-colored frame and wheels, gilt moldings, and neat venetian blinds, drawn by four fine bay horses. A footman was handing out a short stoutish woman, escorting her up the steps, sounding the knocker.

Ushered by the maid into the room, Martha Washington did not even wait for the proper greetings. She came forward, extending her hands.

"My dears, I just heard the news, and I had to come. I stopped first at your house, Mrs. Payne, then, finding you gone, came on here."

No, she would not take tea or any refreshment. This was not a social visit. As they could see, she had come just as she was. Indeed the nation's First Lady did look like an ordinary housewife interrupted in some early morning task, in her simple dark calico and ruffled cap. She had not even bothered to remove her big white apron. The President, she said, had been shocked by the behavior of his young nephew. Not that they objected to his choice of a bride, for Lucy was a most delightful girl, but both of them were so young! And to carry her off without a decent wedding and without her family's consent, it was disgraceful! However, she wanted to assure them that dear Lucy would be accepted and loved by her new family and well taken care of. George Steptoe had come into possession of his father's estate, Harewood, in Virginia. After his brother Samuel's death the President had given his sons a good education and prepared them for careers in law. She wanted them to know that she and the President would do everything possible to atone for the rash behavior of their nephew George Steptoe.

"I imagine," Molly said after their guest's departure, "that some people would feel honored to have their daughter marry into the family of the President of the United States." She sighed. "If only he had been a Quaker! I suppose there's no use hoping, because he's the President's nephew—"

She was right. There was no use hoping. It would have been the same had he been the Prince of Wales. On August 13, 1793, the Minutes of the Philadelphia Monthly Meeting recorded the inevitable decision:

"Friends are appointed to assist women Friends in preparing a testimony against the misconduct of Lucy Washington, late Payne, who had by birth a right of membership among us, having disregarded the wholesome order of our discipline, in the accomplishment of her marriage with a person not in membership with us, before an hireling priest, and without the consent of her mother, after being precautioned against such outgoing. We therefore testify that the said Lucy Washington is no longer a member of our religious Society, nevertheless desiring she may be favored with a due sense of her deviation and seek to be rightly restored."

"Sometime," said John Todd sadly, "Quakers will understand that such acts betray the true spirit of the Children of Light. We should be welcoming others of different faiths into our fellowship, not excluding our own. I fear that sometimes that which we so glibly call the Inner Light may be nothing but darkness."

At least this time the family compensated for the expulsion of one of its members by adding another. Toward the end of summer William

Temple Todd arrived, becoming a member of the Society by right of birth.

Life . . . death . . . always, it seemed, so closely intermingled. On August 19, just six days after the eviction vote was recorded, notice was made of the death of one Peter Aston, the cause a severe case of fever. It was on that same day that Dr. Benjamin Rush, probably the best known physician of Philadelphia, came to a horrifying conclusion. Since the first of the month, when he had seen a child die from fever and jaundice, he had treated several other patients with the same symptoms, all of whom had died, one in only a few hours, none lasting more than four days.

"I am convinced," he told some of his colleagues, "that we are faced with a plague of yellow fever."

They did not believe him. There had been no outbreak of this dread disease in Philadelphia since 1762. It was Dr. Rush's experience then that caused him now to recognize the symptoms. They soon had to agree. On August 22 the mayor issued orders for the removal of all refuse from the streets of the city. On August 29 the governor of Pennsylvania recommended that the city do everything "to prevent the extension of and to destroy, the evil."

Yellow fever, most deadly of all virulent diseases! Starting on the waterfront, it soon overspread the whole city, a veritable plague. Many died on the second or third day, few survived until the fifth. There was no cure. All remedies—quinine, wine, mercury, jalap, blistering, copious bleeding, camphor, purging with calomel, disinfectants such as vinegar, tar, garlic—were ineffective. People were dying by the hundreds.

Where had the pestilence come from? Ships from the West Indies, where it was endemic? "Putrid exhalations," as Dr. Rush surmised, from some damaged coffee left to rot on a wharf? A dead body wrapped in canvas which someone had seen unloaded secretly from a ship called the *Flora?* Not until a hundred years later would it be recalled significantly that Dr. Rush had noted incidentally that in that particular autumn "mosquetoes [sic] were uncommonly numerous." And of course it was not considered important that on August 29 a letter appeared in a Philadelphia newspaper telling how mosquitoes, "those poisonous insects so distressing to the sick, and troublesome to those who are well" could easily be destroyed by pouring a little oil into cisterns and rain-water casks, their breeding places.

On September 8, Thomas Jefferson wrote his friend James Madison, who had gone home to Virginia: "The yellow fever increases. The week before last about three a day died. This last week 11 a day have died. Consequently, from known data, about 33 a day are taken and there are about 330 patients under it. It is the opinion of physicians that there is no possibility of stopping it. . . . The President goes off the day after tomorrow, as he had always intended. . . . Hamilton is ill of the fever, as is said. . . ." Here the Secretary of State seems to have injected a personal note into the political feud which beset the President's cabinet. "His family think him in danger, and he puts himself so by his excessive alarm. . . . A man as timid as he is on the water, as timid on horseback, as timid in sickness, would be a phenomenon if his courage of which he had the reputation in military occasions were genuine. His friends, who had not seen him, suspect it is only an autumnal fever he has. I would really go away, because I think there is rational danger, but . . . I do not like to exhibit the appearance of panic."

Panic! It pervaded the city. People scoured and whitewashed their houses. If they went outside they covered their mouths and noses with cloths soaked in camphor or vinegar, avoided talking with all, even friends, refused to shake hands. A person wearing crape or other signs of mourning was shunned like a leper. Bells tolled. Funerals so blocked the streets that they were ordered to be performed only at night. Prices rose prohibitively. Business was at a standstill. Because of their terror people became inhuman. As Benjamin Rush wrote in his diary, "Parents desert their children as soon as they are infected. Many people thrust their parents into the streets as soon as they complain of a headache. . . . Friendship is nearly banished from our city."

People began leaving in droves, a veritable exodus, as if they were fleeing from the plagues of Egypt. Carts, wagons, coaches, every kind of conveyance, filled with whole families and piled high with possessions, clogged every road out of the city toward some hopeful haven of safety.

Though aware that there was sickness in the city, as there often was in the heat of summer, Dolley had no idea of its nature or extent. The family tried to keep it from her. After a difficult birth, she was weak and confined to her bed for many days. With the city denuded of government officials, Molly had closed her boardinghouse and moved her small family into the Todd home, ostensibly to care for the convalescing mother and the new baby.

"I'm taking thee away," John Todd announced as soon as they felt she could be moved, about three weeks after the baby was born. "With all this sickness and this terrible heat, we should get thee and the children out of the city."

"And thee too," she thought, seeing how tired and worried he looked. Why was it, she wondered, that so many people were needing to have wills made and other legal business attended to in summer? It would be good for the whole family to have a vacation. Molly, too, looked worn out and distraught. Dolley was secretly amused to learn that they were going to Gray's Ferry on the banks of the Schuylkill, near Gray's Gardens, that pleasure spot with its groves and grottos, bridges and flotillas, its public house. How disapproving Mama had been of young people who had made up parties to sail up the river in summer or drive in sledges over ice and snow in winter, to have supper at the inn and dance the night away! Dolley herself had managed to go there more than once, always with a feeling of guilt, even though she had not participated in the dancing.

She had to learn the truth, of course. Borne in the litter that John had prepared for her journey, the new baby in her arms, the rest of the family crowded into the tightly closed carriage, John riding his horse beside her, she saw the loaded vehicles swarming through the streets, the weeping people, the empty houses, the few pedestrians wrapped in cloaks, skulking along, cloths pressed to their faces.

Arriving at the lodging that John had managed to secure in the thronged resort, popular now for its safety rather than its pleasure, Dolley felt profound relief. They were all here together, Mama and Anna and her sister Mary and her brother John and her own John and chubby, healthy eighteen-month-old little Payne and the precious mite, so small and defenseless, all safe from the pestilence. How selfish of her, she thought contritely, to be enjoying immunity when other women were losing husbands and children!

"I must go back," said John regretfully after he had seen them well settled.

"Oh no!" Dolley made swift anguished protest.

"I'm needed there," he explained with quiet firmness. "People are looking for someone to make wills, advise them, bring them peace of mind if possible. And the Quakers seem to be the only ones who show courage and friendship. We have set up a committee to see that people have help in their need. I am a member of it. Besides, my parents are still there. They refused to leave. Believe me, my darling, I'll be back when I can."

He did go back, returning infrequently for hurried visits, looking more harried and tired each time he came. And each time he left her Dolley was almost beside herself with worry. To add to her concern, the baby, puny and delicate from birth, seemed to sense her fear and distress, for he fussed and cried after every feeding. Presently he developed a low fever, and she was terrified. Could he possibly have contracted the dread disease? A letter from James Todd, John's brother, telling of the death of John's law student, Isaac Hastings, and of the sickness of her father-in-law accentuated her fears.

"O my dear brother," she wrote James on October 4, with her too frequent lapses in spelling, "what a dread prospect has thy last letter presented to me! A reveared Father in the jaws of Death, a Love'd Husband in perpetual danger—I have long wished for an opportunity of writing to thee and enquiring what we could do—I am almost destracted with distress and apprihension—Is it too late for their removal?—or can no interfearance of their Earthly friends rescue them from the two general fate? I have repeatedly entreated John to leave home, from which we are so unavoidably Banished—but alass he cannot leave his Father. . . . I wish much to see you, but my Child is sick, & I have no way of getting to you."

When John came he was almost prostrated by grief. His father had died on October 3. Dolley clung to him, begging him again not to return to the city. Surely he had done enough! But he insisted. He must care for his mother, and there were others who needed him. The fever, however, it seemed, was becoming less rampant. The next time he came, he hoped he would be able to stay.

After their father's death James secured a house in the country for his mother and brother to use as a retreat, near the place where he had taken his own family, and they were preparing to set out when their mother was taken ill. After her death, on October 12, John did yield to his brother's urging and spent his nights in the country, finding some release from tension by going out in the fields mornings and evenings hunting, one of his favorite diversions. After one such early morning, a damp one, he came in feeling chilled and unwell. A good environment, it would be surmised more than a hundred years later, for a man to encounter the carrier of the dread yellow fever. Fearful that it might be the plague, he returned to his parents' house, where he had been living. Learning of his brother's sickness, James came and found him there the next day, in better condition than he had expected.

"It's probably just a cold thee caught out in the dew."

John knew better. He knew too what was in store for him, for he had helped nurse both father and mother through the terrible sequence, administering the ineffective remedies—quinine, calomel, jalap—aided in the blisterings, purgings, bleedings; stoically witnessed the progress of the disease through all its agonizing stages—raging fever, chills, delirium, yellowed flesh, bleeding, finally the black vomiting which heralded the end. For one thing he was thankful. He could endure the torture alone. His family need not participate in his suffering. If only—just once more . . . The idea took possession of him. Surely he could do it safely, make sure that none of his beloved family was exposed to the danger. He set off immediately, alone, on horseback, covering the few miles to Gray's Ferry with an urgency like the fever already coursing through his veins.

For Dolley the days of waiting were torture. She went through the motions of living mechanically, nursing the feebly sucking baby, helping her mother prepare the meals with the scant provisions available, trying to keep the lively twenty-month-old John Payne Todd amused, but her senses all the time attuned to the first warning of disaster. It was on October 19 that John came. She was in the upstairs rooms at the lodging when she heard him speaking down in the hall. She almost failed to recognize his voice, it sounded so thick and unnatural.

"I must see her," he was saying with a terrible urgency. "I must see *her* once more! No!" he cried, as she came running down the stairs, arms outstretched. "No nearer! It's in my veins, I can feel it—the fever. Please—just let me look at thee—"

But she did not heed him. Descending the last few steps, she flung her arms about him, resisting with all her strength when he tried to push her away.

They could not persuade him to stay. In spite of Molly Payne's arguments and Dolley's pleadings, he rushed out of the house, mounted his horse, and rode away. Frantic, Dolley would have raced after him, if her mother had not pulled her firmly back. "No, child, there's nothing thee can do. He insisted on going."

"But—he's sick—I must go—nurse him—"

"How, child? We have not even a riding chair here and no horses. As he said, his brother is there. He will see that he is nursed and cared for. Besides, there is thy sick baby. And remember, he was determined to go."

"To die?" thought Dolley helplessly.

She was almost glad when she felt the heat of fever in her own body, heralding some sort of illness, if not the dread plague. At least it meant sensation, pain. She could share something of the agony he must be suffering. She was desperately sick. The yellow fever? Tradition would call it that, though it lasted longer than the usual brief duration of that dread disease. At least, John need not have worried lest he might have infected his beloved through their physical contact, for time would prove the fever noninfective. It was a time when any of the prevalent illnesses accompanied by fever would likely be ascribed to the current epidemic.

Hours? Days? For Dolley time was measured only by a succession of unrelated perceptions, sounds, sensations, and through it all her mother's voice.

Bitterness on her tongue. "I know, dear, it tastes terrible, but just a few more drops to help the fever?" . . . A tugging at her breast. "There, little William Temple, what a long name for such a little bit of a thing!" . . . Stabs of pain. "Oh dear, doctor, does thee have to take so much blood?" . . . Soft coolness on her forehead. "There, dear, doesn't that feel good?" . . . The baby again. "Poor weak little mite! He needs all the strength he can get." . . . More medicine . . . More bloodletting . . . More cool wet cloths. But—pain in her breasts instead of the familiar tugging, emptiness in her arms. . . . Voices somewhere, muted, sounding far away. "God help her, what misfortune! Both dead in the same day!" . . . "Hush, she must not hear. Still out of her head with the fever, poor child. Time enough for her to know, later." . . . A clatter of wheels in the street. "People are going back home. At last, they say the terror is past, no more dying!"

She fought her way finally out of the deep confusion and, as if through dissolving mists, saw her mother's face.

"John? My—baby?" She mouthed the words faintly but clearly.

"Oh, my dear, it's over! Thee is thyself again. Thee will get well. Thee has been so sick, and we have been so worried. The fever it was, though perhaps not the pestilence. The doctor wasn't sure, it lasted so long. But, thank God, thee is back with us again."

"John? My baby?" repeated Dolley with a growing, horrified suspicion. She had had a terrible dream, heard people talking somewhere . . . Of course it had been a dream. It couldn't be true.

Molly tried to avoid the question, be matter-of-fact, but she could not hide her tears. "They—had the fever, too, at least John did. Remember? He went back to the city—I'm sure had the best of care—his brother—sent us word—five days it was after he left here—October 24. And the baby—so sick with some sort of fever, and such a brave little mite—"

Dolley tried to lift her head. Her eyes were mercilessly probing. "Tell me—he too?"

Molly nodded. "We tried so hard to save him, but—he was so little, so weak."

"They—*both?*"

"Ay, child. But—don't think of it now, dear. It's over. Just get well thyself."

Dolley sank back into the pillow. She closed her eyes. Better the depth of confusion, of nightmares, than this awful clarity of understanding. Husband gone, baby gone. What more of misfortune could life possibly bring, what atoning happiness? Nothing. There was nothing left. Why had not the fever taken her too? But it was not too late. She let herself—no, *willed* herself back into the bleak darkness and confusion that were now more despair than physical illness. But, try as she would, she could not regain the comfort of unconsciousness. Never had her mind been more alert. Sensations throbbed painfully behind her closed eyelids, her life suddenly resolving itself into light and darkness, the past and the future. John's arms about her, the look in his eyes when she came into a room, the sound of his voice as he read to her out of a clever book and their laughter together . . . the feeling of a soft warm bundle in her arms, of lips tugging at her breast . . . now, nothing but loneliness, emptiness. Nothing ever again.

"Please, darling—thee must take some nourishment. Just a little of this warm milk—please?"

No. They wanted her to keep on living, when there was nothing to live for. Couldn't they understand? Why wouldn't they just let her go? Deliberately she closed her lips tightly, turned her face toward the wall.

How long she lay so, inert, unresponsive, yet agonizingly conscious, she could not have told. Hours? Days? It seemed an eternity. Time had no meaning, no present, only past and future, the one bright and brief, the other dark and endless. It was a voice that finally penetrated her obdurate withdrawal from reality, faint and piping.

"Mama?"

Startled, she opened her eyes, turned her head. The small eager face was close to hers, blue eyes so like her own brimming with tears, lips trembling. Her beautiful, idolized little Payne.

"Mama?" The blue eyes met hers, eager, hopeful. "Thee get well? Thee come back?"

Nothing to live for? She stretched out her arms. "Yes, darling. Mama come back."

PART THREE

Widening World
1794 – 1797

1

The ravaged city, bereft of some five thousand of its inhabitants by death, many more by flight, slowly subsided to a semblance of normal life. On November 11 only four deaths were reported. The President and Congress returned from their recess to concern themselves with other problems than yellow fever—war in Europe, French mobs, increased British impressment of seamen, neutrality, embargoes, growing tensions between factions in government.

Normal life? Only a semblance! President Washington had entered unwillingly on a second term that year of the plague, persuaded that he was the only one who could keep the dissident factions from disrupting the country. But he was faced with an almost impossible task. Independence had not freed the new nation from embroilment in the confusion of European politics, and the present situation was one of crisis. The French Republic, born of revolution, had turned radical, beheaded the King, defied most of the thrones of Europe, and involved itself in war, not only with England, its traditional enemy, but with Holland, Sardinia, and others as well. An envoy, Citizen Edmond Genêt, had arrived in America, stirring up action to support the French in loyalty to the treaties of 1778, which pledged the United States to military alliance with her revolutionary ally.

The country was in turmoil, its two political factions polarized. Republicans, headed by Thomas Jefferson, lover of France and ardent Democrat, were in sympathy with the new republic, arguing for support of the treaty even if it led to war. Its excesses, Jefferson believed stoutly, were only temporary. Its ideals—liberty, equality, fraternity—would triumph in the end.

Federalists, many of whom had remained Tories even during the Revolution, were all for support of England. The treaty, they claimed, had been made with the King, and the King was dead. Therefore it was void. Not so, asserted Jefferson. A treaty was made with a country, not a person, and was sacred.

Even the Federalists, however, were shocked by some English actions. Britain had long engaged in the practice of stopping American vessels and removing from them seamen who they claimed were deserters from her navy. Now a new act, called an Order in Council, passed in the fall of 1793, proclaimed her right to seize all neutral ships taking goods to British colonies. Soon American ships, most of them from Federalist New England, were being stopped, stripped of their cargoes as contraband, their seamen, whether or not claiming American citizenship, being impressed and forced into the British Navy. Washington declared strict neutrality. An embargo was laid on trade with England. With many Republicans disillusioned with the excesses of Danton and Marat in the new French government and many Federalists at odds with British arrogances, affairs were at an impasse. Still the two political parties remained poles apart.

For Dolley there was not even a semblance of normality. Life as she had known it had ended. The world with its trees stripped bare, its frozen, often snow-encrusted ground was the outer shell of an inner core of coldness. The big three-storied house on the corner of Fourth and Walnut streets which she and John had so proudly bought and furnished reverberated with echoes. Even though Mama and the children had moved in with her, the boardinghouse having fallen victim to the congressional upheaval, it seemed desolate and empty.

Grief she felt, but that was not her only problem. She was struggling desperately to survive. Though John had made a will in July giving and devising "all my estate real and personal to the Dear Wife of my Bosom and first and only Woman upon whom my all and only affections were placed, Dolley Payne Todd, her Heirs and assigns forever," she had received not a penny of her inheritance. John's brother James had taken possession of not only the effects of his father and mother, as was his right, but those of his brother also. Repeatedly Dolley had sent him requests to send her John's papers so that the estate might be settled, but his only reply had been a suggestion that she sell John's books to raise any funds she required. Sell his books, indeed! "I was hurt, my dear Jamey, that the idea of his library should occur as a proper source for raising money.—Books from which he wished his Child improved, shall remain sacred, and I would feel the pinching hand of Poverty before I disposed of them."

She was feeling its pinching hand. In Gray's Ferry there had been barely enough money to bury the baby and secure a chair and horse to bring them back to Philadelphia. The situation was becoming desperate. In spite of all economies, dispensing with servants, she and Molly going to market and purchasing the barest necessities of food, she was hopelessly in debt. Molly, she knew, felt guilty because she and the children were an additional financial burden.

"Thee must not worry," Dolley tried to assure her. "John was not a poor man. Once the estate is settled . . ."

Then one day Molly came bringing a letter. "It's from Lucy." She looked half pleased, half apologetic. "She wants me to come and bring the children. She says they have a big house, this Harewood which George inherited. And he wants us. But—I shouldn't be leaving thee, not now!"

Dolley read the letter. Was it relief she felt? Surely it was an ideal solution. Security and plenty for Mama and the children, for her four fewer mouths to feed! But—to be left alone—no one to share this new, terrible responsibility!

"Of course thee must go." She tried to sound cheerful. "Everything is so uncertain here. Who knows what the future may bring?" She smiled ruefully. "And we thought that was such an unfortunate marriage! Our Lucy was wiser than we were."

It was settled. Molly left with her two youngest children, Mary and John. Anna, to Dolley's delight, preferred to remain with her. Now nearly fifteen, bubbling with lighthearted gaiety and blossoming into youthful beauty, this beloved sister, together with her own little Payne, was a ray of light and warmth in the big empty house.

But in spite of their presence Dolley felt alone and helpless. For the first time in her life she had no one to depend on but herself. Even the two advisers John had commissioned in his will, Edward Burd and Edward Tilghman, had done nothing to solve her problems. Of course she need not have felt devoid of help, for she had many relatives and friends, any one of whom would have welcomed the opportunity to assist. There was Colonel Isaac Coles, her mother's brother, a Congressman residing in the city. There was Aaron Burr, her mother's former boarder, with whom she had become well acquainted. There were Anthony Morris and Eliza Collins, her wedding attendants, and other Quakers at Pine Street Meeting. But she would not, *could* not, ask them for money, even for loans. It would seem like betrayal of John, who had thought he was providing for her. She could not expose family problems to public gaze. Instead she let debts to merchants accumulate, sold a few household effects—but *not* books—resorted to the only marketable asset she possessed, needlework, consenting to create artful costume designs for her Quaker friends, and pinched every penny.

Weeks passed, and still no settlement. On January 14, 1794, a division was made of Mary Todd's clothing, on paper, two thirds to Dolley and one third to James, but she had still received no portion of John's estate. February. And suddenly Dolley knew she had been a dependent child long enough. She hired a lawyer, one of John's respected friends, William Wilkins, to give legal assistance. She sent brother James a letter by messenger, not just pleading this time.

"As I have already suffered the most serious Inconvenience from the unnecessary Detention of my Part of my Mother-in-Law's property and of the Receipt Book and papers of my late Husband—I am constrained once more to request—and if a request is not sufficient, to *demand* that they be delivered this day—As I cannot wait thy return from the proposed Excursion without material Injury to my Affairs.

"The bearer waits for thy answer. Dolley P. Todd."

At last, results. She began to receive her portion of Todd family furnishings and effects. But not until over a year later, under the pressure of an even more obdurate agent than William Wilkins, would a full settlement be made. Before that time she would have lived through some of the most difficult, most bewildering, yet finally most fulfilling days of her life.

It was during that bleak winter of loneliness and uncertainty that an incident occurred that would profoundly affect her future. She was walking to market one day by her favorite route, past the Indian Queen. Even now, troubled though she was, she craved the stimulus of social gatherings, and there was always human interest about the city's finest hotel, congressmen coming and going, fine ladies dressed in the latest Paris fashions, foreign visitors, occasionally an Indian in full regalia. Though usually little Payne was with her, for she could seldom bear to have him out of her sight, today it was cold and windy, and she had left him in Anna's care.

Even the weather that winter had been unkind. Though mild at Christmas, January had brought heavy snow and bitter cold which had persisted into February. Dolley picked her way carefully, for it had snowed again the night before, covering the patches of ice. There were few people about, and the hotel looked deserted except for two men standing talking below the steps. One of them, she thought, looked vaguely familiar. Intrigued, she turned her head to observe them more closely, and she could not help overhearing some of their conversation.

"These resolutions of yours restricting our trade with nations who discriminate against us—people are shouting your praises all over the country!"

"Not everywhere, my friend. Not in New England, where merchants are still clinging to their trade with England in spite of her unjust seizure of our ships and seamen."

Attention diverted, Dolley failed to watch her step. Her foot slipped on a treacherous patch of ice, and she foundered, would have fallen if a strong pair of arms had not encircled her, held her upright.

"Oh!" she gasped. "I—I thank thee, sir!"

She looked into a pair of blue-gray eyes almost exactly level with her own, set in a somewhat sallow face with sober, almost forbidding features. No wonder he had looked familiar. An old sobersides, she had once thought him. When she was firmly on her feet again, the strong arms released her. "Pray, forgive my—shall we say—ungentlemanly presumption, Mistress—?" His voice rose as if in question.

"Todd," supplied Dolley meekly.

"Ah yes, I thought so. And, if I am not mistaken—have we not met before—a long time ago?"

"Many years ago," she replied, wondering how good was his memory.

It was all too good. The gray-blue eyes lighted with that same whimsical gleam. "This time, I guess," he said slyly, "it was I who was one big jump ahead."

Dolley laughed merrily, surprising herself by the sound, for it was the first time she had heard it in months. He insisted on escorting her home, and she did not object. They could get along without her intended purchases, and, as he said, it was not a proper day for a lady to be traveling the treacherous streets unassisted.

Later Dolley marveled at the ease she had felt in the company of "the great little Madison," as people called him, "great" because of his political achievements, "little" because of his slight figure, little taller than Dolley's own five feet five. She had forgotten that he was considered the most important and influential member of Congress, that he was already being acclaimed as the "Father of the Constitution," that he was probably the foremost authority on political history and government in America, if not in the world. When he had expressed admiration for her husband, whom he had known, sympathy for her loss, she had lost all awe and reticence, and she had confided thoughts and emotions as she might have done to her father or an older brother.

"What must he have thought of me!" she exclaimed ruefully when recounting the incident to her friend Eliza Collins. "Prattling away like a silly child, boasting of the clever things Payne says and the bargain I found in market in a Virginia ham!"

"Hm." Thoughtfully Eliza appraised her friend's piquant young face with the glowing brilliancy of its skin, its sparkling blue eyes, its frame of black curls escaping from the demure Quaker bonnet. "Hardly a child," she commented. "By the way," she added with an apparent change of subject, "that lawyer of thine, William Wilkins. I suppose thee knows that he is falling in love with thee."

The blue eyes widened in consternation. "N—no! What makes thee think so?"

"My dear, I don't think, I know. So do half the others at Pine Street Meeting. All we have to do is see the way he looks at thee, waits to speak with thee after service."

"B—But he's my lawyer. He has things to talk about, to explain."

"And doesn't he have some queer name he calls thee?"

Dolley frowned. "He calls me Julia, says I remind him of someone by that name."

"Hm. Someone he cared a lot about, no doubt. But don't look so worried, pet. It's not thy fault. Thee can't help being just about the most attractive young widow that ever walked the streets of Philadelphia."

Dolley *was* worried. Somehow it had not occurred to her that anyone would expect her to remarry. And William Wilkins! True, he had been more than necessarily attentive to her business affairs, but he had been John's trusted friend and she had considered his concern only an expression of loyalty to her husband. She had even thought of making him the guardian of little Payne in case something happened to her. But, no, she must not do that. William might think she was encouraging a more intimate relationship. Henceforth she must be careful to treat him only as a business adviser. Besides, was he really the sort of person to whom she would want to trust the child's future, too much the meticulous and unimaginative lawyer? John had had such dreams for his son! Who, then? Certainly not his uncle James. The first thing he would do would be to sell John's precious library, his son's heritage!

Though Dolley was almost certain Eliza was mistaken about William Wilkins's romantic notions, when she wrote him again about a business matter, she added some personal words which, she felt, would permit no misunderstanding in their relationship.

"My good friend.—I wonder if I have ever properly expressed my gratitude for services which have far exceeded mere professional duty. I know that it is loyalty to my beloved husband which has prompted thy exceptional attention to my interests. I have three older brothers. They have all gone away, so were not here when I needed them most. Thee have been the brother who has taken their place in my need. That is how I shall always think of thee, as a brother. And I do thank thee for thy protective concern. Thy grateful friend and sister, Dolley Payne Todd."

There! If Eliza was right . . . She wasn't, of course, but just in case . . . She was relieved when his letter dealing with the business matter came. It was signed, "Thy friend and brother, William Wilkins."

The problem of a possible guardian for Payne! She felt hounded by the necessity of choice. Life was so uncertain. In a matter of days it had robbed her of in-laws, husband, son, a multitude of friends. She herself had been close to death. Little Payne was the focus of all her hopes, her anxieties. He slept beside her at night, followed her about the house by day, accompanied her on all excursions except when the weather was inclement. Anna complained when he willfully destroyed one of her prize possessions. "He should be spanked," she insisted vehemently, but Dolley only smiled. "Not yet, dear. He didn't mean any harm, and he's such a baby, only two." Anna sniffed. Perhaps she vaguely surmised that similar excuses would be forthcoming when the age was *twenty*-two.

Dolley found the answer to her problem. It came one day when an old friend, Aaron Burr, came to the house to call. He and Dolley had often enjoyed spirited conversations at her mother's boardinghouse. Dolley admired the charming, vivacious senator, famous for his distinguished military career and his brilliant leadership in Congress, and in his presence she felt more animated and less depressed than at any time since John's death. Both of them were lonely, for Burr's wife, an incurable invalid, was back in their New York home with their teenage daughter Theodosia. Burr was as worshipfully fond of his daughter as was Dolley of little Payne, and their conversation soon centered on the fine literary training he was supervising for young Theodosia.

"This country will be proud of her name one day," he asserted confidently. "She has a brilliant mind and is being as well educated as any son of mine could possibly be. I'm making her development my first concern, even above my own career."

Dolley's eyes shone. The idea had come to her with a flash of inspiration. When little Payne came into the room and instantly became the object of the guest's interest and attention, she was sure. She would make a will, as Wilkins was urging her to do, and, if anything happened to her, Aaron Burr would be her son's guardian. Whatever might happen in the future to cast aspersion on her choice, her judgment would be vindicated by one biographer who would write of him, "He had a veritable passion for adopting and rearing children."

Suddenly Dolley awoke to the discovery that it was spring. The chestnuts began to put forth tender leaves, to stream long catkins. Presently other trees foamed white or pink or crimson with blossoms. There was a heady fragrance in the air. Pedestrians on the unpaved streets picked their way around mud holes instead of patches of snow and ice. Housewives who had neglected their outdoor chores during the cold months scrubbed their white stone steps and stoops every Wednesday and Saturday until they shone. And Dolley felt the hard frozen core of her own spirit melting. Not that she had stopped grieving or that the void of terrible loss had even started to fill. But, like the renewed earth, she knew that it was time to live again.

Quakers did not believe in wearing mourning garb, nor did Quaker women confine themselves any longer to the old coarse dull browns and grays. Though simple, even austere in style, the gown beneath the folded white kerchief was often of flowered calico, varicolored silk, or even satin. Head coverings could be caps of fine transparent tulle as well as concealing bonnets with wide rims resembling horses' blinders.

Dolley blossomed like the trees. She took out of her clothes chest some of the gowns she had made of more delicate colors and fabrics, the ones John had liked best. She knew he would want her to wear them. She put on the prettiest one, topped her black curls with a filmy bonnet whose ruffle of lace ended in long streamers tied in a bow under her chin, and went with Anna to an afternoon tea at the home of their friend Sally, daughter of Thomas McKean, a signer of the Declaration of Independence and onetime governor of Pennsylvania. Once more she attended some of Martha Washington's Friday evening levees. She took little Payne to one of William Penn's parks and, regardless of adult stares, ran races with him on the new soft grass. That on her twice weekly trips to market, her route taking her past the

Indian Queen, her trim figure and alluring features attracted unusual male attention, she was either unaware of or happily indifferent to.

"Really, Dolley," Eliza once chided good-naturedly, "thee must hide thy face, there are so many staring at thee."

Dolley only smiled. She enjoyed admiration, but she knew she acted wholly in conformance with the strict Quaker code of morality, which did not require a woman to bury her face within the confines of an ugly sunbonnet. She little guessed, however, that in these days of brief widowhood she was the object of purposeful speculation on the part of more than one widower or bachelor, one in particular.

Until one May day in that year of 1794 . . .

2

As Elizabeth Collins read the note delivered to her by messenger, her bright eyes sparkled with excitement.

"Thee must come to me. Aaron Burr says that the great little Madison has asked to be brought to see me this evening."

So! According to the prevailing social code the communication meant one thing. The most eligible bachelor in Philadelphia was seeking to pay court to the city's most attractive widow. Hastily Eliza packed a portmanteau with one of her best gowns and all its accessories, summoned the family carriage, and set off for Number 51 South Fourth Street. She found Dolley walking the floor in great perturbation.

"My dear, how wonderful! The most brilliant member of the House, they say he is. And wouldn't it be exciting, both of us married to prominent men from Virginia!" Eliza, who was engaged to Richard Bland Lee, another leading Congressman, was looking forward to her marriage in the near future.

"But—he's only coming to call," protested Dolley. "What makes thee think it means—"

"Thee knows very well what it means," interrupted her friend. "When a man approaches a lady through a third party, it means he desires to court her."

Dolley was all the more perturbed. "But—how do I know I want him to court me? I—I scarcely know him."

"Thee will," assured Eliza astutely, "before it comes time to decide. I did. Rather a masterly stroke, wasn't it," she added sagely, "his asking Burr to be his intermediary?"

Dolley looked puzzled. "What—why—"

"My dear, doesn't thee know what people are saying—that once Burr is free, and his wife, of course, is fatally ill, he also is likely to pay court to thee? Madison must know that Burr is likely to be one of his chief rivals for thy hand."

"No!" Dolley flushed hotly. "How can people think that? Why—he's just a friend—"

"A very attentive one," reminded Eliza. "And I have an idea," her eyes narrowed speculatively, "that Burr was willing to introduce Madison to you because he's in debt to him for certain favors. They say Madison has been urging the President to accede to Burr's request to appoint him as minister to France."

Dolley's head swam. *People are saying!* Could one not even keep an association with an old family friend without causing tongues to wag? Suddenly she wondered how much more they would gossip if they knew that she had just signed a will making Aaron Burr the guardian of her son in case the need arose!

"Come now," urged Eliza, "we must make plans. Thee did well to summon me, for of course thee could not receive them alone. I brought one of my best gowns, my buff silk with the peach bloom scarf. What is thee planning to wear?"

When evening came they were ready. As her grandniece Lucia Cutts would report long afterward, Dolley was dressed in "a mulberry colored satin, with a silk tulle kerchief over her neck, and on her head an exquisitely dainty cap, from which an occasional uncropped curl would escape." They received the two guests in the formal parlor, its polished mahogany furniture and the silverware on the refreshment table shining in the candlelight.

In spite of her perturbation Dolley was the perfect hostess. Pouring tea into the fragile cups, her hand did not tremble. Adroitly she guided the conversation to include some of her guests' major interests, Burr's love for his daughter Theodosia, Madison's life as a Virginia planter. When the latter began talking about his ancestral home, which he liked to call Montpelier—meaning "bald hills or mountains," he explained—his sober features brightened, the stern lips relaxing into the warm smile she so well remembered. He was more interested, she noted, in the world around it than in the estate itself.

"You should see the prospect! The Blue Ridge Mountains thirty miles away across a broad expanse of green meadows and sweeping forests, long undulating miles of them! All changing in color and shading every hour! One could watch them for years on end, and they would never be the same. Enough food for the spirit for a lifetime!"

When the two men began talking about political problems—the war in Europe, seizure of vessels by the British, John Jay's mission to England to try to negotiate a treaty—Dolley could relax. Both men were leaders in politics, Burr a senator, Madison a representative, and so close were they to the country's problems that even during this social call they could not rid themselves of responsibility. They were in agreement on many issues. Madison had actively supported Burr's candidacy as minister to France, but without success. James Monroe had received the appointment.

Dolley only half listened to the conversation. They were discussing the mounting grievances against Britain. Bad enough, it was, her failure to give up the western forts in accordance with the Treaty of 1783 and her encouragement of Indian raids on American settlers, but this seizure of commercial vessels, this increased impressment of sailors for the British navy, were stirring up sentiment for war even among New England Federalists, who depended on trade with Britain and her island colonies for their commercial prosperity. President Washington, however, was determined to maintain peace. In April, just a month before, he had sent John Jay, Chief Justice of the Supreme Court, to England to try to negotiate a treaty which would remove the causes of these grievances.

"Let us hope and pray," said Madison, "that he succeeds, but I am not too confident. Jay is too much a staunch Anglophile to press hard for concessions. I confess I expect little justice from Britain."

"Then let us have war!" Burr asserted, his voice loud and authoritative. "Do you realize that a hundred of our vessels have been seized by the British for condemnation as a result of this abominable Order in Council? Britain is treating us again like one of her colonies! You'd think we had never won our independence!"

Madison shook his head. "Not war." His voice was low and mild but firmly penetrating. "Embargo or nonintercourse, yes, proper retaliation for their attacks on our commerce. I believe war at this time, with our dissonant parties, would mean dissolution of our new republic."

Dolley found herself studying the two men with a critical eye. Though they were about the same height, small men, there similarity ended. They were as unlike as two people could possibly be: Burr flamboyant in a suit of blue velvet with a rose-pink waistcoat adorned with buttons of a darker pink shell in silver settings, white silk stockings and silver-buckled shoes; Madison in sober black, ruffled shirt, short breeches with buckles at the knees, black silk stockings and shoes with simple lacings. Burr graceful, charming, vivacious, fluent and impassioned of speech; Madison slow, unemotional in manner, a bit stolid, but with a twinkle in his mild blue-gray eyes. Burr a brilliant member of the Senate, destined no doubt for higher office, perhaps even President; Madison defeated in his contest for senator from Virginia, yet respected for his quiet but potent leadership in the lower House. Suppose, as Eliza had so amazingly suggested, both of these men were to become aspirants for her hand! Which would she choose?

Dolley kept looking at them thoughtfully, shrewdly, as they talked, one glib, argumentative, full of self-assurance, the other slow, mild of speech, deliberate, obviously sure of facts and figures, quietly confident. Suddenly she wished she had not signed the will making Aaron Burr the possible guardian of little Payne.

Slow of speech James Madison undoubtedly was, but he was not slow in pursuing his courtship of the widow Todd. Once the proper approach had been made, it became socially correct for a suitor to call, and he did so, not once but several times. Before the month had passed, through her cousin, Isaac Coles, he made his proposal of marriage, which Dolley received with dignity and gratitude. She appreciated the high honor he had paid her. She did not refuse, nor did she say yes. He had to give her time to consider. The fact that Aaron Burr's wife had died soon after he had brought Madison to her house had nothing to do with her hesitation. If there had been a choice between the two, she had already made it.

Big though Philadelphia was, the largest city in the country, its grapevine of romantic gossip was all-pervasive. It was soon common knowledge that the "great little Madison" was courting the widow Todd.

Presently Dolley received a note from the First Lady inviting her to come to the President's house for tea. It was not an unusual request, since she and the Washingtons were indirectly related through her sister Lucy. Perhaps Martha had received some news from George Steptoe that she wanted to share. She was somewhat surprised, however, to find herself the only guest.

While they were having tea and the maid had left them alone, Martha Washington disclosed the purpose of her invitation. "I hope you won't think me meddlesome," she broached tentatively, "but—I am going to ask you a very personal question. My dear, are you engaged to James Madison?"

Dolley was taken aback. She became so nervous she slopped some of her tea into the saucer. She felt herself flushing. "Why, I—No, I think not," she stammered foolishly, the words disclosing the uncertainty of her own mind.

"I understand," said Martha, reaching out to touch her hand. "You mean that he has proposed, but you have not yet been able to make up your mind. A very natural reaction, since you lost your dear husband so recently. But, my dear, I just wanted you to know how the President and I feel about it. He would make you a good husband, and all the better for being so much older. We both approve of it highly, though the President is always unwilling to give advice in matters of the heart. The esteem and friendship existing between Mr. Madison and my husband is very great, and we do think he would make you very happy."

Dolley thanked her for her concern and left as soon as courtesy permitted. She was heartened by the First Lady's approval of her suitor's proposal yet more uncertain than ever. It was she who must make up her mind, not others, not even the kindly and persuasive First Lady of the land. And if the rumor of her engagement had reached the President's ears, how many others—!

She was soon to discover. At Pine Street Meeting on Sundays she was conscious of pursed lips, speculative, hostile eyes, averted faces. Already they were accusing her for even considering marriage to a man outside the Quaker fold, a "libertine," as they called him, the ceremony to be performed by a "hireling priest." Eliza Collins, on the eve of her marriage to Richard Bland Lee, was encountering the same cold disapproval, but apparently without the same distress.

"Doesn't thee care?" Dolley demanded of her friend when she visited the Collins house to inspect the elaborate bridal finery. "They will expel thee from the Society. Yet thee doesn't seem to mind!"

"Of course I mind," replied Eliza soberly. "But I love Richard, and I'd rather be cast out than to give him up. Besides, I know it's not right, their being so narrow and bigoted. Sometime they will know it too, not in our lifetime maybe, but sometime." She smiled mischievously. "And I won't be the first one to be cast out. How about thy sister Lucy? Is she sorry she made her choice? Isn't she happy?"

"Yes," admitted Dolley.

Still she could not come to a decision. Suddenly she knew she must get away, from Philadelphia, from her attentive and importunate suitor, from friends trying to persuade her, from critics so violent in their opposition that they seemed like enemies. She acted swiftly, renting her house for six months, making plans to spend the summer with relatives in Virginia. Telling Madison she would give him her answer before the summer was over, taking only Anna, little Payne, and a maid, she set out by stage in June for Auburn, the plantation of Great-uncle Isaac Winston, over roads winding across the Susquehanna, through Baltimore, over the Maryland hills, into Virginia, returning at last after eleven years to the familiar rolling hills and green valleys of Hanover County. It was like coming home, for it was near Scotchtown and she had often visited her uncle's family in the old days. Here, free from all conflicting warnings and persuasions, she could surely make up her mind.

But she was not free. Letters kept coming. One of them, from Catherine, wife of her cousin, Congressman Isaac Coles, she found amusing, it was so obviously an attempt at matchmaking.

"Now for Madison, he told me I might say what I pleased to you about him. To begin, he thinks so much of you in the Day that he has Lost his Tongue. At Night he Dreams of you and Startes in his Sleep a Calling you to relieve his Flame for he burns to such an excess that he will be shortly consumed and he hopes your Heart will be calous to every other swain but himself. He has consented to everything that I have wrote about him with Sparkling Eyes. Monroe goes to France as Minister Plenipo—Madison has taken his house. Do you like it?"

Her cousin's wife, Dolley decided, must be gifted with an extraordinary imagination. The restrained and dignified Madison yielding to confession of such excessive degrees of emotion was impossible enough to be laughable.

Congress adjourned in June. Madison, she knew, was now in Montpelier and waiting for her answer. Letters kept coming from him. He was enjoying his family and working hard, one of his tasks translating for a French guest who spoke no English, but he was waiting impatiently for the infrequent posts, hoping . . . hoping . . .

Suddenly Dolley was laid low by fever, malaria the doctor called it, perhaps the same illness that had prostrated her at Gray's Ferry. While heat tortured her body, her mind still struggled with the momentous problem of choice, arguing with herself pro and con, like two adversaries in the red haze of battle, for the first time, it seemed, putting the uncertainty into words.

To be read "out of unity," cast out, no longer one of the Children of Light, like so many others of the family! How can thee? . . . But no one can take away the Inner Light. That comes not from people but from God.

To unite thyself with one so different from thyself, one so brilliant of mind, a deep thinker, perhaps destined to be a great leader? Might not thee become a hindrance? . . . But perhaps he needs someone like thee, someone to provide emotion, laughter, love of people.

Would he be the right father for little Payne? Perhaps Aaron Burr or William Wilkins . . . No, thee knows better. He is thoughtful, loving, a man to set a child the best possible pattern to follow.

The struggle went on and on . . . until finally the fever abated, and along with it the uncertainty. As soon as she felt well enough, even before Aunt and Uncle considered her fully recovered, she left with Anna and Payne for Harewood, where Lucy and her mother had been long expecting her. On the way, stopping overnight in an inn in Fredericksburg to change stages, she wrote two letters, one to James Madison saying that after proper time had elapsed she would become his wife, the other to William Wilkins, her lawyer, asking his advice on financial matters attendant to her marriage.

It was August 18 when Madison wrote his jubilant reply.

"I received your precious favor from Fredericksburg. I cannot express, but hope you will conceive the joy it gave me. The delay in hearing of your leaving Hanover which I regarded as the only satisfactory proof of your recovery, has filled me with extreme inquietude, and the consummation of that welcome event was endeared to me by the *stile* in which it was conveyed. I hope you will never have another deliberation on that subject. If the sentiments of my heart can guarantee those of yours, they assure me there can never be a cause for it."

William Wilkins's reply came almost as promptly. He was warm in his approval and admiration of Madison. "To such a man I do most freely consent that my beloved sister be united and happy. Yes, my dear and amiable Julia, you have my fullest and freest Approbation of the Step you are about to take. No wish is dearer to my Heart than your happiness and Heaven is my Witness that nothing is less selfish than my attachment to you. That I have not been insensible to your Charms ought not I think be regarded as a fault—few persons in similar Situations would not have felt their irresistible influence: but none I would venture to say could have mingled in their emotions more true Respect and more Fraternal Affection than I have."

So . . . Eliza was right. He had been in love with her, obviously still was. She sighed with relief. At least she had managed to impress upon him her desire for a sisterly relationship. The rest of the letter was entirely of business. "You are placed in a critical situation in this

Affair—the Eyes of the World are upon you and your Enemies have already opened their mouths to censure and condemn you." He advised her to place much of her estate in the hands of trustees for the support and education of her son, to become his when he reached maturity.

Her "enemies." Yes, they could be called that, John's relatives who had been making things so hard for her and would certainly oppose her remarriage; the Quaker "friends" who had turned against her at the mere rumor of her marriage to a "libertine" outside the fold. Wilkins was wise, cautious, practical, a good businessman. She would follow his advice exactly. Did it occur to her that if he had been less cautious, more imaginatively assertive, like another of her suitors, she might now be preparing to be Mrs. William Wilkins instead of Mrs. James Madison?

3

It was a happy reunion. Dolley had not realized how homesick she had been for family. She wept in her mother's arms, exclaimed over the growth of young Mary and John, aged twelve and eleven, delighted in the obvious happiness of Lucy and her George. They in turn expressed surprise at little Payne's two-year-old precocity in speech and agility and at the lovely Anna's emergence at sixteen into the full bloom of womanhood.

Dolley had dreaded disclosing the news of her contemplated marriage, fearing an unfavorable reaction. Would they think it was too soon after John's death? That her suitor was too old, seventeen years her senior? Especially, how would her mother feel about another member of the family becoming an outcast from the Quaker fold? Already three boys, husband, a daughter! She need not have worried.

"My dear," said Mary equably, "he is a good man, and I am happy for thee. I could not have asked a better prospect for thy future." Perhaps her months of benefiting from the happy marriage she had so adamantly opposed had taught her the folly of interference in matters of the heart.

Reaction from others in the family was exuberant.

"How exciting! Will he be coming here? Will we see him?"

"Can we come to the wedding? Can I wear my new yellow cambric with the pink flowers?"

"Where will thee live? He's a Virginian, isn't he, like us? Thee will not be away off in Philadelphia?"

"Of course you must have the wedding here," insisted Lucy with possessive pride. "Don't you think it's a beautiful house for a wedding?"

"She's already saying 'you' instead of 'thee,'" thought Dolley, shocked suddenly by the prospect of inevitable change. "Soon I shall have to learn."

"Yes," she said. "It's a lovely house. I shall be glad to have it here. Thee—you are very fortunate, Lucy."

Dolley was happily surprised by Harewood. Samuel Washington, the President's brother, had been considered a poor manager, constantly in debt. Married five times, at his death he had left four children to be supported and educated by his brother George. But Harewood, George Steptoe's inheritance, was now in thriving condition. Though still in his teens, Lucy's young husband was handling his property with the acumen of a responsible adult. The house, though perhaps not a "mansion" like his uncle's Mount Vernon, was large and comfortable, built of rock quarried from a magnificent blue-gray limestone ridge running through the estate. The hauler, it was recorded, had been paid an acre of land for each teamload brought in a day. Dolley delighted in its unusual features, in its staircase which was like that at Mount Vernon but broader and with lower risers, in its elegantly paneled drawing room with walls of watered silk and a gorgeous mantel of greenish marble, one of two that Lafayette had presented to Washington; in its fine woodwork, the pilasters, wainscoting, and cornices all brought from England. Yes, it was a beautiful place to be married in, a startling contrast to the bare stark Meeting House in Philadelphia.

Sharply conscious of the disparity, she felt the old uncertainty returning. How could she change her whole way of life—dress, speech, manner of worship, friends? One day she found her mother sitting alone, sewing on her wedding dress, a gown of white silk cut simply, as became a Quaker bride, with a wide V-shaped yoke about the high neck in lieu of a kerchief.

"Mama, tell me, please—" She hesitated, then blurted, "If thee had felt sure that Papa would never become a believer, would thee have married him just the same?"

Mary Payne laid down her sewing. She considered. Her eyes became soft and reminiscent. "Yes," she said. "In fact, I had no reason to believe that he could become one of us. I could only hope. And—we were very much in love."

In love. Perhaps that was the reason for her uncertainty. Lucy had felt no hesitation about marrying George and being disowned by Meeting, even eloping in defiance of family, and seeing them together, Dolley could understand why. Perhaps that was why she herself had waited so long—five years—to yield to John Todd's importunate suit. She had not been "in love" with him until after their marriage, and even then it had not been this radiant, starry-eyed emotion that shone in Lucy's eyes. Now, mercilessly, she probed her feelings for James Madison, this man who was literally old enough to be her father, vastly superior in intellect, a leader among his peers. Did she "love" him? Could admiration, deep respect, confidence, joy in companionship be called "love," or would it grow into it as with John Todd? Uncertainty again, confusion!

Then suddenly he was there, riding up the path through the grove of honey locusts, being greeted in proper Virginia hospitality by George and Lucy, George's sister Harriot, Molly Payne and her three younger children, lifting two-year-old Payne to his shoulders with the possessive gallantry of a prospective doting father, then later, when the family thoughtfully left them alone, taking Dolley's hands in both his own and looking into her eyes with the same radiance of emotion she had often seen passing between Lucy and her George.

He was eager for an early wedding, but Dolley tried to postpone the actual setting of a date. It was August, and not until October would the first year of her widowhood be ended. She permitted him, however, to place on her finger a beautiful gold ring set with eight rose diamonds. She found him fully agreeable to all the suggestions William Wilkins had made for little Payne's security. Madison was not at all interested in securing any of her estate for himself. It was right and proper that after the $350 mortgage on her house was paid, the rents on it should be used for the child's support and education, all the property to go to him at age twenty-one. Yes, of course he would be willing for the child to be brought up as a Quaker.

"And if"—she hesitated—"*when* we marry, even though the Meeting will probably cast me out, I shall always be a Quaker at heart. Nothing can shake my belief in its emphasis on conscience and the Inner Light."

He nodded. "Of course, my beloved. You must know that for years I have fought in both state and nation for people to be free to worship according to their conscience."

He was patient. At George's and Lucy's insistence he remained their guest while Dolley continued to temporize. She watched him as he quietly, unobtrusively endeared himself to members of the family, riding with George over his estate and giving sage advice about crop rotation and management and markets, contrasting the soil favorably with that of his own plantation at Orange; rousing laughter with his wry humor at the dinner table; telling stories of student pranks at the

College of New Jersey to the wide-eyed Mary and John; bringing a sparkle to Lucy's and Anna's eyes with his thoughtful compliments. Most of all she observed his conduct with her idolized little Payne, senses alert for any signs of resentment at what she knew was her obsessive devotion to the child. But as they walked in the garden, the boy loudly insisting on following, he made no protest, even by a frown, and often hoisted him to his shoulders as they strolled along the paths between the boxwood hedges, set him chortling with glee as he imitated the motions of a cavorting steed. He encouraged the child to climb on his knee when the family gathered at teatime. He smiled indulgently when she followed her custom of remaining at the boy's bedside each night until he fell asleep.

"I know I'm being overprotective, probably spoiling him. But—he's still just a baby, and—he's been all I had left."

"Yes, my dear. I understand."

It was this growing appreciation of his potential as a foster father even more than as a husband that brought her to a decision. She set the date for their wedding for September 15, six weeks before the year of her widowhood was to expire. Time for preparation was short, and the household was plunged into excitement. It would be a small wedding, she insisted, just the family. Madison's sister Nelly and her husband, Major Isaac Hite, were invited, for their home near Strasburg was within driving distance. Others of his family lived too far away to come. Madison secured the services of the Reverend Alexander Balmain of Winchester, who had married his cousin Lucy Taylor.

The day dawned, September 15, 1794. Strange that everything could seem so normal and ordinary, little Payne fussing to be dressed, servants clattering pots in the cookhouse, crows cawing, even the sun rising as usual. Was it memory of her first wedding day that soon sent her to find paper and quill pen and start a letter to Eliza Collins, now Lee, who was still away on her honeymoon at Warm Springs?

"*September the 16th.*" She never noticed her mistake in the date. "I received your precious favor from Bath and should have indulged myself in writing an answer but for the excessive weakness in my eyes —And as a proof, my dearest Eliza, of that confidence and friendship which has never been interrupted between us I have stole from the family to commune with you—to tell you in short that in the course of this day I give my hand to the man of all others I most admire. . . . In this union I have every thing that is soothing and grateful in prospect—and my little Payne will have a generous and tender protector.

A settlement of all my real property with a considerable addition of money is made upon him with Mr. M.'s full approbation. This I know you feel an interest in or I would not have troubled you with it. You also are acquainted with the unmerited censure of my enemies on the subject. . . . Adieu! Adieu!—it is yet uncertain whether we shall see you before the meeting in Philadelphia. Mama, Madison, Lucy, George, Anna, and Harriot join in best love to you and yours. Dolley Payne Todd."

In spite of lingering misgivings, being Dolley, she could not resist yielding to the alluring color and noise and fragrance of the day's excitement. The parlor blossomed into a garden as Anna, Mary, and Harriot brought in great armfuls of fall flowers. Tantalizing odors kept drifting from the kitchens, where succulent meats were turning on spits, great kettles were bubbling, breads, cakes, tarts, and biscuits were baking in the huge ovens. When the fateful hour came and eager but painstaking hands tightened stays, hooked, buttoned, patted, smoothed, straightened, fingered with admiring "Ohs!" and "Ahs!," she took a keen delight in the soft sheen of the white satin fabric daintily patterned with lace. Just as long ago she had lovingly fingered the shining silk of Grandmother Payne's sun-yellow gown, her fingers now stroked the beautiful fabric with a caressing motion.

"Such a narrow waist!" sighed the rather plump Harriot enviously.

"Just twenty-three inches," said Mama proudly.

"And that wreath of orange blossoms," bubbled Anna, "so beautiful on those black curls."

As a final touch Dolley fastened about her neck Madison's wedding gift, a necklace of intricate medallions depicting in mosaics subjects from Roman history, Byzantine temples, tombs, bridges, a Colosseum. Trust him to pick something scholarly and historical! Her fingers lingered on their shining loveliness, eleven pictures joined together by delicate chains, as once they had surreptitiously felt beneath her kerchief for a golden butterfly. Strange—startling!—to think that those rigid rules of discipline would soon be in the past. Did she really want such freedom?

She descended the staircase to where the groom waited, looking up at her with such naked devotion in his eyes that Dolley felt a guilty qualm, fearful that she would be giving less than she was receiving. Was she being fair to him?

He was a groom to be proud of, faultlessly, if conservatively, attired in his usual black but with a short-waisted silken coat, richly embroidered waistcoat, and, instead of a plain white neckerchief, an elaborate jabot of fine Mechlin lace. Distinguished-looking he was, in spite of his slenderness and short stature. Standing beside him, Dolley was suddenly glad that she had chosen satin slippers with low heels so that they seemed exactly the same height. She would have hated to look taller than he.

They entered the parlor where the Reverend Mr. Balmain stood waiting in his ecclesiastical robes, the flower-bedecked fireplace behind him, the family gathered around, the jovial and portly Samuel Washington looking down at everything out of his large square frame above the mantel. All so queer and confusing compared with the stark simplicity of a Pine Street Meeting marriage! What was she doing here in this strange house, standing before this strange person of another faith, this "hireling" priest, committing herself to this man by her side, not a "libertine"—her lips quirked, even the most hardbound Quakers could not call him that!—but almost a stranger?

"Dearly Beloved, we are gathered together here in the sight of God to join this man and this woman in holy matrimony, which is an honorable estate, instituted by God . . ."

What beautiful words! As the gentle voice continued with the solemn phrases, hallowed by time but strange to her ears, suddenly the medley of thoughts, emotions, and confusion of details was absorbed into its quiet cadence. She was conscious only of the voice, of a kindly face looking down at her, of a firm hand holding her own.

"James Madison, Junior, wilt thou have this woman to be thy wedded wife, to live together in the holy estate of matrimony; wilt thou love her, comfort her, honor and keep her, in sickness and in health; and forsaking all others keep thee only unto her, as long as ye both shall live?"

Another voice, low but firm and confident. "I will."

Why, it was not at all strange! It was beautiful. They even used the familiar "thee" and "thou"!

"Dolley Payne Todd, wilt thou have this man to be thy wedded husband . . . ?"

It was here, the final, the irrevocable. No more hesitation, no more turning back. The end of one life, the beginning of another. She looked into the kindly face, felt the reassuring pressure of the strong fingers.

"I will," she said clearly.

It was over. Embraces. Congratulations. A festive supper with a loaded table. Music from a tinkling harpsichord, a fiddler grinding out old familiar tunes like "High Betty Martin," "Money Musk," "Leather the Trap." The three young girls daring with reckless bravado to cut up the groom's jabot of beautiful Mechlin lace as souvenirs of the joyous occasion, apparently with his beaming approval.

Suddenly in the midst of the festivities she remembered little Payne. Always she had put him to bed, stayed by his side until he fell asleep. Stricken with self-reproach, she hurried upstairs. There he was, in her bed as usual, sound asleep, her faithful maid beside him. But there were tear stains on his cheeks, and one small arm was flung out as if in search of something.

"He was good, missy, but he cried a bit. Don't worry. I stay here, case he wake up and miss you. Now you go back where you belong."

Dolley thanked her and stooped to kiss the child, still feeling guilty. The first time in months that he had gone to sleep without her goodnight kiss! But the maid was right. She did belong downstairs with her new husband, and this was her big night—wasn't it?

As she passed the desk she saw the letter to Eliza lying as she had left it. Suddenly she sat down and, picking up the quill, added a hasty postscript.

"Evening. Dolley Madison. Alas! Alas!"

She stared at the last two words. What had made her write them? Her Quaker conscience still secretly prodding? The same foolish indecision that had made her keep John Todd waiting for five years? Starting to cross them out, she hesitated, then with a quick motion she tore the paper to completely eliminate them, not noticing that one of them still remained, causing its readers a century and more later to wonder. Why, on the eve of one of the happiest and most noteworthy marriages in history that strange equivocal word—*Alas?*

4

"Your Jemmy," Nelly Hite told Dolley, "is a most remarkable person. I hope you know that already."

Your Jemmy. Dolley was surprised at how much she liked the sound of the words. "Yes—oh yes," she agreed. "Thee—you don't need to tell me."

Nelly Hite's eyes, slate blue like her brother's, held the same mischievous twinkle. "He's not always the sober, stiff intellectual most people think him. He has a keen sense of humor."

"Yes," said Dolley a bit ruefully, remembering her first encounter with her new husband. "I know."

"I could tell you some of his stories and witticisms," continued Nelly. "Yes, and I must admit some of them are a bit vulgar." And she proceeded to relate one of them.

It concerned Madison's student days at the College of New Jersey, later to be known as Princeton University, where he had pursued courses in law, government, Latin, Greek, Hebrew, mathematics, French, astronomy, and theology under the direction of the famous Scottish Presbyterian, Dr. John Witherspoon, its founder. He was an indefatigable student, rising at five, studying far into the night, averaging no more than five hours of sleep a night, and cramming his junior and senior years into one.

"No wonder he became ill," commented Nelly. "He came home finally to Montpelier believing he had some incurable disease and was doomed to die. Fortunately he had a good doctor who, instead of bleeding and blistering him to death, made him take long walks and horseback rides. But to get back to my story—"

The college was a hotbed of rebellion, directed not only against the arrogant political power of King George in England but against the ecclesiastical power of the Established Church in America. Six years ahead of the Declaration of Independence the students were proving in spirited debate that by the law of nature all men are equal. Madison became one of the early members, perhaps one of the founders, of a student society calling themselves the "Whigs," which enjoyed sharp debates with a more conservative rival group which they called the "Tories." During a "paper war" the two groups engaged in a duel of satire, each trying to outdo the other in vilifying verse. At this dubious art Jemmy excelled, and some of his most execrable verses were read at club meetings held in the chapel.

"I was a meddlesome child," said Nelly, "and one day I got into some of his diaries and wrote down some of his poems." She produced a sheet of foolscap. "Here, read this. It's surely his masterpiece."

> Come, noble Whigs, disdain these sons
> Of screech owls, monkeys and baboons.
> Keep up your minds to humorous themes
> And verdant meads and flowing streams
> Until this tribe of dunces find
> The baseness of their grovelling mind
> And skulk within their dens together
> Where each one's stench will kill his brother.

Dolley read the outrageous little ditty with both amusement and amazement. Such vulgar bombast issuing from the chaste lips which had helped shape the dignified phrases of the Constitution, the gentle but skillful hands which had penned its famous Bill of Rights! She was learning more about this complex husband of hers every day. She was glad they had come here to the Hites' home during their honeymoon instead of going to Montpelier, which was too long a trip, James decided, before their return for the opening of Congress in Philadelphia. Better to meet the members of her new family by degrees rather to be plunged into its confusion all at once.

She felt immediately at home in the Hites' house of dressed limestone in the process of being completed that year and found Isaac Hite (called "our Major" by his compatriots) a genial host. He had been the first student to be elected to the new honor society of Phi Beta Kappa at William and Mary College in Williamsburg. The friendly talkative Nelly liked nothing better than to share details of her family and especially of her favorite older brother.

Jemmy—Could Dolley ever get used to calling him that?—was the oldest son of James Madison, senior, and Nelly Conway Madison, first of their ten children, five of whom had died in infancy. As Jemmy himself would say later of his forebears, "In both the paternal and maternal line . . . they were planters and among the respectable, though not the most opulent class." Unlike his brothers, Francis and Ambrose, he had shown little liking for farming, only for books, and his father had given him the best education possible, first with a Donal Robertson, a Scottish schoolmaster in King and Queen County, later with the Reverend Thomas Martin, rector of the Brick Church at Orange. Jemmy was studying Greek and Latin at age twelve; at thirteen he was reading Virgil, Horace, Ovid, Sallust, Terence, and Justinian. He was also learning Spanish and French, both with a Scottish accent. In 1759, when he was eighteen, he traveled on horseback the three hundred miles from the Virginia Piedmont, through wood trails, over rivers by poled ferries, marveling at his first glimpses of cities— Fredericksburg, Alexandria, Baltimore, Philadelphia—arriving at last at the little town containing the stark gray walls and imposing tower of Nassau Hall, the sole building of the College of New Jersey.

Here he became zealous patriot, untiring scholar, probing philosopher, ribald satirist, and returned home physically debilitated but still ardent student, this time of religious history, international law, and politics, study which, carried on for the next fifteen years, was to make him, according to one of his future biographers, "the best informed man in America on the principles of government and the keenest analyst the world had yet produced of the relationship between government and economics."

At the onset of the Revolution, his health partially restored, he became a full colonel in the Orange County Militia, but because of the possibility of a recurrence of his malady, though an excellent horseman, a fine marksman, and an ardent patriot, he could not enter the Army as a regular. In 1776, however, he was called to a more valuable patriotic service, at age twenty-five assuming his first public office as delegate to the convention called to frame the first Virginia constitution, the first step in the political career which was to involve him for the rest of his life.

"I hope you realize, my dear sister," Isaac Hite said to Dolley, even his smile seeming oversize, his lips were so broad, "what a debt our new country owes to that husband of yours."

"Yes—oh yes," Dolley replied humbly. "I know a little about it, but I need to know much more." Her blue eyes shone with eagerness. "I want to know everything about him."

Isaac laughed. "That's a big order! But at least we can get you started on what will be a lifetime of discovery."

Dolley had been eight, in 1776, when Madison's public life began. Delegate to the convention in Williamsburg, he was appointed to the committee for framing a Declaration of Rights and Virginia's first constitution. As Edmund Randolph said of him at this time, "His diffidence went hand in hand with his morals. . . . In Convention debate his lips were never unsealed except to some member who happened to sit near him; and any one who had once partaken of the rich banquet did not fail to wish to sit daily within reach." Though George Mason wrote most of the Virginia Bill of Rights, it was Madison who fought for and secured the passage of the article on religion. Not just "tolerance," he insisted. The English Toleration Act previously in force in the colony assumed an official religion together with the state's rights to grant or withhold favor from "Dissenters." Equality, not tolerance they must have.

His revised clause stated that "all men are equally entitled to the full and free exercise of religion according to the dictates of Conscience." The Virginia Declaration of Rights became a model not only for the new American states but for revolutionary peoples everywhere. His further attempt to effect a complete separation of church and state, which threatened to dethrone the Anglican clergy and divest them of their special emoluments and privileges, did not pass.

"Not then, that is," Isaac qualified. "But, being Jemmy, he would continue to fight for its passage in Virginia, even if it took years. And it did, ten of them." Isaac chuckled. "He ran for election to the new assembly that fall and was defeated. You never could guess why."

"Then thee—you must tell me," Dolley urged. "Why?"

"Because he wouldn't bribe the voters by treating them to free whiskey! Thought it was immoral and opposed to the country's new democratic principles."

Dolley laughed with him, but her eyes sparkled. Surely her Quaker friends would approve of that action! Perhaps if they understood the character of this man she had married . . .

"Would you believe this?" Isaac continued. "Jemmy never made a public speech until he was thirty. Too diffident and afraid with his weak voice he couldn't make himself heard. And he was thirty-seven before he won his first forensic triumph. It was in 1788, at the convention deciding whether Virginia would ratify the new Constitution. Its fate was still undecided. Eight states had ratified, nine were necessary to establish the new government. Without Virginia it well might fail, resulting in thirteen little warring states or two or three contending confederacies. Jemmy was sick, but he went. And who do you suppose was his biggest opponent, opposed to ratification?"

"Who?" Dolley prompted dutifully, though she thought she could guess.

"That silver-tongued giant Patrick Henry! He thought it would take away some of Virginia's precious rights. They say Jemmy spoke so low that he couldn't be distinctly heard. It was like David facing Goliath! The most powerful orator of his time against the most logical but unimpressive thinker and scholar. Somebody said when Jemmy got up to speak it was as if he had just had a casual thought, stood with his hat in his hand and his notes in his hat, no excitement of debate showing except by a sort of seesaw motion of his body, while Patrick Henry was like thunder and lightning. But who won? Our little Jemmy. Vote was 89 to 79 in favor. I hear they call him the 'Father of the Constitution.' He may well too have been its savior."

Isaac was right, decided Dolley. It would take a lifetime to learn to know this husband of hers. But at least she was making a beginning.

They stayed two weeks at Belle Grove, and Dolley felt herself happily inducted not only into marriage but into her new family. Little Payne was absorbed into the Hite nursery containing Nelly's two surviving children, five-year-old Nelly and one-year-old James Madison, giving the bride more freedom to cultivate her new relationships. That the doting mother did not take full advantage of such freedom, however, was evidenced by a tart comment in one of Nelly's letters, preserved for posterity.

"Then there was *that child,* who would have nothing else but to sleep in their bed with them, as he had every night since they had been man and wife."

The honeymoon at Belle Grove was not ideal. Dolley had a recurrence of the malarial fever which had prostrated her that summer, so severe that a rider was sent posthaste to Winchester to fetch a Dr. Baldwin, whose doses of "bark" (Peruvian cinchona containing quinine) restored her partially to health. They had to return to Philadelphia as soon as possible, decided the anxious husband, where medical help was more readily available. Before they left another tragedy occurred, for Nelly Hite gave birth prematurely to a stillborn child, not the first time such a misfortune had happened.

"We left Mr. Hite's the day before yesterday," Madison wrote his father from Harewood on October 5. "Our time was passed there with great pleasure on our side, and I hope not less on the other. Our departure, however, was embittered by the loss sustained the night preceeding by my sister. . . . In about 8 or 10 days we expect to set out for Philadelphia, and your daughter-in-law begs you and my mother to accept her best and most respectful affections, which she means to express herself by an early opportunity. . . ."

As Madison's new coach took the long road to Philadelphia, crossing the Potomac at Harper's Ferry, the wild blackberry bushes were turning red. The scarlet oaks were a glowing crimson. Beauty was all along the roadside, but the road itself! Ruts, dust, mud, rocky mountain slopes, tree roots and stumps, treacherous streambeds! The "neat and costly" coach in which Jemmy had taken such pride excelled in beauty rather than workmanship. It was soon "a perfect wreck." Fortunately one of his hobbies was carpentry, and he was able to tie and hammer and piece it together. It took all of Dolley's tact and cheerful adaptability to quiet Payne's complaints, soothe Anna's youthful sullenness, and assure her distraught husband that it was much more comfortable than traveling by the public stagecoaches, which were built without springs.

They arrived at last in Philadelphia, to take up residence in the house vacated by Madison's friend James Monroe, who had gone as ambassador to Paris. Furnishings were at a minimum, pieces from her leased house, china and other effects from Montpelier, but, though Madison had commissioned Monroe to purchase draperies, rugs, china, and other household effects from French aristocrats distressed by the Revolution, two years later he would still be looking for them "by every vessel that escapes the British depredations."

Congratulations began to pour in, from Madison's cousin, the Reverend James Madison, the first Bishop of Virginia and President of William and Mary College; from his roommate at the College of New Jersey, Philip Freneau, another member of the "Whigs" who shared his liberal political views; from General Horatio Gates; and, the one Madison cherished most, from his most intimate friend and political associate Thomas Jefferson, who, while rejoicing in his newfound happiness, feared that in the felicity of his marriage Madison might be tempted to retire from public life.

"Hold on then, my dear friend," he wrote from his own Monticello in December, "that we may not shipwreck in the meanwhile. I do not see, in the minds of those with whom I converse, a greater affliction than the fear of your retirement; but this must not be, unless to a more splendid and more efficacious post. There I should rejoice to see you. I hope I may say, I shall rejoice to see you. . . . Present me respect-fully to Mrs. Madison, and pray her to keep you where you are for her own satisfaction and the public good, and accept the cordial affections of us all."

Dolley read the letter with both interest and trepidation. A "more splendid and efficacious post?" What did he mean? Jemmy was al-ready a Congressman, a position of high political responsibility. She had wondered if she could possibly become an acceptable legislator's wife. Now Mr. Jefferson seemed to be urging her to even more terri-fying responsibility!

Back in Philadelphia she felt suspended between two worlds. Strangers were living in her house. She was living in the house of strangers. She avoided her Quaker friends, or, rather, they seemed to be avoiding her. Yet a lifetime of inhibitions prevented her from full participation in other friendships. It was this quandary, she knew, that had been responsible for her long hesitation about remarriage, for the words "alas! alas!" on her wedding day. It had been, was still, a choice, not between marriage and widowhood, but between two worlds. Had she been naïve to hope that she could keep both of them?

Then suddenly the predictable happened. On December 2 the Quaker Monthly Meeting passed a resolution declaring her "out of unity," because, "having disregarded the wholesome order of our Dis-cipline, in the accomplishment of her marriage with a person not in membership with us, before a hireling priest," she could no longer be considered a member of the Society of Friends.

So . . . the choice had been made for her. Regret, yes, but also, strangely enough, relief, a sense of freedom, what Jemmy had tried to put into words, every person's right to worship God "according to the dictates of Conscience." No more having to hide a golden butterfly under one's kerchief! She could belong to both worlds, after all, follow the guidance of her own Inner Light while entering with all eagerness and energy into the new complex life expected of the wife of a James Madison. It would not be hard, since she knew now that she felt for her new husband a warmth of affection which the faithful John Todd had never inspired. And he would ask nothing more of her than just to be herself.

5

The face that looked back at her from the mirror was sweet, young, innocent, demure, framed by a ruffled cap with lacy ribbons that tied under the chin, a few tendrils of curling black hair escaping around cheeks and shoulders. The gown, what little of it showed, was of a sober color, circled about the neck with a lacy white kerchief. The reflection was very like the miniature painted of her just last year by James Peale, brother of the famous portrait painter Charles Willson Peale, who had done so many pictures of the President. James loved the miniature. He called it "my lovely Quaker bride."

Dolley gazed steadily into the mirrored blue eyes. There was more sadness in them, less sparkle, than in the miniature. They still reflected the grief she had felt since the news had come the first of the year. That faithful chronicler, Elizabeth Drinker, had recorded the tragedy in her diary on January 5, 1795. "I heard this evening of the death of two of Molly Payne's sons, Temple and Isaac; the latter offended a man in Virginia, who sometime after shot him with a pistol." Temple had been victim of a fatal sickness. Fever? The family had never been able to discover all the details. Her brothers were all gone now except John, the youngest. Walter had gone to Britain on a ship from Virginia and been lost at sea. Perhaps it was this sense of loss and of betrayal of childhood loyalties that had made her put on this sober Quaker garb when dressing tonight for Martha Washington's Friday levee.

A face appeared beside hers in the mirror, youthful, eager, merry.

"Look!" lilted sixteen-year-old Anna. "How do you like it? Sally helped me pick out the material. She bought some too, a different color, and her seamstress made them for us. She's going to wear hers tonight too. What—what do you think?" There were doubt and a bit of bravado in her voice as well as gaiety.

Dolley gazed wide-eyed, at a loss for words. "Thee—you—" She still resorted to the old Quaker manner of speech in moments of surprise or stress. Suddenly Anna had grown up. She had turned into a beautiful woman. Her gown of purple velvet, tight-waisted and full-skirted, its low-cut neck and short puffed sleeves emphasizing the whiteness of neck and arms, was the perfect complement to her blond fairness and light blue eyes derived from her Winston forebears. "So" —she continued, still almost speechless—"thee—you—and Sally Mc-Kean—"

Her first reaction was shock. Little Anna, her gay beguiling child, a charmer, a heartbreaker! Next came resentment. Donning finery when her brothers were scarcely buried! But here reason asserted itself. Even Isaac had been gone from home when Anna was a young child, and she could hardly remember the older boys. Besides, Quakers did not believe in wearing mourning. Surely—she could not be feeling envy! Jemmy gave Anna a generous allowance, and she had every right to spend it as she chose. And—how beautiful she was!

Dolley smiled and gave her a quick embrace. "You are lovely, my dear. I shall be proud to go with you tonight."

When Anna had gone she returned to the mirror. And what was she doing in this sober Quaker dress when God had made his world so resplendent with color? Suddenly she began changing. If only the hooks and buttons were not so troublesome! The rose-colored satin she had made right after her marriage and not yet worn! It needed pressing from lying in the chest, but no one would notice. Cut low in the neck after the prevailing style, bedecked with many festoons of ribbon, short puffed sleeves—yes, her arms and neck were just as white as Anna's but not so youthfully slender. As a concession to her Quaker heritage she put a filmy wrap of lace about her shoulders and added a soft little cap, not enough to hide the lustrous curls.

It was the look in Jemmy's eyes that made the change worthwhile. Since Congress opened he had been worried about national problems —the heightening tensions between the two emerging political parties, the President's condemnation of what he chose to call "self-created" Democratic Societies, the terms, as yet undisclosed, of the Jay Treaty. At sight of her his features relaxed, his whole face brightened.

"My dear! What a sight for weary eyes! Never have I seen you more beautiful."

Martha Washington's Friday levees were social events, attended by almost everybody who was anybody in Philadelphia. They were media for political tête-à-têtes, for gossip, opportunities for discreet court-ship, expedients for the display of the latest fashions from Europe. Etiquette had been prescribed early in the administration and was formal. While at his own Tuesday afternoon levees, for men only, the President appeared in black velvet coat and breeches, hair powdered and gathered behind in a silk bag, yellow gloves, dress sword, at Martha's he was just a private gentleman in cloth coat, waistcoat, and black small-clothes, and he mingled with the company. The First Lady received seated on a sofa, greeting each guest with some polite observation as he or she was presented.

"Too stiff and formal," thought Dolley. "If I were in her place, I would be up and about, trying to make everybody feel right at home."

Mrs. Washington greeted them warmly. "My dear, how beautiful you look tonight! How lovely you both look! And how is that sister of yours, my charming niece?"

Formal greetings over, Dolley turned with joyful relief to the exciting melee of color, candles, buzz of conversation. As always, she responded to the stimulus of a crowd like a flower opening to the sun. She glowed, sparkled, exuded an interest in every person encountered as if he or she were the only one in the room. But even in the act of listening, sharing, sympathizing with different individuals, she was conscious of others—of Anna surrounded by a group of youthful males suddenly aware of her maturing beauty (Oh dear, must she soon face the heartache of losing her?); of Jemmy, easily distinguished because of his garb, sober black in contrast with flamboyant blues and buffs and crimsons. She was relieved to see him in long, apparently friendly conversation with the President, was distressed when a fellow congressman, Samuel Dexter, an outspoken Federalist, deliberately turned away at his approach. She knew why. Dexter had accused Madison of lack of personal integrity because he had seemingly shifted his position.

"I must invite him to dinner," thought Dolley, "some Sunday soon so Jemmy will have a chance to explain to him that he has not really changed his principles, only his way of applying them." Instantly she began planning what other people she should invite and what foods would best satisfy to repleteness and so create a mellow state of mind.

Already she was becoming increasingly knowledgeable about the political situation. Finding her not only interested but shrewdly understanding, Jemmy was sharing with her some of his problems as a leading congressman. She had read much of his correspondence with his closest friend, Thomas Jefferson, who, after his resignation as Secretary of State at the end of 1793, had retired to his Virginia house. Even in retirement Jefferson was the acknowledged leader of the Anti-

Federalists, the democratic party, or, as they were usually called, Democratic-Republicans, or simply, Republicans. Alexander Hamilton, Secretary of the Treasury during Washington's first term, epitomized the position of the Federalists. The two had clashed in the cabinet, bringing about the schism that had created the two parties. They represented opposing views of government, the Federalists power by the qualified few, chiefly the moneyed and industrial classes, the Republicans power by the people.

"There are three fundamental types of government," Madison explained to her, as he had outlined them in a paper entitled "Spirit of Governments." "There are military despotisms, under which human nature has groaned through every age; there are money despotisms, which pretend to give liberty but really rely on interested partisans to defend the domination of the few over the freedom of the many; and there are republican governments, which it is the glory of America to have invented, and her unrivalled happiness to possess."

Jefferson and Madison had opposed Hamilton on many issues: the creation of a National Bank, which they condemned as both unconstitutional and profitable to merchants and financiers rather than to the mass of the people; the protection of manufacturers by the taxing powers of Congress through subsidies, tariffs, and prohibition of competitive imports; the attempted suppression of democratic societies formed in protest of government policies.

"The right of citizens," asserted Madison firmly, "to enter into voluntary organizations and to censure the government as they see fit, must be inviolable if a people are to remain free."

The opposing views clashed on foreign as well as domestic problems. During the Revolution and the years immediately after there had been strong national affection for France, but as years passed an increasing number renewed their loyalty to Britain. In the Constitutional debate Hamilton, along with other conservatives, had revealed his preference for the British monarchical system. He had lost. Madison, with other democrats, had won. But the French Revolution, with its radical attack on the aristocrats, its bloodbaths, had made the term "republican" anathema to Hamilton and his followers. The common people, the hoi polloi, fit to govern themselves? Nonsense! They were fools.

Jefferson, on the other hand, interpreted the excesses of the French liberationists as indictments not of democracy but of the abuses of monarchy. In his five years as minister to France he had been deeply interested in the events leading up to the French Revolution and keenly sympathized with its aspirations. While deploring the reign of violence that had resulted, he still had hopes that a truly republican government might emerge. As leader of the anti-Federalists he was denounced by Hamilton and his adherents as "Jacobin," "Atheist," "Franconian," "heretic," and his friend Madison was suffering the same innuendos. Distressed by the schism between the two parties, the President had attempted to steer a middle course, but in this, his second administration, he was veering toward Hamilton's concepts of government. His long and close friendship with both Jefferson and Madison had become strained. Dolley knew that this was causing Jemmy much pain and regret.

But his greatest worry, she knew, was not over such disparagement of himself. He was used to that. It was the dangers besetting the country that distressed him. Ships were being constantly seized, American sailors impressed by the British Navy. The nation's commerce was in jeopardy. Like other American officials, Federalist and Republican alike, he was waiting in an agony of hope and apprehension for the result of John Jay's negotiations in London.

"I'm afraid," he confessed to the sympathetic Dolley. "Jay is a strong Federalist. He must have been given his instructions from Hamilton, careful that they should give no offense to Britain. Even if he is able to effect a treaty, what will it be?"

News came at last that a treaty had been negotiated and signed, but when Congress disbanded in March of 1795 its terms were not known. Madison faced the reprieve with a mixture of emotions. Apprehension. What did the treaty say that the administration should postpone announcing its terms? Delight! At last he could show his bride his beloved Montpelier and show *her*, his incredible good fortune, to his parents.

It was a long seven-day journey. Anna, bereft of her young friends, was bored. Payne fussed and cried. Jemmy was by turns preoccupied or exuberant. But Dolley enjoyed every moment, the crossing of wide waters by ferry, the rough rides over muddy rutted roads, even the nights in noisy, drafty "ordinaries." From Philadelphia to Chester, Wilmington, Elkton, across the Susquehanna where the scenery took one's breath away, on to Baltimore, to Georgetown, a glimpse as they crossed the Potomac of the bare bones of the new Federal City soon to be given flesh, then Virginia, her childhood love but parts she had never seen before, up valley sides and over mountaintops.

"The Delectable Mountains," she thought, remembering the adventurous journey of Bunyan's Pilgrim. And at last arrival at the goal of pilgrimage.

"There it is!" Jemmy might indeed have been pointing proudly to the "Celestial City." "Montpellier!" He always spelled and pronounced it so, European fashion, though to most people and in subsequent annals it would be the Anglicized Montpelier.

They whirled up the long, gently sloping drive with a sudden burst of speed, the horses as eagerly sensitive as their master to the familiar stimuli, then, descending, were engulfed in a medley of smiling black and white faces, bows, embraces, greetings both exuberant and dignified.

"It's Massa Jemmy! Massa Jemmy's come!"

"Welcome, son. It's been a long time."

"And our lovely new daughter! Welcome home, my dear!"

"So this is little Payne! What a sweet child! And Anna!"

"Two sisters for you, Fanny! Welcome, all of you."

Montpelier at last. Would she be disappointed, Dolley had wondered. Surely no place could be as divinely beautiful as Jemmy had pictured it. But it was. She loved everything about it, the house, square and solid on its eminence, its transverse hall with rooms on either side, its wainscoting and fireplaces, reminding her of Scotchtown; the broad vistas of fields and woods fringed by the foothills of the Blue Ridge thirty miles away; especially the people in her new family, who received her with more than polite acceptance, with delighted gratitude. Their Jemmy, married at last after all these years, and to an attractive woman of whom they could be justly proud! They admired and fondled and spoiled little Payne, just turned three and cherubic with his wide-eyed smiling face and black glossy curls, as if he had been Jemmy's own. They drew Anna as well as Dolley into the circle of daughters and daughters-in-law, some of whom lived within the bounds of the original estate, acquired in 1723 by James's grandfather Ambrose Madison and his wife, Frances Taylor. This Ambrose, Dolley learned, had died young, leaving the thirty-two-year-old Frances with three young children. She had been equal to the challenge, not only raising and educating her family but improving the five-thousand-acre estate, shipping tobacco, directing her fifteen slaves in wool carding, weaving, shoemaking, and other crafts. Her son James, Jemmy's father, had married Nelly Conway.

"She descended from some of the early settlers," James commented casually. "Her father, Francis, lived near Port Royal in the county of Caroline." He was careful, as always, not to mention that she was descended from Sir Edward Conway, Baron of Ragley, who was knighted by Queen Elizabeth for supervising the sacking of Cadiz. The idea of both the title and the reason for it was anathema to his democratic spirit.

James Madison, Sr., looked a bit crusty and forbidding with his thin patrician features, heavy brows, and strong full lips. But Dolley discovered that the lips could smile, the eyes under the lowering brows twinkle. It was from him that Jemmy had inherited both his reserved demeanor and his wry sense of humor. Now over seventy, James Sr. was still a prominent citizen of Orange County, having been county lieutenant, justice of the peace, vestryman, leading landowner. His wife, Nelly, had borne him twelve children, of whom seven had survived, James, Francis, Ambrose, William, Nelly, Sarah, Frances. Ambrose, who had shared the management of the estate with his father, had recently died.

"She looks like a frail reed," thought Dolley of Jemmy's mother, "ready to blow away in the slightest wind." Indeed Nelly Conway Madison, then in her sixties, was chronically afflicted with malaria and generally enfeebled. But reeds, as Dolley knew, could be tough, resistant to the harshest winds, and Nelly still had a quarter century to live.

The summer and fall of 1795 were a prototype of the four yet to come. Dolley was surprised to see Jemmy, the confirmed scholar, turn farmer, helping his father supervise the growing of tobacco, hemp, clover, experimenting with new crops and fertilizers. And she in turn surprised Jemmy and his family by her interest in gardening, digging and weeding among the tulips, iris, peonies, and nasturtiums as spring brought them to bloom in profusion. Nelly Madison was delighted when Dolley proved her culinary skills by going into the kitchen and baking her favorite seed and layer cakes.

Though life was free and leisurely, activity abounded. Since Jemmy's brothers, Francis and William, lived nearby with large families there was plenty of entertainment for little Payne. He basked in the indulgence of doting elders and the society of admiring peers. Fanny, Jemmy's youngest sister, was an older but congenial companion for Anna. There was company galore, often twenty-five or thirty to dinner. There were quilting parties, dances, though Dolley, still a Quaker at heart, watched these without participating. The hotels in Orange

Courthouse, Sanford's, Bell's, Alcock's, were centers for balls and other social gatherings.

But over all hung a cloud. Jemmy might convulse the company in merriment over some droll story at dinner only to retire into brooding worry once the guests had left. He watched impatiently for the mails, read his letters from Philadelphia with frowning concentration. Dolley knew that he got up from their bed at night to pace the room or go outside to walk. *The Treaty!* It was like a shadow dogging his steps, a huge question mark challenging his every thought and action. What were its terms? Why were they being kept secret? What would it mean for the Republican cause?

Then suddenly his fears were realized. The President summoned the Senate to a special session for June 8. The terms of the treaty, intended to be kept secret until the Senate had acted, were leaked through Benjamin Bache's paper, the *Aurora*. Jemmy received his copy, tore it open, read it.

"It's worse than I feared," he told Dolley in horror. "It renounces for us all freedom of the seas. It forbids our carrying provisions in our neutral ships to ports of the British enemies. It gives no assurance against the impressment of our seamen. It prohibits export of all our principal crops, molasses, sugar, coffee, cotton, to any part of the world outside our own country. Tax preferences to American ships are wiped out. Worst of all is a clause granting favored-nation status to Britain. And all they give us in return," he finished bitterly, "is the promise to surrender the Northwest posts by June of next year, and they promised to do that in the Treaty of 1783! It makes us virtually an ally of England and an enemy of France!"

It was time, Jemmy decided, to take his family on an important journey.

6

They started one day in July, traveling southwest along a rough winding trail that two hundred years later would be indicated on maps as "Constitution Route"—significantly, for it linked together the two men who best personified the genius of that historic document.

It was a long thirty-mile trip, winding up and down the foothills of the Blue Ridge through country sparsely settled, often as wild as uncharted wilderness but breathtakingly beautiful in its summer luxuriance.

"Where are we going, Papa?" three-year-old Payne kept querying, always adding restively, "How much farther? Aren't we almost there?"

"Not yet, son." Jemmy never grew impatient at his incessant questions. "Where are we going?" he repeated once, smiling fondly. "To the top of the world, son, as near to heaven as you're likely to be on this earth."

They came finally to a little town, kept on south and presently were climbing, spiraling, up . . . up . . .

"He calls this 'Little Mountain'?" gasped Dolley. "What would a big one be like?"

Jemmy laughed. "It's only about six hundred feet. It must have seemed big, though, when he arrived here on his wedding night in a raging snowstorm. They had to leave the carriage at the foot and come up on horseback. The servants had thought no one would travel in such a storm and had gone to their cabins. They found the house dark, no food, no heat. But Tommy was undaunted—also his bride. He took her into his old one-room cottage nearby, built a roaring fire, and, remembering a hidden treasure, produced a bottle of French wine that he had stashed away behind a bookshelf."

Arrived finally at the top of the "little mountain," Dolley exclaimed in delighted amazement. Monticello! It crested the height triumphantly, its red brick and white columns blending into its setting of trees and lawns and sky, its proud little dome—first in America, she was to learn—rising into the heavens like a crown. It seemed indeed the top of the world. Even the undulating lines of the Blue Ridge towering behind the toy town of Charlottesville to the west appeared dwarfed in the distance. Dolley stood gazing, speechless.

"No wonder he says," observed Jemmy softly, " 'All my wishes end where I hope my days will end . . . at Monticello.' "

Dolley had seen Thomas Jefferson before, at Scotchtown, in her mother's boardinghouse, on the streets of Philadelphia, for in Washington's first term he had been Secretary of State. But now, it seemed, she was seeing him for the first time. What a contrast they were in appearance, these two whose brilliant minds were in such close accord, the one tall, rangy, bold of features, rust hair already tinged with gray and a bit disheveled, careless, nondescript in dress; the other slender, fine-featured, short of stature, powdered hair carefully combed over the ears and tied behind, black clothes and crisp white ruffles faultless in their neat sobriety! Only the eyes seemed akin, both blue-gray and deep-set, both kindled from the same inner fire.

Jefferson might be indifferent to accepted modes of dress, but he was an epicure in other areas. The house was a veritable museum of choice furnishings, paintings, statuary which he had assembled with consummate taste in Europe. They were served dinner at a perfectly appointed table laden with unusually tempting delicacies—French bread, crisp and tasty, vegetables with piquant flavors, meats with wine sauces, and for dessert a delectable concoction called ice cream.

"He liked French cooking so well," Jemmy told Dolley later with a chuckle, "that he had one of his most able servants, James Hemmings, come to Paris to learn how to cook from a famous French chef."

Later, in the library, Dolley sat and looked and listened while the two men talked, marveling both at her surroundings and at the conversation. Books! Why, there must be thousands of them! Jemmy's hundreds had nearly taken her breath away. She was intrigued by a small portable writing desk standing on one of the tables. It was on that, Jemmy had told her, that Jefferson had labored in agonized travail to create one of the greatest testaments for human freedom of all time, the Declaration of Independence.

She regarded him with mingled awe and curiosity. Was there any truth in the old rumor that he had once been romantically attracted to her mother? If so, it had been but a passing infatuation, for his almost fanatical devotion to his beautiful but frail wife, Martha, was common knowledge. He had given up ambassadorial honors to remain by her side, worried by her bed during her frequent illnesses, nursed her through her last sickness, fainted at her death, vowed never to marry again.

Listening to the two men now, her mind boggled. They were talking with the utmost intelligence about almost every subject under the sun. *Farming.* Both of them had original ideas for improving their big acreages. *Architecture.* Both were planning extensive additions to their mansions, and Jefferson had been asked by Washington to help lay out the Federal City. Both favored the classical styles as promoted by the great Palladio. They spoke glibly of styles Doric, Ionic, Corinthian. *Art.* Was the Italian artist Giuseppi Calendi supplying Madison with all the portraits he desired of America's first discoverers, those copied from the originals owned by the Duke of Florence? *Astronomy.* At last Jefferson had acquired the telescope he had long wanted, also a pair of globes both terrestrial and celestial. Madison wished he could see the wonderful orrery at Princeton, telling the wonders of the solar system. *Archaeology.* Jefferson was tremendously interested in rumors that mastodon bones had been discovered out in Indian country, and he wanted some for his artifacts collection. *Law.* They touched on theories of government from Aristotle and Plato to Montesquieu and Locke. And of course, *politics.*

Dolley had been awed by Jemmy's seeming omniscience. But Jefferson! Why, he was agriculturist, naturalist, astronomer, musician (his violin was his most precious possession), artist, philosopher, architect, legislator, and a dozen other things, to say nothing of inventor. The results of this latter talent were all about her. There was the clock in the entrance hall, indicating not only time but the days of the week by weights descending on one side of the room. He had miscalculated here, however, and holes had had to be made in the floor to permit the weights to show Saturday! In the dining room there was the dumb-waiter connected with the wine cellar and the revolving serving doors with shelves so servants need not enter and little four-tiered tables between the guests so they could serve themselves. He had planned small private stairs leading to each of the bedrooms, saving space used by big expensive staircases. And, most intriguing of all, he had put kitchen, laundry, smoke room, and other work areas usually housed in outbuildings off a long underground passage beneath the mansion!

The whole family enjoyed the days at Monticello, foretaste of many such visits. Dolley found Martha Jefferson Randolph, "Patsy," the image of her father, though six years younger than herself, a congenial companion. (Why, she wondered, were Marthas, including the President's wife, always nicknamed Patsy?) Maria, "Polly," Jefferson's younger daughter, inheritor of her mother's delicate-boned, exquisite beauty, was almost the exact age of Anna, and the two enjoyed adolescent confidences, duets at the harpsichord, strolls in the garden. Payne found an admiring and docile playmate in Anne, Martha's older child, three years old like himself. Martha and Maria, who had both accompanied Jefferson on his foreign ambassadorship, were the sole survivors of the lovely but frail Martha Skelton Jefferson's six children.

But over all hung the shadow of that dark specter, Jay's Treaty. On June 24 the Senate, strongly Federalist, had ratified the treaty by a bare two-thirds vote. Much of the country had been as appalled by its terms as were Jefferson and Madison. John Jay had been hung in effigy, Hamilton stoned on the streets of New York. It was a sellout to England, Jefferson insisted, and if the President was weak enough to sign, Madison might fight its implementation.

Before they left, their host took Dolley aside. "You must keep your husband in public life," he spoke with the sternness of a father addressing a child. "The preservation of our democratic government may well depend on him. Now that he has made such a felicitous marriage he may be tempted to retire to private life and—"

"As you have done," said Dolley with demure but unruffled composure.

"Er—ah—yes." For a moment the great man was nonplussed. Then he laughed. "Touché, my dear. But"—his manner was more pleading now than peremptory—"our country's future may depend on your husband, and your influence may well be important. I hope—"

Dolley looked him straight in the eye. "My husband," she said firmly, "will make his own decisions. But wherever they lead him, I shall accompany and support him to the best of my ability."

Jefferson returned her gaze, not with the whimsical indulgence accorded a child but with the respect due a woman. "Yes," he said. "I believe you will."

Back to Philadelphia in November, not too happy a trip because the horse Jemmy had borrowed from his brother William proved unmanageable, and he had to buy another on the way. Remembering the high cost of feed in the city, he bought twenty barrels of corn in Fredericksburg and had it sent by water, together with two wagonloads of goods from Montpelier. In Philadelphia they moved into a three-story brick house on Spruce Street. Dolley had already ordered the winter's supply of wood, and it was in the cellar. With the furnishings from their previous house, plus those shipped from Montpelier, she made the new home habitable and ready for entertaining.

Madison fought hard with other Democratic-Republicans in the House to prevent the implementation of the unfair and unpopular treaty that Washington had reluctantly signed. As he had said long ago in Number 58 of his *Federalist Papers,* "The House cannot only refuse but they alone can propose the supplies requisite for the support of government." They had the power of the purse. The Executive could make treaties, the Senate ratify them, but it was only the House that could implement them. This was the essence of the whole principle of balance of power, the genius of the Constitution. Yet, though the majority were shocked by the outrageous terms that made the country virtually an ally of England and an enemy of France, that curbed her freedom as an independent nation, Madison and his supporters were defeated by a narrow vote. He was bitterly disillusioned.

Dolley listened, understood, sympathized with his frustration, and wondered how she could best help him. What should be her role as the wife of a partisan leader in Congress, expected to take a prominent place in the social life of the divided and troubled country? Should she permit the political schisms to dictate her actions, the functions she attended, her choice of dinner guests, her attitude toward people? No. Let all argument, rancor, be relegated as far as possible to the halls of government. It was up to her to be a catalyst, not a promoter of discord. Differences, she knew, could often be mitigated, if not resolved, in a quiet encounter at one of Martha Washington's levees or in the give and take around her own dinner table. The decision was not hard, for it concerned *people,* and she liked them all, whether Republicans or Federalists, Southerners or Northerners, foreign dignitaries or rough pioneers from the wilderness.

She and Jemmy had had differences, in background, in religion, and they had become inconsequential, not through argument but through sharing. She had gone to church with him, though not taking communion, and discovered that the Inner Light could be experienced amid stained-glass windows and solemn chants and candles. Though she could not expose Jemmy to the stark austerity of a Quaker Meeting, herself being excluded, he made an avid study of Quakerism, admired its sincerity, included among his most treasured reading matter the writings of George Fox, Barclay's "Apologies for Quakers," Penn's "Counterfeit Christianity Detected."

Dolley still, and always, would consider herself a Quaker. When her father's will was finally probated in January 1796 and she made affirmation to his signature, it was recorded, "This day appeared Dolley P. Madison, of the State of Virginia, Gentlewoman, late Dolley P. Todd, who being one of the People called Quakers, and conscientiously scrupulous of taking an oath, Doth Solemnly affirm and declare, etc." It was only the unimportant features that she discarded, the stern inhibitions, the peculiarities of speech.

For the many social events, such as the President's birthday ball or the Friday levees or the assemblies at Celler's Tavern every Thursday night, formal affairs where no gentleman was admitted "in boots, colored stockings, or undress," Dolley and Anna followed the new French modes of dress, described glowingly in a letter to Anna from her friend Sally McKean when they were vacationing at Montpelier during the summer of 1796. Waistlines were climbing, necklines lowering, and "there is no such thing as long sleeves. They are half way above the elbow, either drawn or plaited in various ways, according to fancy; they do not wear ruffles at all and as for elbows, Anna, ours would be alabaster compared to some of the ladies who follow the fashion!" But Dolley still draped the décolleté necklines with filmy kerchiefs and covered her black curls with simple little caps of fine muslin or lace.

Sally and her father were guests at one of Martha Washington's dinner parties which Dolley and her family attended. Jemmy had wanted to refuse the invitation, since his relations with the President were becoming more and more strained.

"Nonsense!" Dolley chided cheerfully. She knew how the estrangement grieved him. "People can disagree and still be friends. Besides, Anna has set her heart on going." This was a persuasive argument, for Jemmy was as fond of her lovely sprightly young sister as if she had been his daughter.

It was a formal dinner party, with all in festive dress, all, that is, except Jemmy, whose usual plain black was relieved only by a crisp white shirt ruffle. Sally looked especially beautiful in a blue satin dress trimmed with white crepe and flowers, a petticoat of white crepe richly embroidered, and across the front a festoon of rose color caught up with flowers. Anna's dress, though simpler, lavender silk embroidered with pink roses, blended perfectly with her fair fresh complexion and wide merry blue eyes. Dolley was not pleased, however, when the guest of honor, Don Carlos Martinez d'Yrujo, the newly arrived ambassador from Spain, attached himself to Anna's side with obvious fervor of admiration. Oh dear! She felt sudden shock. Why, the child was—no longer a child, but seventeen, a woman of marriageable age. But—oh, not to someone who might take her as far away as Spain, not to this—peacock! Hair powdered to snowy luxuriance, striped silk coat lined with satin, black silk breeches, white silk stockings and buckled shoes, a jeweled smallsword at his side, the hat tucked under his arm tipped with white feathers, the Spaniard was the epitome of confident, if not vainglorious splendor. But Dolley was soon relieved, for presently the handsome ambassador transferred his attentions to the dazzling Sally—and kept them there. Two years later he would still be pursuing her until finally success would crown his efforts and she would become the Marchioness de Casa Yrujo.

Thanks partly to Dolley's quiet diplomacy, the long and cherished friendship between Madison and Washington remained outwardly unspoiled during this last year of the latter's administration. But when the President's Farewell Address was published in September 1796, Madison recognized in it little of the document he had helped write four years earlier when Washington was hoping to leave the presidency at the end of his first term. Some of the phrases showed the unmistakable quill marks of Hamilton.

Meanwhile Jemmy's frustration and disillusionment with the Republican cause, together with conditions that summer at Montpelier, had brought him to a firm decision. He would not run again for Congress. His father, disabled by sciatica and hardly able to walk, needed him badly. He had become intensely interested in experimental farming. He superintended the building of a new flour mill that summer while his parents were away recuperating at the Springs. And he was enthusiastically planning extensive additions to the mansion.

Dolley did not try to dissuade him. She expressed no opinion when Jefferson urged Madison, whom he considered "the greatest man in the world," to run for President on the Democratic-Republican ticket in the 1796 election. Jemmy was adamant in his refusal. Jefferson was older, better known, and much the greater man. Besides, Jemmy wanted to retire. On the Federalist ticket Hamilton was contesting the candidacy with John Adams, Washington's Vice President.

The campaign was hotly contested. Its outcome was still undecided when Madison drove his family to Philadelphia that fall to take his seat in the lame-duck Congress. They arrived on November 21, running into an almost impossible housing problem. They had given up the rent on Spruce Street, and Dolley's house was still rented. They had to move into smaller quarters, even more cramped because Jemmy's sister Fanny had returned with them. By storing some furniture, including the carpets, curtains, and other effects sent by Monroe from France, which had finally arrived, unfortunately brine-soaked from their long journey in a leaky hold, they managed.

It was decided. Adams was elected in the electoral college by a single vote beyond the bare majority, but the Federalist candidate for Vice President, Thomas Pinckney, lost out to Jefferson. This was some consolation. Madison could now retire knowing that the Republican cause had its ablest exponent at the seat of government.

On March 4, 1797, Dolley sat in Congress Hall with the wives of other legislators, some like herself for the last time, and saw John Adams inaugurated the second President of the United States. But the new President, stocky, sober, looking a bit pompous in his elaborate pearl-colored broadcloth suit, sword, and cockade, was not the central figure of the gathering. Nor was Jefferson, imposing in a blue coat over a crimson vest. It was the tall straight figure in black velvet, black military hat with black cockade, which drew all eyes. It was he who received the tremendous applause as he entered the hall, who was given the full attention of the crowd as he rose and with great dignity introduced his successor, finishing by reading his own brief farewell, his presence eclipsing even the great moment of inauguration. All, including the new President, participated in the excess of emotion which swept the crowd. When he had taken the oath, Adams covered his face with his hands, his wrist ruffles wet with his tears. There was scarcely a dry eye in the house.

For it was the end of an era. Washington, the hero of the nation's independence, guide of its first troubled years, symbol of its freedom for all future generations, was leaving them.

Seeing Jemmy's face suffused with tears, Dolley knew that whatever differences had been between them, they had been forgotten. The tears were a catharsis, washing away the discord, leaving only memory of the long years of friendship, of mutual struggle to bring the new nation into being, of collaboration far oftener than disagreement.

Packing, this time for good. Much luggage, sixteen pieces of it, had already been sent by water. A servant from Montpelier had come with extra horses to haul the furniture. They would take several weeks for the trip home, going a roundabout way by Harper's Ferry, Warm Springs, Harewood, Belle Grove.

It was with mixed emotions that Dolley climbed into the carriage. Was she sorry to see it all end? Not when she pictured the broad lawns where little Payne liked to run, the gardens that would soon be a profusion of lilacs, roses, mock orange, jasmine, tulips, the mountain vistas. Certainly not when she saw Jemmy's face, the tense lines gone, eyes alight with anticipation. Her only concern was for Anna, who might miss her young friends and the excitement of the city. For herself there were no regrets. She had long ago learned to say, like the Apostle Paul, "In whatsoever state I am, therewith to be content."

PART FOUR

Washington
1801–1809

1

With February there should have come a hint of spring. One year, Dolley remembered, the buds of the lilacs had been swelled and seemed ready to unfold. Not this year of 1801. The grounds around the house were still snow-covered, the oaks and dogwoods as starkly bare as in midwinter. It was as if the outer world sensed the chilling bleakness behind the walls and, like the members of both worlds, was waiting. Change. It was surely in the offing. But what? Spring or more of winter? More years of comfortable, satisfying life here at Montpelier, like the last four? Or who knew what of excitement and glamour, but also trouble and turmoil? Life—or death?

Father Madison lay in his bed stricken with the sickness that for months had kept him from superintending the estate. Several times he had seemed close to death, and life in the house had been slowed and muted. James had returned from the legislative session in Richmond in December, where he had participated as a delegate to the electoral college, afflicted with an acute attack of rheumatism which had increased in spite of "temperance and flannels." Dolley was at her wits' end, running the household, ministering to its two ailing members, trying to keep Payne, now a boisterous, noisy, mischievous, almost nine years old, from disturbing the occupants of the sick rooms and disrupting the family.

"He should be spanked," complained Anna repeatedly after being victimized by one of his pranks. This time he had put a frog in her favorite reticule and when she opened it, it had jumped almost into her face. But she knew it was no use.

Dolley had not even punished him for one of his most flagrant acts of mischief. It had happened at one of her early receptions back in Philadelphia, when one of the guests, General Van Cortland, had been paying Anna's friend Sally McKean, who was looking especially lovely, a flowery compliment, accompanied by a deep bow. The sight of the gentleman's nobly coiffured head at such close range had been

too much for the small Payne, and he gleefully pulled off the much
becurled and powdered wig. Sally and others had laughed, thought it a
joke. Even the shorn general, bereft of his dignity, had emitted a polite
chuckle. Not the outraged Anna. And certainly not the mortified Dolley. The general had received an abject apology, but the small miscre-
ant merely a mild rebuke. As now.

"Just a silly childish prank," excused Dolley. "He means well, and,
after all, he did no real harm. It's so hard for him, having to keep
quiet. Try to be patient, dear."

Patience. Dolley's own was sorely taxed. The preceding months had
been a succession of quiet and turmoil, triumphs and defeats, and
now, most trying of all, uncertainty. Freedom from the political scene?
It had been a short delusion. A James Madison could not stay aloof
from a national policy that outraged all his democratic principles.
Those Alien and Sedition Acts! Giving power to expel any alien suspected of opposition to the present government? Jailing any person
who spoke about the President or any member of the federal government "with intent to defame them or to bring them into contempt or
disrepute"?

"Where have our liberties gone?" James had fumed. "Where is our
precious freedom of the press? Jailing editors of Republican papers
because they criticize the President!"

Of course he had had to act. His Virginia Resolutions, presented to
the state legislature, declared the right of a state to avow a law unconstitutional and call on its sister states to join in securing its repeal.

"To the press alone," he had maintained, "chequered as it is with
abuse, the world is indebted for all the triumphs which have been
gained by reason and humanity over error and oppression."

In the election of 1800, when Jefferson had run for President on the
Democratic-Republican ticket, James had shared in the calumnies
heaped on his head by the opposition. Jefferson had been accused of
every crime but murder. Dolley still smarted at the memory of the
slanders directed at them both: atheism, cowardice in the Revolution,
hostility to commerce and manufacturers, ruthless ambition, government by the riffraff, the dregs of society. Change, opponents had decried! Exchange Secretary of State John Marshall for a James Madison?

Secretary of State! The very words were frightening, suggesting a
majestic full-rigged ship bearing down on a defenseless little rowboat
—she being the rowboat. Of course, Jefferson had remarked casually

when visiting Montpelier during the campaign, if he were elected Madison must hold the most responsible position in his cabinet. Dolley, startled, had turned confidently to Jemmy, expecting to hear his instant refusal. Why, he was just getting the estate organized here at Montpelier, was immersed in his exciting remodeling plans for the house, had exulted over and over again in the idyllic life they were enjoying! But he had not refused. Demurred, yes. But with a chill of apprehension she had known what his decision would be. Loyalty . . . duty . . . Always they would be his stern mentors, and they would guide him now—loyalty to Jefferson, his more than friend, his other self, duty to his country.

So this was the meaning of that letter long ago when Jefferson had written of their marriage. *I do not see . . . a greater affliction than the fear of your retirement; but this must not be, unless to a more splendid and efficacious post.* And this, doubtless, was the "more splendid and efficacious post." Well, in spite of her fears and self-distrust she had given Jefferson her answer. *My husband will make his own decisions. But wherever they lead him, I shall accompany and support him to the best of my ability.* Loyalty and duty, for her also.

Victory! Whatever its consequences, Dolley had rejoiced with James when Jefferson and Aaron Burr, the Republican candidate for vice President, had won the election. The Federalists were divided. Extremists had turned against Adams because of his reluctance to lead the country into an unnecessary war with France, his promotion of a monstrous land tax, and, yes, his moderation in enforcing the Alien and Sedition Acts. They had hectored and harried him all through his administration. Since all the Republican electors had voted for Burr as well as Jefferson, they were tied for first place, and according to the Constitution the election was thrown into the House of Representatives.

"Of course," James assumed confidently, "it won't come to a vote. Burr, being an honorable man and knowing he was the choice for Vice President, will immediately withdraw from the contest."

"Of course," agreed Dolley, yet, remembering her appraisal of Burr that day she had seen him and James together, somehow she had her doubts.

The triumph was short-lived. Burr was not the honorable man James had thought. Yielding to an excess of ambition and the proddings of Federalists who believed they could control him, he was contesting the election. Now, with the House meeting to ballot on Febru-

ary 11, James was distraught with frustration and worry. Though the
Republican House was unlikely to elect Burr, Federalist influence
might cause a deadlock until after inauguration day and necessitate a
new election. In spite of his rheumatism which made every step a
torture, he dragged himself back and forth, back and forth, along the
new sixty-foot brick portico, eyes focused for the first sight of the post
or of a messenger from the Federal City, oblivious for once of the four
massive Doric pillars of which he was so proud.

Those pillars, his bane as well as his pride and joy! Built according
to his own specifications by his own common workmen, forty feet
high, wood filled with mortar and bricks, they had been ready to be
hoisted three years before. But his carpenters had been powerless to
raise them. To his mortification he had had to send to Monticello for
one of Jefferson's skilled stonecutters. Not until 1799 had they been
hoisted finally into place, fulfilling his dream of a modest little Greek
temple. The 190 French windowpanes and eight brass door hinges that
Jefferson had sent him from Philadelphia had completed the impressive façade. But all building plans were now far from his mind.

The news came at last, brought by a special messenger. James came
limping into the house, calling for Dolley, his face brighter than she
had seen it in days. "Read it, love."

She read. "Ten for Jefferson. I hope you will have the cannon out."

"At last!" he exulted. "The people have won. Now we can see what
a really democratic government can do. Isn't it wonderful?"

Dolley regarded him fondly. It had not occurred to him, she knew,
that the news meant personal honor and prestige for himself. He was
thinking only of the good of his country. "Yes," she agreed, "wonderful, indeed."

So . . . it had come. The change. The end of the comfortable, satisfying four years. The beginning of excitement, trouble, and turmoil.

Jefferson had won, it developed, on the thirty-sixth ballot when
some Federalists, having gained from him assurances on some vital
points of policy, had cast blank ballots. To make sure that such an
anomaly could not occur again, three years later the Twelfth Amendment to the Constitution would prescribe that electors should name in
their ballots the persons designated as President and Vice President,
respectively.

Jefferson wrote, urging Madison to come at once to the new Federal
City in preparation for his coming duties as Secretary of State. No,
James replied firmly. It would not be seemly for him to appear before

his nomination and confirmation. Besides, it was impossible for him to leave with his father so ill. His own temporary incapacity was not even a consideration. He would have gone on crutches if necessary.

Dolley started packing. If she faced the coming change with reluctant resignation, she was the only one. Anna was exuberant. She had missed the excitement and festivity of Philadelphia, for country dances, quilting bees, fish fries, barbecues were poor substitutes for levees, theater parties, assemblies at Celler's Tavern. Perhaps Sally and her Spanish grandee husband would be in the Federal City, yes, and their sister Mary, who a few months before had been married here at Montpelier to John G. Jackson, a Congressman from Virginia. Payne, like any adventurous nine year old, was an enthusiast for any sort of change. They would leave, decided James, directly after the inauguration on March 4, since his father's health seemed to be improving.

But late in February James Madison, Sr., suffered a relapse, and on the last day of the month James wrote Jefferson that "yesterday morning rather suddenly, though very gently, the flame of light went out." He found himself the executor of the estate faced with myriad difficult problems. It took weeks to settle them. He had to apportion the property satisfactorily to his mother, his brother William, his three sisters and their husbands, Nelly and Isaac Hite, Sarah and Thomas Macon, Frances and Robert Rose; to Nelly Conway Madison, the only child and heiress of his brother Ambrose, and the nine children and one son-in-law of his brother Francis. He himself was left with the Montpelier mansion and three farms of about five thousand acres, extending from the Rapidan River to the top of the southwest mountains. His mother was settled in quarters to the right of the front hall, with her own private staff.

Meanwhile in the Federal City, occupied officially only since the preceding November, his friend Jefferson was strolling casually to the Capitol on March 4 for his inauguration dressed "like a plain citizen," delivering his brief address, and returning to his lodging at Conrad's boardinghouse to take his usual place at the lowest and coldest end of the dinner table, smilingly refusing a more honored seat. His inaugural address, when a report of it arrived at Montpelier, was just what James had hoped for and expected. It emphasized the warning that he himself had helped write into Washington's 1783 address against entangling Old World alliances. He especially approved of the conciliatory climax.

"Let us restore to social intercourse that harmony and affection without which liberty and even life itself are but dreary things. And let us reflect that having banished from our land that religious intolerance under which mankind has so long bled and suffered, we have gained little if we countenance a political intolerance as despotic, as wicked, and capable of as bitter and bloody persecution. . . . We are all Republicans, we are all Federalists."

And the new President had immediately put his philosophy into action by freeing all persons who had been imprisoned or were under prosecution by the Alien and Sedition Acts, "without asking what the offenders had done, or against whom they had offended."

James beamed his approval. "At last!" he exulted to Dolley. "Those despicable acts were an ax laid to the very roots of our Constitution. No nation can remain democratic without freedom of speech and of the press."

On March 5, Madison had been nominated for Secretary of State and quickly approved by the Senate, in spite of its Federalist majority. Though he and Albert Gallatin, the Swiss-born Senator whom Jefferson wanted as his Secretary of the Treasury, had been named by the Federalist *Columbian Centinel* as "sons of darkness" who would help Jefferson destroy the Constitution, another Federalist conceded that: "If Madison be Secretary of State there will be more justice and liberality of opinion on party men. He is the best of them all."

When Jefferson visited Montpelier on April 3 on his way to Monticello, he was shocked to find his new Secretary of State in "very indifferent health." But he was fast improving, Madison assured him. They talked together far into the night, the new President deploring the last attempt of the Federalists to maintain their power. Even while balloting for the new President had been going on, the Federalist House in one of its last activities had passed a Judiciary Act creating several new federal districts, requiring at least sixteen new judges to be appointed. President Adams had hastened to make the appointments before the new administration could come into office. On the evening before inauguration day he was still signing their commissions.

"Sneaky!" Jefferson denounced bitterly, his blue-gray eyes sharpening to steel. "I never would have believed Adams, a thoroughly just man, would have so yielded to party pressures. Appointing those new federal judges so late they're already being dubbed 'midnight judges'! Fortunately I found a lot of the commissions still undelivered and forbade their delivery, but there are still too many of them left! I tell you, a President shouldn't have the power, or at least he shouldn't exercise it, of influencing the policies of the country through his appointments of the judiciary for years to come!"

Jefferson stopped at Montpelier again April 26 on his way back to the capital, hoping that Madison could accompany him.

"We'll soon be following," James promised, for with the spring warmth his rheumatism was getting better each day. Not so the roads over which they must travel.

"Don't come the Ravensworth way," Jefferson sent back a warning. "The mud holes would overturn your carriage. Come by Fairfax Courthouse."

The President had not exaggerated. Even by the Fairfax county road it was a fatiguing, jolting journey. The coach swayed drunkenly, sank to its hubs in mud, labored through chuckholes and over swollen streams. Was it a foretaste, Dolley wondered, of the new even more fearsome challenges they would be facing?

2

Washington City, as it was now called in honor of the person who had labored most lovingly and untiringly in its creation, was an ungainly but lusty infant just emerging from the painful throes of birth. As the Madisons rode through a marshy wilderness between the President's House and the Capitol, over rough wheel tracks bearing the incongruous name of Pennsylvania Avenue, their carriage sank in mud as deep as that in the Virginia backcountry. On May 2, following his arrival in Washington, James was sworn in as Secretary of State by Judge Cranch, one of the "midnight judges."

Jefferson insisted that the Madisons stay with him until they could find a place to live. Dolley was captivated by the President's House, bare and half-finished though it was, situated far from the Capitol on an unenclosed piece of barren ground, surrounded by masses of stone, bricks, and other materials used in its construction, looking, as one inhabitant described it, "more like a ruin in the midst of its fallen fragments than a new and rising edifice." Dolley saw it as it would later appear, cleared of the surrounding clutter and of some of the venerable oaks which dwarfed its majestic classic simplicity, its walls of white sandstone giving it an impressive dignity in contrast with the few brick and frame buildings scattered over the raw landscape.

"A castle!" she pronounced delightedly, as once long ago she had exclaimed over the modest magnificence of Scotchtown.

Abigail Adams, moving into the house the preceding November, had used the same descriptive word in a letter to her daughter, though not with the same complimentary intent. "To assist us in this great castle . . . bells are wholly wanting, not one single one being hung throughout the house, and promises are all you can obtain." She had other complaints: lack of a main staircase, leaking roof, insufficient lighting, only a cord and a half of wood to supply the twelve fires constantly required. "Surrounded by forests, can you believe that wood is not to be had, because people cannot be found to cut and cart it? And the great unfurnished audience-room I make a drying room of, to hang up the clothes in." But she had admitted, "It is a beautiful spot, capable of every improvement, and the more I view it the more I am delighted with it."

"I would be grateful," said Jefferson soon after their arrival, "if Mistress Madison would act as my hostess at a little dinner I am giving today."

Dolley was dismayed. Preside at the table of the President of the United States? With some of the most important people of Washington present, perhaps foreign dignitaries? And what could she wear? She and Anna had been living in the country for four years. The Washington ladies would think them hopelessly outdated. Then she remembered. Jefferson had no wife. His daughters were unable to leave their families in Virginia. How lonely and helpless he must feel!

"Of course," she said willingly. "I shall be glad to."

Excitedly she and Anna scrounged around in their meager wardrobe for things presentable. "What will the women think of us?" mourned Anna. "They'll know we're from the backwoods!"

They need not have worried. There were no women among the guests. All were members of Jefferson's cabinet or men closely associated with his administration. Among them were Albert Gallatin, Secretary of the Treasury, a brilliant Swiss immigrant; Vice President Aaron Burr; Henry Dearborn, Secretary of War; Robert Smith, Secretary of the Navy; Attorney General Levi Lincoln; Dr. William Thornton, the city district commissioner, a Quaker whom Dolley had known in Philadelphia; Samuel Harrison Smith, who had come to Washington to establish a Republican newspaper, the *National Intelligencer*.

The dinner was served at a round table in the pleasant south room later to be known as the Green Room. Dolley was impressed with its furnishings, an elegant sideboard with pedestals and urn knife cases, a large mahogany table, two glass cases for the silver and plated ware, fifteen black-and-gold chairs. She noted with satisfaction that there were no rules of precedence. If any guests had titles, they were ignored. Jefferson was dressed neatly but casually, as befitted his democratic code, in twilled corduroy breeches, a scarlet embroidered waistcoat under a coat of more somber color, and comfortable satinette shoes. His servants were more impressive than he in their blue livery coats trimmed with silver lace.

Having been at Monticello, she should have known that the food and table arrangements would also contrast surprisingly with the

President's studiedly informal appearance and manner. The menu was ample, too much so—rice, soup, round of beef, turkey, ham, a loin of veal, cutlets of mutton, fried eggs, fried beef, a pie called macaroni, some kind of a rich crust filled with something like onions or shallots (too strong, she didn't like the taste), and ice cream with a light crust crumbled into thin flakes. And it was faultlessly served. Jefferson had even here provided little tables beside the places so the guests could serve themselves and the servants could be dismissed and the conversation be less interrupted.

But—the conversation!

"Gentlemen," began the President after the main courses had been set on the little tables and the servants had retired, "I would be glad of your opinions on several issues with which we have to deal. And I am sure our Secretary of State would welcome your advice."

Oh dear, thought Dolley, this was turning into a cabinet meeting, not a cosy friendly little dinner! What he needed wasn't a hostess, it was a secretary!

"For instance," continued Jefferson, "this matter of the Dey of Algiers . . ."

"Blast his heathen thievery!" interrupted Secretary of the Navy Smith. "The effrontery of demanding tribute for keeping our ships from being despoiled by those Barbary pirates!"

"True," agreed Jefferson. "But our predecessors started the custom of tribute, emulating European countries, and our payments are three years in arrears."

"Then let us stop the practice," Smith argued hotly. "Let's protect our commerce with warships instead of dollars."

Madison cleared his throat. "Well said," he agreed mildly. "We shall suggest such a measure to Congress immediately. But our promises to the Dey must be fulfilled. If we are three years behind in payments, we must discharge our debts. It is a matter of national responsibility."

"And while we're recommending to Congress," interposed Vice President Burr, "we should do something about that dastardly excise tax on whiskey, which is anathema to our Republican supporters in the West. You know very well it was the principal cause of the Whiskey Rebellion."

"But it's a source of much needed revenue," remarked the Secretary of the Treasury. "While I agree that it's a poor business, can we stand the loss in taxation?"

After some heated discussion, attention shifted to the ever-menacing problem of British depradations on American shipping.

"We've got to stop this shilly-shallying!" proclaimed Smith hotly. "The despicable Jay Treaty did nothing to stop the insulting seizure of our vessels and the impression of our seamen. I say—let's have action."

"But what kind of action?" demanded Jefferson. "Let us hear from our Secretary of State on the matter."

Dolley looked anxiously at James. If only he would inject a little humor into the parley, tell one of his little stories, even one a bit bawdy, to relieve the tension! But he was as sober as a presiding bishop.

"I shall write to our minister, Rufus King, in London," he began in his usual deliberate manner.

"A confirmed Federalist," muttered Smith, receiving a scowl from New Englander Levi Lincoln.

"And express our desire," continued Madison, disregarding the interruption, "to establish entire confidence and harmony of good will between the two countries, which can rest on no other foundations than those of reciprocal justice and respect."

"Hear, hear!" approved Lincoln.

"Poppycock!" snorted Smith. "Nothing but the same old line!"

"But I see no sign," went on Madison firmly, "of a change of conduct taking place on the part of Britain. Therefore American policy can scarcely fail to take some shape more remedial than that hitherto given to it."

"What about this rumor?" demanded Samuel Harrison Smith, "that Spain has ceded all of that vast Louisiana tract to France? And what would that do to our settlements in the West? What if Napoleon has his eye on an American empire out there?"

The conversation grew even more heated, a babel of confusion. Dolley listened with mounting concern. Soon they would be—no, they already *were* at one another's throats. A dinner party should not be like this, and, after all, she was the hostess.

"Mr. Jefferson," she said brightly during a brief lull in the conversation, like an eye in the storm, "why don't you tell the gentlemen about your wonderful clock? It's such a marvelous invention! I'm sure they'd be interested."

Courteously, if reluctantly, Jefferson complied, and soon the guests were chuckling over his mortification in having had to cut through his floor in order to install the weight that completed the week's sequence with Saturday. When serious talk was resumed, there was no more hot argument, only reasonable friendly discussion.

As days passed and no women were included among the invited guests, Dolley was troubled. Surely it was wise for a President to include influential females among his associates. It had been Friday when they arrived, the day of Martha Washington's levees, and, she understood, Abigail Adams had continued the custom. No one had appeared. She waited patiently for the next Friday. Again—nothing. It was Anna, reunited with her friend Sally, now the Marchioness d'Yrujo, who reported the pertinent gossip.

"Listen to this!" her eyes sparkled merrily. "The women waited for an announcement of the usual levee. None came. Then some of them, including Sally, decided to take matters into their own hands, pretending everything was as usual. On the proper day they dressed to the nines and at the customary hour for the levee came to the President's house. He wasn't here so they waited in the oval room, bound to shame him. Presently he came in from his usual horseback ride, dressed—you can guess how, boots, spurs, rough clothes, hair disheveled by the wind! Oh, he received them courteously, acted as if he had been expecting them, freckled face beaming, even had the servants bring refreshments, then explained how he felt about levees. Waste of time, too much like the panoply of Old World kings, not consistent with our new democratic ways. After a reasonable interval he led them politely to the door. They got the message. No more levees."

"Oh dear!" said Dolley. It was even worse than she had thought. The female whispering campaign against the President would have already begun. She could imagine the innuendos. "Country boor!" "Backwoodsman!" "Cheapskate!" "Antisocial!" But he was not like that at all, not antisocial, not niggardly in hospitality. He had a group of guests at his four o'clock dinner almost every day, but—all men! Something must be done.

"I suppose," she remarked innocently to the President, "it is impossible to have the usual levees with the house in its present condition."

"Not impossible," he replied. "Mrs. Adams held court upstairs in the oval room, the one with all the mahogany chairs and the crimson stuff left over from the Washington furnishings. She had it full to the gills. All the stiff formality of the Washington style of entertainment. There was Adams wearing velvet, silver buckles at his knees, hair powdered, bowing from the waist, his wife in all her queenly glory

seated at his side. But," he continued firmly, "there will be no levees in
my administration. They always reminded me of an audience with
royalty. There is no place for them in a democratic society. Two receptions a year will be sufficient, New Year's Day and the Fourth of
July."

"Of course," conceded Dolley, "if you include all kinds and classes
of people in your dinner parties—"

"Certainly. All kinds and classes. Every level of society." He chuckled. "I even had my butcher at one of my dinners. You should have
seen some of the faces. But I made sure he was treated with the same
deference as the most honored guest. I invite them all, Republicans
and Federalists, stiff-necked New England industrialists and Western
pioneers, plumed foreign grandees with gilded smallswords and feathered Indians with tomahawks."

"Men—*and women?*" interposed Dolley with significant emphasis.

He was taken aback. "Why—why, yes, I suppose so." Suddenly his
large firm lips broke into a smile. The twinkle in his eyes seemed to
change them from steel-gray to warm vibrant blue. "Thank you, my
dear," he said humbly. "I got the message."

And he had. During the next few days his dinner parties included
the wives of several cabinet ministers, legislators, diplomats, and common citizens. He was a genial host. Presiding at the table, Dolley
could see compressed lips break into smiles, wary skepticism give way
to a frank, if grudging appreciation. Like herself, the other women
were captivated by his conversation, ranging all the way from astronomy, geology, music, mathematics, to some of the "tall stories" for
which he was famous.

"You would never believe this," he joked once, "but before I went to
France I had some ripe pears sewed into bags and stored, and when I
got back six years later I found them beautifully preserved, all candied
in their own juice."

To Dolley's relief he was proving that he could be as popular with
women as with men. Mrs. Samuel Harrison Smith, née Margaret Bayard, would later record her impressions in a volume entitled *The First
Forty Years of Washington Society*, telling of her own conversion from
prejudice to admiration. She had been told stories of Jefferson's cru-
dity and vulgarity. One day a man came to her house to arrange for
some government printing by her husband's paper. She wrote, "He
turned to me a countenance beaming with an expression of benevolence and with a manner and voice almost femininely soft and gentle.

Something in his countenance and voice just unlocked my heart."
With amazement she discovered that he was not a messenger from the
President's House but Mr. Jefferson himself. "I felt my cheeks burn
and my heart throb," she confessed. Though she was the daughter of a
staunch Federalist, thereafter she became an ardent supporter of the
Republican cause.

Mrs. Smith was also impressed favorably by Dolley, whom she first
met at the President's House on May 26. "She has good humor and
sprightliness," she recorded, "united to the most affable and agreeable
manners."

Dolley had been asked by Jefferson to be hostess on this occasion.
He had written, "Thomas Jefferson begs that either Mrs. Madison or
Miss Payne will dine with him today, to take care of female friends
expected."

Margaret Smith, indefatigable chronicler, preserved her further impressions of this dinner party.

"Since I last wrote I have formed quite a social acquaintance with
Mrs. Madison and her sister; indeed it is impossible for an acquaintance with them to be different. Mr. Smith and I dined at the President's—He has company every day, but his table is seldom laid for
more than twelve. This prevents all form and makes the conversation
general and unreserved. I happened to sit next to Mr. Jefferson and
was confirmed in my prepossessions in his favour by his easy, candid
and gentle manners. Before and after dinner, Mrs. Cranch and myself
sat in the drawing room with Mrs. Madison and her sister, whose
social disposition soon made us well acquainted with each other."

While a guest at the President's House, Dolley was spending much
of her time trying to find a suitable place to live. Jefferson was being
criticized by the Federalists, she suspected, for "taking boarders."
James was spending most of his time in state department business in
what were known as the Six Buildings on the road to Georgetown,
where, as the British legation secretary Augustus Foster chronicled, he
"received foreign ministers in a very indifferent room into which they
were ushered by his clerk." His staff was small, consisting of Chief
Clerk Jacob Wagner and six other clerks, all remnants of the previous
administration. He discharged none of them, preferring "honor and
delicacy" to "political conformity."

Work had been accumulating during his delay in arrival, and he
tackled the most pressing problems at once. On May 15 at his instigation the cabinet voted to fulfill the country's debts to Algeria but

hereafter to protect America's shipping from the Barbary pirates by warships rather than tribute. He made up a list of presents to be sent to the Dey, including four redbirds and two squirrels. He sent dispatches to Rufus King indicating that the Adams policy of tolerating aggressions by Britain had come to an end. He told the French ambassador, Louis Pichon, that if transfer of the Louisiana tract to France from Spain took place, it would almost certainly bring about collision between France and the United States. Navigation of the Mississippi, an essential for western colonists, was maintained in agreement with the Spanish authorities, but with France holding the west bank and attempting to extend her empire, navigation would bring about daily conflicts with the western settlers. Also Madison was being swamped by requests from a myriad of applicants for official appointments. He had no time to hunt for houses.

As Dolley canvassed the city in her carriage, jolting over rutted paths, now a surge of choking dust instead of a welter of mud, crossing makeshift bridges, the few buildings separated by long stretches of woods and marsh, she was nevertheless impressed and delighted with its possibilities. Designed by Major Pierre Charles L'Enfant, a French engineer in the Revolutionary Army, who had had a creative mind and expansive vision, it was laid out in a grandiose design of streets, broad avenues, circles, parks, squares. He had placed the congressional building on Jenkin's Heights, which, he noted, "stands as a pedestal waiting for a monument." For the President's House he had selected a ridge west of the Tiber, a little stream which had been originally called Goose Creek. At the cross axis running south from the President's House and west from the Capitol there was to be a Washington Monument, which he pictured as an equestrian statue and which would be connected with the Congress House by an avenue 160 feet wide.

"It is planned on such a scale," President Washington had approved, "as to leave room for that aggrandizement and embellishment which the increase of the wealth of the nation will permit it to pursue at any period, however remote."

But L'Enfant had proved too headstrong and insubordinate to carry his plan to execution, and, though his design had been largely followed, others had been appointed by the committee to execute it, among them Benjamin Latrobe and Dr. William Thornton, the English Quaker whom the Madisons had known in Philadelphia.

Dolley's search was discouraging. Buildings were few. There were

Thomas Law's nine houses on Capitol Hill near the truncated, half-finished Capitol. Scattered along the main thoroughfare, no better than a country road, were a few straggling buildings with Blodgett's, otherwise known as the "Great Hotel," halfway between the Capitol and the President's House. Between the latter and Georgetown there were the Six Buildings, all strung together, and north of the avenue another complex called the Seven Buildings. Here and there, half-hidden among the trees, were mansions built by older inhabitants, like Daniel Carroll and Motley Young. Most intriguing to Dolley was a new house near the President's designed by Dr. Thornton who had drawn the plans for the Capitol, for John Tayloe. Far more imposing and luxurious even than the President's House, it was built with eight sides and was called the Octagon. If Dolley could have foreseen the part it was to play in her life, she might not have been so intrigued.

It was William Thornton who finally solved the housing problem, urging the Madisons to take temporary lodgings for the brief time before they would leave for the summer vacation. He would find a house for them by the time they returned. They rented a small house in the Six Buildings on Pennsylvania Avenue between Twenty-first and Twenty-second streets next to the Gallatins, Albert and his wife, Hannah, an energetic, high-spirited woman, strongly Republican, who enjoyed political arguments. She and Dolley soon became lifelong friends.

That the widowed Jefferson missed Dolley's gay enlivening presence was evidenced by his admission that he and his secretary felt like "two mice in a church." But the Madisons had hardly got settled in the new house before he was writing on June 4, "Thomas Jefferson was much disappointed at breakfast this morning, not having known of the departure of Mrs. Madison and Miss Payne; he hopes they will come and dine with the Miss Butters, who were assured they would meet them here, and tomorrow with Mrs. Gallatin and Mrs. Mason. Affectionate salutations."

Because of the malarial dangers from the city swamps, most officials left Washington for the summer months. The Madisons waited until after the Fourth of July celebration, then drove home by way of Loudon County to visit Dolley's old friend Eliza, now the wife of Richard Bland Lee. It was wonderful to be together again for an all too short renewal of their long friendship. Then they went on through the burning July heat to Orange. Mail routes were arranged between Monticello and Montpelier, and couriers enabled the President and his chief secretary to exchange important dispatches. They remained in the country until October. It was a pattern they were to follow for the next sixteen years.

Before leaving Washington, James had asked William Thornton to find him a house. He was embarrassed because he was unable to pay the advance rent required for the house that Thornton secured for him next to his own residence, for he had borrowed a thousand dollars to buy household equipment. Nicholas Voss, a contractor, was building the house in question and needed six hundred dollars, the whole of the first year's rent, to finish it. Thornton was good enough to borrow the money himself, putting Voss under bond to complete the house by October 1.

Returning to Washington in October, the Madisons stayed with Jefferson a few days until the freshly plastered walls of the new house had dried. Dolley was delighted with their new residence on F Street, just two blocks from the President's House. Thornton had had the third floor divided into four extra bedrooms with dormer windows, suitable for servants and guests. The family apartments on the second floor, bedrooms, parlor, office-library, small dining room, were soon made attractive with her own familiar furnishings. The first floor, with its reception room, large drawing room, dining facilities, was ideal for entertaining. There was a picturesque cupola on the roof, and the house was equipped with a fire escape. The cellar had been divided into wine and coal rooms. Soon there would be a coach house and a stable for four horses. This was to be their home for the rest of James's two terms as Secretary of State.

Soon the notes began coming again from the President's House. "Thomas Jefferson requests the presence of Mrs. Madison . . ." "Thomas Jefferson would be pleased if Mrs. Madison and Miss Payne . . ." "Thomas Jefferson begs Mrs. Madison . . ." He could have asked other cabinet wives to preside at his table, and occasionally did, but he preferred one whose charm and dignity of manner were balanced by a good-natured humor which put everyone at ease, who was equally cordial with a pompous foreign ambassador or a crude wilderness pioneer, who could converse as sympathetically with an irate Federalist as with a staunch Republican—merely because she liked them all. Though Dolley was never designated as official hostess during the Jefferson administrations, she was so in fact. When one young woman dined with the President in 1803, she noted that the wife of the Secretary of State "in fact appeared to be the mistress of the mansion."

After dinner Dolley took the guests on a tour of the house, even taking them into Jefferson's bedroom and showing them "his odd contrivance for hanging up jackets and breeches."

Jefferson was insistent on observing democratic customs in all his entertaining. This applied to dress as well as table manners. He abhorred the gold lace worn by the French ambassador, said they "must get him down to a plain frock coat, or the boys on the streets will run after him as a sight." He himself sometimes carried informality in dress to an extreme. One foreign diplomat complained that the President received him in a "blue coat, thick grey-colored waistcoat, green velveteen breeches, and slippers down at the heels!" The Federalists made delighted propaganda use of the slippers.

The President formulated a code of manners with fourteen points to govern his conduct with foreign diplomats and other guests. It stipulated that "at dinners, public and private, perfect equality exists between the guests, and to give force to the principle of equal or pele mele, and to prevent the growth of precedence out of courtesy, the members of the Executive at their own houses will adhere to the ancient usage of their ancestors,—gents en masse giving place to ladies en masse."

This code, entitled CANONS OF ETIQUETTE TO BE OBSERVED BY THE EXECUTIVE, prescribed also the proper procedure for visits. Foreign ministers on arriving should pay the first visit to the ministers of the nation; the families of foreign ministers should receive the first visit from all residents; there should be no distinction among foreign ministers, no titles. The President would receive the first visit from ministers, but would not return it, while their families would both receive the first visit and return it. The President and his family would take precedence everywhere, in public or in private.

Dolley felt very comfortable in following this code of manners. It made her roles of President's hostess and wife of the Secretary of State infinitely easier.

Each day at four dinner was served at the President's *round* table, with perhaps twelve, seldom more than fourteen guests. Round, irate Federalists commented, so there could be no precedence. Mrs. Smith thought otherwise. "Round," she wrote, "so that all could see each other's faces and feel the animating influence of looks as well as words, and make for more social enjoyment." Dolley would have agreed.

Jefferson's democratic credo, however, permitted luxuries that could hardly be characterized as "simplicity." He brought from Mon-

ticello furniture purchased in France in styles of Hepplewhite, Shera-
ton, Louis Seize. He had a French steward, Étienne LeMaire, a French
chef, and many servants from Monticello. His wines from Spain and
France were the finest vintage procurable. And his table was set with
delicacies from abroad, waffles from Holland, macaroni from Italy,
almonds and anchovies from France. His *pièce d'occasion* was often ice
cream, served according to a French recipe, in little balls enclosed in
shells of warm pastry.

Dolley's role as hostess was by no means confined to the President's
House. As the wife of the chief cabinet minister she did much entertaining in her own home. Her house also was the resort of visitors,
both officials and personal friends. She set a bountiful table. One member of Congress wrote, "An excellent dinner. The round of beef of
which the soups is made is called 'bouilli.' It had in the dish spices,
and something of the sweet herb and early kind, and a rich gravy. It is
very much boiled and is still very good. We had a dish with what
appeared to be cabbage, much boiled, then cut in long strings and
somewhat mashed; in the middle a large ham, with the cabbage
around. It looked like our country dishes of bacon and cabbage, with
the cabbage mashed up after being boiled till sodden and turned dark.
The dessert was good: much as usual, except two dishes which appeared like apple pie in the form of the half of a musk-melon, the flat
side down, top creased deep, and the color a dark brown."

Madison's scale of living could hardly be called frugal. Often he was
in financial difficulty, as when unable to pay his year's rent in advance.
Though he had many assets, a house in Philadelphia, at Montpelier
1,800 acres of productive land, a farm of 374 acres in Culpepper
County, the whole of the farm adjoining the Montpelier mansion,
several lots in Washington, like many of the Virginia squires, he was
land-poor. His farms absorbed the income they yielded.

In his desire to provide a worthy setting for his own official hostess
he had indulged in some extravagances, purchases of fine porcelain,
plate and glassware, imported wines of rare vintage—Hermitage, Vir-
gin, White Cotillion—besides olives, preserved fruits, and other delicacies. In 1802 he bought a secondhand coach made in Philadelphia for
$510, with an expensive silver-plated harness. He had also indulged
his taste for good horses. Unfortunately his payments were not always
made promptly, and Mr. Voss had to remind him sometimes that his
rent was overdue. But he always paid his bills eventually and was
never accused of avoiding his financial responsibilities. Generously

hospitable, proud of his charming wife, he was determined to be a good provider.

Inured more to Quaker thrift than to luxury, Dolley compensated in many ways for his extravagances. A skilled seamstress, she provided both herself and Anna with costumes in the prevailing styles and at only moderate expense. One admirer gave a detailed description of her dress on one occasion. "She had on her head a turban of white satin, with three white ostrich feathers hanging over her face, very becoming indeed! Her dress too, of white satin, made high in the neck, with long sleeves, and large capes trimmed with swan's down was rich and beautiful. She looked remarkably well, and as much like a bride as a queen, for she wore no colors."

Queen! The word was beginning to appear more and more in descriptive comments about her, in diaries, in letters, in conversations somehow preserved for posterity. Fortunately they never reached her ears. She would have scoffed at their extravagance, hated their suggestions of royalty in a democratic society. And she would have been horrified at one of the most lavish appraisals by the Danish minister who observed her during one of Jefferson's receptions.

"What need you manners more captivating, more winning, more polished than those of that amiable woman? I have, by turns, resided in all the courts of Europe and, most positively I assure you, I never have seen any Duchess, Princess, or Queen whose manners, with equal dignity, blended equal sweetness. Her stately person, her lofty carriage, her affable and gracious manner, would make her appear to advantage in any court in the world. Upon my soul, as I have often exclaimed to myself, as I have seen her moving through admiring crowds, pleasing all, by making all pleased with themselves, 'She moves a goddess, and she looks a queen.' "

A pity both of these commentators could not have seen her after the festive occasions, whatever they were, when as usual she laid aside her finery, satin plumes and swan's down, donned a simple gown of Quaker gray and changed the fashionable turban, which was being copied by women all over Washington, for a modest little cap with ribbons tied beneath her chin.

3

"Yes, as I was saying," the voice resuming conversation was low but vibrantly compelling, and every eye about the table was turned in its direction, "amusing things sometimes happen even in the sober halls of government. As you may know, my department has been badgered by people seeking appointments. One newspaper writer whose virulent attacks on the Federalists have done more harm to our party than to theirs came to me." James smiled mischievously. "I won't mention his name. He thought he deserved a reward. He wanted to be governor of a western territory. 'I'm sorry,' I told him. 'I'm afraid there are others with superior claims to such positions.' 'Oh!' he said magnanimously, 'Well, a collectorship would do.' 'Sorry again,' I replied. 'Then how about a post office job?' Down he kept coming, down—down—until finally he got to his last request. 'Well,' he asked humbly, 'do you have any old clothes you could spare?' "

Amid the laughter which followed Dolley gave her husband an affectionate smile. Trust Jemmy, when arguments became too heated, to ease the tension with one of his droll stories! When the discussion of political problems resumed, it was in a much milder atmosphere.

James could have told them of other less humorous, some near-tragic applications that had caused him worry, but generally he was close-mouthed. He had been asked that some place in the post office, any little place, be found for his old "Whig" college mate Philip Freneau, who was now reported indigent. The French dancing master who had taught his nieces and nephews back in the town of Orange had begged him, "Oh, in pity be kind!" Some editors who had been fined or imprisoned under the Sedition Act felt they should be given offices. One of them suggested that the acts passed by Congress should be given for publication only to Republican papers. But this was not Madison's theory of government. Freedom of information and of the press was vital in a democracy.

He was dealing with other problems more important than appoint-

ments. One, of course, was the spoliations of trade and the impressment of seamen by the British. The list of the latter amounted to near
two thousand, four fifths of them native Americans, and property
unlawfully seized totaled millions. Madison had instructed Rufus
King, the minister to England, to attempt redress of these two grievances. His own policy was simple. He would employ against England
the commercial weapons that he had long advocated, always with an
attempt at peace making.

More serious at present was the problem of French dominion in
Louisiana, which signaled an attempt by Napoleon to establish an
empire in the New World. He had already embarked on reconquest of
Santo Domingo. His control of the Mississippi and of New Orleans
would result in inevitable conflict between France and the United
States. Madison's message to Livingston, the American minister to
France, was clear. More than half the produce of American farmers in
April of 1802 went through New Orleans. If France took possession of
the city and closed the port it would mean inevitable alliance between
the United States and Britain.

Dolley could do little to ease James's worries except provide a sympathetic ear and a social milieu where international problems could be
discussed over tempting food and in an atmosphere of domestic serenity. Tensions between France and the United States, as represented by
Louis Pichon, French chargé d'affaires and the American Secretary of
State relaxed visibly under the mollifying influence of her honey-
sweetened Virginia ham and generous portion of her famous forty-egg
cake.

The house on F Street had become a social center second only to the
President's House. Invitations to Dolley's dinners were prized, and
she was cosmopolitan in her choice of guests. Congressmen, planters,
foreign diplomats, cabinet members, Democratic-Republicans, Federalists, newspaper men of all persuasions, bishops, Quakers, Baptists,
probably some who called themselves atheists, all rubbed shoulders at
her teas and dinners. Afterward in her drawing room there was music
and perhaps a bit of dancing. The men might have a game of brag, the
ladies one of loo. Still loyal to her Quaker traditions, Dolley did not
participate in the dancing. But she enjoyed cards. Samuel Smith once
remarked to his wife that at his first try at loo he had won two dollars
from her, but "felt some mortification at putting the money of Mrs.
Madison into my pocket." Soon Dolley gave up playing for money,
not because she minded losing but because it seemed a betrayal of her

Quaker upbringing. However, she presided over all the forms of gaiety with benign acceptance. In spite of Jefferson's democratic credo, the atmosphere here was more relaxed and informal than in the President's House. It was the most popular social center in Washington.

Jefferson held rigidly to his decision to permit only two celebrations each year, New Year's and the Fourth of July. He adamantly refused to have his birthday, April 13, observed. The birth of his country, he felt, was far more important. And, indeed, he was so inextricably linked to the day marking its emergence as a nation, being the author of the Declaration of Independence, that he might well have felt that they shared the same birthday. July Fourth compensated for all the forbidden celebrations. It was a gala event, with gun salutes, parades, speeches, flag waving, presentations, and, of course, jollity that exceeded the bounds of sobriety.

This year of 1802 it sported an additional feature never seen before or since—the GREAT CHEESE. Only capitals could do it justice. It was a mammoth concoction created by a group of ardent admirers in Cheshire, Massachusetts, who were enthusiastic over Jefferson's interpretation of nationalization laws in his message of 1801. Everyone who owned a cow had contributed all of one day's milk, "only no Federalist must contribute a drop." Hymns had been sung and prayers offered while the cheese was being made. Great kegs of curds had been poured into a huge cider press to congeal. Weighing over twelve hundred pounds, it had been brought in a wagon drawn by six horses to Washington bearing a banner with the words, "The greatest cheese in America for the greatest man in America."

Jefferson had accepted it gratefully but it was against his principles to receive gifts. In his financial accounts he noted, "To bearer of the cheese $200," which was 50 percent more than the current price of cheese. Also, being Jefferson and it being the Fourth of July when the President's House was open to guests, every person who came was invited to share in its consumption, to the detriment of rugs, furniture, draperies, and all the rest of the decor. The monstrosity became the talk of the town, and for days Dolley exhibited what was left of it to curious visitors as she gave them a tour of the President's House. It shared the fascination of other exhibits, such as Jefferson's pet mocking bird, which he had tamed and trained to sit on his shoulder and take food from his lips, also to hop up and down stairs after him. People admired also his deep windows filled with rare plants, his botanical specimens, his beautiful cabinet which flew open at a touch to make available the things he needed when he studied at night—a goblet of water, a dish of light refreshment, a candle.

July again brought adjournment of Congress and general exodus from Washington. Montpelier again at last! But the summer was no holiday for Dolley. Visitors came in droves—diplomats, foreign travelers, neighboring farmers, newspaper reporters, relatives. Among the latter that year of 1802 were Bishop James Madison, Jemmy's cousin, and his son. Other guests at the same time were the William Thorntons, with Mrs. Thornton's mother, Mrs. Brodeau. Dr. Thornton's pretty French wife, Anna Maria, recorded in her diary on September 3, "Arrived at Mr. Madison's country seat about 110 miles from Washington." She described the place as wild, romantic, and covered with flourishing timber, the house as "upwards of eighty feet in length and of a plain but grand appearance more pleasing by displaying the taste for the arts which is rarely found in such retired and remote situations."

The Thornton family and the bishop accompanied the Madisons on their usual visit to Monticello. They arrived at the foot of Jefferson's mountain after dark, and, as Anna Maria noted, "had it not been for the almost incessant lightning we should not have been able to see the road at all." At last it became so dangerous that "all but Mama" walked the last three quarters of a mile, arriving just ahead of a deluge of rain. She described the mansion, always in a litter of rebuilding, as "a place you would rather look at now and then than live in."

Dolley always reveled in the month they spent at Monticello each summer. One of her greatest joys was the presence of children, and Martha Randolph's were near enough to be constant companions both for her and for Payne. It was her greatest sorrow that she and Jemmy had so far been unable to present a little brother or sister to her much indulged young son. Though James could not have been a more loving or thoughtful father, spending long hours teaching the boy in lieu of a tutor, taking him on hunting and fishing expeditions, showering him with more luxuries than he could afford, Dolley knew that he secretly longed for sons of his own. The days at Monticello, with a lot of children all about, filled a void for both of them.

The summers were no holidays for James, either, for in addition to the entertainment of guests and the constant attention to letters arriving, he had to crowd into three months all the responsibility of a year of farming. During his long absences he must trust the responsibility of his farms to his overseer who was paid sixty pounds annually in

Virginia currency plus all living expenses. After paying this salary, clothing his servants, and deducting expenses for repairs, there was little profit left. There had usually been depredation in his absence, especially in his forests, where branches had been broken off and trees barked by poachers who made and sold lampblack. His interest in scientific farming demanded much time in experimentation. In 1803 he became the first President of an association of farm groups organized by him at the capital and called the American Board of Agriculture. For all these activities the only time he could spare was during his summer vacation.

Dolley was overjoyed when Jefferson was able to persuade his daughters to visit him in the fall and winter of 1802. Now Washington would see that he had a real First Lady, two of them, in fact, just as charming and capable as Martha Washington and just as, or almost as intellectually brilliant as Abigail Adams. Like Abigail, who had accompanied her ambassador husband to London, the two girls had been exposed to the cream of European culture when their father had been minister to France. Martha Jefferson, after attending school in Philadelphia, had gone with her father in 1784 to France, had been educated in the school of the Abbaye de Panthemont, then had become mistress of her father's house in Paris. Maria, six years younger, had lived for some time in London with Mrs. Adams, who had been loath to part with her.

"A finer child of her age," Abigail had noted, "I never saw. So mature and understanding, so womanly of behavior, and so much sensibility, united, are rare to be met with. . . . Slighter in person than her sister, she already gave indications of a superior beauty. It was that exquisite beauty possessed by her mother—that beauty which the experienced learn to look upon with dread, because it betrays a physical organization too delicately fine to withstand the rough shocks of the world."

Yes, Jefferson's daughters would qualify in every respect as most beautiful, gracious, and intellectual First Ladies. But Dolley was both glad and sorry when Jefferson showed her a note from Martha.

"Dear Papa . . . will you be so good as to send orders to the milliner—Madame Peck, I believe her name is, through Mrs. Madison, who very obligingly offered to execute any little commission for me in Philadelphia, for two wigs of the color of the hair enclosed, and of the most fashionable shapes."

Of course Dolley was delighted to oblige, but—what a pity to hide those masses of beautiful auburn hair that were Maria's crowning glory! However, wigs were very much in vogue. Dolley herself seldom wore one. Her own glossy black curls were too abundant. But she loved to shop, whether for bargains in furniture—she and Anna Maria Thornton once picked up some beautiful chairs at a sale at the Point for only a dollar each!—or for feminine accoutrements. She hastened to fulfill the commission.

In spite of their hesitancy at leaving the country for the sophisticated society of Washington, Jefferson's daughters became immediately popular and much admired. Thanks to Dolley, who made sure their wardrobes were of the proper cut and materials, equipped with all the frills, spencers, pelisses, reticules which the French styles demanded, as well as the new wigs which she had secured for five dollars apiece, they made the rounds of teas, dinners, receptions with dignity and confidence, charming all they met, Martha with her wit and geniality, Maria with her remarkable beauty. In fact, they became weary with too much socializing. When Mrs. Samuel Smith regretted that she had given no party for them, Martha assured her that they were "heartily tired" of all the entertaining. Mrs. Smith was highly approving of them both.

"Mrs. Eppes is beautiful, simplicity and timidity personified," she wrote, "but when alone with you of communicative and winning manners. Mrs. Randolph is rather homely, a delicate likeness of her father, but still more interesting than Mrs. Eppes. She is really one of the most lovely women I have ever met, her countenance beaming with intelligence, benevolence and sensibility, and her conversation fulfills all her countenance promises."

The high point of their visit was the New Year's party, one of the two social events which Jefferson deigned to approve. The two girls received beside their father in the main reception room, now creditably furnished and finished, no longer a bare repository for drying clothes. Dolley was glad she need not act as hostess, for she and James were grieving over the death of his sister Nelly Hite the day before Christmas. She had no heart for celebration. Even Martha's children in whose presence she had taken such joy were sad reminders of Nelly's two, now motherless, thirteen-year-old Nelly and ten-year-old James Madison Hite.

But for others it was a gala occasion. The elite of Washington as well as Jefferson's favorite commoners took full advantage of the opportunity to inspect the President's House for the first time since the debacle of the Great Cheese. Among the most important guests were heads of departments, foreign ministers, chargés d'affaires, consuls, legislators. The President's daughters looked and acted the part of First Ladies, and their costumes, Dolley noted with satisfaction, while not elaborate, compared favorably with those of the more fashionably dressed guests, including Madame Pichon, wife of the French minister, who had generously coached Dolley not only in her French pronunciation but in the prevailing modes of French fashion, even insisting on giving her some of her own beautiful clothes.

"She has shown me everything she has," Dolley confessed gratefully, "and would fain give me of everything."

None, however, man or woman, could outshine the elegant Spanish minister, the Marquis d'Yrujo, in his silks, feathers, jeweled sword, his crown of powdered hair held high in arrogant defiance of his current unpopularity with most Americans. For in November 1802 the Spanish intendant at New Orleans had closed the port to all but Spanish vessels. A howl went up immediately from western settlers. Madison was furious at the action. Was it the work of Napoleon, dictating to Spain and already embarking on his plan of empire in the New World?

The whole question of ownership of that vast territory stretching all the way from New Orleans to the Canadian border and containing all the land from the Mississippi to the Rockies, had become of paramount importance to the United States. Not that there was any desire to possess it! Its importance lay in its owner's control over the west bank of the Mississippi, the chief trade route of the western colonists. Suppose France got control also of East and West Florida, which belonged to Spain, and gained another foothold in the New World!

France had once owned this territory but had ceded it to Spain in 1763 as payment for her alliance during the Seven Years' War. When Secretary of State, Jefferson had made a favorable treaty with Spain assuring the rights of American commerce on the Mississippi. But France under the dictatorship of Napoleon was now master of much of continental Europe, including Spain. The rumor that Spain had ceded to France the whole vast Louisiana Territory boded ill for America.

Madison sent a sharp protest to Madrid. "To our western citizens," he wrote, "the Mississippi is everything. It is the Hudson, the Delaware, the Potomac, and all the navigable waters of the Atlantic states formed into one stream. Justice, ample justice, to the western citizens of the United States is the only tenure of peace with this country."

The whole West was clamoring for war—with Spain, if that country still owned the west bank of the Mississippi, with France if it was true that Spain had ceded the territory to her. Britain, of course, always at odds with France, was taking advantage of the impasse, with Federalist support, to involve the country as her ally. British chargé Thornton was urging the President to take forcible possession of New Orleans. Even Jefferson, disillusioned in his French sympathies by the ruthless and autocratic Napoleon, who had proclaimed himself First Consul for life, was tempted to military action. He and Madison spent hours in spirited discussion.

Dolley sensed James's tormented anxiety and tried to ease the tension. She invited the French minister Louis Pichon and his wife to dinner, so that the two men could discuss the crisis, hopefully, in an informal and friendly atmosphere. Pichon, a courageous critic of his own government, was proving a wise and honest mediator between the two countries. And to her relief only friendliness prevailed—at first.

"France's position must be made clear," James said mildly. "We want to live in peace, but it looks as if your country won't let us."

"I know," responded Pichon despondently. "One can only hope."

"We are sending a message to Robert Livingston, our ambassador in Paris," Madison continued. "This is what the President says." It was so that James always reported their joint decisions, "The President says," even though he himself was largely responsible for them. "There is on the globe one single spot, the possessor of which is our natural habitual enemy. It is New Orleans, through which the produce of three-eighths of our territory must pass to market. The day that France takes possession of New Orleans we must marry ourselves to the British fleet and nation."

"That," said Pichon with a tightening of his lips, "as you and I well know, would be a disaster for both your country and mine."

James regarded him steadily, the food neglected on his plate. "And as you and I well know," he went on, "many of my countrymen, including members of Congress, are eager for war. They feel that their fortunes lie with England rather than France in the light of your country's actions." His eyes became suddenly challenging. "Shall we lay the foundation for future peace or the hazards and horrors of war, the great scourge of the human race?"

Dolley sensed the increasing tenseness in the atmosphere. The sudden ominous silence was her opportunity. She turned to the ambassador with a smile. Had M. Pichon noticed how admirably his wife was beginning to grasp the English language? And she had not known a word of it when she arrived in Washington! "And she has been helping me so much with my poor French pronunciation! We walk and ride together frequently, as you know, and I consider her one of my best friends. You have no idea how beloved is dear Madame Pichon by the women here in Washington. We are all learning so much from her about how ladies dress in Paris, and, I assure you, she is a model for many of us in fashion. Oh, she is very clever, that wife of yours, M. Pichon!"

"*Non, non,*" demurred Madame, blushing. Though she was fast learning to understand English, she did not yet venture to speak it much in public. "*Ma chère amie, elle est trop aimable!*"

James regarded Dolley gratefully. He bowed in courtly fashion toward the ambassador's young and genial wife. The tension had vanished as if by magic. There was no more talk of international crises.

But the crisis remained, intensified, and when news came that Spain had indeed ceded the Louisiana Territory to France, excitement and clamor for war flamed white-hot. The weeks required to take messages back and forth across the ocean dragged interminably. Jefferson grew grimmer and grimmer, James more restive and taciturn. No matter who held the mouth of the Mississippi, James wrote Robert Livingston, the American ambassador in France, "justice, ample justice to the Western citizens of the United States is the only tenure of peace with this country." There were, or soon would be, two hundred thousand militiamen on the banks of the Mississippi, all ready to march at a moment's notice to preserve the country's right to use the river. But the American ministers, Livingston in Paris and Pinckney in Spain, seemed powerless to solve the dilemma.

Finally Jefferson and Madison decided to send James Monroe as a special envoy having joint powers with the two ministers. They asked Congress for an appropriation of two million dollars for unspecified diplomatic purposes. It was understood, though unstated, that the money was intended for the possible purchase of New Orleans and the East and West Floridas by the United States.

"The Floridas and New Orleans," declared James, "command the only outlets to the sea for the American West and must become a part of the United States either by purchase or conquest."

Monroe sailed with his family to France on March 9, 1803, and landed April 8, fortified with formidable arguments for peaceful negotiations, plus the even more powerful inducement of the two million dollars.

War seemed inevitable. Then came a bombshell. Napoleon, faced with war with England to satisfy his ambition to dominate more of Europe, had decided suddenly that by throwing America into alliance with England he was likely to lose his new American possession to his British enemy. With her strong navy England would be sure to seize it as soon as war was declared. Moreover, he needed more money to fight. Oddly enough, it was mosquitoes that helped bring him to this momentous decision. For in 1801 the army he had sent to subdue the revolution in Santo Domingo sparked by the Negro idealist Toussaint L'Ouverture had been devastated by yellow fever. Out of the thirty-three thousand French soldiers he had sent, he discovered, twenty thousand had fallen victim to the scourge. It had been a deadly drawback to his ambition to establish an empire in the New World. Suddenly, one day in April, before Monroe had arrived in Paris, Talleyrand, Napoleon's foreign minister, called Livingston for a conference.

"How would the United States like to buy the whole of Louisiana?" he demanded bluntly.

Livingston gasped. No! was his first reaction. All the United States wanted was New Orleans and the Floridas.

Talleyrand continued without enthusiasm. He had tried to dissuade Napoleon from this impulsive decision. Without New Orleans, he explained, the rest of Louisiana was of little use to France. "What would you give for the whole of it?"

"Er—ah—say, twenty million francs," gulped Livingston.

"Too little," was the reply. "Think it over, and we will talk later."

Events moved at a breathtaking pace. When Monroe arrived he bolstered Livingston's flagging courage. The agreement was already made, though the treaty had not been signed, when the startling news reached Jefferson and Madison.

They were in a quandary. They had no wish to extend the country beyond the Mississippi. Many Easterners, especially Federalists, thought it was too large already. It would change the whole concept of America as a compact, homespun agricultural country, enlarge her boundaries by more than twice again, make her a continental power! Moreover, it probably wasn't legal. The Constitution might have to be amended before such a purchase could be made. Was not Jefferson, by his every statement and action, the defender of a limited interpretation of national power under the terms of the Constitution? And—fifteen million dollars, which was the price finally agreed on! Congress had been reluctant to appropriate two!

Decision had to be made quickly. Napoleon might change his mind. And Jefferson was not one to hesitate. It was he who decided, though it was Madison who had shaped American policy toward this desirable conclusion, cannily schooled his envoys in their most effective arguments. Like many of his other achievements, this one was not bruited to his glory at the time, merely hidden in the records to be discovered far in the future.

News of the treaty, signed in Paris, arrived in Washington on the evening before July 4, 1803, just in time to be officially announced on the gala day. The capital city came alive. A discharge of eighteen guns saluted the dawn. There was a huge parade celebrating the news that the country had just doubled its size. Dolley was in the crowd that at noon flowed through the doors of the President's House to greet the triumphant leader and to partake liberally of his punch, wine, and cakes.

There was mixed reaction. In many parts of the country, as in Washington, there was wild rejoicing. But Federalists who had been clamoring for war against France burst into criticism. "The administration is bankrupting the country to buy a desert!" "We don't want territory beyond the river. We are too big already!" "Bad enough to have Kentuckians in Congress, but with this treaty in effect, others like thick-skinned beasts will crowd Congress Hall, buffalo from the head of the Missouri and alligators from the Red River!"

"A truly noble acquisition!" was Madison's satisfied appraisal.

There was still anxiety. Not until the treaty was finally ratified by the Senate in October, the debate over constitutionality successfully terminated, and the money for the purchase appropriated could they breathe sighs of relief. But there was unmitigated rejoicing when on December 20, 1803, the Stars and Stripes were raised over the American city of New Orleans. History had been made.

The year brought other excitement to the Madison family. To Dolley's distress the time had come, James insisted, to put eleven-year-old Payne in school. It was some comfort to her that Alexandria was so near, just across the Potomac, and that the school chosen, Alexandria Academy, was the one George Washington, a first trustee, had picked for his nephews, Lawrence and George Steptoe. The fact that Lucy's husband had once studied there made it seem more intimately connected with family. But Dolley delivered him up to strangers with tearful reluctance.

In the fall of 1803 Dolley gathered the cabinet ladies together to help equip Meriwether Lewis, Jefferson's private secretary, and William Clark for the exciting expedition Jefferson had planned for them to explore the great territory just acquired and perhaps the land beyond it, which still belonged to Spain up to the 42nd parallel, and north of this was claimed by both England and the United States. Dolley was very much concerned for their safety on this perilous journey, and under her leadership the women tried to provide everything they could possibly need for comfort and safety. Before the party left they also gave the adventurers many farewell parties.

It was in the winter of 1803 that the celebrated portrait painter, Gilbert Stuart, came to Washington. It became the fashion to have a "Stuart portrait" by this genius who had won the title of the "Portrait Painter of Presidents," and he was soon in great demand. "Stuart is all the rage," a friend wrote Dolley during her absence from the city, "he is almost worked to death, and every one is afraid that they will be the last to be finished." But he kept on taking orders and carried on amusing conversations while he studied his subjects, making them forget themselves and appear simply and naturally. His portraits were especially popular because of the delicate "flesh tint" that marked his work and proved so flattering.

It was during the following months that both James and Dolley had their most widely acclaimed portraits painted, destined to become the most popular among the many to be preserved. The one of James Dolley considered to be "an admirable likeness." She was not so sure about her own, which showed her as a seated figure before a heavily curtained background. Many of her friends felt that she looked too thoughtful, that the smile was stiff and unnatural, failing to reveal her vivacity and charm.

Stuart's power to amuse was never more in evidence than in his portrait of Dolley's sister Anna. It reveals all the beauty and charm that made her one of the most courted and popular young women of Washington. Most marriageable, too, conceded Dolley, dreading the inevitable day of loss. Anna was more than a beloved sister. She was the daughter she and James had never had, the sunshine that had made bearable all the sorrows of her first marriage. Was Gilbert Stuart one of her many suitors? Some seemed to think so. At least he was an ardent admirer who managed to portray all her happy glowing womanhood, high-waisted, low-necked gown displaying her full-bosomed loveliness, cloak thrown carelessly back, a stray curl dropping over her high white forehead.

"I wish you would paint me your portrait," she is said to have remarked during one of her sittings.

"All right, I will" was his rejoinder. Whereupon he placed a curtain in the background of her picture and proceeded mischievously to mold it into his own boldly aquiline profile. It is there today, a humorous self-caricature of the great portrait painter.

Dolley did not have long to dread. The inevitable soon happened. One of Anna's numerous suitors became more and more favored. He was Richard Cutts, one of the most eligible of Washington's bachelors, twenty-eight years old, a democratic member of Congress from Massachusetts, a handsome lawyer who had been educated at Harvard and in Europe, son of a well-to-do family with property in lands and merchant ships. Dolley could not object when they became engaged. Anna's happiness was more important than her own. But, oh, to have her gone for half the year to that far-off outpost of civilization, a district of Massachusetts called Maine! Dolley consoled herself by remembering the Marquis d' Yrujo's attentions and that it might have been Spain!

But as that winter of 1803 brought events that embroiled them both in a furor of unpleasant social exigencies, she could almost have wished that dear Anna was already far removed from the hotbed of bickering and jealousy and intrigue that Washington had suddenly become.

4

Jefferson with his democratic code of etiquette sometimes trod on aristocratic toes. In one instance his policy of equality almost resulted in an international incident.

The new British minister, first since Jefferson had taken office, arrived in America in November 1803. He was Anthony Merry, a rather unassuming man with no title and not much wealth, slow, vigilant, sensible, without imagination. Mrs. Merry made up for all these drawbacks. Large, flamboyant, bejeweled, domineering, she was, as one associate described her, "a fine woman accustomed to adulation." The toes encased in her stylish satin slippers were very aristocratic and very sensitive.

Their voyage had been unfortunate, the ship long delayed by Atlantic storms. Even the presence of the famous poet Thomas Moore on board had scarcely compensated for Mrs. Merry's discomfort. Nor did their arrival in the new developing country augur well for her enjoyment of the commission. She wrote the poet that she laughed every step of the way from Alexandria, where they landed, to Washington, at the "coachie" sent for them. "And the Capital—good heavens, what profanation! Here is a creek too, a dirty arm of the river—which they have dignifed by calling it the Tiber!"

In spite of his milder temperament her husband shared her amazement and disdain. For his official presentation to the President he donned his full regalia, uniform, gold lace, dress sword. Madison, as always conservatively and faultlessly attired, conducted him to the President's House. They found the audience chamber unoccupied. No Jefferson. Presently they encountered him in a narrow vestibule where, crowded against the wall, the new emissary of his Majesty George III was introduced to a person of commanding height and mien, to be sure, but, as he wrote later, "not merely in undress but actually standing in slippers down at the heels, and both pantaloons, coat and underclothes indicative of utter slovenness and indifference to appearance and in a state of negligence actually studied. Shoes actually fastened with a shoe string instead of a bow or buckle! I could not doubt," he reported in a dudgeon, "that the whole scene was prepared and intended as an insult, not to me personally perhaps, but to the Sovereign I represented." He further described his impressions of the country, "Why, this is a thousand times worse than the worst parts of Spain!"

In an attempt to mollify him, Madison assured him that the Danish minister had been received just as informally. The Dane, Merry retorted bluntly, was a diplomat of the third rank, while he was of the second. There was worse to come. The Merrys were invited by Jefferson to a state dinner for foreign ministers and his cabinet on January 2. Good, thought Dolley, for whom James had described the unfortunate confrontation. Now they would see that Jefferson was not the country boor they had thought him, that his table was set with the finest linens and silver, his service irreproachable, and his clothes for such an occasion as proper, if a bit more carelessly worn, than those of foreign dignitaries. Once more Merry appeared in full regalia, his splendor somewhat eclipsed, however, by the flamboyance of the Marquis d'Yrujo, the Minister from Spain. But Mrs. Merry had no competition among the ladies. She was attired in satin, with a long train, a lace shawl at least four yards in length, a diamond crescent brooch, diamond comb, diamond earrings, and a diamond necklace adorning her full bosom.

But Dolley's hopes for pacification were dashed. When dinner was announced, she happened to be standing near the President, and he offered her his arm. "Oh no!" she whispered. "Take Mrs. Merry." But Jefferson was obdurate. Smiling, he conducted Dolley to the dining room and seated her by his side. Madame d'Yrujo took the chair at his left. When Merry started to take the chair next to the marchioness, he was forestalled by a congressman. Madison conducted Mrs. Merry to a place below the marquis. To make matters worse, M. Pichon, the minister from France, a nation with which England was at war, was given a favored place.

Mrs. Merry was furious. She toyed with her food, rose early, and persuaded her equally outraged husband to order their chariot.

"This," breathed Sally d'Yrujo to Dolley as they left the table, "could cause a war."

It almost did. Soon the whole town heard her protests. Madison tried to explain to the affronted minister. Protocol, Jefferson felt, had no place in a democracy. Americans believed in equality, no preference, no titles. "When brought together in society," he expressed the President's view, "all are perfectly equal, whether foreign or domestic, in or out of office. No title being admitted here, those of foreigners are given no preference."

Still James was in a quandary. He wanted to keep peace with England, yet he felt bound to support Jefferson. When Dolley gave a dinner a few days later to which the Merrys were invited, James gave his arm to Mrs. Gallatin, wife of the Secretary of the Treasury. To her horror and disgust Mrs. Merry found herself alone, and the astonished Mr. Merry had to give her his hand. He wrote to his government in England complaining bitterly, and Madison, as Secretary of State, was faced with an international incident. He wrote James Monroe in London, trying to explain the situation and smooth the matter over.

To Dolley's dismay the Marquis d'Yrujo, husband of her dear friend Sally, fanned the smoldering fire into a hotter blaze. He agreed with Merry that first place at presidential dinners be given alternately to his wife and Merry's. Dolley was distressed, feeling that she, the President's unofficial hostess, was the butt of some of the criticism. But she had one advantage. She gave the large and overpowering Mrs. Merry no competition in splendor of appearance. Though both women were more conspicuous than their husbands, Mrs. Merry with her satins and brocades and jewels was supreme.

There was even worse to come. Jerome Bonaparte, brother of Napoleon, had taken an American wife, the beautiful Elizabeth Patterson, niece of Robert Smith, Secretary of the Navy. Here Mrs. Merry met her match. At a grand ball given by the Robert Smiths she costumed herself to the hilt, in dark blue crepe over white satin trailing into a long train, with white crepe silver-spangled drapery falling to her knees, head and shoulders ablaze with diamonds. But little Betsy Patterson Bonaparte stole the show in a gown so décolleté and of such gossamer substance, the thinnest sarcenet, that no one "dared to look at her except by stealth." She was warned by her aunt and other women that she must wear more clothes at the Pichons' dinner the next evening or they would not be there. Mrs. Merry was further incensed at this dinner when Jefferson again insisted on escorting Dolley to the table. Dolley felt like a lamb being led to the slaughter. The international furor over what Madison called "diplomatic superstition," "nauseous," "frivolous," had become a seething cauldron. Writing to Monroe he blushed, he said, at having to "put so much trash on paper."

Jefferson, whose lack of tact had occasioned the impasse, was glad that his daughters were not with him. The brunt of the battle, he wrote Martha, was falling on Mrs. Madison and her sister, "who are dragged in the dirt of every Federalist paper. You would have been the victims had you been here, and butchered the more bloodily as they would hope it would be felt more by myself."

Dolley tried to shield James from knowledge of the most cruel barbs being flung at her in gossip and the press. Was it at this time that embittered Federalists were whispering that Jefferson and Dolley were conducting an affair? Jefferson knew of the slander and was amazed. "I thought," he noted, "that my age and ordinary demeanor would have prevented any suggestion in that form, from the improbability of their obtaining belief." The ridiculous slander almost resulted in a duel.

But it was at this time that there began an even worse whispering campaign, not only against her but against her beloved Anna. Again it came from the Federalist stronghold, rumors assailing their chastity. Apparently someone wildly reasoned that because Dolley had had two children by her first husband and none by her second, therefore she must have "a sexual insatiability resulting from sterility." Aggrieved Federalists evidently forgot that the same reasoning would have applied to George and Martha Washington! Ridiculous as the gossip was, it would still be rearing its head ten years later.

Dolley suffered all such innuendos cheerfully and in silence. James had too many serious problems to be bothered with such trifles. They were as foolish and unimportant as the criticism she heard leveled at her dinners. When it was reported to her that one of them had been ridiculed by the wife of a foreign minister (Mrs. Merry, no doubt) because it was more like a harvest-home supper than the entertainment of a Secretary of State, she laughed merrily.

"Tell her," she commented good-naturedly, "that the profusion of my table is the result of the prosperity of my country, and I must therefore continue to prefer Virginia liberality to European elegance."

But gossip about Anna, with no more justification than the girl's gay, irrepressible friendliness to all, men as well as women, was another story. Fortunately Richard Cutts was too levelheaded to do more than laugh at the silly accusations against both of them. But any attack on Anna was more painful to Dolley than any barb directed at herself. In spite of her dread of losing her sister she was almost glad as the time of the wedding drew near.

Anna was married on March 20, 1804, in the drawing room of the house on F Street by the Reverend Mr. McCormick, pastor of the church in Washington which the Madisons attended. James, who had been like a father to her, gave her away, as he had done five years before for her sister Mary on the occasion of her marriage to Congressman John G. Jackson. It was a scene of great gaiety, with Dolley outdoing herself as a gracious hostess. There was a reception, with many gifts, simple and homemade most of them according to the prevailing custom, tokens of love and friendship, embroideries, pincushions, laces, paintings, original poems. Madame Daschkov , wife of the Russian minister, sent the typical gifts of her country, two wine coolers, one filled with salt, the essence of life, the other with bread, the staff of life.

Fortunately there were still several weeks to the end of Congress, so Dolley need not face loneliness at once. But when the coach had left for Maine on a rainy day she went to her room and wept. Not since the death of John Todd and their baby had she felt so lonely. The skies seemed to be weeping with her.

"One of the greatest griefs of my life," she wrote a friend, "has come to me in the parting for the first time from my sister-child."

There was soon more reason for tears, for even as the wedding festivities went on Jefferson was at Monticello watching by the bed of his beloved Maria, as once he had done by her mother. Again it was a losing battle. Every day he had her carried on her bed out of doors, hoping the fresh air would restore her waning life. But it was no use. Abigail Adams had been right in forewarning that the child's beauty was that "which the experienced learn to look upon with dread, because it betrays a physical organization too delicately fine to withstand the rough shocks of the world."

"A letter from the President," Dolley wrote Anna on April 26, "announces the death of poor Maria, and the consequent misery it has caused them all. This is among the many proofs, my dear sister, of the uncertainty of life. A girl so lovely, so young! (She had been just the age of Anna, twenty-five.) All the efforts of friends and doctors availed nothing."

Dolley quietly went through the motions of living, giving dinners, attending receptions, acting as Jefferson's hostess, greeting dignitaries, turning a deaf ear to criticisms both personal and political, celebrating the country's independence, remaining publicly serene in the face of events both distressing and tragic. James was having political difficulties over the purchase of Louisiana. The Marquis d'Yrujo was displeased over what he called France's betrayal of her promise to Spain not to dispose of the ceded territory and further incensed at Madison's determined negotiations to secure all the Floridas. Though Madison attempted to refute his arguments by reasonable statements about the validity of the treaty between France and Spain, the ambassador was not convinced. "Madison's arguments," he complained to Madrid, "are as full of subterfuges, as they are destitute of logic, solid reasoning, and devoid of that good faith which he always puts on display when speaking and writing, and which squares so little with his political conduct."

His rancor, however, did not affect the long friendship existing between Dolley and his wife, the former Sally McKean. That winter and spring the two often went riding together in the Madisons' new chariot of "neat plain elegance" in which Dolley delighted. Built for them the preceding summer for $594, it was all glassed in and fitted with Venetian blinds. She enjoyed not only taking her friends to ride but in picking up pedestrians along the way—Congressmen and others traveling on foot to the Capitol or the President's House. Though inspired only by friendliness, such services, to political foes as well as friends, could not help but arouse friendly feelings toward the Secretary of State.

The feud between Madison and d'Yrujo reached a climax when Congress passed the Mobile Act in the spring of 1804 extending the revenue laws to all territory ceded by France and embracing some lands in West Florida that the ambassador felt still belonged to Spain. He stormed into Madison's office and denounced him in no uncertain terms. Soon after he broke completely with the State Department and moved to Philadelphia, his wife's home, without calling on the Secretary. Sally came alone to say goodbye to Dolley. "For her and her husband," she commented, "I feel a tenderness regardless of circumstances." From this new vantage the marquis continued to fight the administration in newspaper articles, derogatory letters, and other scurrilous writings, taking full advantage of the American insistence on freedom of the press.

Far more disheartening to Dolley was the dénouement of the quarrel between her old friend Aaron Burr and Alexander Hamilton. Hoping to retrieve his fortunes, eclipsed in the campaign of 1800, Burr had run for the governorship of New York, only to be ignominiously defeated, he complained bitterly, through Hamilton's defamation of his character.

Hamilton had called Burr a "profligate," a "voluptuary," "in his profession extortionate to a proverb," suspected on strong grounds of corruption, guilty of breaches of probity. He had accused him of "constantly siding with the party hostile to Federal measures" and of ambiguity in his political principles, called him "artful" and "intriguing," a "Cataline." Burr challenged Hamilton to a duel unless he was willing to retract and apologize. Hamilton accepted the challenge, refusing to repudiate statements he felt were true. He was resolved, however, to reserve and throw away his first fire, possibly also his second, in the hope that Colonel Burr would "pause and reflect."

They met on July 11, 1804, on the New Jersey dueling ground overlooking the Hudson, facing each other at ten paces. Burr took aim and fired. Hamilton, as he had promised, withheld his shot. He fell and died the next day. Dolley could not believe the news. His wife, Betsey, was one of her friends. She mourned with her and her six children. Grief was all the more poignant because Payne was seriously ill, making her even more sensitive to family tragedy.

"Payne continues weak and sick," she wrote Anna. "My prospects rise and fall to sadness as this precious child recovers or declines." Then she added, her only reference to the event, "You have heard, no doubt, of the terrible duel and of poor Hamilton."

Though dueling was considered a proper mode of settling quarrels, somehow Dolley could not look at the Vice President without seeing blood on his hands. To think that she had once considered Burr the person to whom the future of her child could be entrusted!

James too grieved over the tragedy. Though in recent years he and Hamilton had been at political swords' points, he could not forget how they had once labored together over the *Federalist Papers,* how he had shared with the brilliant, erratic, often headstrong patriot the task of bringing the Union to reality. He hated the whole idea of dueling. A strange and cowardly way to silence the barbed tongue of one's critic! Forced to treat the Vice President with civility, he still could not help regarding him as a murderer.

Dolley, as well as James, welcomed the summer's respite. Was it loneliness or the fatigue of almost constant entertaining or the deadly summer dampness of the malarial marshes or, more likely, the fever which had attacked her idolized Payne when he had come home from school for vacation, that made the prospect of Montpelier seem the promise of heaven? They were unable to leave Washington until July 25. It seemed they would never get there. On the way to Dumfries the carriage horses foundered, and they had to transfer to the cart carrying their baggage. The good horses were sent back from Captain Winston's near Stevenburg to get the carriage. They went on by relays, the journey taking five whole days. Never had Dolley felt so weary. Even the cooler dry mountain air failed to return her to health. Perhaps as the belated result of the steaming marshes she succumbed to the inflammatory rheumatism which had long been her bane and spent much of the summer in severe pain. At least Payne had fully recovered.

The influx of visitors was a constant additional strain. Being Dolley, she insisted on performing her duties as hostess whenever possible, but once, when fifteen or twenty of the family came to dinner, she was unable to leave her bed. The guilt was almost more excruciating than the pain. They had invited the Pichons, who had lost their only child, a baby a year old, to visit Montpelier during the summer, hoping the change would be consolation. They had also invited the Merrys, to somewhat assuage their umbrage, but to Dolley's relief they did not come.

Washington again, with Dolley almost fully recovered, James beset with diplomatic problems, Jefferson attempting to assuage his grief in furious activity, finally deciding to run for a second term. The presidential campaign of 1804 was one of bitter slander against the President in both press and pulpit and equal diatribes against his Federalist opponents. "The high office of the President is filled by an infidel, and that of the Vice President by a murderer," accused Federalist Senator Plumer. But the administration was unbeatable. It had bought Louisiana, lowered taxes, reduced the public debt, cut down the Army and Navy, punished the Barbary pirates. Its great achievement, the Louisiana purchase, anathema to New England Federalists because it threatened to shift power to the West, was popular everywhere else. Jefferson and George Clinton won all but fourteen electoral votes. The Madisons were settled in the house on F Street for another four years.

Jefferson rode on horseback from his white President's House (palace, some called it) to the Capitol and delivered his inaugural address in a voice so low that few heard it. Then he held a levee. "All who chose attended," noted British legation secretary Augustus Foster, adding with disgust, "and even towards the close blacks and dirty boys, who drank his wine and lolled upon his couches before us all."

But no sooner had the address congratulated the country on the blessings of prosperity than problems began to multiply. There were schisms among the Democratic-Republicans, conspiracies in the West fomented by Burr, who was soliciting British help in starting trouble, more impressment of American seamen not only on the high seas but in American harbors.

Once again Dolley was Jefferson's unofficial hostess. Notes kept coming by messenger. "Thomas Jefferson begs Mrs. Madison to take care of female friends expected . . ." Sometimes a commission was requested. "Thomas Jefferson presents his respectful thanks to Mrs. Madison for the trouble she has been so kind to take on his behalf. Nothing more is wanting, unless (having forgotten little Virginia) a sash or something of that kind could be picked up anywhere for her. The amount and the person from whom the earrings and pin were bought, Thomas Jefferson would also ask of Mrs. Madison. He presents his affectionate salutations."

But in July, when this letter was written, Dolley herself was in need of helpful attendance. In some way she had injured her knee. The result was an ulcerated tumor, with a threat of gangrene. On June 4 she had written, "My dearest Anna,—I write to you from my bed, to which I have been confined for ten days with a bad knee; it has become very painful, and two doctors have applied caustic with the hope of getting me well, but Heaven only knows! I feel as if I should never walk again. My dear husband insists upon taking me to Philadelphia to be under Dr. Physick's care, but he cannot stay with me, and I dread the separation."

No Montpelier this summer! The disappointment was almost as severe as the pain. A few days later she was still writing from bed.

"I had a long friendly letter from the President yesterday, begging me to get Virginia's (his granddaughter) wedding garments, also trinkets and dresses for all the family. I shall drive to the shops, but am not able to alight; and so little variety in Georgetown; but I must do my best for them, and have promised to be at the wedding if possible, the last of this month. But I have scarcely a wish, and no expectation of going. . . . I never leave my room except to drive. The Fourth of July I spent at the President's, sitting quite still and amusing myself with the mob. Farewell."

They went to Philadelphia. The journey in the heat was less difficult than she had expected, for she was more comfortable riding than in any other position. "My health and spirits revived every day with the drive, and here I am on my bed, with my dear husband sitting anxiously by me, who is my most willing nurse. But you know how delicate he is. I tremble for him; one night on the way he was taken very ill with his old complaint, and I could not fly to aid him as I used to. Heaven in its mercy restored him next morning, and he would not pause until he heard my fate from Dr. Physick."

The report was good. Dr. Philip Physick, chief surgeon at the University of Pennsylvania, promised to cure her knee—in time. He would not resort to surgery or amputation. He would try to cure the ulcer with splints, leg elevation, rest. They found lodgings in Sansom Street and with James, faithful nurse, constantly at her side, the injured leg bound to a board and projecting from the bed, Dolley reveled in more intimate companionship than they had enjoyed since their honeymoon. Problems of state—with Spain over West Florida and Texas, with Britain over violations of neutrality, with agitations for war with Napoleon, who had made himself emperor—had been left behind in Washington. While Madison wrote a paper on the rights and obligations of neutral nations, in an attempt to persuade England to change her policies, Dolley read or embroidered or wrote letters to Anna or entertained visitors.

"I have the world to see me, and many invitations to the houses of the gentry, but withstand all, to be at ease here. I have not seen where I am, yet, and the longer I stay, the less do the vanities tempt me, though, as you know, I usually like the routs all too well."

Some of her visitors were well-remembered Quakers. When one of them severely lectured her on seeing too much company, she wrote, "It brought to mind the time when our society used to control me entirely, and debar me from so many advantages and pleasures; even now, I feel my ancient terror revive in great degree."

But fortunately there were more moderate Quaker friends, reminders of the quiet seeking after the Inner Light in the Pine Street Meeting. "You ask who is kindest to me here, and I can tell you that, among a number, Betsey Pemberton bears all the palm. Never can I forget Betsey, who has been to me what you would have been."

Dolley welcomed all the visitors, but it was the hours alone with Jemmy that she cherished, rejoicing together over the birth, up in Maine, of little James Madison Cutts, a "little charmer" with such a "beautiful nose," discussing where Payne should go to school next to prepare him for Princeton, Jemmy's own alma mater.

But it had to end. In October, Jefferson wrote that Madison's presence was necessary in Washington to help decide whether an alliance with Britain was advisable to counter the Napoleonic menace. He must go. It was almost their first parting since their marriage. The long weeks following were a torment to them both but a boon to future biographers, providing almost their only love letters in existence.

"A few hours only have passed since you left me, my beloved," she wrote on October 23, "and I find nothing can relieve the oppression of my mind but speaking to you in this, the only way. . . . I shall be better when Peter [their black servant] returns with news, not that any length of time could lessen my first regret, but an assurance that you are well and easy will contribute to make me so." And the next day she was writing, "What a sad day! The watchman announced a cloudy morning at one o'clock, and from that moment I found myself unable to sleep, from anxiety for thee, my dearest husband." And the following day, "This clear cold morning will favor your journey, and enliven the feelings of my darling . . . Adieu, my beloved, our hearts understand each other. In fond affection, thine."

Was it being in Philadelphia again which made the "thee" and "thine" flow so naturally from her pen?

Only when assurance of his safe arrival came did the letters reflect her usual lilting buoyancy.

"I have at this moment perused with delight thy letter, my darling husband, with its inclosures. To find you love me, have my child safe, and that my mother is well, seems to comprise all my happiness. . . . I walk about the room and hope a few days more will enable me to ride, so that you may expect me to fly to you as soon—ah, I wish I might say how soon!"

She even showed an interest in politics. "I wish you would indulge me with some information respecting the war with Spain, and the disagreement with England which is so generally expected. You know, I am not much of a politician, but I am extremely anxious to hear (as far as you think proper) what is going on in the Cabinet. . . ."

James's letters to her were equally loving if more restrained. "Yours of the 1st instant, my dearest, gives me much happiness, but it cannot be complete till I have you again with me. . . ."

On November 17 she was able to write, "Mr. Cutts and Anna arrived last evening, my beloved, and so pleased and agitated was I that I could not sleep. We will leave on Monday if I am quite strong

enough, but I must wait a little your commands. . . . Farewell, my
beloved one."

James's last letter to her contained the good news that Payne, nearly
fourteen, had been admitted to St. Mary's College in Baltimore, a new
school for boys directed by Father Louis Dubourg. "The last mail, my
dearest, that will be likely to find you in Philadelphia, and I am not
without hope that this will be too late."

Dolley's bubbling cup of happiness was almost full. Reunion with
her beloved Anna brought only one regret. Little James Madison
Cutts, aged three months, had been left with Richard's relatives in
Maine. Her arms ached to hold him.

Even with the new pair of sorrels bought in Philadelphia the coach
seemed to crawl. "Faster, faster, Peter!" she wanted to urge, while
knowing that the frozen road with its deep ruts required caution. The
last time she had taken this journey from Philadelphia eleven years
ago she had welcomed slowness. It had suited her mood of agonized
indecision. Now she could not move fast enough. Washington again at
last. Past the Capitol, high on its hill, along Pennsylvania Avenue with
its new paving stones and sidewalks and its double rows of poplars
which Jefferson had recently ordered planted. Then—F Street at last.
She was out of the carriage, running. As if summoned by her eagerness he was there to meet her. It was over at last. She was back in his
arms.

5

To Dolley's delight Martha Randolph, concerned for her father's lone-liness after the death of his beloved Maria, came to Washington to spend the winter of 1805–6, bringing her five daughters and one son. Once again the testiness of the indefatigable Mrs. Merry reared its head.

"Does she come as the President's daughter," came her inquiry, "or as the wife of a Virginia gentleman? If the latter, she would expect to make the first call, if the former, to receive it." Tongue in cheek, Martha wrote back that she was in Washington as the wife of a Vir-ginia gentleman, and as such should expect the first call from the wife of the British minister, as the canons of official etiquette drawn up by her father declared that all strangers to the city should be visited first by all residents of Washington. The Merry incident came to an abrupt end when his Majesty's government, loath to make an issue of his complaints, informed Merry to his amazement that his request for a recall was granted.

The Merrys were not the only foreign diplomats who brought zest to Washington life as well as problems for its government. There was General Louis Marie Turreau, the French minister who arrived in November 1804, startling the populace with his huge black mustache, his fiercely crimson face, and beetling eyes, shocking them by the visits of his gold coach to the red-light district and his repeated beatings of his wife. Dolley, of course, entertained them both and made friends with the unfortunate Madame Turreau.

"She is good-natured and intelligent, generous, plain and curious," she wrote Anna. "We ride, walk together and visit sans ceremony. I never visit her chamber but I crack my sides laughing—I wish I could tell you on paper at what."

Then there was the Tunisian ambassador, Sidi Suliman Mellimelli, who arrived in November 1805, bringing four Turkish attachés, negro servants, and an Italian band, his impressive figure clad in scarlet and gold silks, his eight-inch black beard dwarfed by a twenty-yard turban of white muslin. He came on a sensitive diplomatic mission, hoping to counter Jefferson's firm refusal to pay tribute to Tunisia to avoid having American ships pirated. He called at once on Madison, followed by his interpreter and the carrier of his four-foot pipe. Everything was satisfactory, he told the Secretary of State, except for one thing. He needed some concubines. After some hemming and hawing Madison supplied the deficiency with a professional designated as "Georgia a Greek," her services charged to the State Department. Later he would write in another connection but with undoubted reference to this exigency, "Applications to foreign intercourse are terms of great latitude and may be drawn on by very urgent and unforeseen circumstances."

Mellimelli's arrival coincided with that of numerous tribes of Indians come to pay honor to the Great White Father—Osages, Pawnees, Sacs, Missouri, Creeks. All these diverse elements met in Dolley's drawing room, where dissident factions, not only foreign but among the warring Indian tribes, were amazed to find that their enemies were rather decent people after all.

All converged too on the President's House at the New Year's reception, along with the "citizens, cobblers, and tinkers" who so disgusted certain Federalists. The Osage chiefs were there in full regalia, also the resplendent Suliman Mellimelli in his gold tunic and crimson doublet, accompanied by his Greek interpreter and four secretaries. Jefferson was fortunately able to converse with him in Italian. The Tunisian minister obligingly took off his turban to show the Osages that his head was shaved like theirs except for a little tuft on the crown. He was the center of a curious audience watching him smoke his exotic four-foot pipe or dip into his snuff deeply scented with attar of roses. He seemed quite indifferent to the admiration of the crowd and stood for the most part aloof, until, suddenly spying a corpulent black servant coming from the kitchen with a platter of cakes, he rushed toward her and with great enthusiasm threw his arms around her, exclaiming in Turkish, "The handsomest woman in America! You look like one of my wives, the best and most expensive one—a load for a camel!"

One day the two groups met again in the Madisons' parlor, the Indians as gaudy with their painted faces, feathered topknots, brilliant blankets as was the crimson-robed and elaborately turbaned Mellimelli with his attachés and servants. The Tunisian was more interested in the Indians' religion than in their strange appearance.

"Whom do they worship?" he demanded. "Abraham, Muhammad, or Jesus?"

One of the chiefs answered through an interpreter, "We worship the Great Spirit with no one between us and him."

"Vile heretics!" denounced the devotee of Muhammad. But later when an Indian remarked about the death of an Osage chief, "God being God, it was His work," Mellimelli acknowledged that there must be some good in them.

The Washington women were fascinated by the colorful visitor and crowded around him wherever he went. He basked under their attention, catering to their curiosity by unwinding his twenty-yard white turban and showing them how it was draped. He had brought lavish gifts, including a crimson velvet caftan for Dolley, weighted with gold, and four Arabian pedigreed stud horses for the President. But his largesse won no concessions for Tunis as to tribute, and his presence cost the country not only the expense of his upkeep at Stelle's old hotel, complete with "Georgia a Greek," but of a multiplicity of presents to speed him on his way, also the responsibility for three of his entourage who deserted, his cook, secretary, and barber.

It was well that Dolley and Jemmy could share the humor of events as well as their serious political implications, for he was struggling with harassing problems. The Florida controversy with Spain was no nearer solution. A General Francisco Miranda was attempting to secure American aid for a Venezuelan revolt against Spain. There were rumors that Aaron Burr was conspiring with Britain and sympathetic Federalists to make trouble in the West. And James's statement on the rights of neutrals, exposing startling figures on the British seizure of ships and the impressment of sailors, was being opposed in Congress through the efforts of John Randolph, one of his own Virginians.

Napoleon owned most of Europe. Britain controlled the seas. And America was a little neutral power trying to survive in a world at war. English ships were capturing hundreds of cargo ships merely on the suspicion that they were carrying goods to French destinations. Almost more debasing was the British practice of stopping American ships and kidnapping members of their crews.

"We are only taking our own deserters," Britain claimed when the United States protested. Sometimes this was true, for British sailors were deserting in large numbers, preferring the more humane treatment of American officers. But over and over again they were taking native-born Americans. It was a reprehensible practice which not many years later would help cause an eruption into armed conflict.

The presence of Martha Jefferson Randolph and her family during the winter of 1805–6 was a blessing. Jefferson was elated. He stole moments from affairs of state to play with his grandchildren. Mrs. Smith wrote, "While I sat looking at him, playing with these infants, one standing on the sofa with its arms around his neck, the other two youngest on his knees playing with him, I could scarcely realize that he was one of the most celebrated men now living, both as a Politician and Philosopher."

Dolley enjoyed the children as much as did their grandfather. She delighted the younger girls by giving each of them a new doll, then making additional dresses for them. She introduced Ann Jefferson Randolph, a blonde of remarkable beauty and superior education, to society, and later was proud as a parent when the girl was able to translate a confusing paper that had baffled Madison and his state department. But most of all she was thrilled by the birth during the winter of James Madison Randolph, first baby to be born in what was later to be known officially as the White House, though its sandstone outer walls in contrast with its drab surroundings had long inspired the designation. "The white Palace," Mrs. Smith had once called it in her diaries. Two little James Madisons born in the year! If he could not have sons, at least Jemmy would have namesakes!

In fact, there was no dearth of young life in their own families, and James gave no sign of feeling deprivation for their lack of children. Not only was he a devoted father to Payne. He shared her concern for Anna's and Lucy's children, her joy over the birth of Mary's, her grief over the death of the latter's little Dolley. Presently their greatest worry was for her brother, John, the only one still living. Now twenty-three, he had never settled down. For a time he had lived in Kentucky negotiating lands once owned by his father. His greatest problem had been addiction to liquor. It was James now who suggested a possible remedy for his inertia and shortcomings.

"You know we're planning to send George Davis of Norfolk as Minister to Tunis," he told Dolley. "What would you think of John's going along as a member of his staff? It might broaden his horizons and give him an incentive to make something of himself. Also, I believe," he added with a wry smile, "it's against the Mohammedan code to indulge in liquor."

Dolley happily agreed. There were consultations in the family. John was delighted. James made the necessary arrangements, and after some time John left for Norfolk to join the future ambassador. A letter from Mr. Davis sent her hopes soaring.

"I received John as a brother, and feel most confident that his new situation will at least call forth those energies of mind which have been cramped by want of action, and open an extensive field for advancement. You may rest assured his interest and happiness are very dear to me."

Remembering Mellimelli and "Georgia a Greek," Dolley had momentary qualms. Would John be subjected, perhaps, to temptations more insidious than a too opulent thirst?

Spring came that year with its usual renewal of life and activity. The "Tiber," that insignificant little stream that Mrs. Merry had so ridiculed, emptying into the Potomac at the foot of Seventeenth Street, became a respectable torrent. Triumphantly Jefferson reported that he had recorded the first shoot from a tulip bulb, then the first appearance of a bluebird. His Lombardy poplars along the avenue sprouted their fuzzy catkins. Logs were piled into mud holes, making a passable corduroy road. Soon Payne would be coming home from school. The weeks at Montpelier were in the offing.

Dolley should have felt the joy of anticipation that spring usually inspired. Not this year. James had fallen down the front steps late in January and had dislocated his ankle. Though it was slow in healing, she knew it was not wholly responsible for his dragging steps. He had become the butt of the opposition's persecution and was suffering maligning attacks by John Randolph, once friend but now implacable political foe, and from his Federalist henchmen. Already they were looking toward the election of 1808, bent on preventing Jefferson from consenting to run again and Madison from being his successor. That staunch Federalist Timothy Pickering was demanding, "Shall the feeble timid Madison or the dull Monroe extend the system under which fools and knaves will continue to be the general favorites of the people until the government is subverted?"

Nor were the slanders confined to James. Again the whispers were circulating against the morals of Dolley and her sister Anna. Randolph was even writing of his suspicions to London, suggesting how "the respectability of any character may be impaired by an unfortunate matrimonial connection." Dolley, hearing the old gossip revived, was less concerned about her own reputation than the sorrow it would cause James if he should hear of it. Not that either he or her friends would believe any such foolishness! But she could not bear to cause him extra pain and worry.

If James was disturbed by the torrent of abuse, he did not show it. It was after one of Randolph's most severe attacks that they visited Samuel Harrison Smith and his wife, Margaret, at their farmhouse called Sidney, a little distance from Washington. "Mrs. Madison," wrote Margaret, "was all that was tender and affectionate and attractive as usual; Mr. Madison was in one of his most sportive moods."

Perhaps it was memory of the part he had played in bringing her and Jemmy together that made Aaron Burr's treachery, when it was finally proved, seem to Dolley like personal betrayal. By the fall of 1806 there was indisputable evidence that Burr was conspiring to found a separate nation in the West, collaborating with Britain to take the Southwest out of the United States by armed revolt. His partner in the conspiracy seemed to be General James Wilkinson, commander in chief of the American Army and governor of Upper Louisiana, who, realizing finally the perfidy of his fellow conspirator, notified the President and caused Burr's arrest.

"I suppose you have heard that Burr is retaken, and on his way to Richmond for trial," Dolley wrote Anna on March 27 of the following year. "This is all I know about him." It was but a brief sentence in a letter that told at length of James's sickness with a bad cold, the President's daily headache which necessitated his retiring to a dark room at nine each morning, weddings and dinners attended. And it was the only time she mentioned in writing an event that must have caused her intense distress and soul-searching. Though the trial, conducted by Chief Justice Marshall, a strong Federalist and opponent of the administration, was inconclusive, acquitting Burr of the lesser charge of high misdemeanor, ₃etting on foot an expedition against Mexico, James was convinced that in reality it was a case of high treason and was harsh in his condemnation of the Chief Justice for his narrow interpretation of the treason clause in the Constitution and his dismissal of the evidence on technical grounds.

"The trial was a farce," he denounced bitterly, "a circus, politicians juggling for Marshall's favor."

For Dolley life these days seemed to bring nothing but loss. Loss of the honor of a man she had once respected and admired, given the possible responsibility of educating her son, to whom she owed the fortuitous meeting with the supreme love of her life. Loss of her beloved mother, who had been staying with her youngest daughter, Mary, in Clarksburg, West Virginia.

"It is with grief unutterable," John Jackson, Mary's husband, wrote Madison in October 1807, "I communicate to you the painful intelligence that ere you receive this our beloved and Most respected Mrs. Payne will be no more." Her illness had come on suddenly, a violent stroke of the dead palsy. By the time the news reached Washington the burial had already taken place.

Dolley was grief-stricken. Her mother gone, beloved mentor, shining example of courage, best guide to her own experience of the Inner Light! Two weeks later she was writing her friend, Mrs. Henry Dearborn, "Deep affliction, my dear friend, has for some time past arrested my pen. My beloved and tender mother left me forever. . . . She was in Virginia with my youngest sister where she died without suffering or regret. . . ."

More tragedy was to come. Mary Jackson, herself the victim of long illness, probably tuberculosis, grew steadily worse. Her one desire was to pay a visit to her three sisters. Since she was unable to ride in a carriage, Jackson bought a light wagon in which she could lie full length, intending to carry her over the mountains, first to Lucy's, then to Dolley's in Washington, where Anna would be visiting. They never made the trip. Late in November when he was leaving the courthouse, he was clubbed almost to death by henchmen of criminals he was prosecuting. He received a fractured skull and other injuries. By the time he recovered Mary was dying. All their children but the last born had died. Dolley, who had wept over each one of them, wept again now over the letter the bereaved husband wrote to James.

"You knew my Mary well, yes, you gave her to me at the altar, you witnessed our union and our happiness. You saw the little prattlers that she gave me. In the short period of seven fleeting years all these things took place, and all, all but one—and the dearest of all has been torn from me in the same period."

But tears had to be shed in secret. James was too harassed by problems of state to be burdened with her personal grief. And in that year of 1808 events were moving inexorably to a time of momentous decision. Jefferson had refused a third term. It was common knowledge that he wanted Madison to be his successor.

No! Dolley protested silently, not this time because she feared her own incapacity as helpmate. For eight years she had been an understudy for the role of First Lady, whether successfully or not, it did not matter. But Jemmy! His responsibilities as Secretary of State had driven him to a sickbed time and again. What would the burden of complete responsibility for his country's welfare do to his delicate constitution? Jefferson was tough and sturdy, impervious to winds and storms like one of his stout poplars lining the avenue. Crises, opposition, slanders—he could stand straight, unbending before them all. Jemmy was no strong tree. He was more like a sensitive plant, susceptible to the full impact of every wind and storm. Eliza Trist, daughter of his landlady in Philadelphia, had once said of him, "He has a soul replete with gentleness, humanity and every social virtue, too amiable to bear up against a torrent of abuse." Dolley, of course, knew better. She had seen him accept abuse, contempt, and slander, calmly, without flinching. Yet she knew the pain suppressed behind tight lips and a steady, unyielding gaze.

"I shall not ask for it," she had heard him tell Jefferson, "certainly not fight for it. Lord knows I would rather go back with my dear wife to Montpelier, live out our life there together. It is for the people to decide. If they really want me—"

"They will," Jefferson had returned promptly, "if they know what's good for the country. And of course you will do your duty."

Of course. Dolley sighed, even while smiling in apparent agreement. He would do his duty, even if it killed him.

James was too much embroiled in affairs of state to be concerned, even interested in the coming election. As repeatedly through the eight years, he was laboring to keep the country out of armed conflict with one or the other of the warring European nations and still preserve national integrity. Both France and England were bent on destroying American commerce, each to the detriment of the other, France with its 1807 Decree from Milan, declaring that all ships paying a tax to the British government or allowing themselves to be searched by British cruisers were "good prize"; England by its Orders in Council forcing neutrals to trade with all its enemies through British ports, paying duties on "enumerated articles," including cotton, sugar, tobacco, molasses. England was still impressing American seamen.

Then in June 1807 had come the attack by the British ship of war *Leopard* on the American frigate *Chesapeake,* killing three and wounding eighteen, and removing four alleged deserters who proved to be United States citizens. It had put the country in an uproar. Congress, at Jefferson's urging, had passed an embargo act on all foreign commerce of the country. New England Federalists, always partial to England and seeing their commerce jeopardized, were bitter in their attacks on Jefferson and especially on Madison as the favored candidate for the Democratic-Republican nomination.

Even on their brief holiday in May the storms accompanied them, not only in politics but in the equally hostile elements. "My limbs yet tremble with the terrors and fatigue of our journey," wrote Dolley eleven days after they started on Thursday, May 7. A high wind incapacitating the Potomac ferry forced them to go by the new bridge below Little Falls. Friday they were stopped by the high waters of the Rappahannock and had to cross in a boat. At Captain Winston's Madison was writing three days later, "I continue rain-bound, and how I am to cross the waters before me I know not." Later he wrote, "I got home on Friday night by taking my carriage to pieces and making three trips with it over Porter's mill pond in something like a boat and swimming my horses."

No wonder that after this experience Dolley was laid up for three weeks with the old inflammatory rheumatism! "Never had I more extreme sickness and pain," she wrote Anna when she was finally able to move her arm. "Dr. Willis bled me and gave me medicine—Nelly [Nelly Madison Willis, Ambrose's daughter] and Mother Madison nursed and waited on me with great attention and kindness—What in this world can compensate for the sympathy and confidence of a mother and sister—nothing but the tie that binds us to a good husband. Such are ours and we ought to be satisfied."

There was satisfaction also in a letter received from John Payne, Dolley's only brother left, from his post as American consul in Tripoli. It brought relief that her worries over his dissipation were apparently at an end.

Back to the bitter contest, the partisan fervor, the slander, the lies. James was not immune from the latter even in his own Virginia. John Strode, a wealthy farmer friend who had bought his 1807 wheat crop was accused in the news of being dunned for payment and of replying, "Tell Madison if he will take off the embargo I'll pay him for his wheat." Instead of dunning him, Strode protested indignantly, Madison had told him personally when prices fell because of the embargo that he would be the last to ask him for payment!

"Sickly, valetudinarian, and subject to spasmodic affections" ran the innuendos. Slave to France, enemy of England, indecisive, timid, inept in office. But his supporters were just as eloquent. "Whether we contemplate his irreproachable morals, or solid talents," affirmed editor Samuel Harrison Smith, "we are supplied with the strongest reasons for approbation. While in public life he has invariably sustained the unassuming character of modest merit, his discharge of public duty has been no less distinguished by intelligence, fidelity and zeal. Amidst the various public scenes in which he has been engaged, he has invariably displayed a dignity and moderation which are at once the best evidence, and the surest preservative of republican principles."

James had meant it when he said he would not ask, would not fight for the presidency. For two months that summer he tended his farms, harvested his crops, far from the raging political tempest. Gratefully Dolley saw his eyes brighten, his pale cheeks tan, his joking and laughter with the constant influx of guests become more spontaneous. When it came time to return, she knew that they were ready.

By late November victory was assured. As one historian was to write later, "Madison's election was a verdict of approval on his work and Jefferson's in guarding America's welfare and safety in a world convulsed by warring giants. It was a testimonial to the steadfast faith of the people in the principles of the Jeffersonian party. Above all, it was a tribute to Madison's reputation as an honest man who loved his country and could be trusted to defend it. Integrity of character broke the shaft of slander, and an informed electorate carried him to victory against odds which in appearance were insurmountable."

At Jefferson's last New Year's reception Dolley, radiant and vibrant as always when surrounded by a crowd of people, found herself beside the President.

"Do you know what I just heard somebody call you?" demanded Jefferson.

"No. What?" she asked innocently.

"The Queen-elect."

"Oh—no!" She looked up at him in dismay. What must he think of her! A queen! Anathema to his democratic society!

But his eyes were twinkling. "Don't worry, my dear. There are many kinds of queens, and they don't all sit on thrones. How about a queen of hearts?"

PART FIVE

The White House
(1809 – 1817)

1

It was March 4, 1809. To Thomas Jefferson's vast relief the country had a new President, one of his and its own choosing and one he loved like a son. He was jubilant. When someone commented on the contrast between his gaiety and the careworn appearance of his successor, he replied, "Can you wonder at it? My shoulders have just been freed from a heavy burden, his just laden with it. I feel like a prisoner released from his chains."

Washington was in a gala mood. Optimism prevailed. Jeffersonians were glad because his most intimate friend and disciple was succeeding him. Even Federalists rejoiced because the Embargo was to be lifted, trade would again flourish with Europe, and the "arch-fiend of democracy" was out of office. Shopkeepers and hotel owners rejoiced over the crowds pouring into the capital, on horseback, in coaches, in chariots, even in country wagons. Among the shopkeepers were Mrs. Sweeney, who informed the ladies of Washington that she had commenced the "millinery and mantua making business," and Mrs. Walker, who apprised the ladies that "on Monday morning, in the Front Room of Mr. Peltz's house near the Centre Market, she opened and offered for sale a Fresh and Elegant assortment of Fashionable silk velvets, Turbans, Pelisses, coats, etc."

Only the barbers mourned because the election had brought no change in parties. The Federalists wore much powder on their hair and long curls, Democrats short hair and queues tied carelessly with a ribbon. "The country is doomed," lamented one barber. "What Presidents we might have had, what queues they have got, sir! as big as your wrist and powdered every day! But this little Jim Madison, with a queue no bigger than a pipe stem! Sir, it is enough to make a man forswear his country!"

Thousands were lining Pennsylvania Avenue as Dolley rode to the sumptuous new chamber of the House, soon filled to overflowing. Sitting in her reserved seat, she watched as the bipartisan committee of senators led the new President into the hall, her eyes only for the slender figure dressed in plain black clothes as usual, but this time in a full suit of American manufacture made of the wool of merino sheep raised in this country. Colonel David Humphreys, Washington's comrade in the Revolution, had obtained the sheep while serving as consul in Algiers. Jemmy looked very neat, very dignified—yes, and very small and vulnerable. She drew a long breath as he rose to deliver his inaugural address. Oh dear! He was actually pale and trembling when he began, and one could hardly hear him. But soon he began to gain confidence, and his words were audible.

"The present situation of the world is indeed without parallel," he reminded the audience, "and that of our country full of difficulties." He wanted peace above all else. He wished to maintain neutrality and would seek diplomatic negotiations rather than appeal to arms. But— and here his voice penetrated to the farthest corner of the big chamber —he was determined to exclude foreign intrigues from the country and would continue to foster the independent spirit of a people too proud to surrender their rights. Central to his speech was his devotion to the Union and emphasis on civil liberties, chief among them freedom of speech and religion.

Dolley drew another long breath, this time in relief. There was loud and prolonged applause, even from some Federalists. Chief Justice Marshall administered the oath, guns sounded, and the ceremony was over. For her, however, the day was just beginning. Back home to F Street, where they would be holding open house this afternoon. Her first test as hostess in the role of First Lady.

It was Margaret Smith who, as so often, preserved that event for future generations. "Today after the inaugural we all went to Mrs. Madison's. The street was full of carriages and people, and we had to wait nearly half an hour before we could get in—house completely filled, parlours, entry, drawing room and bedroom. Near the door of the drawing room Mr. and Mrs. Madison stood to receive their company. She looked extremely beautiful, was dressed in a plain cambric dress with a very long train, plain around the neck without any kerchief, and a beautiful bonnet of purple velvet and white satin, with white plumes. She was all dignity, grace, and affability."

There! That was over. For Dolley the day seemed to be one long breath of relief after another. Still to come was the grand ball at Long's Hotel, followed by a supper. She felt no fatigue herself. Excitement and crowds always revivified her. But Jemmy! More hours of unrelieved standing, of hand shaking, of the trivial repartee which he hated except with his intimate friends in an informal milieu.

Margaret Smith, faithful chronicler, was at the ball also.

"When we went," she recorded, "there were not above fifty persons in the room. We were led to benches at the upper fireplace. Music struck up Jefferson's march, and Mr. Coles entered. Madison's march was then played, and Mrs. Madison led in by one of the managers and Mrs. Cutts and Mr. Madison. She looked a queen. She had on a pale buff colored velvet, made plain, with a very long train, but not the least trimming and beautiful pearl earrings, necklace and bracelets. Her headdress was a turban of the same coloured velvet and white satin (from Paris) with two superb plumes, the bird of paradise feathers. It would be *absolutely impossible* for anyone to behave with more perfect propriety than she did. Unassuming dignity, sweetness, grace. It seemed to me that such manners would disarm envy itself and conciliate even enemies."

Dolley, however, was not as confident as she seemed. When one of the managers presented her with a card to lead the first number, she was at a loss how to respond. "But what shall I do with it?" she asked helplessly. "I do not dance."

"Then give it to your neighbor," the manager suggested.

"Oh, but I couldn't do that. It would look like partiality."

"Then I will." He gave it to Anna Cutts, who was standing at Dolley's side. The more youthful Anna, freed from Quaker inhibitions at an earlier age, took it without hesitation and proceeded to take Dolley's place in the quadrille.

The room soon filled, became so crowded that people had to stand on the benches to get a view of the moving masses. Dancing! It was scarcely possible to elbow one's way from one side to another. Dolley was almost pressed to death, for all crowded around her, peering over others' shoulders to get a peep at her. It became unbearably hot. Finally someone broke the glass in upper parts of the windows to let in air. Her head ached. Her hand felt crushed in a vise. The velvet dress clung to her like a steaming compress. Still she kept smiling, remembered each person's name and made some appropriate personal remark or inquiry as she greeted them, but all the time worried for Jemmy, trying to get a glimpse of him.

Margaret Smith, who happened to be standing near him, was also concerned, for he looked spiritless and exhausted. "I wish," she said, "with all my heart that I had a little bit of seat to offer you."

"I wish so too," he replied wistfully. When one of the managers came to ask him to stay for supper, he assented, but remarked unhappily to Margaret, "I would much rather be in bed."

Still something of his wry humor emerged. When she told him they were moving to their country place that week and were having a well dug, he observed, "Remember the old saying, 'Truth is at the bottom of a well'? I expect when you get to the bottom of yours, you will discover most important truths. But I hope," he continued with a whimsical smile, "you at least find water."

Dolley was led to supper by General Turreau de Garambouville, the French minister, Anna by the Honorable David Erskine, the British envoy. At the crescent-shaped table Dolley sat in the center between the two, feeling like a dove between two hawks.

"I chose a place where I could see Mrs. Madison to advantage," remembered Margaret Smith. "She really in manners and appearance answered all my ideas of royalty. She was equally gracious to both French and English and so affable to all. Though I suspect that Mrs. Robert Smith, wife of the new Secretary of State, did not like the superior position at the table [given] to Anna Cutts."

At last. Dolley could leave after supper and take Jemmy home. If this was a foretaste of the next four years, she feared for both his health and his sanity. And the social melee was but a trifle of the office's responsibility compared with the political burden resting on his shoulders. No wonder Jefferson had been so carefree and gay and witty all that day of his release. Once, as admiring ladies had pressed about him, a friend had jested, "You see, they *will* follow you." "That is as it should be," Jefferson had retorted, "since I am too old to follow them. I remember when Dr. Franklin's friends were taking leave of him in France, the ladies almost smothered him with embraces. On his introducing me as his successor, I said that among the rest of his privileges, I wished he could transfer this one to me. 'No, no,' he said, 'you are too young a man.' "

After the inaugural festivities Jefferson hastened to vacate the President's House. He sent his household goods ahead in a wagon drawn by six mules and four horses accompanied by eleven black servants, an imposing procession. He himself left in a phaeton attended by a single servant, happy as a schoolboy just released for vacation. A few days later he wrote back to the Madisons, "I had a very fatiguing journey, having found the roads exceptionally bad. The last three days I found it better to be on horseback, and traveled eight hours in as disagreeable a snowstorm as I ever saw." He had found no oats or tobacco sown and not much done in his garden. Nothing was in leaf but the red maple, weeping willow, and lilac.

Dolley saw the homesick longing in Jemmy's eyes. He was wondering if anything had been planted at Montpelier and if his own trees, chestnuts, weeping willows, silver poplars, were in leaf and near to blooming. Smiling brightly, she began chattering about the plans she and architect Benjamin Latrobe were making for the refurbishing of the President's House. They had moved in on March 11 to find need of many improvements and new furnishings. In a mellow mood Congress had authorized the expenditure of twelve thousand dollars for repairs and improvements and fourteen thousand "for the accommodation of the household." Madison had appointed Latrobe, the official Surveyor of Public Buildings, to superintend the work. Already immersed in affairs of state, he left the whole matter of improvements to Dolley and the architect.

If some had accused the new President of being weak and indecisive compared with Jefferson, a mere rubber stamp of his predecessor, they were soon disproved. As a matter of fact, Madison had studiously represented his own decisions on foreign policy as Jefferson's out of respect for his superior. Now he alone could be held responsible for executive policy. A crisis soon came. The governor of Pennsylvania had declared his intention to call out the militia to resist a decree of the Supreme Court. While Madison was conciliatory, he was unyielding. He would enforce the court's decision in whatever manner became necessary. It was the supreme law of the land. A dangerous threat to the Union was nipped in the bud.

Even in compromise he showed strength rather than weakness. When in order to gain Senate approval for his appointment of the brilliant and competent Albert Gallatin as his Secretary of the Treasury, he was obliged to forgo his desire of James Monroe as Secretary of State in favor of Robert Smith, brother of the powerful Senator Samuel Smith, there was advantage as well as loss in his decision. Because of the weakness and incompetence of his new appointee, Madison could virtually act as his own Secretary of State.

He was fortunate to have as his own personal secretary young Edward Coles, who at twenty-three was not only remarkably efficient and committed to the administration's democratic policies but imbued with family loyalty. The son of Dolley's uncle, John Coles II, he was well known to her from childhood days, when she had gone with her parents to visit Uncle John, his wife, Rebecca, and their ten children at Enniscorthy. Ned and his sister Sally had been her favorites. Though she had had nothing to do with his appointment, she was delighted to have him in their official household.

Before he had been two weeks in office Madison had approached both belligerent nations, France and England, offering repeal of the Nonintercourse Act in exchange for that of the British Orders in Council or the French Berlin and Milan Decrees, all of which waged relentless war on American commerce. Ambassador Erskine agreed. The Orders in Council would be withdrawn, he promised, on June 10. Madison's proclamation that after that date trade with Britain would be resumed made him extremely popular, with Federalists as well as Democrats.

While James was struggling with such problems, Dolley was working with Latrobe to refurbish the President's House. There were many gaps. Much of the furniture was shabby. First they tackled the great East Room, scarcely more presentable than when Abigail Adams had used it to hang her wet clothes. The worn carpet was sent to the Capitol to do service in the House of Representatives, being of the same pattern. Two handsome mirrors and some beautiful hanging lamps were provided. Curtains, chairs, sofas upholstered in yellow satin damask, plus a gorgeous "rising sun" in the same fabric, made the drawing room where she would do much of her entertaining an attractive center. A pianoforte costing $458, even a guitar, were added for musical interludes, and, of course, adequate supplies of linens, china, glassware, and for the laundry one of Yarwood's efficient washing machines. All of these, of course, became public property. But the beautiful new chariot which Robert Fielding made for the President in Philadelphia, with harness for four horses, was paid for out of James's own purse. It cost fifteen hundred dollars.

Dolley and Latrobe did not always agree. She objected to having the Stuart portrait of George Washington hung in the dining room and argued the point with the architect by correspondence when he was on business in Philadelphia. He was sorry to "have counteracted any wish of yours as to Genl. Washington's picture" but went on to explain, "The dining room is properly the picture room, and in speaking to the President as to the furniture of the room, I understood it to be arranged that not only the Genl. but the succeeding Presidents should have a place there . . . But if you have the slightest wish to the contrary remember that the Motto of my family, of my art, of my duty, is *tutto si fa,—tout se fait. . . ."*

Dolley gracefully yielded on the matter of the picture. Not so with another of his objections. "The curtains! Oh, the terrible red velvet curtains!" the architect exclaimed at one point. "Their effect will ruin me utterly, so brilliant will they be." Dolley only smiled. Bright colors, especially those the hue of God's sunlight or his crimson roses or red maples surely belonged in a house meant to enclose joy and cheer. He had agreed on the color of the chariot which would be "a very beautiful reddish brown according to your wish," though he shuddered at having to pay eleven dollars a yard for its cloth lining.

Bells were installed in each room and thirty servants hired, for Dolley knew there would be much entertaining. The nation's guests would of course be her guests. One person became her indispensable helper. Jean Pierre Sioussat, "French John," had been employed in the household of British minister Merry. When the latter left, he had preferred to remain in Washington, and now he became a majordomo in the White House. Yes, it was really being called that now, informally if not officially. General Henry Dearborn had used the words only a few days before, on May 19, symbolic for the executive department of the government. "The materials of which the white house and other large houses are composed," he had observed, "are pretty well known and many of our best friends are more uneasy than I think they have any good grounds for." A much better term than the President's House, certainly than the President's Palace!

There! She was ready. The improvements had been rushed to completion. Now for her first real experience as hostess. There had been a big dinner back in March but this would be the first really big reception. What should it be called? A levee? That had been Martha Washington's term, and Abigail Adams had followed her example. Jefferson, of course, had had nothing of the sort. Hers would be different, not stiff and formal like theirs, but an occasion where people could be free to enjoy themselves, with joking, light talk, refreshments, music; where men could talk politics if they wished, ladies could wear their best gowns, young men and women meet and fall in love. An "open house"? Better, why not a "drawing room"? It was formally announced that on Wednesday evening at eight o'clock on May 31, Mrs. Madison would be in her drawing room to receive friends, and on every Wednesday after that when she was in the city. No invitations were issued. All who wished might come. If only it would be a good day!

It wasn't. Rain poured, and the mud hole outside the gate, one of the worst in Washington, was a morass. Several carriages broke down, causing the occupants to be relayed to the house by more fortunate friends. All conveyances arrived spattered and bedraggled. But the house was warm and bright and glowing. Fires blazed on the hearths. The new chandeliers dazzled with their hundreds of wax candles. At least two hundred people came, the women in low-cut gowns, ruffs, plumes, jewels; the men, all except James who wore his usual black, in colored coats, crimson, green, blue with gilt or pearl buttons, starched neckcloths, fine cambric shirt frills, patent leather pumps with buckles. Boots were banned for evening occasions, since the mud on them might soil the ladies' skirts.

"The public," reported one British guest, "greatly relished the honor of seeing the President and his lady." His description of the two, however, was less than flattering. "Mrs. Madison plump, tall, affable and showily but tastefully dressed, whereas Mr. Madison the President is a very small thin pale-visaged man of rather a sour, reserved and forbidding countenance. He seems to be incapable of smiling, but talks a great deal and without any stiffness. He was in black, his hair dressed in a very oldfashioned style—a large club highly powdered, his locks long without any curl or fizzing and his hair combed down on his forehead."

Dolley would not have appreciated this description of her Jemmy. It was she who carefully combed and powdered his hair each day in what she considered the most becoming style, puffing it a little over the ears and drawing it down over the bald places above his forehead, then combing it back into a short queue tied with a ribbon, requiring no service of barbers. And as for his incapability of smiling—!

William Thornton, who was something of a poet, wrote an amusing rhyme to celebrate this first "drawing room" of Dolley's, satirizing some of Washington's young men who attended. The first stanza ran:

> Tom Tingey, Tom Turner, Tom Ewell, Tom Digges,
> All go to the palace to eat up the figs.
> How different the conduct of Romulus Riggs
> Forever engaged with his schooners and brigs!
> The ladies go thither, but cannot dance jigs,
> Lest the motion of dancing should loosen their wigs.

> Some go as Federalists, some go as Whigs,
> Some as philosophers, some few as prigs.

The British observer should have seen the sober President guffaw when he heard it.

It was with satisfaction and anticipation that the Madisons left for Montpelier on July 20. Dolley felt comfortable in her new role of First Lady. Already she had hosted a half dozen Wednesday "drawing rooms," as well as several small dinners, all as successful as the first. They had settled in living quarters in the southwestern corner of the White House, and to her delight Anna and her family would occupy apartments in the southeastern part. To have Anna and her children nearby, under the same roof, was joy unspeakable. And Richard Cutts and his family were coming to Montpelier with them.

James too was feeling well satisfied with the first four months of his administration. On June 10 restoration of the trade with Britain had been celebrated with great fanfare, and on the same day six hundred ships had sailed for England. He had every reason to believe that Napoleon would reciprocate by repealing his Berlin and Milan Decrees under which he had seized ten million dollars worth of American ships and cargoes in retaliation for the Nonintercourse Act. True, Turreau, the French minister, had left Washington in high dudgeon because of the new agreement with Erskine without a word to Madison or his Secretary of State. But the move was inspired also by personal desires. Having divorced his wife, he was ardently pursuing the famous Baltimore beauty, Elizabeth Patterson Bonaparte, whose marriage to Napoleon's brother had been abruptly annulled by the Emperor. For the moment prospects for peace with the two European belligerents seemed hopeful.

James became increasingly excited as they turned into the long curving road leading up the hill to Montpelier. All through the fall and winter brick kilns had been kept fired by Jefferson's brickmaker Hugh Chisholm while James Dinsmore, carpenter and draftsman, and his workmen made repairs and additions to the house. A good start had been made, though it would be at least two years before the work was completed. One-story wings were being added on each side of the house. A beautiful "temple" was being built over the sunken icehouse, one of the first in Virginia, that kept cool drinks and ice cream on hand for the many visitors. The additional room would make possible a separate wing for Mother Madison and her household. William

Thornton had helped to draw the plans, and Latrobe was aiding in the construction.

In spite of the confusion guests, invited and otherwise, kept coming and were always made welcome. On August 2, Samuel and Margaret Smith arrived after spending some days at Monticello.

"Oh!" exclaimed Dolley regretfully. "Why didn't you bring your little girls?"

"We were afraid they might incommode people," replied Margaret, "so many of us."

Dolley laughed. "Why, I shouldn't have known they were here among so many, for right now we have only three and twenty people in the house, and are always glad for more."

"Everything," recorded Margaret, "bespoke comfort, no restraint, ceremony. Hospitality is the presiding genius." Most of the guests, she noted, were near relatives, Madison's brother William and his wife, Anna, and her family, and others, "all plain country people, but frank, kind, warm-hearted Virginians."

Dolley would have blushed could she have read Margaret's description of her.

"Mrs. Madison, uniting to all the elegance and polish of fashion, the unadulterated simplicity, frankness, warmth and friendliness of her native character and native state. . . . When the servant appeared with candles to show me my room, she insisted on going upstairs with me, assisted me to undress and chatted till I got into bed. How unassuming, how kind is this woman. How can any human being be her enemy? Truly, in her there is to be found no gall, but the pure milk of human kindness. If I may say so, the maid was like the mistress; she was very attentive all the time I was there, seeming as if she could not do enough, and was very talkative. As her mistress left the room, 'You have a good mistress, Nany,' I said. 'Yes,' answered the affectionate creature with warmth, 'the best I believe in the world. I am sure I would not change her for any mistress in the whole country.' The next morning Nany called me to a late breakfast, brought me ice and water (this is universal here, even in taverns) and assisted me to dress. We sat down between 15 and 20 persons to a most excellent breakfast—tea, coffee, hot wheat bread, light cakes, a pone or corn loaf, cold ham, nice hashes, chickens, etc."

But the euphoria of vacation ended suddenly. A messenger came from Washington with the upsetting news that the British government had repudiated the Erskine agreement. Foreign minister Canning had told the House of Commons that Erskine had disobeyed his instructions.

"How!" fumed James, all his hopes for settlement with England dashed. "The British government seems to have reverted to monopoly and piracy." He was surprised "in spite of all their examples of folly." Perhaps, he commented, they had yielded to the demands of London smugglers in sugar and coffee.

As a matter of fact, Erskine had grossly misrepresented the conditions under which the agreement had supposedly been made. He had made only a partial revelation of his instructions, making no insistence on the three conditions that his government had stated must accompany the withdrawal of their Orders in Council: that the United States reopen its harbors to British warships, renounce all trade with enemies of England and its colonies, and permit the British navy to capture American trading vessels doing business with enemies of England. Madison could never have agreed to these conditions. As one biographer was to say of him later, "He was not a pacifist President who stood aloof from decision. He was an unsentimental bargainer in a hard-boiled age."

"I have to return to Washington," he told Dolley bleakly.

He left on August 4, taking only two and a half days for the journey. In spite of the multiplicity of guests requiring constant attention and a smiling serenity which Dolley did not feel, the house seemed empty and desolate. Only in those troubled weeks of sickness in Philadelphia had she experienced such devastating loneliness. Jemmy had been so distraught, so hopeless. Presiding at endless meals, promoting light talk as they sat rocking on the sixty-foot long veranda in the evening cool, even playing with the children, her pleasantest pastimes of all, Dolley was miles away in the heat and stress and contention of Washington. That he also was finding the White House empty and lonely was evidenced by his letters.

"My dearest," he wrote once, "everything around and within reminds me that you are absent, and makes me anxious to quit this solitude."

Though he was in Washington only four days, they seemed like as many weeks. He had handled the distressing situation with courage and dispatch, signing a new proclamation on August 9 restoring all the restrictions of trade with Britain according to the Nonimportation Act. His fellow Republicans stood by his decision, also some of the more moderate Federalists. But the conservatives poured abuse on his head. He had betrayed the British government, deceived the American people, played into the hands of that despicable Napoleon!

Erskine was recalled by his government, and a new ambassador, "Copenhagen" Jackson, so-called because he had once prepared to blow up Copenhagen if it did not yield to his demands, was assigned. He was noted for his harsh treatment of neutrals. He came with one object in view, to spank this infant nation into submission to its superiors, also to discipline its upstart President for disparaging remarks he was reported to have made against his erstwhile sovereign. He and his wife, a Prussian baroness, arriving on September 11, checked into Washington's most expensive hotel to await the arrival of the Madisons from Montpelier. Here they were confounded to find that the words "gentleman" and "lady" were used by the servants to describe the innkeeper and his wife. And when the wife visited Mrs. Jackson and actually shook her hand, amazement was overwhelming. Then to discover that she and Mrs. Erskine had been in the habit of exchanging visits! But of course the former envoy's wife had been an American.

Jackson wrote home, "Pray send me something that is English. Everything that breathes this air gets a tendency to become American."

On Madison's arrival the first of October the new minister and his wife made their way to the White House in a new carriage with liveries which, Jackson was sure, "quite astonished the natives, who never before saw such a one—a landau barouche." Jackson found Madison, he reported, "a plain and rather mean-looking little man." But the baroness found to her amazement that she actually liked Dolley in spite of what friendly Federalists had told her was her "low origin." The First Lady, she commented, was *"une bonne grosse femme de la classe bourgeoise,* very fit to grace the President's table; without distinction either in manners or appearance, but, to be just, she is also without pretensions." Jackson, also primed by Federalist friends, judged that "she must, however, have been a comely person when she served out the liquors at her father's tavern in the state of Virginia." Shades of her chaste childhood and Quaker ancestry!

The new envoy was happily surprised when he was invited to dinner at the White House. Foolish, Madison had decided, to follow Jefferson's stubborn credo on that "foolish question of precedence." He conducted Mrs. Jackson to the table while the envoy took Dolley. The dinner in cuisine and service was more than could be expected of a boorish primitive society. Jackson commented, "I do not know that I had ever more civility and attention shown me."

But he found the President far less amenable at the conference than at the dinner table. The "plain and rather mean-looking little man" showed remarkable strength in resisting either the blandishments or the bullyings of the new British minister. No, his country would not yield to Canning's three conditions for abrogation of the Orders in Council. He would not acknowledge the right of his Majesty's government to disavow the Erskine agreement. And he refused to compromise, even when offered satisfaction over the affair of the *Chesapeake,* which, still unsettled after many years, was still a rankling sore in the American flesh.

"Madison is as obstinate as a mule!" exclaimed the frustrated envoy.

The euphoria accompanying the first months of the new administration had indeed ended, not for a brief vacation interval, but for many years to come.

2

"Ah, you are fortunate, sir. This is Wednesday, and this evening Mrs. Madison will be holding one of her famous drawing rooms. Everybody who is anybody in Washington will be going to the Palace. You really must attend."

The young man who had just arrived at the inn nodded eagerly, then frowned. "What a piece of good luck! But—I wonder how I can get there. Here it's almost evening already, and I'm away out here in Georgetown. My letters of introduction are all to persons miles away on Capitol Hill, and there is the President's House halfway between. But"—his eyes flashed with determination—"I swear I'll get there!"

He mounted to his room, as he expressed it later in a letter to a friend, "resolved to put on my pease-blossom and silk stockings, gird up my loins and sally forth on my expedition, and like a vagabond errant trust to Providence for success and whole bones."

The landlord met him as he descended the stairs. "Great good fortune, sir! There is a party of gentlemen just going from the house, and one of them, a Mr. Fonatine Maury of New York, offers his services to introduce you at the Palace."

Good! The young man, as he described it in the same letter, "cut one of my best opera flourishes; skipped into the dressing room, popped my head into the hands of a sanguinary Jacobinical barber who carried havoc and desolation to the lower regions of my face; mowed down all the beard on one cheek and laid the other in blood like a conquered province; and, thus, like a second Banquo, with 'twenty mortal murthers on my head,' in a few minutes I emerged from dirt and darkness into the blazing splendor of Mrs. Madison's drawing room."

"Here," his letter continued, "I was most graciously received; found a crowded collection of great and little men, of ugly old women and beautiful young ones, and in ten minutes was hand in glove with half the people in the assemblage."

Introduced by name to the hostess, his eyes strayed to the book she held under one arm. Of course, it was too much to hope . . . he was only a very young author . . . No, it was *Don Quixote* she was holding.

"Oh! Mr. Washington Irving!" she repeated the name eagerly, sapphire-blue eyes agleam with excitement. "Had I known you were coming, I would have been carrying your fascinating Knickerbocker's *History of New York.* You are the writer of it, aren't you? Or is it supposed to be a secret? My husband and I have been enjoying it. You have such a wonderful sense of humor."

The guest was surprised and flattered, for he was a very new author indeed, both his books written under pseudonyms, and it would be years before he was recognized as one of America's foremost men of letters. "Then you take time to read, Madam, with all the rest of your duties?"

She laughed deprecatingly. "Not much," she confessed. "Just between you and me, I often carry a book in my hand, like this fine copy of *Don Quixote,* which I have been rereading. It gives me something not ungraceful to talk about, in fact makes a very good topic of conversation. It's my husband who is the reader, and, oh, such dry heavy tomes he devours! Hundreds of them, and remembers every word! Not nearly so entertaining as yours, dear friend. I call him a walking library."

Dolley was being unduly modest. As a matter of fact, she did a good deal of reading. She especially enjoyed the writings of Addison, Pope, Swift, and Scott, also translations of the plays by Molière, with their shrewd satires on human nature. Just the year before, in 1810, George Watterston, writer of novels and histories, had brought out the first of his poetic romances, *A Wanderer in Jamaica,* and had dedicated it to Dolley with the words: "Madam, I have presumed to address this poetical effusion to you, from the reputation you have acquired of being desirous to promote the cause of general literature." So pleased was Madison with this author's capabilities that at the earliest opportunity he would appoint him librarian of the Library of Congress.

Washington Irving was more impressed with Dolley than with the insignificant-looking little man with the sober, careworn features. His letter of January 13, 1811, written four days later, was hardly complimentary to his country's President.

"Mrs. Madison is a fine, portly, buxom dame, who has a smile and a pleasant word for everybody. Her sisters, Mrs. Cutts and Mrs. Washington, are like the merry wives of Windsor; but as to Jemmy Madison —ah, poor Jemmy!—he is but a withered apple-john!"

Sometime later Irving was writing to his brother that he was not too sanguine about getting the diplomatic appointment he had sought in coming to Washington, but that "the President on its being mentioned to him, said some very handsome things of me, and I make no doubt will express a wish in my favor on the subject, more especially as Mrs. Madison is a sworn friend of mine, and indeed all the ladies of the household and myself are great cronies."

If he expected Dolley to use her influence in his behalf, however, he did not know her. She rigidly refrained from interfering in the making of appointments. That was James's business. When Irving later boasted that he felt her favor would win him the post of secretarial assistant to Joel Barlow when the latter was to be sent as American plenipotentiary to France in the hope of securing a favorable commercial treaty, he was sadly mistaken. He did not get the appointment.

A pity the future noted novelist could not have seen his "withered apple-john" through the eyes of the Baron de Montlezun, who wrote of the President sometime later: "But when he can disengage himself for a moment from the cares attached to the painful honor of being the chief of republican government, the wrinkles smooth out of his face, his countenance lights up; it shines with all the fire of the spirit and with a gentle gaiety; and one is surprised to find in the conversation of the great statesman as much sprightliness as strength."

The new French minister, Louis Sérurier, who arrived in February of that same year, 1811, would have characterized him in this way after attending one of Dolley's little dinners. It was in such intimate environs that Madison's innate humor, normally tight-locked in the bud, blossomed into gems of droll wit, sometimes a bit more colorful than Dolley approved. He was able to converse with the new envoy in his native language.

"Have you noticed that my French has an odd accent?" he asked M. Sérurier at one point. "If so, it wouldn't be the first time." He went on to tell a story about his college days. A Frenchman had come to Princeton and wanted to converse with the college President. Not knowing French, Dr. Witherspoon had asked if anyone could act as interpreter. Madison had loftily volunteered. As the relieved foreigner began glibly to speak, James had caught a few words, communicated them to the President, and attempted to translate his reply. The poor Frenchman had not understood a word he was saying.

"I might as well have been talking Kickapoo at him!" he said glee-fully, his bluish eyes sparkling. "You see, I had learned French from my Scotch tutor, read it to him as we did Greek or Latin, that is, as a dead language, and this pronounced with his Scotch accent, which my tongue had probably caught, besides a twang of my own which was no more French than Caesar's Latin!"

Dolley relaxed, laughing with the rest. Occasionally his college sto-ries smacked of the crude vulgarity of his old Whig ditties. At least this had been chaste, if self-derogatory. Jemmy loved taking jibes at himself.

It was remarkable, she thought, that he had the heart to jest, so beset was he by political dilemmas, crushed in a vise not only between the two belligerents in Europe bent on his nation's subjugation but between two contentious elements in his own country, one trying to propel him into an unwanted and disastrous war, the other threaten-ing secession with his every attempt to avoid it.

The year had started out with hope, the New Year reception at the White House as brilliant as the glittering golden coach of the French minister Turreau, that great gold ball on wheels, the footmen resplen-dent in gold tinsel and cord, with golden swords. France had seemed to symbolize hope as well as brilliance. The preceding year Congress had passed what was known as Macon's Bill, named for its sponsor, Congressman Nathanael Macon, chairman of the House Committee on Foreign Affairs. Ending the long experiment with nonimportation, so disruptive to American commerce, it reopened trade with both belligerents, but provided that if either France or England revoked its edicts, the British Orders in Council or the French Berlin and Milan Decrees, the President might prohibit commercial intercourse with the other.

In the preceding August, Napoleon had apparently accepted the invitation extended by the Macon Bill. John Armstrong, the American envoy in Paris, had announced that the Berlin and Milan Decrees would be revoked as of November 1. On November 2 Madison had proclaimed nonintercourse with Britain subject to the repeal of her Orders within ninety days. There had been other favorable develop-ments. Peace with both warring nations seemed to be in the offing.

Dolley also had radiated hope and optimism in her rose-colored satin with its ermine trimmings and her turban of rose velvet, a jew-eled crescent holding the white ostrich plumes in place.

The new French envoy, Sérurier, though noncommittal about this commitment by the emperor, was a welcome change from the wife-beating "butcher" Turreau. Tall, thin, looking younger than his thirty-five years, in spite of a "pallid cheek and rather a dark melancholy countenance," he was an attractive addition to Washington society. Dolley liked him at once. James was less cordial. He wanted to know why American ships were still being arrested under the French decrees. Sérurier claimed to know of no arrests but admitted that the Emperor was doubtless waiting to make sure either that Britain repealed her Orders in Council or that Madison fulfilled his promise to reinstate the nonintercourse act against her.

Hope was short-lived. Britain did not repeal the Orders, and restoration of the nonintercourse act against her was arousing bitter debate in Congress. At one point it almost resulted in a duel between John Randolph, Madison's old opponent, and his ardent supporter, Congressman John Eppes. The duel, Sérurier reported, "was converted into an accommodation by Mrs. Madison." Just how Dolley accomplished this miracle was never documented, but probably by her usual technique of smoothing out disagreements, getting the belligerents together in a corner at one of her drawing rooms or at an intimate little dinner. Randolph and Eppes announced in the press that they no longer felt moved to resort to pistols.

Yet Dolley's genius as a hostess could not be explained in terms of technique. It was merely the natural expression of her friendly, loving nature. She was tactful because she was sensitive to people's needs, vivacious because she loved life and wanted everybody to relish it as she did. She remembered people's names not because she relied on a peculiar system but because she was personally interested in every person she met. No one introduced to her at one of her crowded teas or drawing rooms ever required a second introduction on meeting her again. Each one had the satisfaction of being recognized and addressed by his or her own name. She was conciliatory because she was distressed by any kind of dissension, and when hot argument occurred, she would often quietly leave the room for a few moments, returning to find the hint taken and peace restored.

"I would rather fight with my hands than with my tongue," she sometimes said.

Of course she must have had enemies. Any woman with a high-bred manner and refinement would scarcely commend herself to those to whom mediocrity was at a premium. Her love of pleasing, of making everybody happy must have been called insincerity, even toadyism by those who could not understand the pain given her by an unkind word. But except for those whispers of scandal based more on political prejudice than on personal animosity, contemporary appraisals were remarkably kind, some extravagantly so. Typical of the latter is a description by Eliza Trist, friend of both the Madisons in their Philadelphia days.

"She had a sweet, natural dignity of manner which attracted while it commanded respect; a proper degree of reserve without stiffness in company with strangers, and a stamp of frankness and sincerity which, with her intimate friends, became gaiety and even playfulness of manner. There was, too, a cordial, genial, sunny atmosphere surrounding her, which won all hearts—I think one of the secrets of her immense popularity. She was said to be, during Mr. Madison's administration, the most popular person in the United States."

Somehow she always managed to make people feel at ease. At one of her drawing rooms she saw a youth, obviously from the country, withdrawn into a corner and evidently tortured by embarrassment. Greeting one person after another, she drifted toward him. In spite of her effort to be casual, his embarrassment became overwhelming. The saucer of the cup of coffee he was holding dropped to the floor. He tried to crowd the cup into his pocket without success.

"What a crowd!" Dolley observed lightly. "One can't help being jostled, can one?" She began asking about his family, where he came from. Did he have brothers and sisters? When he went home he must take her regards to his mother and invite her to visit Washington. He was soon talking to her eagerly, his discomfort, even the broken saucer on the floor forgotten. Meanwhile a servant had unobtrusively swept up the pieces and at her bidding brought the guest another cup of coffee.

A shy, embarrassed person attending one of her drawing rooms drew her like a lodestone. On one occasion, spying a young man skulking to the edge of the crowd as if intent on retreating from the brilliant scene, she hurried toward him, a warm smile mitigating what must have seemed the formidable magnificence of her high turban and stiff brocade, and extended her hand. Her instinct for spotting familiar faces was as true as her memory of names. "Aren't you William Campbell Preston, son of my old friend and most beloved kinsman, Sally Campbell?" she inquired cordially, and when he nodded, "Do sit down here beside me, my son, for you are indeed like my son." Her eyes sparkled. "I believe I am the first person who ever saw you in this world." She proceeded to introduce him to a bevy of young girls, among them "your kinswoman, Sally Coles." Sally was her cousin, daughter of Colonel John Coles of Ennisworthy. She also insisted on young William Preston's moving into the White House for the rest of his stay in Washington.

Dolley was rejoicing during these years at having many members of her family near her. Edward Coles, son of her great-uncle John Coles, was private secretary to Madison. "A thorough gentleman," one friend described him, "and one of the best natured and most kindly-affectioned men it has ever been my fortune to know." One of Washington's most eligible bachelors, too, for he had never married. His one ambition, it developed, was to migrate to the "free" state of Illinois, where he could take his slaves and free them. Meanwhile he resisted all of Dolley's attempts at matchmaking, while acting as invaluable assistant to both her and the President. She placed him opposite herself at most formal dinners to assist in the conversation and spare the more reticent President the responsibility of guiding the social intercourse.

Also in the White House family were both Anna, with her family, and Dolley's younger sister Lucy, whose husband, George Steptoe Washington, had recently died after a long siege with tuberculosis. George had remained happy and high-spirited to the end. In fact, during one of his visits before his death Dolley had written, "I enjoyed the sound of Virginia hilarity echoing through the house. George coughs incessantly, looks thin and hoarse, but has no idea of dying." His death had occurred when he was on a horseback trip in North Carolina, trying to regain his health. For the first time in many years the three sisters were all together, Lucy, in spite of her grief, included in Washington Irving's apt description of "the merry wives of Windsor."

Lucy was responding to the cheerful influence of her sisters and, at least on the surface, displaying her usual gay and friendly manner. At thirty-five she was maturely gracious and attractive and was receiving several offers of marriage, one persistent suitor being Judge Thomas Todd, Justice of the Supreme Court from Kentucky. But Lucy was reluctant to consider a second marriage after the romantic happiness of her first, and Dolley, though an inveterate matchmaker, did not urge her. She remembered too well her own hesitation after John's death. Besides, she wanted to keep both sisters with her as long as possible, and Kentucky seemed as remote as that faraway district of Maine.

Dolley's days followed a regular pattern. She rose very early, as she had done all her life, then planned the day's activities with her faithful French John Sióussat. Then he would send the house steward to the Georgetown markets to make purchases. She tried to keep accurate accounts of expenditures and worried over the high prices. A turkey cost seventy-five cents, a side of mutton two dollars, a whole hog three dollars, canvasback ducks fifty cents each. Two shad could be bought for a quarter; potatoes were forty cents a bushel. She could hire an extra waiter for an afternoon or evening party for thirty-five cents. Sometimes the food bill for a day amounted to fifty dollars. Though great quantities of food were consumed at Montpelier, much there was produced on the estate; here everything must be purchased. While the President's salary of twenty-five thousand dollars had seemed princely, in reality it barely paid their expenses.

When guests were present the table was always bountifully laid in the manner of the "harvest home" Mrs. Merry had so ridiculed. Though French John could have vied with the royal chefs of Europe in creating gourmet dishes, the Madisons preferred to serve only American viands. Dolley tried to have the different sections of the country represented on her menus—New England fish and clam chowders, crab soups from the Carolinas, fried chicken from Maryland, Pennsylvania pepper pot, and, of course, smoked ham from Virginia. Ice cream made popular by Jefferson was often served for dessert. At her more informal teas her own recipes for soft gingerbread and Roman punch won warm approbation.

Occasionally in the morning she would accompany other ladies to the Congress halls to listen to proceedings, but not often. She did not enjoy the hot contention, particularly in these days when Democratic-Republicans and Federalists were at one another's throats. While others "delight to listen to the violence of evil spirits," she wrote, "I stay quietly at home (as quietly as one can be who has so much to feel at the expression for and against their conduct)." Better to hear from Jemmy's lips what political problems he chose to share with her. She certainly was glad she had not been in the Capitol when her cousin Isaac Coles, who had been Jefferson's private secretary, horsewhipped a member of Congress who had maligned the President. At least a whip was preferable to the pistol which had wounded Dolley's brother-in-law John G. Jackson, her sister Mary's widower, when he had been challenged to a duel for defending the President! James had issued a harsh denunciation of the whole practice of dueling.

Afternoons were spent in returning calls and entertaining at the informal or state dinners held late in the day. When the lighted candles were brought in, it was customary for the ladies to retire to an adjoining room while the men remained for additional wine and conversation, some of it no doubt unfit for female ears. When James held his cabinet meetings, Dolley also liked to gather the wives for what she called "Dove Parties," intimate little sessions with conversation geared to feminine interests. At such gatherings, however, she saw to it that other topics were discussed than the latest Paris fashions and current romancings, certainly than unfriendly gossip, which she hated.

Sarah Gales Seaton, a visitor, once wrote, "After the dinner was over we adjourned to the tea room, and here in the most delightful manner imaginable I shared the pleasure of Mrs. Madison's conversation on books, men and manners, literature in general, and many special branches of knowledge. I never spent a more rational or pleasing half hour." So much for future appraisers who would categorize the fourth First Lady in such terms as "party-queen," "clotheshorse," and other simplicities!

In spite of her rigid schedule Dolley was always available for any guest, distinguished or not, who might unexpectedly arrive. For instance, there were the two old ladies from the country, determined to meet the First Lady. But how? As they arrived in Washington late one night and had to leave early the next morning, they were puzzled. At least they could see where she lived. Meeting an old gentleman in the street, they asked if he could tell them the way to the President's house. Sure, he replied, he would take them. Yes, and since he knew Mrs. Madison well, he would make sure that they met her.

Dolley and the family were at breakfast when they arrived, but she left the table to welcome the strangers. Their astonishment was apparent. This august personage coming to meet them in a plain stuff dress of dark gray, protected by a large white apron, a linen kerchief pinned about her neck! Such simplicity, together with her friendly manner, conquered their awe completely, and they were soon chatting with her as if she were a country neighbor.

"Do—do you suppose," one of them dared to suggest before leaving, "that is, would you mind if I—if I kissed you—just so I could tell my girls about it?"

Dolley laughed delightedly. "Of course I wouldn't mind." And she gracefully embraced and kissed each of the old ladies, who, adjusting their spectacles which had been set awry, departed in a flurry of happy excitement.

Could her visitors have seen her a few hours later, dressed for dinner, they would have wondered if it was the same person. Once she herself had questioned if she were not two people, the housewife who put on Quaker garb each morning or the hostess who wore silks and feathers and jewels, who no longer covered her white arms and shoulders with even a filmy kerchief, who, after the prevailing custom for women in society, carried, and used, her dainty little snuffbox. But she had stopped wondering. All these things were externals, trappings of the body, not of the spirit. Religion was a matter of the heart, not of dress. After all, wasn't one of God's maples the same sturdy tree whether clothed in sober green or in flamboyant crimson? She could even point a little fun at some of the unimportant inhibitions that had obscured rather than kindled the flame of Inner Light. Once, when toasts were being given at a farewell dinner for an old Quaker Philadelphia friend who was their guest, she rose, held out her glass, and said with a twinkle in her eyes: "Here's to thy absent broad brim, Friend Hallowell!"

Quick as a flash, he came back at her and without a trace of embarrassment replied, "And here's to thy absent kerchief, Friend Dolley."

Often, after the social events of the day, when she retired to her sitting room, she liked to remove all the finery and don once more the familiar Quaker gray. Jemmy joined her here whenever possible, sure of a bright story and a good laugh, as refreshing, he sometimes said, as a long walk. He needed all the diversion she could furnish during these troubled months, for events seemed to be moving toward some frightening climax.

He was beset by problems both domestic and foreign. Admission of the state of Louisiana into the Union was being hotly opposed by the Federalists. One of the most vocal opponents, Josiah Quincy of Massachusetts, claimed that it was cause for dissolution of the Union. The Constitution had been written for territory already owned. "You have no authority," he shouted in Congress, "to throw the rights and liberties and property of this people into a 'hotch-pot' with the wild men on the Missouri" or the Anglo-Hispanic-Gallo Americans—good, bad, and indifferent—who basked on the sands of the Mississippi. Once let a state be formed west of that dividing line and there would be no stopping short of California and the Columbia River! To Quincy and other strict Federalists everything beyond the Appalachians was foreign, uncouth, and, worse, menacing to the rights of Eastern industrialists. Madison, who had helped frame the Constitution, believed that enlargement of the sphere of government was the surest safeguard against tyranny. In other words, acquisition of more territory would mean for America an expanding Union, not, as it had done for Britain, a colonial empire.

Foreign affairs were still at an impasse. The French Berlin and Milan Decrees were again—or still—in force, the British Orders in Council unchanged. British ships were blockading New York Harbor, impressing seamen at will. The ruthless Napoleon was seizing every American vessel that tried to enter a Continental port. It was an intolerable situation. Madison was desperately attempting to avoid war with either country, playing one against the other, endeavoring to temper the rising war fever of Western militants in Congress, like young Henry Clay from Kentucky. Obliged to oust the inefficient Robert Smith from his cabinet and substituting James Monroe as Secretary of State, whom he had wanted in the first place, Madison was suffering scurrilous attacks by the outraged Smith and his sympathetic Federalists.

In May there was a violent encounter between an American vessel *The President* and the *Little Belt,* a British ship blockading New York Harbor. Clay and his militant Democrats were jubilant, Federalists scandalized. In July, Augustus Foster, a new minister from Britain, arrived. His instructions were firm. The Orders in Council would be maintained until France not only repealed her Decrees "absolutely and unconditionally" but also dropped her regulations that sealed Continental ports to British commerce. His coming did not improve relations.

Even the prospect of two months on their beloved mountain brought little hope of release from the grueling pressures. The Baltimore *Federal Republican,* a Federalist bastion, gave him a parting blast.

"The opinion is gaining ground rapidly that Mr. Madison will be impeached. . . . A doubt nowhere exists that it is in the power of Robert Smith to disclose further high crimes and misdemeanors . . . throwing far into the shade the crimes of Charles II of England. . . . In some countries a summary mode of justice would be pursued for crimes which whiten into virtue when compared to his."

But at least Montpelier brought some respite. They could delight in the near completion of the new wings on the mansion, increasing its spread to 150 feet. The enlargement made entertaining much easier, though the guests who came—Monroe near the end of August, bringing many papers, Jefferson in September, Navy Secretary Paul Hamilton's son with dispatches from Europe—brought problems rather than relaxation. For Dolley no anxiety over political affairs could outweigh her joy at having Payne home for his vacation. He had matured into a tall, handsome youth with charming manners, a talent for attracting admiration whether from foreigners used to the courtly ways of European society or from plantation slaves. But still at the excellent school in Baltimore, he was not yet ready for Princeton.

"He's still so young," Dolley returned to the old excuse. "Just give him a little more time," she pleaded.

But James's lips tightened and his eyes narrowed as he observed the youth haunting the stables, spending his days riding instead of showing interest in the farms, dallying with the daughters of neighboring squires, partaking too liberally of the contents of the wine cellar.

"He's nineteen," he replied briefly, remembering that at that age he was crowding his junior and senior years at Princeton into one. But he could not bear to quell the proud radiance on Dolley's face. He had never told her of the additional payments he had sent the bursar of Father Dubourg's Academy to defray certain questionable expenses incurred by their easygoing and too convivial son.

Though Secretary of State Monroe had warned that in the delicacy of the political situation it might be wise to forgo their usual visit to Jefferson's lest Madison seem to be too much under the influence of the former President, James refused to change his custom of many years. With Dolley, his secretary Ned Coles, and Payne, he drove to Monticello in September. Unfortunately they missed witnessing the climactic moments of the total eclipse of the sun on September 17, because Jefferson's watch happened to be slow. An embarrassing failure for the clever old scientist-inventor who had succeeded in harnessing a week's time with his astounding clock!

"We spent two months on our mountain," Dolley wrote her friend Mrs. Joel Barlow, whose husband had gone as American plenipotentiary to France in an effort to negotiate a commercial treaty with Napoleon and secure indemnity for confiscated property, "returning the first of October to a sick and afflicted city." Fortunately a milder fever epidemic than the one that had devastated her life so long ago!

But they returned to a political atmosphere even more fraught with uncertainty and danger than miasmic marshes. Relations with both England and France had reached an impasse. Britain's Orders in Council were being more rigidly executed. Redress for confiscation of American ships had been withheld. A British warship had attacked an unarmed vessel on American shores with "blood unfortunately shed in maintaining the honor of the American flag." While France too had failed to implement fairly the repeal of her decrees, the country had far greater and more serious grievances against England.

The whole nation anxiously awaited Madison's annual message to Congress. So important was it considered that it took only a little over eight hours, sixteen miles per hour on horseback, to carry it to Philadelphia. It was a mixture of force and conciliation. Nature had made England and America friends, was its theme, and "they will again be friends, whenever the British government shall reciprocate to us our treatment of her." But the country must be ready for countermeasures if such a change in British policy did not take place. France too was pursuing a policy which might require retaliation.

"With this evidence of hostile inflexibility in trampling on rights which no independent nation can relinquish, Congress will feel the duty of putting the United States into an armor and attitude demanded by the crisis, and corresponding with the national spirit and expectation." Therefore he recommended an immediate increase in the Army, enlargement of military supplies, stockpile of naval materials, consideration of such provisions for the naval force "as may be required."

It was clear that the President had definitely enunciated a policy that would lead to war if Britain did not yield to American conditions which included repeal of the Orders in Council and reparations for at least the attack on the *Chesapeake*. But it also invited peace and friendship as an alternative. Unfortunately Foster, the British envoy, was listening to a minority of Federalists who depicted the President as a weak and vacillating creature, a tool of an unstable Congress. "How little it is to be dreaded that this country will originate measures of hostility against us," he wrote his government. He could not have been more wrong in his estimate both of the President and of Congress. Had he been wiser in his interpretations of American policy to his government, history might have been changed.

Added to Dolley's anxiety over James's dilemma was a sense of loneliness and deprivation. Anna was not in Washington but far away in Maine. Richard, his shoulder injured in a carriage upset, could no longer endure the long journey from Maine to occupy his seat in Congress. Though his family had not been living in the White House since the first few months of the administration, they had been occupying a rented house little more than a block away, and Dolley had seen them almost daily. She missed the children almost as much as she did Anna, especially little James Madison Cutts, now six, who seemed like the son she and Jemmy had never had. Of course Lucy was still with her, as ambivalent as ever about a second marriage, but it was Anna who seemed like her other self.

"I believe there will be war," she wrote her sister on December 20. "Mr. Madison sees no end to the perplexities without it, and they seem to be going on with preparations." But the dread prospect did not keep her from more trivial concerns. "I wrote by the *Hornet* to Mrs. Barlow and begged her to send me anything she thought suitable in the way of millinery. I fear I cannot obtain a new-fashioned pattern for you, but will make you a cap such as is much worn."

The country was in upheaval. New young blood was in Congress, their leaders Henry Clay and John C. Calhoun of South Carolina. Speaker Clay, tall, raw-boned, powerful, was all for war, and his supporters, three to one Democratic-Republicans in the House, were soon dubbed the "War Hawks." The explosive thunder of John Randolph, the militant opponent of the administration, was muted after a day in November 1811 when he had strolled into the House with his huge pet hunting dog at his heels, creating much disturbance. Speaker Clay had ordered the dog out, and she did not reappear. After that Clay's power rose, Randolph's faded. The House was preponderantly in favor of militant resistance to Brisith demands. New England Federalists, of course, always pro-British, were horrified. England was their source of profit. Their presses thundered opposition to the President. Even the old scandals about Dolley and Anna were revived. For a time they refused to enter Madison's door, until, as Dolley recorded after one of her drawing rooms, "Our rooms were crowded with Republicans and such a rallying of our party has alarmed them into a return."

Lucy's troubled romance was worrying Dolley almost as much as the possibility of war. "She is in deep distress," she wrote Anna, "and my nights are miserable and so are my days." Judge Todd was still her most promising and persistent suitor. Was it because he was so much older that Lucy kept dillydallying? But look at Jemmy and me, Dolley could not help reminding her, seventeen years between us, and surely no marriage could be happier! At last Lucy acted. She rejected the judge's suit, sent him away to Kentucky disconsolate. Then suddenly she changed her mind, sent a messenger posthaste to bring him back.

"My beloved sister," Dolley wrote Anna on March 20, 1812, "before this reaches you, Lucy will be married to Judge Todd of Kentucky. You are, I know, prepared for it and reconciled to her choice of a man of the most estimable character. Their home is now to be in Lexington, but as a Supreme Judge he is obliged to come here for two months every winter." But the war clouds were still overshadowing any sunshine of romance. "The world seems to be running mad, what with one thing and another. . . . The war business goes on slowly, but I fear it will be sure. Where are your husband's vessels? and why does he not get them in? Congress will be here until May, and perhaps longer."

The wedding took place on Sunday evening, March 29. Phoebe Morris, daughter of Anthony, Dolley's old friend in Philadelphia, was one of the bridesmaids. She had been visiting Dolley that winter and spring. Edward Coles and Payne were groomsmen. "The Judge," Phoebe wrote her father, who had been an attendant at Dolley's first wedding, "is very rich, very handsome." James gave away the bride, as he had given away Mary and Anna. The *National Intelligencer* reported: "At the residence of the President of the United States Justice Thomas Todd of the United States Supreme Court has married Mrs. Lucy Washington." The next morning the couple left for a week at Harewood, Lucy's former home, where they would pick up her boys to drive to Pittsburgh, then down the Ohio River to Kentucky. It was the first wedding to take place in the White House.

The war crisis was coming to a head. In fact, war was already practically existent. New York was blockaded. American ships were being seized. American sailors were being impressed. On March 15 Speaker Clay requested "that the President recommend an embargo to last, say, thirty days, and that a termination of the embargo be followed by war." Of course according to the Constitution only Congress could declare war, but the President could make recommendations.

Foster, the British minister, proceeded to inform the American government that "the great foundation of the maritime interests of the British Empire must be preserved." No threat of war could deter it from asserting its rights. Having faint hope in a British change of policy, Madison recommended the embargo. British seizure of eighteen richly laden American ships, worth $1,500,000, was "alone sufficient for an embargo." The bill was passed by Congress 70 to 41.

Madison read his war message behind closed doors in Congress on June 1, listing all the many grievances. Only one speech was made in Congress in opposition and that occurred before his message. "John Randolph," wrote Dolley on May 29, "has been firing away at the House this morning against a declaration of war, but we think it will have little effect." For hours he defended before full galleries the British blockades, accused the administration of base slavery to France.

Dolley's emotions these days were both acute and ambivalent. She agreed with James, of course, as to the indignities the country was suffering. She nodded in sympathy when Henry Clay gathered a group about him at one of her drawing rooms and thundered denunciations of traitorous elements who were attempting to divide the country. Then, hoping to subdue the resultant tension which threatened to turn her reception into a verbal free-for-all, she approached Clay with a smile and proffered her dainty little snuffbox of platinum and delicately tinted lava, first taking a little pinch herself. For was not the snuffbox the Portuguese olive branch and the production of it a conciliating gesture? Drawing out a man's handkerchief from her reticule, she remarked gaily that she kept it for "rough work," while the dainty wisp of lawn and lace with which she dusted off her face was her "polisher." The ruse worked. The militant Clay accepted her offer and vented some of his belligerent eloquence in a mild sneeze.

As Thomas Wyatt observed in one of his articles on "Illustrious Characters," "The magic influence which the tender of her snuffbox exerted won from the most obdurate a relaxation of hostility; for none partook of its contents, so generously and kindly offered, and retained a feeling inimical to its owner."

Dolley could not forget the teachings of her Quaker heritage. War. Violence. Surely there were better ways to settle arguments between nations as well as individuals. After all, countries were people. If only Jemmy and that British foreign minister Castlereagh could sit down together and talk things over, perhaps around her dinner table!

Even after Madison made his war speech, he was still hoping for peace. It would take only the British decision to repeal the Orders in Council in response to the French making final their repeal of the Berlin and Milan Decrees to make war unnecessary, though Henry Clay insisted that the impressment of seamen, which would probably continue even after repeal, would still constitute just as serious aggression.

On June 4, 1812, the House voted for war, 79 to 49. On June 17 the

Senate concurred with the vote, 19 to 13. That evening British legate Foster went to Dolley's drawing room. The President, he noted, "looked ghastly pale—he made me three bows—he was remarkably civil." Commenting on the pallor, he observed, he "very naturally felt all the responsibility he would incur."

On June 18 the declaration of war was signed by Madison.

It was one of the great ironies of history. For on June 17, the very day the Senate was completing its vote for war, Britain's Orders in Council were suspended.

3

A century and a half later historians would still be arguing over the wisdom of that War of 1812 and of the man on whose slender but resolute shoulders rested the burdens of the commander in chief. Was it "unnecessary, impolitic, untimely, rash," a grievous blunder? Was it the action of bold and supremely confident young "War Hawks" who persuaded a reluctant President to declare war in return for their backing of his reelection bid? Or was it, as some would say, America's "second war of independence," a prerequisite for her final emergence into a respected and self-reliant member of the family of nations? One thing was certainly possible. If Dolley could have had her way and gotten together about her dinner table her peace-loving husband and the leading framers of British policy, the war might have been avoided.

The argument was bitter at the time, threatening to disrupt the country. In fact, the Union so painfully achieved in the Constitutional Convention was about as much in danger of dissolution as half a century later when another administration which also called itself Republican would plunge the country into Civil War. The man who would go down in history as the "Father of the Constitution" might easily have been remembered as its destroyer. But, convinced of the justice of his momentous decisions, he was willing to take that risk.

Federalists, especially in New England, as might be expected, were bitterly opposed to what they called "Mr. Madison's War." They asserted that it was started by the "Virginia cabal" and the "madmen of Kentucky and Tennessee" in order to ruin the flourishing commerce of the country; that it was a base alliance with the tyrant Napoleon in his schemes to shatter the British Empire. New Englanders hung their flags at half mast and tolled their church bells. American contractors in Vermont and New York continued to keep the British troops in Canada supplied with beef. The governors of Massachusetts and Connecticut refused to call out their state militias to protect American shores, acts barely short of treason.

"If they can frustrate national authority even in a state of declared war," Madison denounced in his first wartime message, "it is obvious that the United States are not one nation for the purpose most of all requiring it."

No nation could have been more ill prepared for war or the odds it faced more unequal. It was like a puny but bold David challenging a heavily armed giant Goliath. Great Britain had more than a thousand warships, seven hundred of them at sea. Seventeen vessels constituted the navy of the United States, three of them frigates in such bad condition that rebuilding would take many months. The country had only six thousand-plus regulars in its old regiments, and only five thousand recruits had been raised. Congress was slow in making appropriations and in authorizing a larger army. Both supporters and opponents of the war were unwilling to pay its costs.

In spite of these almost insuperable problems Madison and Dolley revealed an outward calm. As Congressman Jonathan Roberts wrote in a letter to his brother, "The President preserves his cheerfulness wonderfully, a strong evidence of his virtue. The factious temper of the Senate is enough to cast a gloom over a mind of more than common strength. Mrs. Madison has acted with singular discreetness during a very embarrassing season. By her deportment in her own house you cannot discover who are her husband's friends or foes."

Madison was beset by problems. He had to choose his generals either from aging Revolutionary veterans or from young officers who had had no war experience. The first great source of danger was from British troops controlling the Great Lakes and lower Canada, with tribes of hostile Indians as their allies. A Detroit campaign was being forced on the government, and William Hull, with an unsurpassed Revolutionary record, was chosen to lead an army of twenty-five hundred into Canada, assuring the President that he could take his troops across the Detroit River and down the north shore of Lake Erie to the Niagara River. Congress was refusing to raise the necessary taxes, except through the painless method of taxing imports, and unfortunately there were no imports. The struggle to secure appropriations for building new ships was frustrating.

Madison's problems were not all military. He was besieged by requests to proclaim a day of public humiliation and prayer for victory. A flagrant encroachment, he believed, on freedom of religion and separation of church and state, the rights he had labored for so valiantly. Finally, so great was the demand, that on July 9, three days after Congress adjourned, he issued a proclamation, but instead of calling on the people to observe the day, he declared that he was acting in response to a request from Congress, "to enable the religious societies to offer at one and the same time, their common vows and adorations to Almighty God, on the solemn occasion produced by the war, in which he has been pleased to permit the injustice of a foreign power to involve these United States." This last was a satirical jibe at Governor Strong of Massachusetts, who had called for prayers against the war that it had "pleased the Almighty Ruler of the world to permit us to be engaged in against the nation . . . which for many generations has been the bulwark of the Religion we profess."

"I wonder," James commented acidly to Dolley, "why the Governor's Pilgrim ancestors fled from such a staunch defender of their religion!" Since he had not asked the people to pray, only suggested a day for "a voluntary concurrence of those who approved a general union on such an occasion," the proclamation satisfied his conscience.

The drab muted tones of that summer's canvas were streaked with one bright splash of color when on August 6 a large number of Indian chiefs, escorted by General William Clark, superintendent of Indian affairs in their area, arrived in Washington in full regalia, feathers, tomahawks, and even war paint, representing the friendly Sac, Fox, and Osage tribes from Missouri Territory.

"They appear to be very respectable," reported the *National Intelligencer*, "and are remarkable for their gigantic figures and fine proportion of their forms."

Since they were at war with one another, the superintendent desired the President to act as their peacemaker. He also thought the tribes might be persuaded not to yield to further seduction by the British Army.

Dolley entertained twenty-nine of the Indian guests at dinner, together with five interpreters and the whole cabinet. "We sent off our red children," she wrote young Phoebe Morris gleefully, "and had a frolic that would have delighted you."

On August 15 a large delegation of Sioux arrived, and on the seventeenth Dolley gave another dinner for these "terrific kings and princes." Later the two sets of chiefs entertained the President, his family, and cabinet with "an Indian feast, war dance and war whoop" on Greenleaf's Point, the popular Washington resort for such events.

Dutifully James tried to promote peace among them and steer them away from alliance with the British.

"My Red Children," he admonished, "you have come through a long path to see your father, but it is a straight and clean path, kept open for my red children who hate crooked walks. . . . I had heard that the nations west of the Mississippi shut their ears to the bad birds hovering about them for some time past. This made me wish to see the principal chiefs of those bands. I love to shake hands with hearts in them."

He hoped his efforts at peacemaking among more primitive peoples were more successful than those with his own warring white tribes. On August 12 news had arrived of the June action suspending the Orders in Council, but it was to be void unless the American nonintercourse act was revoked immediately. What would happen now? Did it mean hope for peace? But the nointercourse act could not be repealed until it was learned what effect the Declaration of War would have in England.

It was during this influx of Indians that Dolley had a disquieting experience. After one of her dinners, when all the guests including the Indians had presumably left and she was getting ready to retire, she looked in her mirror and saw there reflected, standing behind the door, an Indian in all his war paint. So! Her first panic dissolved into calm reasoning. Careful not to catch the intruder's eye, she walked quietly into the next room, rang a bell, and returned to her toilet as if she had noticed nothing. Presently a servant arrived, and together they somehow, without benefit of his language, persuaded the surprised and no doubt frightened visitor that he had been left behind by his comrades, become lost, and wandered by mistake into this private room. Dolley saw to it that he was guided helpfully to his lodging place.

At last! They were able to get away to Montpelier on August 28, but they did not get far. That evening, when they had reached Dumfries, they were overtaken by a hard-riding horseman. He brought bad news indeed. General William Hull had surrendered his entire army of twenty-five hundred men to the small British regiment at Detroit. He had not fired a shot.

"I must go back," James said tersely. And the next morning he was on the road to Washington.

It was Dolley who put into words his profound disgust and dismay. "Do you not tremble with resentment at this treacherous act?" she wrote Edward Coles, who was on sick leave. "Yet we must not judge the man until we are in possession of his reasons."

They soon were, and there was no disputing the treachery. Even the British general was amazed at his easy victory. "Twenty-five hundred troops have this day surrendered," he reported jubilantly to his superior, "without the sacrifice of a drop of British blood. I had not more than seven hundred troops including militia, and about six hundred Indians to accomplish this service. When I detail my good fortune Your Excellency will be astonished."

General Hull was court-martialed. His excuses that resistance was futile were obviously a cloak for cowardice and blundering inefficiency. But almost immediately after the fiasco came the heartening news that on August 19 Captain Isaac Hull, General William's bolder nephew, commander of the frigate, *Constitution,* had captured, burned, and sunk the British frigate, *Guerrière.* The country's first sea battle and an amazing triumph! The little navy of only seventeen ships had scored a victory over Britain with its thousand warships! Nor was this the end of the good news. In October six hundred miles east of Norfolk the eighteen-gun *Wasp* took as a prize the equally matched *Frolic.* The puny little David's stones leveled at the powerful sea Goliath were hitting their marks!

Dolley's satisfactions these days were not wholly from naval victories. Payne had finished his courses at Baltimore with more or less success and, postponing entrance into Princeton, was serving as James's secretary in the absence of Edward Coles. She was reveling not only in his daily presence but in his maturity and charm which were taking Washington society by storm. Heir to her Irish blue eyes and glossy black hair, he was a handsome youth, and his faultless manners as well as his position as the President's stepson made him the city's most popular and eligible bachelor. If James found his new secretary's abilities less than adequate, further curtailed by social engagements, riding, betting on the races, dallying with pretty girls all too eager to win the favor of the "crown prince," he suffered the inconveniences in silence. The war was causing Dolley enough worries these days. Not for the most perfect of secretaries would he have quelled the radiance Payne's presence brought to her eyes.

And for Dolley, pleasure in her gay, charming, if wayward son outweighed her worries. He was as devotedly attentive to her as to his young female favorites, always planning little surprises to intrigue her. Once he brought back from a trip a cage containing a huge, handsome, flamboyant bird which opened its broad beak and gave her a harsh but friendly greeting.

"Oh!" she gasped. "How beautiful! But—what is it? A—a parrot?"

"Not exactly," he replied, "though it belongs to the same family. It's a macaw. Makes a grand pet, they say. I saw it in a shop and thought you might like it."

"Oh—I do! What gorgeous colors—like sunlight and blue sky! You know how I like birds. And how all the children will love it!"

The bird became her cherished pet and the delight of both nieces and nephews and other neighborhood children who trooped to the house each day to watch her feed it. It was a bright harbinger of fun and beauty in a milieu that was becoming increasingly ominous.

The election of 1812 was bitterly contested, the campaign vicious in its innuendos. Federalists and other opponents of "Mr. Madison's War," supporting DeWitt Clinton, subjected Madison to every possible calumny, calling him "Jefferson's slave," "Napoleon's puppet," "base wretch," "coward," "weak pitiful creature," "imbecile." New England openly threatened civil war, or, worse yet, secession.

"Should Virginia persist in fastening upon the middle and eastern states the obnoxious and fatal administration of Mr. Madison," announced one article quoted in the Alexandria *Gazette,* "we may bid adieu to the Union, and prepare for the horrors of intestine commotion, civil war, and all the calamities that have desolated the old world."

Some Federalists, however, like John Adams, were strong in the President's defense, storming at their fellows for opposing a "just and necessary war." All their bluster, Adams maintained, was for the purpose of putting some weakling in his place. "I own I prefer Madison."

Dolley could almost have wished James would refuse to run, such heaven it would be to retire to the haven of Montpelier, far from the grueling uncertainties of war! But of course James was not that sort of person. Whether as student or farmer or President, he was not one to set his hand to a plow and leave another to break his furrows. He refused, however, to take any part in the campaign, remaining silent, apparently unmoved in the face of all the slanders. Only she knew how they hurt him. Not until November 4, the day after the election, before the returns were known, did he make any defense of his position, presenting in his message to Congress all his negotiations of peace with Castlereagh, America's readiness for peace after the repeal of the Orders in Council, British refusal to stop impressments during an armistice period, facts that could not have failed to influence the election in his favor. The vote when finally counted would stand: Madison 128, Clinton 89.

Dolley would have been astonished and appalled could she have known of a statement the statesman James G. Blaine would make about that election many years later. "She saved the administration of her husband, held him back from the extreme of Jeffersonism and enabled him to escape the terrible dilemma of the War of 1812."

She would have been the first to decry the very idea. How could anything she had said or done possibly have changed the course of history? She had merely seen to it that people of every class and conviction, even deadly political enemies, had a chance to share their conflicting views in an informal and, hopefully, friendly atmosphere, that Jemmy had been exposed to an interplay of the ideas and emotions activating his enemies as well as his political friends. If this had modified the rigid implementation of his convictions, made him more amenable to understanding and compromise, that was not her doing. It was the natural result of people's sitting down together and getting one another's point of view. Perhaps if she could have got that stubborn Lord Castlereagh and Jemmy at her round dinner table sharing some of her sour cream ginger cake and British tea!

During all the stress she continued calmly to conduct her drawing rooms and dinners, welcoming friends and foes with equal cordiality. Mrs. William Seaton, wife of the co-editor of the *National Intelligencer,* described one dinner she attended that November.

"William and I repaired to the palace between four and five o'clock. . . . It is customary, on whatever occasion, to advance to the upper end of the room, pay your obeisance to Mrs. Madison, courtesy to his Highness, and take a seat. . . . Mrs. Madison very handsomely came to me and led me nearest the fire . . . by her own ease of manner making her guests feel at home. . . . When dinner was announced Mrs. Magruder, by priority of age, was entitled to the right hand of her Hostess; and I in virtue of being a stranger, to the next seat. . . . The dinner was certainly very fine; there were many French dishes, and exquisite wines. During the desserts ice-cream, macaroons, preserves, and various cakes are placed on the table, which are removed for almonds, raisins, pecan nuts, apples, pears, etc. . . . I would describe the dignified appearance of Mrs. Madison, but I could not do her justice. 'Tis not her form, 'tis not her face, it is the woman altogether. She wears a crimson cap that almost hides her forehead, but which becomes her extremely, and reminds one of a crown from its brilliant appearance, contrasted with the white satin folds and her jet black curls; but her demeanor is so far removed from the hauteur generally attendant on royalty, that your fancy can carry the resemblance no further than the headdress."

The American Navy, that puny David, continued its startling stone throwings at the British Goliath. In late November Dolley set off with her houseguests for a naval ball at Tomlinson's Hotel in honor of Captains Hull, Morris, aud Steward over their victories at sea. They rode past brightly illuminated houses and wildly cheering crowds, for at five o'clock that very day an extra had announced the capture by the frigate, *United States,* captained by Stephen Decatur, of the British frigate, *Macedonian* west of the Canary Islands, bringing it back to Rhode Island. It was an astounding victory, for the *Macedonian* was new, the largest frigate in the British Navy, faster than the *United States,* its oak timbers far stronger than the American's fir. If America was joyously astounded, Britain when she heard was scandalized, enraged. "In the name of God," demanded the London *Times,* "what is being done with a naval strength between Halifax and the West Indies seven times as great as the entire United States Navy?"

The naval ball was a triumph for Dolley as well as the victorious captains. During the course of the evening Lieutenant Hamilton, son of the Secretary of the Navy, brought the official dispatches telling of the victory to Madison, who had remained at home to work. From there he hastened to Tomlinson's Hotel bearing the captured *Macedonian*'s standards and flag. Assisted by captains holding the four corners of the flag, he paraded it around the room to the tune of *Yankee Doodle,* then laid it at the feet of Dolley. The crowd went wild. Though she received the honor with gracious calm, Dolley felt her cheeks flaming, thereby eliciting an interesting comment in the diary of that same Mrs. William Seaton.

"Mrs. Madison," she wrote, "is said to rouge; but it was not evident to my eyes, and I do not think it true, as I am well assured I saw her color come and go at the naval ball when the flag of the *Macedonian* was presented to her by young Hamilton."

New Year's Day, 1813. The White House was opened to all, and even Federalists came in droves. There was a dense crowd, its noise almost drowning out the music of the marine band in the anteroom. Dolley looked very queenly in a rose-colored satin gown trimmed with ermine, her turban—always a turban!—fastened by a crescent out of which towered white ostrich plumes. Surely, she thought, this new year held more hope and promise of peace than had the old! If only this second term could be smooth and serene without all the bickering and fighting of the first!

But at first the year brought few signs of serenity or peace. The old whispering campaign against Dolley was not only revived but put into scurrilous print by certain editors who, without mentioning names, tried to exploit by innuendo the theme of "sexual infidelity in the wife of an allegedly impotent husband," with the implication that "where there is smoke there must be fire," an attempt that inspired the eminent Charles Carroll of Carrolton to write, "The attack on Mrs. Madison is very reprehensible and the calumny unfounded."

Dolley was annoyed, of course, but realized that such slanders were merely an underhanded means of attacking her much maligned husband. She was far more distressed when news came in mid-February that Joel Barlow, American minister to France, who had been summoned by Napoleon to meet him in Poland to discuss mounting tensions between the two countries, had died tragically at Cracow of inflammation of the lungs. It brought deep sorrow, for both of the Barlows were close personal friends. James was both grieved and incensed.

"The idea," he fumed, "of making the ambassador take a painful journey of twelve hundred leagues to accomplish nothing!"

Dolley found it hard to express congratulations to French minister Sérurier over the safe return of the emperor Napoleon to Paris after his unfortunate attempt to extend his ruthless conquests into Russia. How could she rejoice at the safety of the despot responsible for their dear friend's death!

James insisted that his second inaugural be simpler than the first. No guests were invited, but of course he could not prevent half the city of Washington from attending. He merely put his hand on the Bible and swore to uphold the Constitution. Though Federalists claimed that he looked thin and harassed, his inaugural address revealed the firm confidence of the commander in chief in the struggle he had undertaken.

"As the war was just in its origin, and necessary and noble in its objects, we can reflect with proud satisfaction that, in carrying it on, no principle of justice or honor, no usage of civilized nations, no precept of courtesy or humanity has been infringed. . . ."

However, as Mrs. Seaton recorded, "the chief Magistrate's voice was so low and the audience so very great, that scarcely a word could be distinguished. The little man was accompanied on his return to the palace by the multitude, for every creature that could afford twenty-five cents for hack-fare was present. The major part of the respectable citizens offered their congratulations, ate his ice-cream and bon-bons, drank his Madeira, made their bow and retired, leaving him fatigued beyond measure with the incessant bending to which his politeness urged him, and in which he never allows himself to be eclipsed, returning bow for bow, even to those *ad infinitum* of Sérurier and other foreigners."

Dolley wished she could spare him the wearying formality of the inaugural ball at Davis's Hotel, where there was "a most lively assemblage of the lovely ones of our district," a triviality he found especially distasteful in the present crises. At least, standing by his side, she could protect him from those trying to embroil him in political dispute. She was adept at guiding conversation away from controversial issues.

Just as James entered on his second term, there was sudden hope of peace. Emperor Alexander of Russia offered his services to mediate a settlement between Great Britain and America. Federalists immediately dubbed it a hoax. They would rather wreck a peace proposal than have it result in peace with benefit both to the country and the party in power. But it was not a hoax. Madison, declaring that Russia was "the only power in Europe which can command respect from both France and England," appointed peace commissioners to Russia to act with the American envoy there, John Quincy Adams. He proposed moderate terms for a settlement, chiefly security from impressments and evacuation of all American territory still occupied by the British. Albert Gallatin, Secretary of the Treasury, was appointed as the best possible man in finance and diplomacy. In order to make it bipartisan, James A. Bayard, a Federalist, was chosen as the third member of the team.

Dolley heartily rejoiced in all these developments until suddenly James made a startling proposal. "What would you say, my dear, if Payne were made a member of the team as an attaché to Gallatin?"

She gasped. Her Payne crossing the ocean, that vast expanse fraught with danger from battleships and sinking vessels, to encounter nobody knew what evils on a strange continent beset by war and chicanery and—yes, perhaps even worse, insidious temptations? But—what an opportunity for him! Exposure to all the culture, history, art of the

Old World—and if he had one absorbing interest besides horses and racing and—yes, gambling, it was art! He was rebelling against going to Princeton. Perhaps if—*when* he returned, he would have grown up and would feel the need of more education. She must not deprive him of enriching experience just because of her own selfish fears and wishes.

"Yes," she said calmly. "It will be a fine thing for him to do."

He sailed with Gallatin in May, bound for St. Petersburg with all expenses paid by the Russian government, his vanity tickled by a decoration conferred on him by the same.

"I suppose," commented James wryly, "they think he's the nearest thing to an American czarevitch!" An inauspicious beginning, they both wondered, for the process of growing up?

His absence meant a new career for Dolley. Edward Coles was still ill in Philadelphia, being treated by Dr. Physick for a tumor that had returned on the scar from a previous operation. Though he wanted to resign as Madison's secretary, James would not hear of it. Meanwhile Dolley took over some of his secretarial work. It was not too difficult, mostly letter writing, some of it to Ned Coles, keeping him posted on all developments in Washington.

And they were neither few nor encouraging. That spring Admiral Sir George Cockburn (pronounced Co'-burn) began ravaging towns all along Chesapeake Bay, burning, pillaging, carrying off hostages. After destroying Havre de Grace and other towns above Annapolis, he was suddenly threatening to despoil Washington. He intended, he stated brashly, to "make his bow at Dolley Madison's drawing room before burning the White House and other government buildings."

"No danger," scoffed Secretary of War Armstrong. "The British have no land troops or artillery. The city is perfectly safe."

But others, including Madison, were not so sure. He sent two regiments to Norfolk and ordered Governor Winder of Maryland to strengthen Fort McHenry, at Baltimore, with forces of his state militia.

Hearing of the brutal depradations of this marauding Cockburn, who was stealing horses, cattle, pigs, carrying off slaves, burning houses, Dolley felt history repeating itself. It was Bloody Tarleton, the Butcher, all over again, sweeping through Virginia with his Hessian "savages." In vivid memory she crouched once more beside Isaac in the hedge, watching the red tide sweep up the hill, heard the clatter of horse's hoofs as the arrogant leader rode up the steps of Scotchtown. But her calmness of mien betrayed no hint of such emotion.

"If I could," she wrote Coles on May 12, "I would describe to you the fears and alarms that circulate around me. For the week all the city and Georgetown have expected a visit from the enemy, and were not lacking in their expressions of terror and reproach. Yesterday an express announced the pause of a frigate at the mouth of the Potomac. . . . We are making considerable efforts for defense. . . . The fort is being repaired and five hundred militia, with perhaps as many regulars, are to be stationed on the Green near the windmill. The twenty tents already look well in my eyes, who have always been an advocate of fighting when assailed, though a Quaker. I therefore keep the old Tunisian sabre within reach." Silly old relic! Had it come with that heavily bearded and retinued Mellimelli, a gift to the Secretary of State? Whatever had happened, she wondered, to his present to her, that red velvet caftan weighted with gold bullion and the twenty-yard white turban? The gold, of course, had gone to the State Department to help defray the emissary's huge hotel bill. Funny the things one suddenly remembered!

"One of our generals," she continued her letter to Ned, "has discovered a plan of the British; it is to land as many chosen rogues as they can about fourteen miles below Alexandria, in the night, so that they may be on hand to burn the President's house and offices. I do not tremble at this but feel hurt that the Admiral (of Havre de Grace memory) should send me word that he would make his bow at my drawing room very soon."

In spite of her interest in and knowledge of all these political developments, Dolley, as always, was careful not to participate actively in official decision making. Certainly in their discussions together she spoke her mind freely, and James always respected her opinions. But she seldom attempted to influence him. Many times during the presidency she had been approached by friends and even by strangers begging her to intercede in their behalf, for appointments, for special privileges, but, while dutifully relaying such requests to her husband, she had refrained from urging any specific action.

For instance, there was the letter she had received from Theodosia Burr Alston back in the early days of the presidency, begging her to intercede with the President to permit her father to be reinstated as an American citizen after his trial for treason. One day Burr himself had surreptitiously approached her, leaping over the low fence enclosing the grounds when she was out watering roses. As he had argued with her, reminding her of their past friendship, she had silently and seriously listened. But she had given him no encouragement and had refused to even present his case to the President.

Only once could she be accused of really interfering. During the war the son of her old friend from childhood Quaker days, Debbie Pleasants, had refused military service as a conscientious objector and been imprisoned. When Dolley heard about it, she begged James to intervene in his behalf.

"My dear—I'm sorry, of course, but that is really the prerogative of the military—"

"Of which you are the Commander in Chief," returned Dolley swiftly. Though she continued quietly, her blue eyes shot sparks of challenge. "He is a Quaker, you know, and his 'inner light,' that which is God within him, tells him that it is wrong to fight and kill, just as it did my father. Tell me, isn't he practicing the religious freedom which you worked so hard to put into that first amendment of our Constitution?"

Debbie Pleasants's son was released from prison.

Dolley soon had more personal worries. James became severely sick with his old malarial fever, and she was obliged to cancel her usual drawing rooms and other social activities to nurse him. Even the war and possible attack paled into insignificance while his life hung in the balance. And she was not the only one to be deeply concerned. On June 21 Sérurier wrote the Duke de Bassano, the French foreign minister, "The thought of his possible loss strikes everybody with consternation. It is certainly true that his death, in the circumstances in which the Republic is placed, would be a veritable calamity. The President who would succeed him is a respectable old man, but weak and worn out. All good Americans pray for the recovery of Mr. Madison."

On July 2 Dolley wrote Edward Coles, "For the last three days his fever has been so slight as to permit him to take bark every hour and with good effect. It has been three weeks since I have nursed him night and day. Sometimes I despair; but now that I see he will get well, I feel as if I should die myself from fatigue."

Even from his sick bed, however, James had carried on the country's business, dictating to Dolley, combating the Senate's refusal to ratify his nomination of Gallatin for the peace commission as long as he remained Secretary of the Treasury. She, as well as James, bore the brunt of the problem. "You can have no idea," she wrote Mrs. Gallatin on July 29, "of its extent and the despair in which I attended his bed for nearly five weeks!" And retarding his convalescence were "the disappointments and vexations heaped upon him by party spirit. Nothing however has borne so hard as the conduct of the Senate in regard to Mr. Gallatin."

It was the beginning of a long struggle between the executive and legislative branches of government as interpreted by the Constitution, between an Executive who regarded the Senate, in relation to appointments, as "a Council only to the President," and a Senate who regarded itself as the "greatest power in the Constitution." Even from his sickbed Madison had halted the most ambitious attempt yet made to make the President subordinate to the Senate in their mutual activities.

The attack on Washington had not come, and the war seemed to be at a stalemate. At last in August they were able to get away to the mountains. "I concluded my journey early on the fourth day after I left Washington," James wrote. "I gained strength on the road, notwithstanding its badness." By the end of August he reported his health "greatly advanced towards its usual standard." But he needed another month on the mountains, Dolley insisted. She barely had time to write because of "the crowd of company with which our house has been filled ever since our return to it."

Nothing had been heard from the peace commissioners, but a galloping messenger brought good news on September 23. The dispatch was from Master Commandant Oliver Perry, who had engaged the British in battle on Lake Erie. He had written, "It has pleased the Almighty to give to the arms of the United States a signal victory over their enemies on this lake. The British squadron, consisting of two ships, two brigs, one schooner and one sloop, have this moment surrendered to the force under my command after a sharp conflict."

The message would later go down in history in simpler words. "We have met the enemy and they are ours."

This triumph, commented John Adams, was enough to revive Mr. Madison if he was in the last stage of consumption. Nothing like it had been seen since the surrender of Lord Cornwallis.

Was it really the beginning of the end? wondered Dolley, almost more thankful for the healthy sparkle in Jemmy's eyes than for the military victory. She had felt that this year of 1813 held hope and promise. Surely this distressing war would be over before its end!

She could not have been more wrong.

4

1814. Another New Year's reception. This time it held even more hope and promise than the preceding one. For just the day before, the British dispatch schooner *Bramble* had brought news not only of Napoleon's decisive defeat in mid-October, but, more encouragingly, a dispatch "rather of a pacific character" from Lord Castlereagh. Though Britain had rejected the offer of Russian mediation, she was suggesting direct negotiation.

Before going down to the assembled guests Dolley gave herself a last sober appraisal in the pier glass. She could picture the crowd waiting below, the gentlemen in their crimson waistcoats and laces, the women in flowers, feathers, gloves, and towering headdresses. Were the ostrich plumes on her new white satin and velvet turban too high, would they make her look taller than the slender, black-clad figure beside her? She hoped not. That was one reason she chose turbans, which did not accentuate her height. She was glad that the new gown from France, a soft satin in her favorite pink color, suggested the rosy promise of hope, springtime in winter. And the winter had been long indeed with the war dragging on depressingly, more defeats than victories, through its second full year.

"You look beautiful, my dear."

She turned eagerly. It was all she needed, ever, that relaxing of his tense features, the brightening of his tired, worried eyes. She was ready to go down now, to take her place by his side, to beam and smile, to act as if this year must bring the hope of peace to fulfillment.

Early in the year Madison reappointed the peace commission, this time to deal directly with Britain. It included the former members, James Bayard and John Quincy Adams. Unfortunately the Senate had not confirmed Albert Gallatin, insisting that he could not act as commissioner and retain his office as Secretary of the Treasury. In his place Madison appointed Henry Clay, arousing alarm in hard-line Federalists who feared he would take too harsh a stance in dealing with England. Jonathan Russell, who became also the new minister to Sweden, completed the peace commission. Now there was nothing to do but wait.

Dolley anxiously scanned every letter and dispatch from Europe, as avid for news of Payne as of the commission's activities. Most of the details she would learn much later. It seemed that he was making great progress socially if not in other areas. In St. Petersburg he had been treated almost like royalty, a "crown prince," so to speak, in a country unused to the standards of democracy. He was invited to attend grand balls from which most Americans were excluded. While his superior, Gallatin, sat in the gallery watching proceedings, Payne had danced with ladies of the court at elegant parties. From July on through the summer of 1813 the commission had marked time in Russia, waiting vainly for the return of the Czar, who had gone off to fight Napoleon. Late in October he had still been absent, leaving the prospect of his intervention for peace in limbo. Still in Russia, Payne had joined a jubilant throng gathered for a Te Deum at Kazan Cathedral to celebrate the final defeat of Napoleon at Leipzig.

Then had come the news that Britain, rejecting Russian mediation, had proposed direct negotiation, with Göteborg, Sweden, chosen by Madison as the meeting place. Later the site would be changed to Ghent in Belgium. The commission had left Russia, hoping to join with British negotiators at Göteborg.

Surely, thought Dolley, now that Gallatin was expected home to resume his position as Secretary of the Treasury, Payne would be coming soon! But in January Mrs. Gallatin received a letter from her husband saying that he might spend the winter in Europe. Then, according to a subsequent letter, Payne had left St. Petersburg for Göteborg ahead of Gallatin, going by way of Copenhagen. Why? Knowing her son's yen for adventure, Dolley could only guess.

"I am distressed at Payne's leaving Mr. Gallatin," she wrote Hannah, his wife. "What could have led him to do so? Nothing but anxiety to get home, I hope."

She hoped wrong. He apparently had no strong desire except to extend his social triumphs to as many European spheres as possible. But when she received word from Mrs. Gallatin that from Göteborg he had gone on a visit to Paris and would rejoin her husband in three weeks, in spite of her worry she was mollified because "my precious Payne's going to France" with all its many advantages of art and culture.

James sympathized with her concern over Payne, but he could do little to allay her anxiety. And he was burdened with far greater worries. The prospect of peace negotiations did not mean that the war was over, or even retarded. Indeed, the defeat of Napoleon and his abdication, ending her war with France, had only intensified Britain's thirst for "punishment of America," and she was now free to expend all her energies in that direction. The British were strengthening forces not only in the lake area to the north but also along the coast. Word came that a new commander, Admiral Sir Alexander Cochrane, was on his way to American waters, proclaiming from Bermuda a naval blockade from Maine to the Mississippi. Madison was struggling with new untried young generals and a weak cabinet. His Secretary of War, General John Armstrong, was especially difficult and perverse. He made plans for unwise military engagements in the northern area without consulting his commander in chief. He promised promotions in his own name to gain credit if they materialized or blame for the President if they did not. He was weak and vacillating in carrying out Madison's suggestions for the protection of the eastern seaboard, especially of Washington. Still James hesitated to replace him. It would be like changing horses in the middle of a tumultuous stream.

No news came from the peace commission.

"The more I see of the complexion of the late events and projects in Europe," he commented dubiously, "the less ground remains for sanguine expectations for the peace commission." Though at first he did not share his fears with Dolley, the ruthlessness of the proclamations of Cochrane convinced him that a more intense phase of the war was in prospect, culminating possibly in a devastating attack on Washington itself. Finally, on May 24, he made this fear public. But no one in his cabinet agreed with him. Armstrong again scoffed at the idea. Navy Secretary Jones thought other points "more inviting to the enemy."

Some Washingtonians, however, were alarmed. Admiral Cockburn's forces were still at the mouth of the Chesapeake, marauding, burning, despoiling. Confidence in Armstrong was declining. A committee headed by Mayor Blake complained about the city's "defenseless state."

Though the British had no important land forces in Chesapeake Bay, Madison forced his cabinet on July 1 to consider the defense of Washington. Brigadier General William Winder was charged with the defense of Maryland, the District of Columbia, and Virginia's northern neck. But all of Winder's attempts to increase the military strength for Washington met with only half hearted approval by Armstrong.

In spite of the prevailing mood of anxiety Dolley pursued her usual routine. On July 4, as customary, she presided at the reception at the White House. A young girl visiting from New England later described her impressions of the First Lady on that day.

"I can see her now. As we entered she was crossing the crowded vestibule, conducted by two fair girls, one on each side. Where they were conducting her I do not know, but she had evidently surrendered to their sprightly guidance with her usual benignant sweetness. She stopped to receive our greetings, and that gave me time to admire the tasteful simplicity of her dress. White—but of what material I forget. Her hair hung in ringlets on each side of her face, surmounted by the snowy folds of her unvarying turban, ornamented on one side by a few heads of green wheat. She may have worn jewels, but if she did they were so eclipsed by her inherent charms as to be unnoticed."

But Dolley was not as immune to anxiety as she seemed. "Such a place as this has become!" she wrote Mrs. Gallatin. "Among other exclamations and threats they [the British] say that if Mr. Madison attempts to move from this house in case of attack they will stop him and that he shall fall with it. I am not the least alarmed at these things, but entirely disgusted and determined to stay with him."

August. Would they get to Montpelier that summer? The brief month they had been able to escape in April and May seemed but a dim memory. The farm needed attention. He could not say, James wrote his eighty-two-year-old mother, when they would be able to make the usual visit, but certainly it would be as soon as possible. "Dolley as well as myself is in good health," he assured her. No mean boast, for the malarial season in still marshy Washington was at hand.

The war had intensified as Madison had expected. Britain's pacific offer of negotiation so hopefully accepted had been empty words. Conquest of Napoleon had left her free to concentrate on America, and public opinion waxed hot. Her erstwhile child must be severely punished for insubordination. Grimly James contemplated the ultimatum delivered by Parliament. "Vigorous war with America! We repeat— vigorous war!" Until America agreed to certain conditions there could be no peace. These were appalling. They included new boundaries with Canada, banning all trade with the West Indies, exclusion from fishing rights on the Grand Banks, resigning all claim to the Spanish-owned Floridas, cession of New Orleans to Britain to give her full

access to the Mississippi, and other impossible demands. And the arrival on August 17 of a British fleet of warships, fifty-one vessels, at
the mouth of the Patuxent River just below Benedict, was evidence of
deadly purpose.

James's warning of a month earlier that Washington was in danger
became suddenly dire possibility. Remembering the depradation of
"Cockburn the marauder" along the coast, the more timorous inhabitants were terrified, and many fled the city.

General Winder was encountering annoying and unnecessary delays
in his belated attempts to rear fortifications and provide troops for the
city's defense.

"Oh yes," replied Secretary Armstrong when the general warned him
that the enemy's strength must mean serious attack. "Oh yes, they would
not come with such a fleet without meaning to strike somewhere, but they
certainly will not come here. What the devil would they do here?" Baltimore, he believed, would be their goal. It was of much more
consequence.

Madison, Secretary of State Monroe, and Winder took matters into
their own hands, regardless of Armstrong's lassitude. On August 20
Winder ordered two Baltimore regiments to Washington. Militia cavalry were sent to block the roads to Benedict by felling trees. But the
latter measure was too late. That evening Madison received word that
the British had landed at Benedict. Movement against Washington
seemed assured. Yet even when under Madison's orders papers of all
government offices were being moved to safety, Armstrong observed
that he thought they were acting under unnecessary alarm.

Sunday, August 21. Monroe, who had ridden out to investigate the
enemy's movements, reported them advancing both in barges up the
river and by road. The marching columns were estimated as four
thousand with one thousand more in the barges.

The city was in turmoil. People were pouring out in every sort of
conveyance. No church attendance this morning! And Dolley missed
it. She needed all the spiritual succor available to keep a calm head
above the tense fear attempting to paralyze her body. She must not
bother James with questions or demands. At least Anna was close by,
living in the house she and James had once occupied during Jefferson's
administration, just a little distance away on F Street. Though disaf-
fections in New England had caused Richard Cutts to lose his seat in
Congress, Madison had appointed him Superintendent of Military
Supplies, and his family was still in Washington. Summoning her car-

riage and taking with her only her maid, Sukey, Dolley started for the Cutts's house.

The streets were clogged with carriages, carts, and drays piled high with personal possessions of fleeing inhabitants. As her driver halted at the gate, waiting for a chance to join the moving stream, another carriage stopped just in front of them, and a woman, whom Dolley recognized as the wife of one of James's bitterest Federalist opponents, stood up and loosened her hair, which was long and beautiful. Dolley had often admired it.

"You!" the woman cried in a voice clearly audible above the clatter of traffic. "See this hair of mine? I would pray that I might part with it if it could be used to hang Mr. Madison!"

Her carriage moved on, and Dolley's driver was finally able to move forward into F Street.

"It's all right," Dolley quieted the shocked and terrified Sukey. "She didn't really mean it. People say strange things when they're frightened."

She found Anna's house also in upheaval, for the family was packing. "Richard insists that we leave," her sister announced unhappily. "I don't want to. I can't bear to think of you here without us. But—"

"Of course you must go," agreed Dolley, hoping her dismay was not evident. "You must think of the children, and especially the one to come." Richard had arranged for them to go to their friends the Forrests in Maryland.

Dolley returned home to find James gone for another conference with his cabinet. The house, usually so bustling with activity, seemed empty and bereft of life. Never had she felt more lonely or vulnerable.

Monday, August 22. A report arrived from Monroe from Winder's headquarters, "the Woodyard." The enemy had entered Nottingham, halfway between Benedict and Washington. James was not too alarmed. He thought it strange that, if their force was not greater than it seemed, they should venture so far from their ships. "But they might be counting on their speed and our want of precaution," he admitted, "to take a grave risk."

"Tell me, my dear," he said anxiously to Dolley, "do you have the courage, or perhaps I should say the firmness, to stay here until I return tomorrow, or even the next day? I feel I must go and see what is happening."

Dolley drew a long breath. "Of course," she returned calmly. "I have no fear except for you and the fate of our country."

"Then take care of yourself." In his effort to stifle emotion his voice sounded almost curt. "And guard all the cabinet papers, public and private."

There was no lack of emotion in his long, almost suffocating embrace. Then he was gone.

She went with him in thought which was nearly visual, east from the Navy Yard bridge, to Long Old Fields, nine miles from Washington, where Winder was stationed. Far more concerned for his welfare than for her own precarious situation, she knew the anomaly of the pressures he was undergoing, and her heart ached for him. A scholar, an able administrator, a statesman, a man of peace, but certainly no military expert, what irony of fate for him to be thrust into this impossible role of commander in chief!

Late that afternoon Sérurier wrote of the day's events as they appeared to him. "It was learned with fright this morning that the English had left their ships and advanced boldly overland on Washington. The inhabitants are fleeing in wild disorder, the roads are covered with them. The President has gone to the camp to encourage, by his presence, the army to defend the capital. It appears that the idea of fighting the English in the field has been rightfully abandoned, in view of the poor quality of the troops, and that they will limit themselves to disputing the crossing of the Eastern Branch at Bladensburg, six miles from the capital."

Meanwhile in the State and War offices Clerk Stephen Pleasonton was packing books and papers into linen bags. These included valuable documents, the Declaration of Independence, correspondence of General Washington, laws, treaties, diplomatic correspondence. They were to be conveyed in carts and wagons to Leesburg, some thirty-five miles west of Washington, and stored in a safe spot.

Wednesday. August 23. Dolley received a note from James, somewhat allaying her fears.

"My dearest. I have passed the forenoon among the troops who are in high spirits and make a good appearance. The reports of the enemy have varied every hour. The last and truest information is that they are not very strong, and are without cavalry or artillery, and of course they are in no condition to strike at Washington."

But a second penciled note was far less hopeful. Dolley's mood changed from hope to apprehension, arousing frantic action.

"The last is alarming," she wrote hastily to her sister Lucy, "because he desires that I should be ready at a moment's warning to enter my carriage and leave the city; that the enemy seemed stronger than had been reported, and that it might happen that they would reach the city with the intention to destroy it. . . . I am accordingly ready; I have pressed as many cabinet papers into trunks as to fill one carriage; our private property must be sacrificed, as it is impossible to procure wagons for its transportation. I am determined not to go myself until I see Mr. Madison safe, and he can accompany me—as I hear of much hostility towards him. . . . Disaffection stalks around us."

To Dolley's vast relief James came home that evening, but she saw little of him. He was rushing about holding conferences, making frantic last minute attempts to defend the capital. Armstrong, forced at last to admit his negligence and fearing for his reputation, was doing his best to improve his image, even predating an order to bring a regiment to Washington "with the utmost dispatch." At nine o'clock General Winder came to the White House. He had brought his poorly equipped army on the run to the city and was camping near the Navy Yard. His Baltimore brigade, already worn out with marching, he had sent back to Bladensburg.

Able finally to get her weary and distraught husband to sleep, Dolley was forced to wake him at midnight when a messenger brought a note from Monroe. "The enemy are in full march for Washington. Have the materials prepared to destroy bridges. You had better remove the records."

He would have gone out again to accost Armstrong with the emergency, but she persuaded him to send the note to him instead. "Come, love, there's nothing you can do before morning. The records are already attended to. Please—try to get a little rest."

Finally he fell into a troubled sleep, while she lay, taut and wide-awake, beside him, ears tensed for the sound of—what? Guns? Battle cries? Screaming shells? But there were only the muffled beat of hoofs, the dull clatter of wheels as more and more carriages bore their terrified exiles from the city. Did she sense somehow that it was the last night they would ever spend in the White House?

Wednesday, August 24. The sun rose blazing like a red-hot coal, presaging stagnant heat. Before noon the thermometer would climb far past ninety. When James embraced her before leaving again, she tried not to show her fear by clinging to him. "Where?" He did not know. To General Winder first at his headquarters at the Navy Yard. He had had word that Secretary Jones would be there, waiting for counsel, and—his lip curled—hopefully, Armstrong. Then he would probably go to Bladensburg where the first attack was likely to come. His presence might at least give courage to the troops. He hoped to be back by three for the dinner to which the cabinet and other guests had been invited. He smiled bleakly. By that time perhaps there would be good news.

Seeing him ride away on his horse, a brave but defenseless little figure haloed by a cloud of dust, hearing the hoofbeats die away, merge into the dull sounds of other traffic, Dolley wondered if she would ever see him again.

Fortunately there were things to do, the dinner to be ordered in case it could ever take place, more papers and other valuables to be packed. . . . But she spent much of the morning watching through a spyglass from the window of her sitting room. There was little to be seen, only the conveyances relentlessly moving half-hidden in dust, groups of soldiers seeming to be roving about haphazardly. Toward noon, to pass the time of interminable waiting, she sat again at her desk and tried to chronicle the events for Lucy.

The letter she had started yesterday lay unfinished, its last sentence echoing her present mood. "My friends and acquaintances are all gone, even Colonel C. with his hundred, who were stationed as a guard of this inclosure. French John with his usual activity and resolution offers to spike the cannon at the gate and lay a train of powder which would blow up the British should they enter the house. To the last proposition I positively object, without being able to make him understand why all advantages in war may not be taken."

Except for the faithful Sióussat, her maid, Sukey, Paul Jennings, Madison's fifteen-year-old mulatto servant, a cook, gardener, and coachman, she was alone. She took up her pen and with a steady hand began to write.

"Wednesday morning, twelve o'clock.—Since sunrise I have been turning my spyglass in every direction, and watching with unwearied anxiety, hoping to discover the approach of my dear husband and his friends; but, alas! I can descry only groups of military, wandering in all directions, as if there was a lack of arms, or of spirit to fight for their own fireside."

The heat was stifling. Already the thermometer was well above ninety. The long gray, high-necked Quaker dress which she always wore in the morning clung to her body. Even her pet macaw in the cage above her head was feeling the heat, or somehow sensing the tension, for he was moving from perch to perch and making raucous sounds of protest.

"Poor bird," she murmured. "I believe you're worried about him, too, wondering where he is."

Suddenly he cocked his head as if listening, blue-and-yellow feathers puffed, strong beak upraised. Were his ears attuned to sounds she could not hear—guns, perhaps? She moved again to the window and in spite of the heat and dust, flung it open. Yes, she could hear it, definitely the sound of cannon. How far away would it be? If six miles, that could mean fighting at Bladensburg.

So . . . it had started. As if she had heard a trumpet call, she was roused to action. Whatever happened, there were things to do to make ready. If there was victory, they might be back to dinner. If not . . .

In the dining room, as if it were an ordinary day, Paul Jennings was laying the places for dinner for the number of guests invited. Already he had brought up the Madeira and other wines from the cellar and placed them in the silver coolers. But it was not an ordinary day. Even if the cannon portended victory, she knew there would be no big company dinner. Already some of the prospective guests had sent their regrets, like Mrs. Jones, wife of the Secretary of the Navy. "In the present state of alarm and bustle of preparation for the worst that may happen, I imagine it will be more convenient to dispense with the enjoyment of your hospitality."

"Take off most of the place settings, Paul," Dolley ordered abruptly. "Leave only enough for the President and any men he may bring with him. And pack the best silver in bags, also the rest of the plate. If we need it later, we can always bring it back."

Suddenly everything seemed to be happening at once. Mrs. George Campbell, wife of the acting Secretary of the Treasury, came, bonnet awry, out of breath as if she had been running.

"Really, my dear Mrs. Madison, you must not stay here. You're in grave danger. We all are. I just heard from an official in the War Department that—that the British will be here in two hours. I have a carriage outside. Please—come with me."

Dolley thanked her for her concern but said she could not go now. She was waiting to hear from her husband. If the city was really in danger, he would come or at least let her know what to do.

Mrs. Campbell was followed by others, Mayor James Blake and Charles Carroll of Bellevue, their very good friend, all bringing warnings, urging her to go, and to her annoyance Carroll insisted on staying until she followed his advice. "Not until my husband returns," she told him firmly, "or until I receive a message from him."

But she proceeded with preparations to leave. French John had managed to procure a wagon large enough to hold the boxes of papers she had so carefully packed, but there was room for little more. The silver, of course. The house was so full of treasures, things she and Latrobe had so lovingly picked. Those beautiful crimson velvet curtains in the oval drawing room, the ones Latrobe had considered too gaudy! A woman's foolish whim, probably, but they would take up little room, perhaps even protect the silver and papers. She told French John to take them down and stood watching while he climbed a ladder and did so, then helped him fold them carefully and pack them in the bags of silverware. And a little French clock of cloisonné which she treasured. There was room for that too.

A clatter of hoofs sent her running to the nearest window. James? Oh, let it be James! It was James, yes, but another one, James Smith, a free black man who had accompanied the President this morning. Seeing her, he waved his hat. "Clear out! Clear out!" he cried. "General Armstrong has ordered a retreat!" Without further explanation he wheeled his horse and rode away, shouting the news as he went.

The city burst into fresh pandemonium. As if most of its eight thousand inhabitants had not presumably left, the streets became even more clogged with traffic, carts, carriages, people running, soldiers no longer straggling and milling about but moving with obvious purpose, with seeming intent to put as much distance as possible between themselves and whatever military action was taking place. Cowards, she thought; then she irrationally hoped that she might see Jemmy running with them.

"Mrs. Madison, I must insist . . ."

"Thank you, Colonel Carroll. Just a little longer—please."

Not until two messengers came, horses sweating, clothes and faces grimed with dust, did the exigency finally penetrate. They brought word from James. She must leave at once.

"Yes," she assured the importunate Carroll, now fuming with impatience.

Still she hesitated. Something seemed to tug at her attention. She felt as if she had forgotten something. She wandered as if by instinct into the state dining room, where the table was still half-laid. Of course. There it was on the wall, the portrait of General Washington, the fine one by Stuart that the government had purchased back in

1800! There he stood, the instrument and symbol of the country's freedom, hand outstretched over the table bearing that sacred document, the Declaration of Independence. It must not be left for the British to find, gloat over, perhaps desecrate. She went to it, seized the frame in both hands. It was fastened to the wall, would not move. Impossible to get the thing carried to safety.

Swiftly she gave orders to the faithful John Sióussat. It would take too long to unscrew the portrait from the wall. And, besides, the frame was incredibly heavy. He was to get Tom Magraw, the gardener, to help him. They must cut it from the frame.

"My dear Mrs. Madison!" Charles Carroll was frantic in his insistence. "You must come. Your carriage is waiting. I can't vouch for your safety if you wait longer."

"Yes, yes," she agreed. "Please be patient. Just a few more minutes."

While the two men were removing the picture she returned to her sitting room and, perversely, still hoping for James to return, sat down again at her desk. It was madness, perhaps, to continue with the unfinished letter, but she would not leave until assured that the picture was safe.

"Three o'clock.—Will you believe it, my sister? We have had a battle, or skirmish, near Bladensburg, and here I am still, within sound of the cannon! Mr. Madison comes not. May God protect us! Two messengers, covered with dust, come to bid me fly; but here I mean to wait for him. . . . At this late hour a wagon has been procured, and I have had it filled with plate and the most valuable portable articles belonging to the house. Whether it will reach its destination, the 'Bank of Maryland', or fall into the hands of British soldiery, events must determine. Our kind friend, Mr. Carroll, has come to hasten my departure, and in a very bad humor with me, because I insist on waiting until the large picture of General Washington is secured, and it requires to be unscrewed from the wall. This process was found too tedious for these perilous moments; I have ordered the frame to be broken, and the canvas taken out."

She ran back to the dining room. The picture was there, out of its frame, lying on the floor. Charles Carroll had been busy. Going outside, he had found two men passing in a carriage, a Mr. Jacob Barker and a Mr. Robert Depeyster, a Quaker banker who had helped the government financially during the war, and had brought them in.

They had agreed to take the picture to safety. Still hoping James would come, she returned to her letter.

"It is done, and the precious portrait placed in the hands of two gentlemen from New York, for safe keeping. And now, dear sister, I must leave this house, or the retreating army will make me a prisoner in it by filling up the road I am directed to take. When I shall again write to you, or where I shall be tomorrow, I cannot tell. Dolley."

Picking up the sheets of foolscap, she thrust them into her reticule. Then, without a backward look, head held high, Charles Carroll guiding her, her little maid, Sukey, following, she left the house and entered her waiting carriage.

French John Sióussat was the last to leave the house. About to lock the front door and hearing a raucous sound, he remembered Dolley's macaw. Taking the cage, he ran with it to the house of the French minister Sérurier, who was living in Colonel John Tayloe's house, the Octagon. Returning, he locked the house carefully and took the key to the house of André de Daschkov, the Russian minister, knowing that both these places, protected by their countries' flags, would be immune to attack.

Had Dolley waited a little longer, she would have realized her wish, for in the wake of Winder's retreating rabble of an army rode the President, dead tired, for he had been in the saddle since dawn. With him were Monroe and Attorney General Rush. Soon came Colonel Laval with a detachment of dragoons. They found the White House empty, open, for locks were no more protection from roaming looters than from a foreign enemy. Madison and his companions entered, took what refreshment they could find, but dared not stay. Watching from the Octagon not far away, the French minister saw them come and go and wrote of it to his superior, Talleyrand.

"It was then, my lord, that the President, who, in the midst of all this disorder, had displayed, to stop it, a firmness and constancy worthy of better success, but powerless in regard to militia which more than once, in the War of the Revolution, had drawn after it in flight the illustrious Washington himself, coolly mounted his horse, accompanied by some friends, and slowly gained the bridge that separates Washington from Virginia."

Some hours later, about six, Admiral Cockburn, brash with triumph from his victory at Bladensburg, rode into the city with the vanguard of his victorious troops. Their first objective was the Capitol, still unfinished, its two magnificent wings connected by a long makeshift section of unpainted wood. It was told later that the admiral climbed to the rostrum in the House and conducted a derisive mock trial, demanding, "Shall this harbor of Yankee democracy be burned? All for it will say aye!" The chorus was overwhelming. Torches performed the job, and the wooden area was soon a blazing tinderbox. The Congressional furniture, carpets, drapes, the precious books accumulated for the Library of Congress, all were flung on the blaze.

The company moved on, to the Navy Yard, to the Treasury Building, entering, plundering, firing all the public buildings in their way. Later a British subaltern recorded the scene with appreciative zest. "The blazing of houses, ships, and stores, the report of exploding magazines, and the crash of falling roofs, informed them as they proceeded, of what was going forward. It would be difficult to conceive a finer spectacle than that which presented itself as they approached the town. The sky was brilliantly illumined by the different conflagrations; and a dark red light was thrown upon the road, sufficient to permit each man to view distinctly his comrade's face."

It was nearing eleven, according to Sérurier, when he "could see a column, preceded by torches, moving toward the President's House." Rumor had it that they found a table laid for a sumptuous meal and partook of it with gusto. At least they managed to find food and wine, which may have sparked the impossible story. The admiral, it was reported, insisted on his troops "sitting down and drinking Jemmy's health." He found a few trophies to take away, an old hat that belonged to the President and "a cushion off Mrs. Madison's chair," which inspired pertinent comments, as Margaret Smith reported, "too vulgar to repeat." Then the furniture was piled up, the torches applied, and the house became another beacon of flame.

Weeks later Dolley once more recounted her experiences of that August 24, this time to her friend, Benjamin Latrobe's wife.

"Two hours before the enemy entered the city, I left the house where Mr. Latrobe's elegant taste had been so justly admired, and where you and I had so often wandered together, and on that *very day* I sent out the silver (nearly all)—the velvet curtains and Gen. Washington's picture, the cabinet papers, a few books, and the small clock —left everything else, our own valuable stores of every description, a part of my clothes, and all my servants' clothes, etc., etc., in short, it would fatigue you to read the list of *my* losses, or an account of the general *dismay,* or particular distresses of your acquaintance. . . . I confess that I was so unfeminine as to be free from fear, and willing to remain in the Castle. If I could have had a cannon through every window, but alas! those who should have placed them there fled before me, and my whole heart mourned for my country! I remained nearly three days out of town. . . ."

The hours that followed her escape from the city on that fateful August 24 became almost as confused in her memory as the disparate accounts that would go down in history. Her mind retained them as pictures, disconnected, unrelated, like the haphazard incidents in a dream. . . .

Her horror on that first night, eyes fixed hour after hour on the angry red glow in the sky. Did she watch it, dry-eyed, spellbound, through the parted folds of an army tent, as some reported, or through the window of a friend's house where she had managed to find shelter? It did not matter. Surroundings were of little account when witnessing the end of one's world. Retreating soldiers, other exiles like herself fleeing from the city, brought reports of what was happening. So it was *her* home, *her* beloved possessions, worse yet, Jemmy's precious books, which helped kindle that ugly flaming in the heavens. So the blustering admiral had made good his threat "that he would make his bow in Mrs. Madison's drawing room." That was the least of her concerns. All she really wanted to know was, Where was Jemmy?— and was he safe?

The jumble of disconnected impressions continued into the next day. Her kind reception in homes, first of Charles Carroll at Bellevue, then at Rokeby, the home of her good friend Matilda Lee Love above the Little Falls of the Potomac . . . Matilda's distress and her own embarrassment for her friend when, asked to bring a cup of coffee to their distinguished guest, the cook replied, "I make a cup of coffee for you, Mis' Matilda, but I'm not gwine to hurry for Mis' Madison, for I done heerd Mr. Madison and Mr. Armstrong done sold the country to the British." It was all right, Dolley assured her distraught hostess. The poor woman just didn't understand. . . . Then at last word from Jemmy. He was safe, and he wanted her to meet him at the tavern in Great Falls! In fact, he had been traveling about all night, trying to find her. . . . No, she could not wait, even to spend the night. He might be waiting for her. She must go on. . . .

On the road again, this time hopefully . . . The tavern at last, a haven after hours of slow travel over dirt roads so clogged with loaded wagons and carriages that they could barely inch their way along. Only twenty-four hours since leaving home, yet it seemed a year!

Grateful, deadly weary, going upstairs, only to hear the proprietor of the hostel, discovering her identity, screaming after her, "Mis' Madison! if that's you, come down and go out! Your husband has got mine fighting, and _____ you, you shan't stay in my house; so get out!" More outbursts from other women in the house who had also been driven from their homes, many of whom had often enjoyed the hospitality of her drawing room . . . "Come, Sukey, we must go on, find some other place. We can't stay here."

The road again, this time into driving wind and rain, a storm on that evening of August 25, 1814, such as had seldom visited that part of the world. Thunder crashed, trees were uprooted. In the capital there were winds of near tornado violence. As one British observer reported it, "Our column was completely dispersed; some of the men flying for shelter behind walls and buildings, and others falling flat upon the ground to prevent themselves from being carried away by the tempest; nay, such was the violence of the wind, that two pieces of cannon which stood upon the eminence were fairly lifted from the ground and borne several yards to the rear."

Arriving at another inn at last, Wiley's Tavern, she was permitted to enter, drenched and bedraggled, and that was where that evening Jemmy finally found her. But, though wet and exhausted after almost three days of fifteen to twenty hours each in the saddle, he had to leave again with his companions, Colonel Graham, General Mason, Secretary Jones, and Richard Rush, to ride toward Baltimore in an attempt to rejoin whatever army was left. It was almost harder seeing him go than being uncertain about where he was and when he would come back, for she knew what tortures he was enduring, an overstrain for a man half his age and in perfect health. And, she suspected now and would learn later, he would be accused in merciless censure and revilement of fleeing from danger instead of laboring continuously for others' safety and sticking with the Army whenever possible. She was to remain there, he had told her, until she heard from him. The waiting became sheer torment.

It was Saturday, August 27, when he wrote her from Brookeville, Maryland.

"My dearest,—Finding that our army had left Montgomery Court House, we pushed on to this place, with a view to join it or proceed to the City. . . . I have just received a line from Col. Monroe, saying that the enemy were out of Washington, and on the retreat to their ships and advising our immediate return to Washington. We shall accordingly set out thither immediately. You will of course take the same resolution. I know not where in the first instance we are to hide our heads, but shall look for a place on my arrival. Mr. Rush offers his house in the Six Buildings, and the offer claims attention."

The enemy gone! Retreated! It was wonderful—but why? Others would ask the same question and pose a variety of answers. Because of a superstitious fear aroused by the terrible storm? Because they had heard rumors of a vast buildup of troops about to swell the ineffective Army? Or merely because they had accomplished all they had set out to do in the capital? It seemed too good to be true.

It was. Arriving in Washington in late afternoon of the twenty-seventh, Madison had learned that the British fleet was moving to capture Alexandria. But his follow-up letter to Dolley advising her to remain in her present quarters was sent too late. She was already on her way to Washington.

As her carriage approached the city she felt mingled hope and apprehension. Even at a distance she could see the forms of buildings and, high on its hill, the square solid shape of the White House. It was Sunday morning, and its walls gleamed white in the bright sunlight. Perhaps the devastation was not so great, after all. She would go there before trying to find other shelter.

But, coming to the river, the carriage found its way blocked. To her dismay the long bridge had been burned at both ends, all that was left of it a useless skeleton. A man whom she recognized, Colonel Fenwick, was busily transporting munitions of war across the river in the only boat in sight, a barge being poled by several blacks.

"Ask him if he will take us over," Dolley told her driver.

He returned shaking his head dubiously. No, Colonel Fenwick was busy, and anyway, he would not allow any unknown person, especially a woman, to cross in his boat with her carriage. It was a quandary. For safety's sake Dolley had followed friends' advice and disguised herself as a farm woman. She was not using her own carriage, too well known to escape undue attention, but had hired a conveyance belonging to an acquaintance, Mr. George Parrott of Georgetown. There was nothing to do but disclose her identity. Descending from the carriage, she approached the barge as it was being loaded close to the bank.

"Colonel Fenwick," she called, at the same time removing the wide-brimmed bonnet which hid both her features and the crown of glossy black curls. "Please—I beg you—"

He gaped in surprise and embarrassment. "M—my dear Madam, I

d—did not dream—! Of course. Just wait until I make room for your carriage, and—please forgive me!"

The carriage crossed in safety, and as they rode into the city Dolley's heart sank. The devastation was calamitous. Though most of the private houses were still standing, for the British had destroyed only public buildings, a pall of desolation mantled everything. Streets were littered, walls blackened, the air tainted with noxious fumes.

"We'll go to the President's House," she told her driver stubbornly.

Her young companion, Edward Duvall, protested. "But, Mrs. Madison, are you sure you want to see—? It's bound to be a terrible sight. Why not wait—?"

But she insisted. However, as they drove into the grounds and up the incline, only sheer obstinacy kept her from cowardly retreat. The four square walls were still there, but blackened almost beyond recognition. Only the bright sunlight had made them look white from a distance. The windows, most of them broken, grinned at her like gaps in rotting teeth. The roof was gone. Silently, lips tensed to keep from moaning aloud, she descended from the carriage and entered the doorless opening. The house was a shambles. The rooms that had been so beautifully decorated and furnished were gutted, the ceilings cracked, the walls discolored by heat and flames. Piles of ashes disclosing remnants—the lovely furniture she and Latrobe had so carefully chosen, the choice draperies, worst of all, Jemmy's precious books—littered the floors. It was all she could do to keep from weeping. No, tears were too mild a release. She wanted to scream, to cry out in indignation against this insult, not to herself, she cared nothing for her own losses, but to the country she loved. How could they!

She would find out in time that the orgy of destruction aroused almost as much shock and outrage in Britain as in America. It violated her gentlemanly code of ethics in warfare. While burning, pillaging, despoiling of private property, even murder and rape of civilians could be condoned, swept under the rug, so to speak, destruction of the citadels of government, even those of a despised little upstart nation which had once been her vassal, was an indignity to be deplored.

"Willingly would we throw a veil of oblivion over our transactions in Washington," noted a British newspaper. "The Cossacks spared Paris, but we spared not the Capitol of America."

Dolley did not cry. She did not scream or give vent in any way to her emotions. Returning to the carriage, she told her driver to take her to Richard Cutts's house on F Street. To her relief she found her brother-in-law there, though Anna and the rest of the family had not returned from their refuge in Virginia. Jemmy also, she learned with delight, had been there and would soon return.

When he came, sheltered once more in his arms, she did finally weep, but they were tears of joy. The worst was over. Whatever happened now, they could face it, boldly, courageously, as long as they were together.

5

"Oh, say, can you see by the dawn's early light,
What so proudly we hailed at the twilight's last gleaming?"

Dolley read the whole poem, printed in the *National Intelligencer,*
with shining eyes. It was beautiful! She agreed with the comment
made by the editor: "Whoever is the author of those lines, they do
equal honor to his principles and his talents." And perhaps, she
thought, she herself might take a little credit for them. If she had not
called James's attention to the need of sending someone to try to
secure the release of Dr. William Beanes from his imprisonment by
the British, he might never have sent Francis Scott Key on that mission.

William Beanes, a physician whose house at Upper Marlboro,
Maryland, had been taken over by the enemy as their headquarters,
had been promised safety if he took no action against the British. But
he had been accused by a spy of helping to arrest some marauding
soldiers, dragged from his bed, and made a prisoner. All pleas for his
release had failed. Francis Scott Key, a Georgetown lawyer, had desired to secure the President's permission to seek the doctor's release.
Dolley had suggested that her husband approve Key's undertaking,
and Madison had done so.

Because he had brought letters from battle-wounded British prisoners in Washington telling of their good treatment by the Americans,
General Ross reluctantly agreed to Dr. Beanes's release but detained
him and Key lest they disclose the British plan to attack Fort Mc-
Henry. From his post on a nearby boat Key watched the ensuing
battle. Though Cockburn had claimed he could conquer the fort in
two hours, for twenty-five hours the bombardment continued.

"Is the flag still there?" questioned Dr. Beanes eagerly as the dawn
of September 14 began to break. He was an old man and his eyes were
dim. "Can you see it?"

His companion peered into the slowly lightening sky. "Yes," he cried joyfully. "It's still there!" In his happy emotion words began flooding his mind, and in the half-light he wrote them down on the back of a letter he had in his pocket. Later, in a tavern in Baltimore he revised them to fit a popular tune, "Anacreon in Heaven," little dreaming that a hundred and seventeen years later both words and tune would become his country's national anthem or that the same flag, weather- and battle-scarred, would be enshrined among the nation's treasures for future generations.

It was no wonder the patriotic young Key strained his eyes in the dawn of that September 14, for had not the flag been flying it would have meant the fall of Baltimore and possibly a disastrous turn of the war. But other victories were soon to follow. From Lieutenant Thomas Macdonough, in charge of naval operations on Lake Champlain, came news of a battle which resulted in the capture of a frigate, a brig, and two sloops of war. Jubilation in the capital almost drowned out the sighs and moanings over the signs of demolition. It was a personal triumph for Madison also, for he had insisted on the building of the brig, *Eagle,* launched just three and a half weeks after its timbers had been cut, one of the vessels that enabled Macdonough to win the decisive victory. Had the British won, the whole Hudson Valley would have been open to their advance.

Dolley was having her personal reasons also for rejoicing, for on September 16 Anna gave birth to little Mary Estelle Elizabeth Cutts. After four boys, James Madison, Thomas, Walter, and Richard, this was Anna's second girl. The first, Dolley Payne Madison Cutts, born in 1811, had elicited raptures of delight. "I claim her as my pet, my darling daughter!" Now Dolley felt doubly blessed. Anna's children, six of them still living, were the sons and daughters she had never been able to bear for James. She reveled in their nearness during these days of upheaval.

Change . . . indecision . . . uncertainty. The last months of 1814 were rife with turbulence. In Europe the peace commissioners, Bayard, Adams, and Clay, having traveled from Russia to Göteborg, then finally to Ghent, were struggling to reach fair terms with a Britain toughened to triumph over the humiliating blow delivered the enemy by the burning of Washington and making arrogant demands such as would be imposed on a defeated nation. In Washington, Congress, meeting in special session in temporary quarters, was heatedly arguing over the capital's future. Should it be rebuilt on its present site or moved to some other city? In New England hard-line Federalists were congregating in a convention at Hartford, secretly formulating proposals that stopped just short of secession. Meanwhile Dolley had moved from Anna's house into new presidential quarters where, calmly and confidently, she was attempting to restore a semblance of normalcy to the official life of the devastated city.

The Octagon, designed by William Thornton for the wealthy Benjamin Tayloe and built in 1800, was a gem of architecture. Only the President's House was larger and more luxurious. Built of brick instead of the prevailing sandstone, it was fitted into a pie-shaped lot not more than a block from the White House, hence its unusual shape. Though not strictly eight-sided unless one counted the semicircular front as two sides, the aptness of its name was never questioned. And, though all in its vicinity, including the President's House, would be altered almost beyond recognition, both name and building would remain unchanged through ensuing generations. A hundred and fifty and more years later tourists would be able to see it in all its original uniqueness, enter its doors and inspect the rooms where Dolley had persistently continued her teas and dinners and drawing rooms, see in the foyer a little table she once owned and gave to her dressmaker, climb the stairs and peer into a room where James signed a document that ended what some called America's second war of independence.

With the threat to Washington, Benjamin Tayloe had persuaded the French minister Sérurier to occupy the Octagon during that summer of 1814, ensuring its safety by reason of the French flag. Now, through the persuasion of William Thornton, Sérurier generously relinquished his claim and Tayloe gladly rented it for the presidential temporary residence.

Dolley delighted in the spacious circular foyer with its elegant staircase, the drawing room on the main floor with its magnificent chandelier and mantel, reminding her of the carved marbles she had so loved at Scotchtown. In spite of the smaller size of the house, there was plenty of room for Siôussat and Paul and Sukey Jennings in the bricked kitchen quarters downstairs, and the circular chamber above the foyer became James's office and study.

On New Year's Day, 1815, she was ready for her first reception, modest compared with those in the White House because of the small space, but equally splendid in hospitality. A few articles of finery had apparently been salvaged in her flight, along with the crimson curtains and clock, for one guest recorded that she wore "a robe of rose-colored satin trimmed with ermine, and a white satin turban on her head, whence sprang a tiara of white ostrich plumes."

Always beneath the glittering surface of her drawing rooms ran the steady undercurrents that often determined the course of momentous decision making. To say that she did not interfere in politics was no implication that she did not subtly influence their course. Certainly the conciliatory atmosphere of her gatherings helped heal animosities, soften the opposition's derisive revilements of "that servile hypocrite Madison," and promote national unity. And tradition says that through her influential drawing rooms and persuasive little hints and parleys she was instrumental in keeping the nation's capital where it was.

"Have you noticed how much healthier the city has become since so many trees were cut and the bogs and marshes have begun to dry up? There was almost no malaria at all last summer. . . . Have you seen Latrobe's designs for the new capitol? General Washington would be pleased with them, I know. This was really his dream city, remember? . . . What a blessing Jefferson's beautiful Lombardy poplars along the avenue were spared by the fire! . . ."

After much hot debate, on February 9 the House cast its vote, 78 to 63, to repair the public buildings and keep Washington the capital of the nation.

But the New Year had brought even greater causes for rejoicing. On January 8 General Andrew Jackson defeated the British forces at New Orleans with an astounding victory. On the following Saturday, when the news reached Washington, the city went wild with joy. Unlike the destructive conflagration of August, the countryside was ablaze with the flames of thousands of torches, lanterns, bonfires, and candles. The engagement at New Orleans had presented one of the most amazing contrasts of losses in modern history—seven hundred British killed, fourteen hundred wounded, but only seven Americans killed and six wounded. Jackson became a hero overnight. Ten days later what British forces were left at the mouth of the Mississippi returned to their ships.

Though the news of this defeat had not yet reached England, other developments had softened Castlereagh's demands. Late in October the startling news of the defeats on Lake Champlain and at Baltimore had arrived in London. Moreover, England was becoming tired of fighting, her citizens restive. The mercantile interests were agitating because of their heavy losses of merchant ships, and negotiations of the great European congress in Vienna were threatening the renewal of European war. After weeks of patient negotiation at Ghent, the peace commissioners had come to an agreement on Christmas Eve. Rumors of a possible peace sent American speculators scurrying south to buy up tobacco and cotton before the prices should go up. But nothing was sure until on the evening of February 14 Secretary of State Monroe came to the door of the Octagon. He held out a packet.

"The treaty," he said simply.

Dolley, standing beside her husband to greet the guest, saw James's lips tighten, his shoulders stiffen. His fingers closed about the packet, but he made no move to examine it. It might have been any ordinary missive. She would have broken the seal, torn it open, to learn immediately its portentous contents! After a leisurely exchange of amenities the two men went upstairs to the office above the foyer. Though there were other guests in the drawing room, Dolley did not return to them but paced the foyer, back and forth, round and round, arms hugging her body to keep from shivering, watchfully alert for some movement on the stairs. She felt like a prisoner in the dock waiting to hear the judge's verdict—death or life, war or peace.

What were the terms hidden in that sealed packet? The fact that the commissioners had agreed to them meant little. They were tired, frustrated, even in conflict because of their own special interests, Adams concerned with the Newfoundland fisheries, Clay with navigation of the Mississippi. If the British were still insisting on their extreme demands—more territory, control of the West, dominion of the seas— James would never sign it. Mild he might be, conciliatory, and he was. But in a matter of principle he was adamant.

There was motion on the stairs. She stood still, frozen, her eyes probing into the candlelit duskiness, searching his face as he came down leading the way. She drew a long breath, and the coldness of her body melted into tingling warmth, for he was smiling.

The terms of the treaty implied neither victory nor defeat for either side. As the *National Intelligencer* stated, "Its general principle is a restitution and recognition of the rights and possessions of each party as they stood before the war." Disputed boundaries would be settled later by joint commissions. No grievance was addressed, no concession made. The matter of impressment, a prime cause of the war, was not mentioned, but with the cessation of war in Europe it had ceased to be an issue.

The Prince Regent in Britain had already ratified the treaty. In the oval room above the foyer, surrounded by his cabinet and others—senators, congressmen, and diplomats—the President signed it, the room ever after to be known as the "Treaty Room," the round desk holding the writing easel, the inkwell, brass holder, and quill pens, the chair where he had sat—all preserved in place for history. Twenty-four hours later the treaty was unanimously ratified by the Senate.

And how would history assess the struggle that ended that day? A futile, inconclusive conflict entered upon by a weak and timid President? Some would think so. Yet in that same year of 1815 Justice Joseph Story wrote: "Never did a country occupy more lofty ground; we have stood the contest, single-handed, against the conqueror of Europe; and we are at peace, with all our blushing victories thick crowding on us. If I do not much mistake, we shall attain to a very high character as well as crush domestic faction."

And more than a century later another historian, Irving Brant, would write: "It was under the guiding hand of President James Madison that the struggling young country won an equal position among the free nations of the world, and began its long climb to leadership." The youthful nation had come of age. "Mr. Madison's War," a derisive term, had become an accolade, or, as one historian would call it, "a determinant of the nation's destiny."

So . . . the war was over. Washington was jubilant. And Federalist guns were spiked, if not silenced. The delegates from the Hartford Convention, arriving in Washington to present its demands to the "little pigmy" of a President, made no effort to do so. They would have received nothing but ridicule. Two of them attended Dolley's next Wednesday's drawing room, "presented their respects to him and talked of nothing." The third, Harrison Gray Otis of Boston, refused to attend this function where, as he wrote his wife, "all was tinsel and vulgarity," and because, he complained, "we have received no dinner invitation from Mr. Madison. What a mean and contemptible little blackguard!"

Dolley welcomed the two dissidents with her usual impartiality and did not miss the third. No amount of opposition could have dampened her euphoria or aroused her indignation. Her sole desire was to exert all her energies in acts of healing and reconciliation. But she had always done that.

Along with her joy over the end of the conflict was another satisfaction almost as great. Payne would be coming home. There had been a letter from him to the President in November which had brought her great joy. He had been in Ghent watching with trepidation the slow progress of the peace negotiations. One section was especially gratifying. She had read it over and over.

"We received ten days ago the very painful intelligence of the destruction of the public buildings in Washington. This barbarous act meets with universal excoriation. It has induced the Paris journals for the first time to come forth against what were supposed to be the inclinations of the British government. My absence from Washington I most deeply regret if for no other reason than that I might at least have been useful to you and my mother. I shall have opportunity to write her by the *Herald*. . . ."

Now Dolley eagerly questioned Henry Carroll, Clay's secretary, who had brought the text of the treaty from New York. Had Payne perhaps had some important part to play in the negotiations as Gallatin's aide? At least he could bring her news of her son. Carroll was vague. So far as he knew Payne had not been in Ghent during the decisive days. He had seemed to prefer Paris. At least, Dolley comforted herself, he would be coming home with the peace commissioners. He had gone for six months, which had stretched into two long years!

There was plenty of activity to help bridge the interval of impatient waiting. In March they were able to get away for a brief respite at Montpelier, the first time in eleven months. Change, yes, but by no means rest. World events followed them—news that Napoleon, rallying his forces, had again secured control of France, posing questions of further danger to neutral rights; nearer home, that Andrew Jackson, flushed with his victory at New Orleans, had continued martial law there in peacetime, and, though at the President's insistence he had rescinded the order, a lawsuit had resulted. Wisely Madison judged the general with "a liberality proportioned to the greatness of his service, the purity of his intentions, and peculiarity of the situation."

Back in Washington, Dolley learned with disappointment that Gallatin was remaining in Europe long enough, hopefully, to secure a favorable commercial treaty with Britain. Another delay for Payne! Now Payne would never be with them in this jewel of a house, the Octagon, for they were moving again. Madison knew that Tayloe wanted to return to his own home now that the war was over. Moreover, he disliked being under obligation to a person who was what Margaret Smith called "an outrageous Federalist."

In June they moved into the corner house at the Seven Buildings, at the juncture of Pennsylvania Avenue and Nineteenth Street, the property of the late Vice President, Elbridge Gerry. It was an adequate house with some fine features—twenty-seven windows of hand-blown glass, four dormers over a beautiful cornice, and a front door with a splendid fanlight. It seemed strange, however, to be living so close to the street, reminiscent of the houses back in Philadelphia when they had scrubbed the steps twice a week and gathered on the front stoop when the work was finished.

But Dolley enjoyed even the lack of privacy. Schoolchildren would gather outside one of the windows to watch her feed her pet macaw, rescued from the fire by Sióussat and ready with a raucous greeting when they moved into the Octagon. She welcomed the children and cajoled the bird into the antics she had taught him to entertain her small nieces and nephews. One of these children was to write later, "She as well as her pet was very engaging. I can clearly recall her as she appeared in her inevitable turban."

It was a comfortable house but—oh, so small! When she gave a reception on General Jackson's first visit to Washington after his great triumph, the place swarmed like a beehive. The general, besieged by his ardent admirers, was almost suffocated. Dolley longed for the amplitude of the East Room with its generous space and softly glowing chandeliers. The torches she had provided to supplement the inadequate lighting of the drawing room turned the small place into a sweltering oven. But people were good-natured, and the evening was pronounced a superb climax to the general's days of celebration.

As in the Octagon, Dolley had a clear view of the wrecked President's House and of its amazingly slow rejuvenation. Soon it became in reality as well as in deference a "White House"; for the sandstone walls, though stoutly resistant to the fire, were so stained and blackened that the only remedy was to paint them white. In time all its other designations—President's House, palace, castle—would fall into disuse, and it would be known for all future time as the White House. But as the renovation progressed at a snail's pace, with little to show for it except fresh paint and a few replaced windows, she despaired of ever living in it again. The Capitol, of course, was more important, with Congress crowded into the only building of any size, Blodgett's Hotel. Benjamin Latrobe, who for years had been the surveyor of public buildings, had been called back to the city to repair its damage. It would be eight years before the repairs and new building were finally completed, the two wings refurbished, the center portion, formerly only rough boards, constructed, and the whole surmounted by the majestic Bulfinch Dome, the crowning concept of its architect, Charles Bulfinch.

Already Jefferson had offered to compensate for one of the Capitol's greatest losses, the Congressional library, for when the British had been approaching, the only conveyance available for salvaging had been a wagon drawn by four oxen, large enough to hold only the national records and a few books. Just a month after the burning Jefferson had written Samuel Harrison Smith, husband of the avid chronicler, Margaret, offering his whole library, which he called "the choicest collection of books in the United States," to Congress at whatever terms they might consider proper.

It turned the British vandalism almost into blessing, for the old library had contained only some three thousand volumes, while Jefferson's was twice as large, chosen to fit the needs of scholars and statesmen. In January 1815, in spite of some die-hard Federalists who decried some of the library's iniquitous ingredients ("French, irreligious, immoral!"), representing the "principles of a man who had inflicted greater and deeper injuries upon our country than any other person, except Mr. Madison," Congress voted to purchase the library of some six thousand volumes, "good, bad, indifferent," for a modest $23,950. Eventually the books would arrive at the capitol in a long wagon train, brought by a contractor who was paid $5.00 a day for the trip, his wagons, and mules.

"The next generation," reported the *American Register* with prophetic insight, "we confidently predict, will blush at the objections made in Congress to the purchase of Mr. Jefferson's library."

At last! The *Neptune* arrived at Havre de Grace, bringing home William Crawford, minister to France, and some of the peace commissioners—but not Payne! Only his baggage. Dolley was disconsolate. Naturally Mr. Gallatin had remained in Europe to conclude the commercial treaty, but surely Payne was no longer needed.

"I am so miserable," she wrote Hannah Gallatin, "and astonished at the entire silence of Mr. Crawford." Did the Gallatins know when Payne would return? Why did his baggage come without him? Crawford had given no information except that Payne had missed the boat. Fortunately she did not have to tell James that her son had written Richard Cutts asking him to send him a thirty-day draft for two hundred and fifty pounds to be received from his mother. James might not understand the needs of a young man of Payne's artistic tastes in a cultural environment like Paris. But even she did not know that during his two years in Europe he had expended ten times the amount of his allotted expense money, borrowing the excess from Baring Brothers of London, the banking firm that had loaned the United States money to pay its European debts.

Finally Gallatin, having concluded the commercial treaty satisfactorily, arrived in New York, and Payne with him. "You will find Todd in good health," he wrote Madison, "but he has spent a longer time in Europe and more money than I wished. He owes twelve hundred and eighty pounds sterling, with interest from 1st June last, to the Barings, for which I made myself responsible, and which should be remitted as soon as possible."

Madison sent a check for sixty-five hundred dollars, which included 17 percent interest, an amount he could ill afford. Though he was not pleased, he forbore telling Dolley of this latest demand, unwilling to mar her ecstasy in the presence of her tall, handsome, courtly, and exceedingly Frenchified son, whose conversation exuded famous names—the Czar, dukes and duchesses, Napoleon, Madame de Staël —rather than details of the political mission on which he had been sent; impressions of French viands, theaters, card parties, races, rather than of Old World philosophy and culture. With one of his pursuits, however, even Madison could find no fault. He had commissioned him to purchase some works of art for additional furnishings at Montpelier. Payne's choices had been faultless. Both James and Dolley were delighted with them.

Payne balked at going to Princeton. What could a university teach him that his superior experience had not already compassed? Perhaps because Dolley was so happy at having him home, Madison did not force the issue. He would let Payne act as his secretary again for a time. Ned Coles had realized the dream he had long had of moving to Illinois where he could free his slaves. James had reason to hope that his foster son would come to his senses. He agreed with John Quincy Adams's appraisal of the youth's continued lassitude. "It's surprising! He has sufficient talent to succeed in anything he undertakes."

Dolley's days now were happily full. One of her pleasantest tasks, for it involved children, was helping to establish an orphanage for boys and girls made destitute by the war. She was elected the first directress of the association of women formed in September of 1815 to provide an asylum for this activity, and she remained head of it as long as she was First Lady. She contributed twenty dollars and a cow to the organization and also used her skill as a seamstress in cutting out dresses for all the children and directing the women who did the sewing.

"How can you stand all that extra work with all the other things you have to do?" marveled one of her friends. "Don't you get tired of it? And don't your lovely hands get sore with all that rough cutting and sewing?"

"Oh!" replied Dolley joyously. "The work is delicious. I haven't ever enjoyed doing anything so much."

Her concern for the young was not confined to children. Youths of both sexes were drawn to her like moths to a glowing flame. And she was an inveterate matchmaker. Now, with Payne at home, she had an even more vital personal interest. Surely he would pick a wife soon among the eligible young beauties who frequented her drawing rooms or visited her from Virginia or Philadelphia. Her own choice was Phoebe Morris, daughter of her old friend Anthony. Phoebe was not only beautiful, a lovely blonde to complement Payne's dark good looks, but, like him, she had traveled in Europe when her father had been minister at Cadiz. She was musical and artistic. During her frequent visits Dolley had come to think of her as "dearest daughter."

But Payne remained restless and showed no signs of settling down either to marriage or to serious labor. He did as little secretarial work as possible. Almost as popular in Washington as in Europe, he cut the same splendid figure, attended receptions, teas, dinners, patronized the theater and the races, and, to Dolley's fortunate ignorance, indulged his propensity for gambling and intemperance which had caused John Quincy Adams, who had been with him in France, to note in his diary, perhaps by way of excuse, "The tendency to dissipation at Paris seems to be irresistible. There is a moral incapacity for industry and application."

Washington was in the mood for gaiety. Peace had brought not only the end of fighting but burgeoning prosperity. Opposition to the administration had almost vanished. An "era of good feeling" had arrived. The new commercial treaty was favorable. The economy was booming. The Federalist party was dead, or at least moribund, the Union saved. "Mr. Madison's War" had become the complimentary "Mr. Madison's Peace." The President had suddenly become almost as popular as his wife had always been. These last months of his second and final term promised an end of the turmoil that had characterized all of those preceding. Not that the President took the mood of euphoria for granted. He was too canny a politician, too wise a philosopher, to underrate the fickleness of the public in spite of his stubborn trust in its ultimate wisdom. Warily he followed the principle which he so impressed on Dolley that she was to write years later in a hand become unsteady with age these "warning words of my husband": "Be always on your guard that you never become the slave of the public nor the martyr to your friends."

But she had never depended on public approval for self-fulfillment. She was now, in this atmosphere of harmony, just as she had been in turmoil, gay and understanding companion, concerned friend, thoughtful hostess—in other words, herself. Nor was she at all dependent on her material environment or circumstances. Mrs. Benjamin Crowninshield, wife of the new Secretary of the Navy, arriving in Washington in December and calling on Dolley in the Seven Buildings, was amazed to find no carpets, the floors covered with dark gray cloth and the window curtains made of "embossed cambric, damask pattern, with red silk fringe," the furnishings obviously secondhand and nondescript. When William Lee, charged with furnishing the renovated President's House, made an invoice in 1818, he found that only two pier tables, a few chairs, and a sideboard were fit to use. But Mrs. Crowninshield noted also that at the drawing room she attended on December 6 no one seemed to notice the meagerness of the setting. Dolley's radiant personality transcended all deficiencies.

Not that she was at all indifferent to her own appearance! Mrs. Crowninshield noted that on this occasion the First Lady wore "a sky-blue striped velvet,—a frock,—fine elegant lace round the neck and lace handkerchief inside and a lace ruff, white lace turban starred in gold, and white feather."

On New Year's Day, Dolley once more stood before the pier glass (a borrowed one) and thoughtfully considered her reflection. Their last full year in the presidency. Was it vanity that prompted her to choose unusual fabrics and styles that people would admire, copy, and that history would perhaps remember? Or the desire to please? Or, perhaps, just the impulse that long ago had caused her to hide a thing of beauty beneath her Quaker kerchief? At least the urge was as much a part of her as her sparkling azure eyes, her warm smile, her contagious joy in living.

The creation she now saw reflected was one of the simplest yet loveliest she had ever worn. She regarded it with satisfaction, a bit of pride also, for it was of her own designing. History would again be indebted to the admiring Mrs. Crowninshield for a description. "New Year's Day, midday celebration, 1816. Mrs. Madison was dressed in a yellow satin embroidered all over with sprigs of butterflies, not two alike in the dress; a narrow border in all colors; made high in the neck; a little cape, long sleeves, and a white bonnet with feathers."

But Dolley would have been startled, humbled, probably a little horrified, could she have foreseen that one hundred and fifty and more years later the dress she wore that day would be exhibited, accompanied with the above description, in one of the nation's most beloved treasure houses, The Smithsonian. The mannequin wearing it, however, would be a lifeless thing, with bland insipid features, bearing little resemblance to the vivid, spirited woman, still radiantly attractive if a bit plump, in her prime at age forty-seven.

She took one last critical look at her reflection, stuck out her tongue at it saucily, snatched up her little lava and platinum snuffbox, and went down to greet her guests.

The last year sped by.

February. It was said later that Dolley's drawing room on the sixteenth was the most brilliant ever held in the executive house. The justices of the Supreme Court were there in their sober gowns, Justice Marshall, now more amenable to the administration, leading them. The peace commissioners, Gallatin, Clay, and Russell, were there, also some of the heroes of the war, generals in their gold-encrusted uniforms. The new era of goodwill was attested by the presence of the new minister from England, Sir Charles Bagot. Though the hall and two parlors were so crammed with guests that the servants had trouble squeezing through with their trays of wine, punch, and cakes, no one seemed to mind. With the blazing pine torches supplementing the feebler lighting, the house was so brightly illuminated that it would be remembered as "the house of a thousand candles."

Never had Dolley felt more at ease. No need longer to walk a mental tightrope, carefully balancing attentions between friends and enemies. Republicans and Federalists were, if mildly, in agreement. Prosperity was proving an effective unifier of emotions. With the mollifying presence of the genial Bagot and his glamorously beautiful wife, even the animosities of the recent war seemed to have vanished. Dolley exemplified the mood of the occasion in a rose-colored gown trailing a white velvet train lined with lavender satin and edged with lace. A little gold-embroidered coronet circling her white velvet turban may have inspired Sir Charles Bagot's enthusiastic comment that "she looked every inch a queen."

March. Came the presidential caucus of the Democratic-Republican party, with the vote going to Secretary of State James Monroe, in spite of prejudice against another President coming from Virginia. Though Madison could easily have been chosen for a third term, his refusal was adamant. George Washington had set the precedent. And Madison himself had fought in the Constitutional Convention against the faction dangerously advocating a presidency for life, a sure threat to democracy. Dolley was as pleased as James. The choice was a confirmation of Madison's administration, which, as most now seemed to agree, and one historian would later express it, "had set the country on the road to internal developments, national strength, and economic independence, without weakening the fabric of self government."

April. Her favorite month of all the year, when the world was bursting with new life. It was the first spring since the coming of peace, and the unfolding leaves were surely a more tender green, the willows a deeper gold, the redbud and lilacs and violets and hyacinths all a richer more vibrant color. It was fitting that Easter should come just now, in this season of awakening.

Dolley delighted in the celebration of Easter. It was part of her release from childhood inhibitions. Like other dissenters from the Established Church—Baptists, Presbyterians, Puritans—Quakers had not observed the ritual festivals of Christmas and Easter, believing that they were of pagan origin. She longed for St. John's Church now in the building to be finished, so its altar could be decked with the greens and flowers that symbolized the Resurrection. At least she could fill their own small house with blossoming fragrance. It was Payne who suggested another outlet for her imaginative zeal.

"You should see how some people celebrate Easter in Europe," he told her gaily, never loath to exhibit the superior knowledge gleaned in his travels. "Did you know eggs are supposed to be a symbol of the Resurrection, and when they are dyed red they represent the blood shed on the Cross?"

"No," marveled Dolley, instantly interested. "I never heard that."

"They tell in France," continued Payne, "that the church bells, which never rang during Passion Week, went to Rome to get the Pope's blessing and when they came back, on Easter Eve, they brought with them some eggs dyed red like a cardinal's cloak. They gave them out to be distributed among the children. And in England on Easter Monday, Pasch Monday they call it, they used to have egg-rolling contests when the children rolled hard-boiled eggs colored red down a hill. The child who rolled the greatest number of eggs without cracking them won."

"Oh—what a good idea!" Dolley's eyes sparkled. "And how the children must have loved it! I wish—"

"I know what you're thinking," teased Payne. "I can just see it taking shape, like two big round eggs, in those telltale eyes of yours."

He was right. Already she was picturing the scene. All those children who came crowding around her window to watch her feed her pet macaw! Getting them together, that would not be hard. Tell one, and they'd soon all know. But—getting all the eggs—*how?* And *where?* There would have to be a hill steep enough . . . She began to plan. Her next Wednesday drawing room, of course. She would tell all the mothers. They would get together and boil and color the eggs. And the Capitol hill with its terraces! Even though the building wasn't finished, the grounds were still there.

Being Dolley, she made it happen. On that Easter Monday, April 15, 1816, a custom was initiated that was to persist with only a few interruptions through the decades to the present time. Somebody who witnessed that first gala celebration left an account of it for future generations.

"At first the children sit sedately in long rows; each has brought a basket of gay-colored hard-boiled eggs, and those on the upper terrace send them rolling to the line next below, and those pass on the ribbon-like streams to other hundreds at the foot, who scramble for the hopping eggs and hurry panting to the top to start them down again. And as the sport warms, those on top who have rolled all the eggs they brought finally roll themselves, shrieking with laughter. Now comes a swirl of curls, ribbons and furbelows, somebody's maid indifferent to bumps and grass stains. A set of boys who started in a line of six with joined hands are trying to come down in somersaults without breaking the chain. On all sides the older folks stand by to watch the games of this infant carnival."

Dolley, of course, was among the spectators. She was delighted, not because she had engineered a wonderful project, but because the children had had such a good time. She hoped somebody would plan the same kind of celebration next year. A pity to have it happen only once!

May . . . June . . . Off to Montpelier for a long vacation, the first in many years, a foretaste of the simpler but delightfully leisurely life soon to come. Next year, Dolley reflected happily, she would be able to see the crape myrtle spring into leaf and bud instead of already blossomed into its deep purple-red blaze of color, help Mother Madison dig and weed in her beloved little kitchen garden, watch all the fruit trees burst into bloom.

July. A huge Fourth of July dinner, as usual, spread under an arbor on the lawn with a great crowd of family and friends attending. Not till later did they learn that at the same time in Washington Benjamin Lear was giving an oration, and Madison was being toasted as "a ruler more respected for his merit than his power, and greater in the simple dignity of his virtues than the proudest monarch on his throne."

Hardly had the remains of the feast been cleared away when a note arrived from Monroe saying that the new French minister, Jean Guillaume Hyde de Neuville, was about to arrive at Montpelier. A test for Dolley's genius for hospitality, since she had not been told that he was bringing his entire staff! But with the help of her skilled French cook, Pierre Roux, she managed to entertain the diplomat and his entourage with competence and aplomb, and Madison put the legate at his ease, as de Neuville reported, by talking "as if Louis XVIII had just succeeded Louis XVI," in other words, as if the obnoxious interim between the two rulers, especially the French nation's domination by Napoleon, had never existed.

August. One of the coldest and driest seasons in memory. "The year without a summer," James complained bitterly. His corn yield would be no more than a third, and the tobacco not much better. But next year! He could hardly wait to enjoy all the duties—and even the distresses—of a full-time farmer.

September. More guests. Attorney General Rush, who reported "riding through the drooping cornfields" from Washington to Montpelier, also that he had "never seen Mr. Madison so well fixed anywhere, not even before he was burnt out here," that he was "an excellent farm manager, a model of kindness to his slaves, lived with a profuse hospitality, and was never developed to me under so many interesting lights as during the week I spent under his roof. Perhaps I should add that French cooking and Madeira that he purchased in Philadelphia in '96 made a part of every day's fare!" Madison did not disclose even to this friendly guest his secret hiding place for his old wines—the hollow pediment of the front portico!

October. Back to Washington again for the last time. The season of the fall races, when Washingtonians swarmed to the track four miles from the city, three or four thousand of them, "black, and white, and yellow; of all conditions, from the President of the United States to the beggar in his rags; of all ages and both sexes." Once Dr. Thornton and Jemmy had owned a racehorse, Wild Medley, and in those days Dolley had never missed a race. But now, knowing it might be the last time, she found it almost as exciting to watch Thornton's Herod Eclipse, a beautiful animal, go tearing around the racetrack.

November . . . December. Election returns showing an overwhelming victory for Monroe, who had carried all states except Massachusetts. If Madison had been the candidate, asserted John Adams, he would have carried all New England. Then, not long after Christmas, the first service in newly completed St. John's Episcopal Church just across the square from the White House. No more worshiping in makeshift quarters like the Hall of Representatives! It was a beautiful brick building, designed by Benjamin Latrobe in the form of a Greek cross. Sitting beside James in worship, Dolley could well understand why Latrobe had written in a letter to his son, "I have completed a church that has made many Washingtonians religious who had not been religious before." The President had been offered one of the high-backed front pews, but he had chosen a very ordinary one well back, Number 54, which would remain the President's Pew for years to come. Every President thereafter would worship there on some occasion and be seated in this same pew.

A long way, thought Dolley, looking up at the jeweled stained-glass windows, listening to Dr. Wilmer in his silk gown preaching in the high wine-glass pulpit, from the stark little Cedar Creek Meeting House—a whole lifetime in fact! But never had she been more conscious of the Inner Light. Its Presence, she had long since discovered, was not dependent on anything external. You could experience it dressed in crimson silk or Quaker gray, sitting in a cushioned pew or on a hard, uncomfortable bench—anytime, anywhere.

1817. Only two months more. She felt like William Thornton's Herod Eclipse, thundering down the homestretch. Sixteen years racing to an end! She was not sorry. They had been good years—and bad, fortunately ending with the good. She wished vaguely that she might have had just a few more weeks—or even days—back in the White House. Never had the rooms in the Seven Buildings seemed more cramped and crowded than in these last drawing rooms. But at least Elizabeth Monroe would be able to enjoy the refurbished President's House. Tall, beautiful, graceful, with stately manners cultivated in the most polished court of Europe, she would be a far more eminent and elegant First Lady than Dolley had ever aspired to be.

Then suddenly it was March. The Madisons moved in with Anna and her family temporarily so the Monroes could hold a reception in the Seven Buildings on March 4, Inauguration Day. It dawned fair and mild after a winter of unbelievable cold and wind, the latter perhaps more noticeable because of the cutting of so many trees to make room for prospective building. Francis Hall, a British dragoon who visited Washington in that period, noted in his *Travels:* "It used to be a joke against Washington that next-door neighbors must go through a wood to make their visits, but now there is scarcely a tree between George Town and the Navy Yard."

Monroe took his oath of office at noon before Chief Justice Marshall, delivering his inaugural address in the open in front of the temporary Hall of Congress, because the House and Senate could not agree on which of their chambers should be used. The House with its hard wooden chairs? No! scoffed the Senators. The Senate chamber with its velvet-covered seats? No! balked the frugal-minded Speaker Clay.

The new President listed an imposing array of national blessings and lauded his predecessor "under whom so important a portion of this great and successful experiment has been made." And two days later Mayor James Blake and a committee presented Madison with the resolutions of a Washington mass meeting. They were complimentary to the point of flattery.

"We come, sir," read Blake, "to mingle congratulations and regret —congratulations as Americans participating in the untarnished glory that accompanies you." The regret was for their personal loss. "We shall never forget that when our city felt the tempest of war, it was your wisdom and firmness that repaired the breach." Violence and injustice, he continued, had made necessary a resort to arms, resulting in "a solid peace, a name among the nations of the earth, a self respect founded upon justice and common strength, and, above all, a conviction that the Constitution you were so instrumental in framing is an enduring guarantee of freedom."

There were other addresses equally verbose and flattering. James, who had received similar excesses of verbiage in vilification, received all these encomiums with healthy skepticism, but Dolley, always ready to forgive and forget past indignities, was delighted. Both of them would have been far more gratified by the less glib and flattering but honest and generous appraisal of the administration by James's Federalist predecessor John Adams.

"Not withstanding a thousand faults and blunders, his administration has acquired more glory, and established more Union, than all his three Predecessors, Washington, Adams, and Jefferson."

Dolley was especially delighted by a letter written to her by her old friend Eliza Collins Lee.

"My dear Friend.—On this day eight years ago, I wrote from the retirement of Sully to congratulate you on the joyful event that placed you in the highest station our country can bestow. I then enjoyed the proudest feelings—that my friend, the friend of my youth, who never had forsaken me, should be thus distinguished, and so peculiarly fitted for it.

"How much greater cause have I to congratulate you at this period, for having so filled it as to render yourself more enviable this day than your successor, as it is more difficult to deserve the gratitude and thanks of the community than their congratulations. . . . You will retire from the tumult and fatigue of public life to your favorite retreat in Orange County and will carry with you principles and manners, not to be put off with the robe of state. . . . Talents such as yours were never intended to remain inactive; on retiring from public life, you will form a more fortunate arrangement of your time, be able to display them in the more noble and interesting walks of life. You will cherish them, my dear friend, in a more native soil. . . .

"I remember at this moment, in my last conversation with my venerable uncle, your father's friend, he said of you, 'She will hold out to the end; she was a dutiful daughter, and never turned her back on an old friend, and was charitable to the poor.' "

Dolley reread the long letter again and again. It was fitting that this friend who had shared so many important events of her life should add her blessing to this climactic hour.

It was a month before they could finish packing and leave, a month filled with invitations to balls, dinners, and other honors. At one of the affairs in Georgetown the walls were covered with "transparencies, paintings, and verses executed on white velvet and richly framed," all destined to decorate Madison's favorite room at Montpelier. His farm overseer, arriving in Washington with a train of wagons, was entrusted with carrying all their personal possessions home by land. They themselves, leaving on April 6, traveled by a new means of transportation, "like the Wise Men," thought Dolley humorously, "who went home by another way."

"I accompanied him in the steam boat as far down the Potomac as Aquia Creek," recorded James K. Paulding, secretary of the Navy Board, "where his carriage waited for him, and if ever man rejoiced sincerely in being freed from the cares of public life it was him. During the voyage he was as playful as a child; talked and joked with everybody on board, and reminded me of a schoolboy on a long vacation."

If Dolley had any regrets at leaving the glamorous stage where she had played such a star role for the last sixteen years, they were all dispelled by the relief and joy in Jemmy's eyes.

PART SIX

Montpelier
1817–1837

1

Dolley was happily content, starting with this year of 1817, to spend the rest of her life at Montpelier. She felt no sense of loss, only relief and fulfillment. It was like passing long years of wandering in the wilderness and coming at last into the Promised Land. Even nature embodied the new freshness of life—soaring mountains, ninety miles of the Blue Ridge foothills, instead of dull square buildings; green sloping fields and fresh country air instead of fevered swampland, and, most liberating of all, guests who were unvaryingly friendly instead of sycophants, office seekers, gossips, political opponents. She felt no nostalgia, certainly no envy, only pity at thought of the new First Lady, especially when Margaret Smith wrote that Monroe was attempting to restore to the President's House the stately formality which had prevailed in Washington's regime, that his wife and daughters paid no visits and had received no woman callers except Anna Cutts and a committee from the Orphan Asylum.

Poor Elizabeth Monroe, thought Dolley. Imagine her having lived in Washington for the last seven years yet having almost no personal friends! Even the idolized Washington had been criticized for what some people had called his formality and stiffness, so it was no wonder that Elizabeth had been unpopular with her attempts to introduce the European manners she had found so appealing as the wife of the American minister in Paris and in other Old World capitals. Yet to believe that stuffy European court life would be welcomed in this raw new republic!

Dolley liked and admired Elizabeth, and the two had always been friends. The new First Lady was such an elegantly handsome woman in her furs and velvets, and so courageous! When in France during the Revolution she had actually dared to visit Madame Lafayette in prison when the wife of the gallant young general had been incarcerated as a member of the nobility and was in danger of being guillotined. With only her servants with her in her carriage, Elizabeth had gone to the prison and, demanding to see the prisoner, had been admitted. Because of this indication of official American interest Madame Lafayette had been set free. A pity Elizabeth Monroe was not so popular now in her own country as she had become in France, where she had been called "la belle Américaine!" But Washington with all its problems, even those of her successor and admired friend, seemed to Dolley gloriously far away.

Montpelier. The very name set one's spirit soaring. A "castle," the child Dolley had once called Scotchtown. A "palace," people had liked to call the President's House. But for Montpelier Dolley could find only one word—"heaven."

Her contentment was visible for all to see.

"My beloved friend," wrote Eliza Collins Lee not long after their retirement, "do you know?—or do you now know, my beloved Dolley, that your absence from this city is more and more lamented; that your urbanity, benevolence and cheerfulness will be long sought for *in vain*. But you are happier and oh! that I could witness that superior happiness painted by Mrs. Miller. . . . She says, 'I spent two days with Mr. and Mrs. Madison. Her soul is as big as ever and her body has not decreased. Mr. M. is the picture of happiness. They look like Adam and Eve in Paradise!' "

Dolley was as proud of the finished house—"mansion," some liked to call it—as was James, who had labored for years over works of architecture and made his own original plans, adding wings at each end, designing the stately Palladian portico with its four stuccoed columns, long and wide enough so that in stormy weather he could walk his allotted number of miles for exercise, Dolley usually by his side. When children were there, which was often, it made a wonderful place to run races or play hopscotch or marbles, as spacious as the big attic at Scotchtown. At forty-nine Dolley was still agile enough to give Anna's younger boys, Walter and Thomas, a challenge, and had to temper her pace not to win too often over Dolley, age six, and Mary Estelle, just a chubby adorable four year old. When Richard and Anna visited Montpelier that first summer, Dolley's sister was expecting her seventh child. There was still a sense of loss accompanying her visit, for her fourth son, Richard, little "Dicky," had died after a long wasting sickness at the age of five.

It was the only flaw in Dolley's newfound happiness that Anna and her children were so far away and could visit only a few weeks in the summer, dividing their time between Montpelier and Richard's home in Maine. He had just been reappointed second comptroller of the Treasury and they were preparing to build a permanent house in Washington on the northeast corner of the square opposite the President's House. Dolley was thrilled. Richard's shipping business had suffered reverses during the War of 1812, and she had been afraid he would be obliged to move his family permanently to Maine, which seemed off the face of the earth. With renewed assurance of profitable employment in Washington they would be at least near enough to visit frequently. Together she and Anna pored over the plans for the new house, which would have two stories, a big double drawing room, and a fine garden in back. Of course she had no idea what part this house was to play in her own life.

She always considered Anna's children as her own, especially James Madison Cutts, now twelve, and little Dolley Payne Madison Cutts, a replica of herself at six, namesakes she had never been able to give to Jemmy. But she reveled in all of them, romped with them on the lawns, played dolls with the little girls and hopscotch and marbles with the boys, helped them gather grapes and figs and peaches in Mother Madison's big fruit garden, went with them into the slaves' cabins to listen to stories and songs reminiscent of their ancestors' lives in other centuries and other African climes.

When the children had gone the house seemed desolately empty, but it was in reality far from that. There were Madison relatives living nearby, James's brother William, his sister Sarah Macon, children of his deceased brother Francis. Seldom a day but guests came thronging, relatives, friends, strangers. Someone would be watching through the telescope on the front portico and the cry would go up. "Horse coming!" "Carriage!" "Lordy, see all de dust! Mus' be a whole army dis time!" And all within hearing distance would rush to the front passage and portico to watch the progress of the visitors up the long winding road from the gate which was left always open. Who this time? They came in all sorts of conveyances and at all times—political acquaintances bent on milking the wisdom of the respected patriarch of government, foreign diplomats, old friends and neighbors from Washington, tourists on the road to Virginia Springs who, stopping at Orange Court House, were told that they were only five miles from the ex-President's House, and, though hesitating to intrude on his privacy, could not resist the temptation. All were received with lavish hospitality.

"There are few houses in Virginia," reported one contemporary writer, "that gave a larger welcome or made it more agreeable than that over which 'Queen Dolley,' the most beloved of all our female sovereigns, reigned and wielded as skillfully the domestic sceptre as she had done worthily and popularly the public; everything that came beneath her immediate and personal sway, the care and entertainment of visitors, the government of servants, the whole policy of the interior, was admirably managed with equal grace and efficiency."

And why not? Dolley would have demurred with practical modesty. The house seemed designed for entertaining. The drawing room opening out of the front passage and extending the whole depth of the house was far more inviting than the crimson-curtained room in the President's House where she had held her famous receptions. Its carved marble mantel had been imported from France. The Parisian rugs were colorfully gay. The silk draperies at the triple-hung windows did not hide the view of the rear gardens where roses and jasmine vied in color with the myriad trellises lush with scarlet and yellow vines. Comfortable chairs, French sofas upholstered in crimson damask, walls hung with mirrors and paintings, six of them by Gilbert Stuart—all invited the guests to relaxation and enjoyment, caused them to remain often far longer than intended.

"It was a charming room," Margaret Smith approved in her ubiquitous records, "giving activity to the mind, by the historic and classic ideas that it awakened."

And the dining room! Its big polished mahogany table and huge sideboard decked with china and silver were shining foils for the great platters of delectable foods that came up from the basement kitchens. Descriptions of some of the meals served were preserved for posterity.

"The table was not only abundantly, but handsomely provided," reported one guest, Charles Ingersoll; "good soups, flesh, fish, and vegetables, well cooked, dessert and excellent wines of various kinds; and when Mrs. Madison was prevailing on me to eat hot bread for breakfast, she said, 'You city people think it unwholesome, but we eat heartily, like the French, and never feel ourselves worse for it.'"

Hot bread? It was one of the smallest breakfast items. Breakfast on one occasion, served to fifteen or twenty guests, consisted of "tea, coffee, hot wheat bread, light cakes, a pone or corn leaf, cold ham, nice hashes, chickens, etc."

The French influence in the meals had doubtless been inspired by Thomas Jefferson and the years when Dolley had been his hostess. In his house she had been introduced, like others, to macaroni and vermicelli, anchovies, olive oil, vanilla, citron fruit, Parmesan cheese, European nuts and figs, the ices and creams which Jefferson's French chefs, Julien and Lemaire, had produced and which their own cook, Pierre Roux, continued to provide.

But now, mistress of her own kitchens once more, Dolley was able to serve favorite dishes of her years of early homemaking, even prepare some with her own hands. Guests exclaimed over her croquettes, made of finely chopped meat, seasoned with onion, mace, or nutmeg, coated with crumbs and fried, her sour cream ginger cake, her crab omelet served with parsley and thyme; her seedcake rich with currants and caraway seeds; her soft gingerbread, made with beef drippings and sprinkled with powdered sugar and which she called her "Jefferson gingerbread."

But guests were treated with aesthetic as well as culinary fare. Seated at the great table they could feast their eyes on walls hung with rare engravings depicting characters and incidents in the life of their host—Washington, Monroe, Adams, Jefferson—French and Dutch prints, Steel's engraving of the *Battle of New Orleans.* Conversation was more sparkling and stimulating than the wines. It roamed the whole gamut of human concerns—politics, literature, art, philosophy, religion—and the genial host ("old sobersides," Dolley had once called him!) provided much of the spice and pungency that made it sparkle.

J. K. Paulding, secretary of the Navy Board, who visited them in 1817 and had known James for thirty years, would have scoffed at the eminent historian who would deplore over a hundred years later, "If James Madison had had a sense of humor!"

"He was a man of wit, relished wit in others and his small bright blue eyes would twinkle most wickedly when lighted up by some whimsical conception or association."

Dolley exulted in Jemmy's happiness even more than in her own. At sixty-six, the burdens of sixteen years sloughed off his shoulders, he seemed as many years younger. The oil portrait painted by Joseph Wood in 1816, when his cares had lightened and retirement was in the offing, in spite of its sober expression, revealed something of this new calmness. Eliza Lee, for whom Dolley had had duplicate portraits painted, both of herself and of James, said of Madison's, "It almost breathes, and expresses much of the serenity of his feelings. In short, it is himself."

She was not so complimentary about Dolley's, which showed her in a white gown ruffed high at the neck, a crimson shawl, with crisp black curls escaping from the inevitable turban.

"Your likeness, my dear friend, is not so satisfactory *to me*. To a common observer it is sufficient and instantly recognized—but I lament the absence of that expression of your eyes which speaks *from* and *to* the heart, the want of which robs your countenance of its richest treasure."

But no artist was ever able to capture the essence of that elusive magic which was radiation from an Inner Light. It could no more be pictured than the fragrance of a rose or the sound of a child's laughter.

Visitors during those retirement years were surprised to discover that the eminent statesman-scholar-philosopher was also a vigorous and efficient agriculturist—farmer, Madison called it. James Paulding saw this other dominant interest of his friend in full play. Each morning, after sitting on the portico and conversing on political, literary, or philosophical subjects for a time, they would set out on horseback to examine the fields. Paulding was intrigued by the "matchless dexterity" with which his host opened gates without dismounting, using only a crooked stick, a trick he tried vainly to match. On one ride they inspected a field where a flash flood had caused havoc with deep deposits of gravel.

"A bad business, Tony," commented Madison to the old slave who had come with them.

"Oh yes, massa, ver bad." The black man shook his head mournfully, "ver bad indeed. I tell you what, massa—I think Gor Almighty by an' large, he do mos' as much harm as good."

Since the 1780s Madison had been studying scientific methods of agriculture, accumulating an extensive library, importing plants and seeds from all over the world, working with Jefferson to improve farm equipment, including the much admired "Jefferson plow." He himself had built a new threshing machine, which, he had informed Jefferson gleefully, required "only five or six hands to operate." In Washington Madison had become President of the first American Board of Agriculture. Now, master of his five thousand acres, no longer dependent on overseers to carry out his plans, he was in his element, as absorbed in theories of land cultivation as in those of history and government.

The year of his return he was elected President of the Albemarle Agricultural Society, covering five counties, and proceeded to startle his fellow farmers with a statement of policy and methods which a hundred years later would still be considered revolutionary. Nature's balance, he warned, must be maintained if the earth was not to be ruined. If man overused its resources, he would threaten his own survival. He advocated contour plowing, irrigation, natural fertilizers, tree conservation, reforestation, rotation of crops, scientific breeding of cattle. As one historian a century and more later commented, his first address to the body might have been entitled: "Will the human race destroy the earth it lives on?" Jefferson, himself an agricultural innovator, humbly styled him "the best farmer in the world."

Doubtless guests were even more amazed to see the woman who for sixteen years had epitomized the fashions of Washington out digging in her favorite garden wearing a hideous shade hat given her by the friendly garrulous wife of the French gardener Beazée, her "Beazée bonnet" she called it. The couple had come to Virginia during the Revolution and, employed now by Madison, had made themselves popular with the plantation's servants, taking pains to teach them smatterings of French, much to the amusement of Dolley, who laughed heartily over their jargon. The horseshoe-shaped terraced garden edged with boxwood which Beazée laid out, patterned after the Hall of Representatives, was her pride and joy. It contained not only flowers of all kinds—roses, jasmine, tiger lilies, mock orange, pink oleanders, larkspur, phlox, snapdragons—but also fruits, pears, figs, grapes, strawberries, rare plants many of them. Especially did Dolley love the cape jasmine, and as new buds appeared on the plants she gave them names of people dear to her, first, of course, husband, sisters, and son. Each morning she went the rounds in her Quaker gray gown and ridiculous bonnet, and if she found one dead it was a source of genuine grief.

Far different this riotous profusion of color from Mother Madison's own separate garden, laid out by her own gardener in prim old-fashioned style. Nothing new or different there, any more than in the routine followed through most of her going-on-ninety years. Still spry, erect, mentally keen, Nelly Madison pursued her well-ordered life in her own apartments at the right of the house, ate her meals cooked in her own basement kitchen and served by her ancient servant, Old Sawney, with hands shaking far more than her own. At two o'clock each day she received callers, guests as well as family, seated in state on a couch in the center of her large sitting room, the table at her side containing her Bible, prayer book, and knitting. Fruits of the latter in the form of innumerable gloves and hosiery with names knitted in were presented to the guests she favored.

Though as different in personality and way of life as their two gardens, she and Dolley lived in perfect harmony and sincere affection. One of the qualities which endeared "Grandmama" to Dolley was her love and tolerance of all the children of the family, especially of Payne.

"Give him time," she would echo Dolley's indulgent excuses for the foster grandson whom she had seen grow from a charming cherub to an equally charming but indolent youth in his late twenties. "He will settle down and make something good of himself."

"Yes—oh yes!" agreed Dolley gratefully.

Of all the blessings in this new environment one of the richest was hope for her son. He had accompanied them, willingly enough it seemed, to Montpelier. Here in the wholesome countryside, Dolley was convinced, away from those city temptations that seemed to be his weakness, he would mature into the fine responsible manhood of which he was certainly capable. When he showed considerable interest in Madison's plans for land development, both she and James were delighted. The plantation would be his someday. He would soon marry, thought Dolley happily, settle down, and bless her with armfuls of grandchildren. But as problems began to frustrate James's farm labors—first floods, then a long summer of drought, a market recession which plunged the cost of corn from $1.46 to $0.80 a bushel, then to $0.39—his interest waned. To Dolley's distress he began absenting himself more and more frequently, not merely to the dances, races, and other amusements in the vicinity—Dolley could understand his need for excitement—but for many days at a time. She wondered where he went. To Baltimore, Washington, Philadelphia? She hoped the latter, for it might mean revival of friendship with little Phoebe Morris, her favorite hope for a daughter-in-law.

Then, suddenly, he returned, fresh and alert, blue eyes so like Dolley's own alight with purpose. He had an idea. He wanted land of his own. Richard Chapman had 104 acres he wanted to sell, just a few miles from Montpelier. Payne had seen silkworms being grown in Europe. Why not do the same here in America? Look at the white mulberry tree next to Papa's Greek temple! It had enough leaves to feed thousands of caterpillars! He would plant mulberry trees, hundreds of them. It would be easy, far more profitable than corn and tobacco plummeting in price. He would become rich!

Dolley was overjoyed, James skeptical. He knew Payne's volatile enthusiasms, also his aversion to hard labor. But, he reasoned wryly, Payne was not the only one who could gamble. They examined the property. Even its name was propitious, Toddsberth. A man named Todd had stopped there on his way to explore the Shenandoah Valley with the Knights of the Golden Horseshoe, that band of cavaliers which, early in the eighteenth century, had gone on a trip to explore the country beyond the Blue Ridge Mountains. When they returned Governor Spotswood of Virginia had presented to each of them a small golden horseshoe inscribed with the words, *Sic juvat transcendere montes.* So the expedition had got its name.

James approved, and Payne, who had a small income from his Philadelphia property, paid Chapman $540 for the land. Then, before planting any mulberry trees, he sent to France for silk workers. He needed experts, he felt, to proceed with the complicated project. Meanwhile he marked time by continuing his restless wanderings, his occasional returns home, his piling up of gambling debts.

Fortunately both ignorance of his whereabouts and mounting duties kept Dolley from excessive worry. Guests continued to pour in.

"I have just received yours, dearest Anna," she wrote on July 5, 1820, "and rejoice that you are well and have your friends about you. Yesterday we had ninety persons to dine with us at one table—put up on the lawn under a thick arbor. The dinner was profuse and good, and the company very orderly. Many of them were old acquaintances of yours, among them the two Barbours. We had no ladies except Mother Madison, Mrs. Macon, and Nelly Willis. The day was cool and all pleasant,—Half a dozen only staid *[sic]* all night, and are now about to depart. President Monroe's letter this morning announces the French minister, we expect him this evening, or perhaps sooner— though he may not come until tomorrow; but I am less worried here with a hundred visitors than with twenty-five in Washington,—this summer especially. I wish, dearest, you had just such a country home as this. I truly believe it is the happiest and most true life, and would be so good for you and the dear children. Always your devoted sister."

A rustic retreat far from the world? Hardly. For the world came to Montpelier.

Though he was never again to enter Washington, James was almost as cognizant of events there as when he was President. Legislators came to ask his advice. The *National Intelligencer* and other papers arrived regularly. He was constantly in correspondence with Richard Cutts and others in the capital. Foreign visitors brought news of international import. Through letters and visits to and fro he kept always in rapport with his colleague Jefferson. And President Monroe did not hesitate to question his predecessor on matters of diplomacy.

Madison approved full recognition of the independence of Argentina in its struggle against Spain. Countries must be free to choose their own form of government. European colonialism had no place in the New World. He rejoiced when Spain finally ceded Florida to the United States, climaxing his own sixteen years of effort. He deplored the mounting tension over slavery and only grudgingly countenanced the compromise of 1820 which attempted to balance slave states with free. He hated to see the country so divided. It boded ill for the future.

Slavery. Both he and Dolley hated the institution, considered it not only a denial of democracy but a grievous, unpardonable sin. Yet, like Washington, Jefferson, and other Southerners who condemned it, they were caught in its toils. But what could be done? James could not countenance freeing them wholesale. With the prejudice existing, their condition would be far worse than now, a change from one kind of oppression to one even worse. Emancipation should be gradual, he believed, and slaves should be returned to the continent of their origin. In 1816 he had helped to organize the American Colonization Society. He had a plan for financing universal emancipation, the government raising six hundred million dollars by selling three hundred million acres of its western land to free the million and a half slaves in the United States and send them to Liberia.

Meanwhile he treated his own hundred slaves with an almost lavish care and consideration. Paul Jennings, his faithful body servant, attested to this manner of living in his remarkable *Colored Man's Reminiscences of Madison,* published in book form in 1865.

"Mr. Madison, I think, was one of the best men that ever lived. I never saw him in a passion and never knew him to strike a slave, although he had over a hundred; neither would he allow an overseer to do it. Whenever any slaves were reported to him as stealing or 'cutting up' badly, he would send for them and admonish them privately, and never mortify them by doing it before others. They generally served him very faithfully."

Emancipation, yes. But that was a long-term hope. Meanwhile another of his fondest dreams was partly coming to fruition.

For years both he and Jefferson had been agitating for a national university, as had Washington before them. No success. Now with Jefferson's prompting a university was planned for the state of Virginia, nearer the center of the state than William and Mary College.

Madison rode with Jefferson to Rockfish Gap to choose a site for the new institution. Dolley hated to see him go. It was the first time they had been separated for more than a few days since that terrible summer of her illness in Philadelphia. After much hot argument with colleagues who preferred another location, Jefferson won. The Central College at Charlottesville was chosen to become the site of the new university, with Jefferson as its architect and first President. Madison was elated. Education was to him the very lifeblood of democracy. He and Jefferson, as nearly always, were in full agreement. Professors for the new institution must be chosen with consummate care. Since it was to be government-supported there must be no religious bias or affiliation. His fundamental credo of separation of church and state was always paramount. He had fought hard enough for it in Virginia, his quiet insistence winning even over the fervid thunderings of Patrick Henry. Government funds would support any institution allied with religion over his dead body!

The regular visits to Monticello continued to be some of Dolley's greatest joys. Though Martha Randolph's children were all grown, there were grandchildren now to take the place of her own absent nieces and nephews. She was equally beloved by them. One of Martha's grandchildren was to write of her, "Mrs. Madison helped the older girls with their darning and fancy work, made clothes for the dolls, told such lovely fairy tales and was so sympathetic and kind that the youngest never hesitated to call on her kindly aid."

She listened to children with the same courteous attention as to adults. Once little Benjamin Franklin, who was sitting next to her at breakfast, was having difficulty managing his muffin. Dolley took her knife to cut it for him, but, laying his hand on hers, he protested, "No, no, that's not the way!"

"Well! How then, Master Ben?" she inquired good-naturedly.

"Why, you must tear him open and put butter inside and stick holes in his back and then pat him and squeeze him and the juice will run out!"

Dolley laughed merrily and gleefully followed his instructions.

James also had a keen understanding of children and was a favorite with all the numerous progeny who visited the plantation, Dolley's nieces and nephews as well as his own. He was especially fond of Anna's youngest boy, another little Dicky, the child Anna had been carrying the first summer of their retirement. As early as age three, little Richard Dominicus was showing a greater interest in farming pursuits than any of the other boys. Perched in front of Uncle Jemmy on the latter's big horse, he would ride with him each morning on his rounds of the fields, listening with sober intelligent concern to explanations of why land needed to rest between crops, like "tired people," and how James had found a kind of wheat that the Hessian flies did not like so well, "Lawless" it was called, and why plants needed to be fed nourishing food, "fertilizers," just like children.

After a rain Dicky loved to run to the big tin cup Madison had embedded in the center of the gravel walk to the first gate, measuring the amount of rain that had fallen with a little stick, and bringing it back triumphantly, finger on the exact spot, to show Uncle Jemmy. James gave him a small plot of land which he planted with tobacco and carefully tended during the summer.

"Richard Cutts, Tobacco Planter, Washington." James addressed a letter to him after the family's return home. His whole tobacco crop, James advised him, was harvested and ready for marketing (net weight three ounces). Where did Master Cutts want it sold? In England or here at home? If it was to be manufactured, did he wish it to be pigtail or twist for chewing, or made into snuff? Madison was enclosing a penny as partial payment. When Master Cutts came again, he must bring his sisters, Miss Modesty and Miss Taciturnity. And, he added, "All your friends, white, yellow, and black, send compliments."

Both James and Dolley, especially Dolley, needed all the happiness they could derive these days from others' children because they were receiving so little from the only one they had.

Payne's venture into sericulture was no more productive than his other forms of gambling. The expert workers arrived from Europe. Larvae were secured—and died. The climate was not suited to silk production. Dolley sympathized with him wholeheartedly in his disappointment. Poor boy! He had tried so hard and with such bad luck! James, though sincerely regretful, regarded the failure with less sympathy. He had questioned his foster son's willingness to apply himself to such a complicated and exacting business.

Payne accepted the result with his usual debonair cheerfulness and applied himself to other interests, most of them pursued in places offering more opportunities for excitement than Toddsberth or Montpelier. Dolley reconciled herself to his absences through hoping that somewhere he would meet a fine girl who would tempt him to marry and settle down. Surely it would happen soon. And look what a good marriage had done for her youngest brother, John Coles Payne, who had had a serious drinking problem until he married Clara Wilcox and James had loaned him one of his farms to settle on and run! A sober and hardworking man now with five children, one of them her namesake, Dolley.

Hope soared in the early spring of 1820 when Payne announced that he was going to visit the home of Anthony Morris, Dolley's old Quaker friend, in Philadelphia. Phoebe! She had always hoped Anthony's daughter and her son would be attracted to each other. They had been friendly for many years, for Phoebe had visited the family both in Washington and at Montpelier. Now she wrote Phoebe a loving letter, hinting, inveterate matchmaker that she was, of Payne's interest in their friendship and his need of understanding and affection in this crucial period of his life. Then she settled down to wait . . . and wait . . .

Months passed. It was July when Anthony, not Phoebe, wrote that his daughter had not written because she was in "daily expectation of seeing Mr. Todd . . . about concluding him a false knight, and was actually preparing a denunciation of him to you, when he suddenly appeared at Bolton to speak for himself, which he has done so amiably and satisfactorily that he has silenced all censure and made the most favorable impression on our hearts, indeed, my excellent friend, I can't convey to you the pleasure his company affords to us all."

More hope. More waiting. Finally a letter from Phoebe herself to "her dearest Mrs. Madison." Payne had stayed only four days. Probably their home was a little too quiet for one used to city excitement.

"I dare say he has been sufficiently wearied of my questions, for I was so glad to see him and to know everything about you, how you looked, what you did, what you put on, etc., etc., all the minute details which I thought my long absence would make reasonable. However, I think I have extracted this satisfaction from him, that you are still my own Mrs. Madison, blooming, gay, and affectionate as ever."

Dolley sighed. So it was not to be Phoebe, at least not yet. But she was never one to give up hope. And if not Phoebe, then someone else. Payne's whereabouts were often in doubt. Though she never knew where to send them or if they would ever reach him, her letters went out almost as constantly as her loving thoughts and prayers.

"I am impatient to hear from you, my dearest Payne," she wrote in April 1823, "had I known where to direct I should have written you before this; not that I had anything to communicate, but for the pleasure of repeating how much I love you, and to hear of your happiness. . . ."

And in December 1824: "I have received yours, my dearest Payne, of the 23 and 24 November and I was impatient to answer them yesterday (the day of their reaching me) but owing to the winter establishment for the male [sic] no post leaves until tomorrow morning. Mr. Clay and two members of Congress left us yesterday after passing 2 days. Mr. C. inquired affectionately after you, as does [sic] all your old acquaintances whom I see,—but my dear son it seems to be the wonder of them all that you'd stay so long from us!—and now I am ashamed to tell when asked, how long my only child has been absent from the home of his mother! Your Papa and myself entreat you to arrange your business with those concerned to return to them when necessary and let us see you here as soon as possible.

"Enclosed 30$ instead of the 20$ which you mentioned, and tho' I am sure 'tis insufficient for the journey, I am unable to add to the sum today. I recently paid Holloway 200$ on your note with interest for 2 years. . . . The 'occurrence' you allude to, I hope, is propicious [sic] and if it were for your good, we might rejoice in your immediate union provided it brought you speedily to our arms, who love with inexpressible tenderness and constancy. Your own Mother."

2

Adam and Eve in paradise? Dolley smiled wryly. Not if Eden was supposed to be the state of unmitigated bliss depicted in the old story, that is, until the serpent practiced his wiles. During those years of the 1820s life became increasingly complicated and beset with problems. And worry over Payne and his delinquencies was only one of the serpents infesting the garden.

In spite of James's enthusiasm, expertise, and hard labor the farm was not prospering. All over Virginia plantation owners were struggling to make ends meet. Many were losing their lands. During the first ten years of his retirement there were nine crop failures, due to a succession of hot, rainless summers, broken only by disastrous downpours. Droughts were aggravated by unmanageable insect pests. Plunging farm prices and stagnant overseas markets added to the problems. There were typhoid epidemics affecting not only the servants but, on one occasion, Madison himself. A company he had invested in to promote highway construction failed, and he had to help defray the twelve-thousand-dollar debt. He compensated for some of the losses by shifting to manufacturing for domestic use, producing woolens and linens. Expenses for the huge ménage were incredible. Sometimes he had to buy ten thousand pounds of meat at one time to feed the household properly, and Dolley would order calico by the bolt.

James would have been able to solve these problems in time except for a further complication which was especially distressing to Dolley. Richard Cutts, who had lost his shipping fortune because of the embargo he had supported in Congress, had attempted to recoup his losses by speculation with twelve thousand dollars, much of it loaned by Madison. The venture failed. It was in the spring of 1824 that Dolley learned he was on the verge of bankruptcy. She was horrified for the sake of Anna and the children. Suppose they lost their house and had no place to live! For once she decided to act without James's permission. She wrote Richard a letter. "Secret," it was headed.

"It is with inexpressible grief, my dear brother, that I understand (in confidence) the situation of your affairs! I will not insult your sensibility by descanting on the devoted friendship and affection for you and yours ever felt by Mr. Madison and myself because you know it! But if ever you reciprocated—which we never doubted—I entreat you to secure to me the amount of *all the money lent you* in a house, lots or some other property, in case you have at this unlucky moment to part with what you possess in Washington. It is only in such a case, where other creditors may take *all,* that I would remind you of the *debt.* Yes, it is more for your sake than mine that I now write to ask you, for G___ sake, to do this just thing that you and your children may profit by it, for be assured that you may afterwards command this sum with all that could be desired from every source to rescue or to enrich you for more fortunate speculations. . . ."

But this attempt to save something for Anna was doomed to failure. The loaned money had been used to build the house on President's Square, and this was taken by the Branch Bank of the United States in mortgage foreclosure. To Dolley's horror Richard was sent to debtors' prison for a time, only regaining his freedom by declaring bankruptcy. To be sure, many respectable people had endured this ignominy— Robert Morris, who had helped finance the Revolution, Thomas Mann Randolph—but for Dolley, knowing Anna's sensitivity, it was an unspeakable humiliation. Even worse was the fear that her sister's family would be left destitute.

"We must do something!" she mourned to James.

He agreed. In spite of his own financial problems he arranged with Richard's creditors to buy the house on President's Square, Cutts promising to meet the payments out of his comptroller's salary. At least the Cutts family would have a place to live. It would cost him between five and six thousand dollars, an amount he could ill afford. Lucy also came to the Cutts's assistance, and the sum of twelve thousand dollars was set up in a trust fund for Anna P. Cutts or her survivors, furnished by Lucy P. Todd and "others of her kindred and friends."

As if one disaster were not enough, payment was delayed on a tract of land Madison had sold on Panther Creek in Kentucky, part of his inheritance from his father. Then a bill came from a Baltimore shop which had run up a large unpaid account with Payne during his school years, another for a debt of five hundred dollars he had incurred with a Washington lottery house. James kept the news of these delinquencies from Dolley and against his better judgment paid both bills, as he had done many times before. He could not risk the irreparable hurt it would cause her if her son also went to debtors' prison. Meanwhile she was pursuing him with her usual loving letters, begging him to come home, and sending him drafts of money for his stage fares.

Madison's letters to his stepson during the ensuing months were scarcely more condemning. "I would not attempt to describe your mother's distress, but I now hasten to a subject which if disclosed to her would inflict new tortures." He hoped that the landlord in Philadelphia to whom Payne was in debt for his board and whom James was at present unable to pay would let him come home instead of sending him to prison. "Come then I entreat and conjure you to the bosom of your parents who are anxious to do everything to save you from tendencies and past errors and provide for comfort and happiness."

But Payne neither returned home nor wrote.

In spite of financial stresses and family worries, Montpelier's gates remained wide open. Guests continued to flock, and Dolley welcomed them all with no indication that their entertainment was a further drain on the plantation's limited resources. In November 1824 she saw James ride off by himself to Monticello without, for once, a feeling of loss and loneliness. Her time would be full making ready for the most important guest she had ever entertained.

The Marquis Marie Joseph Paul Yves Roch Gilbert du Motier de Lafayette had arrived in America in August, idol of the country whose independence he had helped to win. Madison had hastened to write this friend whom he had not seen since they had traveled together in 1784 to witness the conclusion of the Indian treaty at Fort Stanwix.

"I this instant learn, my dear friend, that you have safely reached the shores where you will be hailed by every voice of a free people. That of no one springs more from the heart than mine. May I not hope that the course of your movements will give me an opportunity of proving it by the warmth of my embrace on my own threshold?"

Yes, Lafayette had replied. He would visit, first Monticello, and then Montpelier. His two months of travel through the country, often visiting towns named Lafayette, his progress attended by parades, receptions, salutes at dawn, balls and fireworks at night, a celebration at

Yorktown, a visit to Mount Vernon and the tomb of Washington in the company of George Washington Parke Custis, had brought him at last, a thousand riders in his train, to a rousing welcome at Charlottesville. Then, escorted by a guard of honor, he had wound his way up the mountain, descended from his barouche to clasp in his arms his old friend Jefferson, now stooped and frail, who had once helped him outline a plan for the new French constitution.

In the intervening years Lafayette had endured imprisonment, torture, degradation, and time had left its mark on the gallant intrepid youth who had crossed the ocean to fight beside his beloved hero Washington.

"My old friend," Madison wrote Dolley, "embraced me with great warmth. He is in fine health and spirits but so much increased in bulk and changed in aspect that I should not have known him."

James shared in the adulation when four hundred guests gathered in the University Rotunda at Charlottesville. The sight of two former Presidents plus the hero of the Revolution aroused much comment and admiration. "Mr. Madison," wrote Levasseur, Lafayette's secretary, "stood out among all of them for the originality of his mind and the delicacy of his allusions." Toasts in his honor called him the "ablest expositor of the Constitution" and declared that "his commentaries on it "will be forgotten only with the text."

"Happy the people," he replied simply, "who have virtue for their guest and gratitude for their feast." He was greeted with thunderous applause. But unfortunately his compliments to Lafayette were delivered in such a small voice that almost no one heard him.

He returned home not knowing when Lafayette would arrive. He came so suddenly that Senator Barbour had barely time to assemble his Orange County Volunteers to accompany the entourage to Montpelier. But Dolley was ready. To her surprise she found the famous guest far easier to entertain than most foreign dignitaries. He remained four days. Evenings were often spent discussing slavery with farmers in the vicinity when the visitor "never missed an opportunity to defend the rights that all men without exception have to liberty." He was surprised and delighted to find how many Virginians agreed with him.

He spent much time in Dolley's garden and promised to send her seeds of some of his favorite tiger lilies when he returned to France. And he could not get enough of visiting the slave cabins in what they called Walnut Grove, marveling especially at one old slave, Granny

Milly, 104 years old, the head of a household of daughters and grand-daughters, the youngest of them nearly seventy, and all happily retired. He made friends with Old Sawney, who had gone with James to Princeton in 1768 and later managed one of his farms. Now at age 90 he was humored as majordomo in Mother Madison's apartment, though, as Mary Cutts was to note, he "went to sleep in handing her a glass of water, almost his only duty." The visitor was intrigued by the efforts of Madame Beazée's eager pupils to jabber to him in their crude French.

In fact, all the prevailing French motifs in the house and grounds delighted him, but most of all he was fascinated by Madison's beautiful little temple built over the icehouse on the front lawn, its pillared architecture and rounded dome based on the Temple of Venus at Versailles.

There was a big dinner for two hundred on November 19 in Orange Courthouse. Madison himself gave seven of the formal toasts, the one to Lafayette reminding the group "of what we all owe, of what the nation itself owes, to its great benefactor whom we are gratified with having now for our guest," and ending with homage to "the divine rights of self government and its immortal champions."

Other visitors followed Lafayette at Montpelier, first Mr. and Mrs. George Tichnor and Daniel Webster. Tichnor commented that Madison, now almost seventy-four, was "certainly the gayest person of that age I ever saw," looking ten years younger than when harried by problems of the presidency.

Then came the Wright sisters, Camilla and her much-talked-about sister Frances (Fanny), who was arousing shock through the ideas she espoused in her lectures—insistence on a rational basis for all beliefs, including religious creeds, support of political action by working men, and, more controversial still, equal education for women and their right to speak in public before any and every kind of audience!

Madison, with his staunch commitment to freedom of speech, received her with great cordiality and found himself in almost full agreement with her views on slavery. Fanny had come to America with Lafayette to further her plan for slave emancipation, the slaves to be freed gradually, by public purchase or private manumission, then moved to a western tract she planned to purchase for the settlement of the freed slaves during a transition period to prepare them for more normal life. Madison was heartily in favor of her project until he learned that free love and racial amalgamation were among her accepted precepts.

"With her rare talents and still rarer disinterestness," he wrote Lafayette, "she has I fear created insuperable obstacles to her plans in defying established opinion and vivid feelings."

Lafayette, near the completion of his tour of the United States, came to Virginia again in 1825, joining Monroe and Madison at Monticello. It was a momentous occasion, uniting three past Presidents and one of the few surviving military leaders of the Revolution. But Dolley was shocked by Jefferson's look of feebleness. He had shown signs of increasing weakness for a long time, but now his tall figure was stooped, his features drawn and waxen—like the life masks, she thought, which the sculptor John Henri Isaac Browere had made that year for his busts of her and James.

She did not like the one of James. He looked as sober and patrician as one of his ancient Roman statues, cheeks sunken, lips turned down, no sign of that sly twinkle in his eyes. Browere was proud of the fact that his busts showed his subjects exactly as they were, wrinkles, pockmarks, lines, everything, not the way portrait artists portrayed them. Dolley was glad he had not delivered the one of her to Montpelier. The curls escaping from her turban looked like corkscrews, and even the slight smile on her face did little to soften its severity.

Charles Henry Hart, who reproduced these busts in pictures, differed in his estimate of James's but agreed heartily with her unfavorable opinion of her own.

"The bust of Madison is very fine in character and expression, but that of Mrs. Madison is of particular interest as being the only woman's face handed down to us by Browere. Her beauty has been heralded by more than one voice and one pen, but not one of the many portraits that we have of her . . . sustains the verbal verdict of her admirers; and now the life mask by Browere would seem to settle the question of her beauty in the negative."

Dolley would have been amused, not hurt, by this observation. She had always scoffed when people had called her beautiful.

James had recommended Browere to Jefferson, so in October of that year, 1825, the sculptor arrived at Monticello. Assured that the process of molding would take only twenty minutes, the aged Jefferson reluctantly consented. As he told his even more reluctant family, "he could not find it in his heart to refuse a man so trifling a favor, who had come so far."

But all did not go as predicted. Apparently the sculptor attempted a new method of molding, doing neck, shoulders, and head all at once, with unfortunate results.

Jefferson had a keen sense of humor, especially at his own expense. Three days later he was writing Madison a semiserious description of the proceeding. "I was taken in by Browere. He said his operation would be about 20 minutes and less unpleasant than Houdon's method (poured on plaster of Paris). I submitted therefore without enquiry, but it was a bold experiment on his part on the health of an octogenarian, worn down by sickness as well as age. Successive coats of thin grout plastered on the naked head, and kept there an hour, would have been a severe trial of a young and hale person. He suffered the plaister *[sic]* also to get so dry that separation became difficult & even dangerous. He was obliged to use freely the mallet and chisel to break it into pieces and get off a piece at a time."

There was more to the story. Jefferson's seventeen-year-old grandson George, looking through the window to watch the process, saw his grandfather sitting with his head encased in gray plaster, while the visitor appeared to be pounding him with a hammer and chisel. He ran to report that grandfather was being killed by an assassin. Martha rushed to the scene with three housemaids, all noisily attempting to prevent the murder, interfering with poor Browere's final task of separating the remaining plaster from the old man's ears.

"There became real danger," Jefferson continued to Madison, "that the ears would separate from the head sooner than the plaister *[sic]*."

"Oh dear!" Dolley did not consider the episode humorous. "And you recommended the man so highly!"

"No real harm done." James found the rest of the letter reassuring. "After a half hour's rest our friend was as good as new. He invited the sculptor to dinner and to spend the night, and the two joked over the adventure."

The resulting sculpture proved to be worth the suffering it caused, for it was one of the artist's finest works. But the episode was not forgotten. Nearly a century and a half later it would be remembered in an article with the intriguing title, "The Day Jefferson Got Plastered."

James and Dolley made their usual visit to Monticello in September of that year. As usual, it was a meeting of minds between the two past Presidents, as had been all their relationships for the last half century. Their collaboration had been one of the wonders of the world. But this visit brought sorrow as well as joy. Jefferson was only a shadow of the gigantic heroic figure who had dominated national politics for two generations. Since a fall in 1823 he had lost the use of his right hand. He could no longer hoist himself into the saddle, though he still managed his daily ride on old Eagle by being lowered into it from a higher elevation. But physical difficulties were not his only problem. Like many Virginia planters, in fact like Madison himself, he was nearly bankrupt. He had been twenty thousand dollars in debt on leaving the presidency. Though sale to Congress of his huge library had yielded him almost twenty-four thousand dollars, a debt he had signed for a relative had wiped that out completely. His plan to recoup his fortunes by selling land had failed, fertile western lands being far more desirable than poor Virginia soil.

"He's talking of trying to sell almost everything he owns, including Monticello," Martha Randolph confided to Dolley with surprising calmness.

Jefferson himself was not at all despondent. With Madison he discussed new plans for the university which was now his prime interest in life. He was bent on living to celebrate on July 4, 1826, the fiftieth anniversary of the signing of the Declaration of Independence, his noblest achievement. In fact, he had been invited to go to Washington to take part in the celebration.

James and Dolley returned home more saddened than cheered by the visit. They would have been even more distressed had they known it was the last time they would see the hero of American democracy alive.

They could not know, either, that the letter he wrote James on February 17 was the last he would receive.

"The friendship which has subsisted between us, now half a century, and the harmony of our political principles and pursuits, have been sources of constant happiness to me. . . . If ever the earth has beheld a system of administration conducted with a single and steadfast eye to the general interest and happiness of those committed to it . . . it is that to which our lives have been devoted. To myself you have been a pillar of support through life. Take care of me when dead, and be assured that I shall leave with you my last affection."

Jefferson did not attend the celebration in Washington on July 4. He died that very day soon after noon. Strangely enough, while the citizens of Quincy, Massachusetts, were celebrating the same fiftieth anniversary, John Adams, his predecessor in the presidency, died. As years passed, the political differences between the two leaders had become less marked, and they had been in near complete agreement. Flags were lowered to half-mast, and the nation grieved. And no wonder. It was the end of an era. James Madison was now almost the sole survivor of the nation's architects.

James and Dolley received the news of Jefferson's death too late to attend his funeral. It did not matter, he told the grieving Dolley. They had been together so constantly in life that they would remain so in spirit. The letter he wrote Nicholas Trist, Jefferson's grandson-in-law, was his own funeral eulogy for his friend.

"We are more than consoled for the loss, by the gain to him; and by the assurance that he lives and will live in the memory and gratitude of the wise and good, as a luminary of science, as a votary of liberty, as a model of patriotism, and as a benefactor of human kind. In these characters I have known him, and not less in the virtues and charms of social life for a period of fifty years, during which there was not an interruption or diminution of mutual confidence and cordial friendship for a single moment in a single instance."

So ended one of the most remarkable partnerships in history, the "Great Collaboration," one future historian was to call it. People would be trying to compare the two for the next hundred and more years. How were they alike? How were they different? And how could they be so different and yet so alike? "Madison appears less studied, brilliant and frank, but more natural, candid and profound than Jefferson," one person noted. "Mr. Jefferson has more imagination and passion, quicker and richer conceptions. Mr. Madison has a sound judgment, tranquil temper and logical mind." "Madison seems happier," commented another, "friendlier, better informed on current affairs and more resilient to change than the Sage of Monticello." All such contrasts were superficial. The truth was they were two sides of the same coin, metal fused in the heat of their democratic idealism, and spent without stint in its pursuit.

Take care of me when dead. James knew what he had meant. Keep on where I leave off.

James was the only beneficiary in Jefferson's will other than relatives and freed slaves. "I give to my old friend, James Madison of Montpelier, my gold-mounted walking-staff of animal horn, as a token of the cordial and affectionate friendship which for nearly now an half century has united us in the same principles and pursuits of what we have deemed for the greatest good of our country."

James accepted it gratefully and humbly, knowing that his old friend had intended it as a symbol. A king's scepter passed on to a beloved son? Hardly. Jefferson would turn over in his grave at the idea of royalty! Better, a shepherd's rod. He felt like a pigmy delegated to fill the shoes of a giant.

His first duty in the line of succession came with his appointment as rector of the University of Virginia, a position that combined the duties of a President with those of a board chairman. As a member of the governing board he had worked closely with Jefferson on the project, choosing the faculty, many of them European scholars, establishing a curriculum according to their liberal philosophy—all elective subjects, no fixed work required, self-discipline by students, certificates of efficiency instead of academic degrees.

He had suffered with Jefferson through the first year, horrified by the influx of undisciplined youths from wealthy families, who had attacked professors, frequented taverns, turned the dormitories into gambling dens, even thrown a stink bomb in one professor's house. With two other ex-Presidents of the United States, Jefferson and Monroe, and other eminent leaders, he had attended the meeting in the university rotunda where the crisis had been met head-on.

Never could one forget the scene. The students had determined not to yield, or give up one another's names, even to submit, if need be, to expulsion in a body. They stood before the board, looking their defiance. Silence. Then Jefferson arose. He looked on them with the tenderness of a father, trying to repress his emotions. He tried to speak, burst into tears, and sank back into his seat. Shocked, the students submitted, acknowledged their faults, answered all questions. Abashed by the great man's tears, they had willingly subscribed to a new disciplinary system.

Dolley's worry over the new responsibility was mitigated by the fact that she could go with him to all the meetings of the Executive Committee and the Board of Visitors, when they stayed with the Randolphs at Monticello, and that Nicholas Trist, the new secretary of the university, was soon able to take most of the duties from James's shoulders. For three years now James had been working on the editing of his papers, chiefly his voluminous notes on the Constitutional Convention of 1787, and, though she tried desperately to help him by assuming other responsibilities, even by acting as his secretary, she was in constant fear for his health.

There were other worries. Lucy's husband, Judge Todd, had died in that same year of 1826. Mother Madison was growing increasingly weaker and needed more attention. And of course there was always Payne. Dolley thankfully feasted on each small crumb of hope he tendered while only partially satisfying her maternal hunger through her constant rapport with nieces and nephews.

"Your letter, my dearest niece," she wrote eleven-year-old Mary Cutts in July 1826, "with the one before it, came quite safely, for which I return many thanks and kisses. . . . I trust you will yet be with me this summer, when I shall see your improvement in person also, and enjoy the sweet assurance of your affection. . . . I received by the last post a letter from your cousin Payne, at New York; he writes in fine health and spirits, and says he will be detained only a few weeks longer in that city. I sincerely hope to see him soon, though it is impossible for him to prefer Virginia to the North. If I were in Washington with you I know I could not conform to the formal rules of visiting they now have, but would disgrace myself by rushing about among my friends at all hours. Here I find it most agreeable to stay at home, everything about me is so beautiful. Our garden promises grapes and figs in abundance, but I shall not enjoy them unless your mamma comes, and brings you to help us with them; tell the boys they must come too. Alas, poor Walter, away at sea! I can scarcely trust myself to think of him,—his image fills my eyes with tears. Adieu, and believe me always your tender mother and aunt."

Was she just a trifle homesick for the city's bustle and excitement that she added a postscript? "P. S. We are very old-fashioned here. Can you send me a pattern of the present sleeve, and describe the width of dress and waist; also how turbans are pinned up, bonnets worn, as well as how to behave in the fashion?"

In February 1827, hearing that his former secretary and Dolley's cousin Ned Coles was going to Philadelphia, James wrote begging him to try to persuade Payne to return home. Because of crop losses and failure to sell part of his land, he was finding it almost impossible to pay the thirty-six hundred dollars he had promised on Payne's debts. A note that he had sent Payne in December for thirteen hundred dollars had not been acknowledged. Could the youth have misappropriated it instead of applying it to his debts? Time would show that he had indeed.

"His career must soon be fatal to everything dear to him in life," James wrote Ned Coles, "and you will know how to press on him the misery he is inflicting on his parents. With all the concealments and alleviations I have been able to effect, his mother has known enough to make her wretched the whole time of his strange absence and mysterious silence; and it is no longer possible to keep from her the results now threatened."

Somehow he managed through tobacco sales, mortgages, loans, to pay Payne's outstanding debts. But what of the future? Ned Coles, powerless to influence Payne, made his contribution to the problem by loaning Madison two thousand dollars, raised by selling his own bank stock.

It was Ned who, hearing that Madison, always the overmodest, while editing his papers was burning certain documents, sent him a sharp letter of protest.

"Every letter you consign to the flames diminishes the means whereby posterity may derive that intimacy with you on which your best title to their affection and gratitude will rest. . . . Indulge not those principles of delicacy and tenderness. . . . towards the feelings of others which have always characterized you."

Already James was being credited publicly with the title often privately ascribed to him. In a toast given him in absentia in Philadelphia a speaker declared, "If General Washington was father of our country, Mr. Madison should be considered the father of the Constitution. To the health and happiness of James Madison."

To Dolley's distress James was unwilling to relinquish what he considered his duties even when afflicted with his recurring rheumatism or other illnesses. In December 1827, when the university board held its winter meeting, he insisted on going though he had a high fever. To make it worse, there was such a heavy snowstorm that he had to go alone on horseback. It was well she did not know that after his arrival he was confined to bed for several days, his chair at the meeting vacant. He wrote home only after he was up again and back at the meeting, his keen mind as usual governing every important decision.

Frantic with worry until his letter came, Dolley wrote back in relief. "My beloved, I trust in God that you are well again, as your letter assures me you are. How bitterly I regret not going with you. . . . May angels guard thee, my best dear friend!"

When he attended a university meeting in July the following year, Dolley fortunately could go with him. Though they stayed at Monticello, the beautiful mansion seemed bleak and bare, for much of its furniture had been sold at auction to help defray Jefferson's accumulated debts. It was like seeing an old beloved friend wasted by sickness, reduced to skin and bones. The stately rooms echoed with ghostly footsteps and voices. Jefferson's marvelous clock seemed to be measuring past days instead of present. Knowing that James had been obliged to borrow two thousand dollars more that spring and sign a note for another twelve hundred, Dolley wondered if the same bleak bareness would sometime prevail at Montpelier.

But Martha Randolph welcomed them with open arms, cheerfully practical as usual, and all the children and grandchildren swarmed around, her four daughters, all grown up now, four sons, the youngest only twelve. Dolley missed the oldest daughter, married to Nicholas Trist, and her seven daughters, for they were living on his father's farm.

"You'll just have to excuse the things we are lacking, enough chairs for us all to sit down, for instance," said Martha with simple dignity. "You know everything that has happened." And somehow the bleak bareness did not matter. Jefferson's spirit, animating, dominating, transcendent, seemed to permeate the place, dispelling its emptiness.

To Dolley's relief, James, engrossed in university business and a convention called in Charlottesville to discuss the country's internal improvements, seemed healthier and more cheerful than on previous visits. In fact, one reporter comparing his appearance with that of the younger James Monroe, remarked, "Mr. Madison, I think, looks very well, though Mr. Monroe is the most perfect figure of woe I ever beheld—exceedingly wasted away and manifesting the most fixed melancholy."

Home for more company, this time Margaret Smith, with her husband and little daughter Anna, especially welcome since she had not visited Montpelier for many years. Dolley exulted in her company. It was almost like being back with her old friends in Washington.

"I have no notion of playing lady visitor and sitting prim in the drawing room with our hands before us," Margaret announced on arrival. "You have work to do, I'm sure, so let's just sit and work together."

Dolley took her to her own chamber, pulled up a comfortable French armchair for her, settled herself on a sofa where her sewing lay, and with Anna beside her looking at picture books, reveled in the presence of her guests.

"I reclined at my ease," Margaret would record in her diary, "while we talked,—and, oh, how we did talk. We went over the last 20 years and talked of scenes long past and of persons far away or dead. . . . She certainly has always been, and still is one of the happiest of human beings. . . . Time seems to favour her as much as fortune. She looked young and she says she feels so. I can believe her, nor do I think she will ever feel like an old woman."

She was equally entranced with her host at dinner, which lasted from four to six, so rich in conversation that she did not even mention food.

"Mr. Madison was chief speaker, and his conversation was a stream of history. . . . Every sentence he spoke was worthy of being written down. The formation and adoption of the Constitution, the Convention and first Congress, the character of their members and the secret debates. Franklin, Washington, Hamilton, John Adams, Jefferson, Jay, Patrick Henry and a host of other great men. It was living History!"

Conversation continued after dinner on the portico, then in the drawing room over coffee.

"Some of Mr. M.'s anecdotes were very droll, and we often laughed very heartily. His little blue eyes sparkled like stars under his bushy grey eye-brows and amidst the deep wrinkles of his poor thin face. Nor have they lost their look of mischief that used to lurk in their corners, and which vanished and gave place to an expression ever solemn, when the conversation took a serious turn."

During the evening Dolley took Margaret into Mother Madison's apartment. The guest found it hard to believe that the sprightly old lady, her pink cheeks not nearly as wrinkled as her son's, pressing into her hands a pair of gloves she had knitted, was ninety-seven!

"How are you?" inquired Margaret solicitously.

"I have been a blest woman," replied Nelly Madison serenely, "blest all my life and blest in this my old age. I have no sickness, no pain; except in my hearing my senses are but little impaired. I pass my time in reading and knitting." She turned, smiling, to Dolley. "You," she said with deep affection, "are *my* mother now, and take care of me in my old age."

The visit was an idyllic interlude for Dolley. The presence of Anna, whom she called "my little girl," was like having her own Anna back with her as a child. "Come," Dolley said once, taking her hand, "let us run a race here on the portico. I do not believe you can outrun me. Madison and I often run races here, when the weather does not allow us to walk outside."

"And she did run very briskly," noted Margaret, "it was more than I could do, had I attempted it." Both James and Dolley were sorry when the Smiths left the next morning after lingering over the break-fast table.

Though all guests were received hospitably, to Dolley all were not as welcome. Some seemed unable to know when to leave. Dolley was heard to remark, "I have scarcely a moment to breathe."

Not only was the constant entertainment a financial drain, but it infringed on time, especially the long hours they needed—ten to three of each day they hoped to use—in getting Madison's notes on the Constitutional Convention in proper form for publication. Even rela-tives were at times *de trop.*

"Of course I shall make the best of it," Dolley wrote Anna at one time when Madison's sister was coming with her family for an ex-tended visit, "but I can't help wishing she didn't come just now, as it is *terribly* inconvenient. . . . I feel as full as if the world rested on my shoulders."

Of course Mother Madison required more of her care and attention as time went on, but Dolley did not begrudge a moment of that. On February 6, 1829, Madison wrote that his mother "remains with little change except the inevitable increase of weakness." Five days later, suddenly, peacefully, she was gone. Dolley missed her, mourned. But her going was like the sloughing away of rose petals when the time for blooming was over. It was time in the natural order of life.

Far less natural and certainly worse than the death of one who had lived richly and happily for nearly a century was the shock that came a few months later in news that reached them from Philadelphia. Payne was in prison! This time James could not keep the news from Dolley. She hastened to pour out her grief to Anna.

"June 6, 1829. I inquired of you if you had heard from or of my dear child—you say nothing. . . . I received one letter from him in which he tells me that he is boarding within prison bounds for a debt of 2 or 300$. He has submitted to this horrid institution—it almost breaks my heart to think of it. . . . I don't know that I shall send this letter—in truth I feel as if I could not write another letter—my pride —my sensibility and every feeling of my soul is wounded. Yet we shall do something—what or when depends on Mr. Madison's health and strength to do business. His anxiety and wish to aid and benefit P. is as great as a father's, but his ability to command money in this county is not greater than that of others."

James of course did do "something." He arranged to have the debt paid. He urged Payne to come home, and again Dolley waited . . .

and waited. He did not come. Still her letters followed him. When Anna's daughters sent good news of him from Washington, she rejoiced and congratulated him.

"Dolley and Mary wrote me yesterday that you were popular in the City. I should like to be with you to witness it, as the respect and love shown my son would be the highest gratification the world could bestow on me. . . . Adieu, my son, may Heaven preserve and protect you."

3

There was a new President in the White House. In the election of 1828 General Andrew Jackson had been swept to victory over John Quincy Adams, whose one term had been plagued by sectional grievances culminating in what was dubbed the "Tariff of Abominations." Jackson was a populist President, propelled into office by the burgeoning democratic West, Eastern laborers just beginning to demand their rights through organized unions, Southerners who were suffering from oppression by the tariffs imposed by the powerful industrial interests of the North. "Down with the aristocrats!" had been the campaign rallying cry. He was the champion of the masses and the common people.

Dolley well remembered Jackson, the hero of New Orleans, tall, slim, straight as an Indian, thick gray hair that stood defiantly erect, and his wife, Rachel, a lovely, gentle, unassuming woman with mild dark eyes that seemed to plead for friendship and understanding. She had entertained them back in December 1815 when she and James had been living in the Seven Buildings. In doing so she had defied the prevailing prejudice of Washington grand dames, who whispered darkly of an old scandal and refused to visit the general's wife. Jackson and Rachel had married back in 1791, the year of Dolley's own first marriage, believing that her divorce from her first husband had been finalized. Two years later, finding that it had only just been granted on grounds of adultery, they had hastened to go through the ceremony again. During all these years Rachel had endured the slights and innuendos until, revived venomously during the presidential campaign, the gossip had presumably been the cause of her death on Christmas Eve following the election. At least Jackson had blamed his political enemies for the physical decline which led to her death. And the white dress Rachel had purchased for the inaugural ceremonies had been her burial gown! Remembering the softening of Jackson's eagle eyes when they rested on his wife, Dolley suffered with him now.

At least, she thought gratefully, she had shown her own defiance of the cruel prejudice in small acts of friendliness.

"You should have been here for the inauguration!" wrote Anna. "You never would have believed the sight."

From Anna and others in Washington, Dolley heard of the raucous scene following the inauguration. Crowds had flowed into the city, farmers, backwoodsmen, Irish immigrants, all the disgruntled proletariat who had swept the new President into power. They poured into the White House through windows as well as doors, upset trays of food, broke china and glassware, overturned furniture, stood with their muddy boots on the upholstered chairs to get a better look at "Old Hickory." Jackson's soldier comrades had had to make a barrier to protect him. Refreshments had been prepared for twenty thousand. Finally punch had to be carried out on the lawn to serve the horde.

"A rabble, scrabbling, fighting, romping!"

"What a pity, what a pity!" wrote Margaret Smith.

"A Saturnalia!" one Congressman lamented.

But others disagreed. A Jacksonian editor called it "a proud day for the people. General Jackson is their own President." And Francis Scott Key, watching the inauguration, exclaimed, "It is beautiful, it is sublime."

Madison had mixed feelings about the new President and his brand of democracy. When Dolley deplored the damage to the White House, declaring that nothing like that could have happened in the last six administrations, he chuckled. "My dear, have you forgotten the Great Cheese? Remember, Jefferson also was the people's President."

Though he agreed with many of Jackson's policies—opposition to a national bank and a high tariff, belief in the political integrity of the common people—he was not in sympathy with a brand of democracy so much in contrast with Jeffersonian republicanism. He had refused, however, to act as an elector for the opposing party of which Adams was the nominee and so had aided in Jackson's election. Now he viewed with dismay the policy of patronage immediately adopted by the new administration, the practice of partisan appointments soon to be known as the "spoils system." Between March and June of 1829 three hundred postmasters were turned out of office. Heads of departments, military officers, diplomats, clerks, and secretaries were replaced. Still he was able to poke fun at the hordes of office seekers bombarding the new President.

"I'm afraid a lot of them are going to be disappointed," one of his guests commented.

"Yes," replied Madison with a sly twinkle. "I suspect there are more pigs than teats, and there can't fail to be some squealing."

But he found no solace in humor when in 1829 the *Telegraph* announced the replacement of three public servants in the Treasury Department, one of them Richard Cutts.

"*Le règne du Neros est commencé,*" wrote Nicholas Trist.

Dolley was devastated. Even Payne's delinquencies faded for the moment into lesser importance. Already worried because Anna had been ill with fever, she was now plunged into deeper anxiety. What would happen to her and the children now that Richard had no job, no salary? Would they be forced to leave their home and Washington?

No, James assured her. The house was mortgaged, but he himself would have to take over the monthly payments that Richard had been making from his salary. He did not tell her what an increased financial burden it would be in his already straitened circumstances, with many of Payne's debts still outstanding. He wrote Cutts that, though he was in desperate financial straits, he would not force a sale of the property on President's Square (now named after Lafayette) unless he found it absolutely necessary to save his own property, Montpelier and its lands, in Orange.

Worries multiplied that spring and summer. James had another bout with malaria. Anna's sickness persisted. "My dear sister," Dolley wrote her. "I'm afraid of your being in the night air. It would throw you back into the agues and destroy you. Oh, that I could come for you and take care of you myself!" Even the birth of another little James Madison, John and Clara's eighth child, was small comfort, for John was drinking again. The earth scorched and blistered through another drought, and crops languished. Letters from Washington brought news of party dissension, moral scandal. Still at Montpelier flowers continued to bloom, birds sang.

"I would rather hear the birds sing," Dolley wrote Anna, "than listen to the whirlwind of men's passions."

But she and James were suddenly drawn into the whirlwind. Though he had persistently refused active participation in politics since leaving the presidency, that fall James became a delegate to the convention called to frame a new Virginia constitution. The issues at stake, he felt, were too important to permit noninvolvement. Dolley accompanied him to Richmond. It was the first time she had traveled beyond the neighborhood of Montpelier for a dozen years. Suddenly she was once more in the center of excitement, caught up in a social whirl, and she reveled in it. Though invited to stay at the executive mansion with Governor Giles, Madison refused. The governor was an extreme states rights proponent, who had been a harsh critic of James's "nationalism." They stayed at Retreat, the home of Speaker of the House Andrew Stevenson, whose wife, Sally Coles, was a cousin of Dolley, a sister of Edward, who had been Madison's private secretary.

Dolley was in her element. She might have been back in her early thirties, presiding over the teas and receptions in the President's House instead of a matronly sixty-one, emerging into the public eye after long retirement. And once more she was an object of public curiosity.

Anne Royall, a controversial journalist, was covering the convention. Her bold and blatant techniques of gathering information and her brutal frankness in dispensing it had won her the sobriquet in some quarters of "that nuisance." Her outspoken language in oral as well as written expression had even resulted in her arrest and conviction as a "common scold," to the embarrassment of her many friends but more to her own amusement than chagrin. She had escaped the punishment, the ducking stool, only because two fellow reporters on the *National Intelligencer* had paid her debt. But she was an honest, if merciless chronicler of events and actions. What, people wondered, would she say about the former First Lady? She described in vivid language the interview she was finally able to enjoy with the noted visitor. After walking for three miles to find the Stevensons' Retreat and being told that Mrs. Madison was not at home, she persisted in such a loud voice that Dolley, hearing, said she would be down in a minute.

"I listened for her step," reported the importunate journalist, "and never was I more astonished. I expected to see a little old dried up woman; instead of this a tall, young, active, elegant woman stood before me. 'This Mrs. Madison?—impossible!' She was the selfsame lady of whom I had heard more anecdotes than any family in Europe or America. No wonder she was the idol of Washington—at once in possession of everything that could ennoble woman! But chiefly she captivates by her artless though warm affability. . . . Her fine full eye and countenance display a brilliancy found in no other face. She is a stout, tall, straight woman, muscular but not fat, and as active on her feet as a girl. Her face is large, full and oval, rather dark than fair; her eye is dark, large, and expressive; her face is not handsome nor does it appear ever to have been so. . . . but her power to please, the irresistible grace of her every movement sheds a charm over all she says and does. She was dressed in a plain black silk dress, and wore a silk checked turban on her head and black glossy curls. But to witness how active she would run out—bring a glass of water, wipe the mud off my shoes and tie them. . . . She appears young enough for Mr. Madison's daughter. . . ."

Ann Royall was equally impressed by James, whom she watched intently during the convention proceedings. "Seventy-eight and not a large man, but what force! He was dressed in a plain Quaker-colored coat and his hair was powdered." (Combed carefully each day by Dolley, had she but known it!) "He was leaning forward and seemed to listen to the delegates with deep attention."

Another attendant found Madison "in tolerably good health, thin of flesh, under common size, walks without a staff, visage pale, small wrinkles, head bald on top but powdered, showing point in front."

He did listen—carefully, and, as usual, spoke seldom. But when he did others listened. It was a stormy session, with bitter dissension between the east and west portions of the state over the extension of suffrage and whether to count slaves. When on December 2, with a snowstorm raging outside, Madison rose to make his first speech, "No sooner was he on his feet," reported the *Enquirer,* "than the members from all parts of the Hall . . . gathered round him to catch the lowest accents from his tongue. . . . His voice was low and weak; but his sentences were rounding and complete; and its enunciation, though tremulous and full of feeling, was distinct to those who heard him."

"Justice, humanity, and truth," he said, "require that slaves should be considered, as much as possible, in the light of human beings and not as mere property."

Though he tried to effect a compromise by proposing the three-fifths basis of accounting slaves to apply to one house only, in order to placate the West, his efforts failed. Easterners were determined to retain their favored position as slave owners. He was discouraged. "A government resting on a minority," he deplored, "is an aristocracy, not a Republic." Slavery, he saw, had become a grave threat to the survival of republican government. The preservation of the Union might well be at stake.

It was over at last, three months of excitement, frustration, high society, conflict, physical and emotional stress. "We reached home the

fifth day after leaving Richmond, much fatigued, and with horses almost broken down by the almost impassable state of the roads."

But Dolley returned with high hopes. Surely they would find Payne
at home! He was not. The months dragged. Winter merged into
spring, and still he had not come.

"Imagine if you can," she wrote her namesake niece, Dolley, whom
she liked to call "Dolché," "a greater trial to the patience of us farmers than the destruction of a radiant patch of green peas by frost! It
came last night on the skirts of a storm. . . . But away with complaints, other patches equally radiant will arise, and I will mourn no
longer over a mess of peas or pottage."

There was soon a far worse cause to mourn. In May, Anthony
Morris wrote that Payne was again in prison, but that his creditors
would release him for six hundred dollars in cash and notes. Fortunately a lawsuit in Madison's favor brought him nearly three thousand
dollars, enough to pay Payne's debt and make his annual purchase of
ten thousand pounds of pork from farmer David Weaver, who guaran-
teed that his hogs were fatted on Indian corn and that if they "ante as
meney as you want I can git more."

And at last, on the Fourth of July, Payne was released from prison
and came home, replete with repentance and promises of future recti-
tude. For Dolley it was a perfect summer, with Anna and her younger
children, Lucy, and her beloved Payne all together for weeks at a time.
Even nature cooperated, for rains were plentiful and the crops were
good. It was well that she had this halcyon summer. It was the last
such perfect one she would enjoy for many years.

After the Convention James became involved in his last, and perhaps the most important battle of his political life. A group of Southerners headed by Senator Robert Hayne of South Carolina, outraged
by legislative measures that seemed to favor the industrial North, were
enunciating a doctrine of nullification, claiming that the states, not the
federal government, were all powerful and could nullify any act of the
latter which they chose. It was a dire threat to the Union, implying the
right of secession. Shocked by the accusation that he and Jefferson had
countenanced such an interpretation of the Constitution in their Virginia and Kentucky Resolutions of 1798, Madison hastened to publish
a long paper refuting both the claim and the whole doctrine of nullification.

"For this preposterous and anarchic pretension there is not a
shadow of countenance in the Constitution; and well that there is not,

for it is certain that, with such a deadly poison in it, no constitution could be sure of lasting a year." Of course, he insisted, the federal judiciary was the supreme agent, its actions superseding any laws passed by the judiciary of any state.

"The idea that a Constitution which has been so fruitful of blessings, and a Union admitted to be the only guardian of the peace, liberty, and happiness of the people of the states comprising it, should be broken up and scattered to the winds, without greater than any existing causes, is more painful than words can express."

His paper was hailed as the last word in the argument all over the country. Ned Coles called it the clearest exposition of the Constitution ever written. Chief Justice Marshall asserted, "Madison is himself again." As if he had ever been anything else!

Though this particular crisis passed, he was gravely disturbed. Did he have a premonition that less than thirty years later the sleeping giant of nullification would again rear its head, leading both to secession and to civil war?

But the long months of exertion took their toll. All through 1831 he was so crippled with rheumatism that he was confined to bed. Still he kept writing, unable to move his wrists, his fingertips holding a fine twill pen, twitching painfully to form the letters. "In explanation of my microscopic writing," he wrote Monroe, "I must remark that the older I grow the more my stiffening fingers make smaller letters, as my feet take shorter steps." In addition to the disabling rheumatism he had such a severe attack of his old bilious fever that he could hardly walk from one bed to another.

Dolley seldom left his side. No more running together, even walking, on the portico! For eight months she did not leave the enclosure around the house. She soaked his poor swollen limbs in tepid salt baths, then kept them wrapped in bandages of oiled silk. In spite of increasing weakness in her eyes, she wrote reams of pages at his dictation, sometimes letters, often notes on the constitutional convention records that he was bent on working into final shape. Sometimes, during the winter, when he was able, with his bed drawn close to a window, she would sit beside him, a music box playing a merry tune, and they would look out over the grounds to the snow-covered foothills of the Blue Ridge Mountains.

But the worst of his illness passed. By March 1832 Dolley was reporting in relief that he looked nearly well, had a fine appetite, and was in good spirits.

However, he was still confined to bed when President Jackson visited him in July. In spite of their differences, chiefly Madison's dislike of the spoils system, the two enjoyed a friendly relationship, and Jackson had given unequivocal support to Madison's fight against nullification. "The Federal Union—" he had averred emphatically at a Washington dinner dominated by States Righters—"it must be preserved."

When Dolley took a tray of refreshments to the guest room that evening, she found the President sitting at a table, a book open before him and beyond the book a miniature of a beautiful woman. He looked up with a smile.

"My Rachel's prayer book," he said simply. "I read from it every night."

Yes, thought Dolley, noticing that the miniature was attached to a strong black cord, and you wear that picture hung about your neck. Her eyes misted. Suddenly she understood why the President had flown in the face of Washington female society by defending Margaret "Peggy" O'Neill Eaton, wife of his Secretary of War, whom the self-righteous women of the capital, Anna included, were boycotting on what they called moral principles. Some accused her of having been too intimate with Major Eaton while still married to another man. Others based their prejudice on the fact that she had married "too precipitately" after her first husband's death. Very likely no sooner than she herself had remarried, reflected Dolley! She liked Peggy, who had grown up in Washington, and she knew her well. Once as First Lady she had gladly crowned the pretty girl at a dancing school performance where she had won first prize. Dolley shrewdly suspected that the real reason Washington ladies boycotted the Secretary's wife was what they considered her lowly origin, for she was the daughter of the keeper of a tavern, a respectable one to be sure, the Franklin House, patronized by an important clientele, but a tavern nonetheless. Unable to snub Mrs. Jackson, the women had settled their grievance on the unfortunate Peggy.

No wonder, thought Dolley, the President, knowing what suffering whispers of scandal could do to a possibly innocent woman, had taken her part with a vengeance, even precipitating a rupture in his cabinet that would lead finally to a duel between his Secretary of War and his Secretary of the Treasury, fortunately not fatal to either. The trouble a group of gossiping women could cause! Dolley wished fleetingly that she were still in Washington so she could invite Peggy Eaton to her house and defend her in every possible way.

Henry Clay was also in Virginia and, as James knew, was planning to visit Montpelier, but on his way downstate he kept riding past, returning only the day after the President left. It was just as well, Madison confided wryly to Dolley, that their visits did not coincide, for they were presently keen rivals in the campaign for the presidency.

James remained hopeful and buoyant through all his sickness. His humor sparkled in a letter thanking Speaker of the House Andrew Stevenson for a warm cap and pair of gloves sent by his wife, Dolley's cousin Sally, which, "being the work of her own hands will impart more warmth to mine."

"Mrs. Madison," he went on, "has also provided well for my feet. I am thus equipped cap-a-pie, for the campaign against Boreas, and his allies the frosts and snows. But there is another article of covering which I need most of all and which my best friends cannot supply. My bones have lost a sad portion of the flesh which clothed and protected them, and the digestive and nutritive organs which alone can replace it, are too slothful in their functions."

Dolley had other worries, for Anna too was having one bout after another of sickness, starting with an attack of dropsy in the spring of 1830.

"Beloved sister," she was writing in August 1832. "Mrs. Mason has just written to me to say that you are a little better, and those dear daughters of mine, Mary and Dolley, whom I shall ever feel are my own children, have often consoled me by their letters. . . . Do, dear sister, strive to get well and strong for my sake and your children's; what should we do without you? As soon as my eyes are well I will write to dear Mrs. B. Adieu, my dear, ever and always, Your loving sister."

Two days later she received word of Anna's death.

She was numb with grief. Her little sister-child Anna—gone! Dearest in all the world to her except her husband and son—almost her other self! Of course she loved Lucy, but they had never been as close. Suddenly Dolley seemed to age ten years. Friends said that for the first time she lost her bright cheerfulness. Every task, even the tender ministry to her beloved Jemmy, was performed with effort rather than as a joyful privilege. But she hastened to fulfill the saddest of all duties.

"Dear Brother," she wrote Richard on August 5. "The heart of your miserable sister mourns with you and for your dear children. Come to us as soon as you can, and bring them all with you; I am as deeply interested in them as if they were my own. Where are her remains? I will myself write my gratitude to the kind friends who were privileged to do what I could not for my lamented sister.

"Mr. Madison partakes in our sorrows, and in my wish to see you all here. Show this to Dolley and Mary, please, as I cannot write to them at this moment. Yours came yesterday. Affectionately your Sister."

Life went on, of course. Days . . . months . . . years. There were pleasant intervals, some quite long stretches of time, when it became almost normal. James was remarkably well again. He rode over his farms, always one of his chief joys, especially since he was so fond of his horses. Again he and Dolley were able to take three-mile rides. By selling three of his farms and sixteen of his slaves to a kinsman "to whom they gladly consented to be transferred," he was able to pay debts up to six thousand dollars, though still several thousands short of what he owed, so, as Dolley said, "he stills talks of the last resort, 'the house in Washington.' " Not as long as Richard and his children needed it, however!

Dolley's nieces, Mary and Dolché, and brother John's daughter Anna came for visits, Dolché now in her early twenties, keeping feet dancing to the tunes of her guitar, and Mary capturing all the changing moods of gardens and mountains with her paints. And to Dolley's great joy Payne was at home for an extended time. An outcropping of marble had been discovered on his land at Toddsberth, and with the same exuberance that had begotten the silkworm fiasco he was exploring its possibilities to the limit. At last he had found his purpose in life! He would quarry the rock vein, provided it proved deep enough, and become rich!

Dolley joined in the project wholeheartedly, tramping over the ground, securing rock samples, washing them, testing for quartz or granite, exulting when some displayed the beautiful pink-white luster of marble. Surely now Payne, late blooming for he was past forty, was developing into the steady purposeful maturity of which he had so long given promise. No wife in the offing for him, however, to Dolley's disappointment, as rumors had once indicated.

"As I told you," she wrote Mary in March 1833, "I hear nothing more of his liking to the young lady report gave him for a wife, and I'm sorry for that." She hoped the girls had been able to see Jackson's second inauguration, then, in closing, put her beloved niece into the care of "Him who is able to lead us safely through all the allotments of his wisdom."

The allotments did not continue in this happy sequence. Payne's interest in the strain of marble, which did not run as deep as expected, waned, and he was off again. In the winter of 1833 James was again ill, suffering from a violent itching eruption over his entire body. His only exercise for months was in a chair he had purchased "for exercise by rocking." Reluctantly he came to a most unwelcome decision, resigning his position as rector of the university. Fortunately he recovered from this ailment, largely through a lotion recommended by a Dr. Dunglison. The welts disappeared, and he was free of pain. Even the rheumatism in his hands lessened so that he was able to write once more in his fine legible script. He used this new versatility to express his continued worry about the future of the country.

"What is more dangerous than nullification," he wrote Ned Coles, "or more evident than the progress it continues to make, either in its original shape or in the disguises it assumes? Nullification has the effect of putting powder under the Constitution and Union, and a match in the hand of every party to blow them up at pleasure."

Especially was James alarmed by the agitation among certain Southerners for a second Constitutional Convention. If they should succeed in calling one, it might well mean disaster. The whole Constitution could easily be put on the bargaining table and be torn apart by political extremists and powerful interest groups. Even if the main body of the document were left intact, there might be amendments proposed that would tear to bits the Bill of Rights, with its precious elements of religious liberty, with its complete separation of church and state, freedom of speech, the right of privacy. He hastened to express himself most forcibly.

"Having witnessed the difficulties and dangers experienced by the first Convention," he wrote, "which assembled under every propitious circumstance, I would tremble for the result of the Second."

It was a statement which, more than a hundred and fifty years later, would be quoted when the same danger would again rear its head.

Dolley was too busy to concern herself seriously with the state of the Union. That was Jemmy's province. Hers was the smooth management of the multiple household, nursing its ailing master, ministering to the constant flow of visitors.

Some of the latter were more welcome than others. It was a high point of the year when in 1834 nephew James Madison Cutts brought his bride, Ellen O'Neale, whom he had married at her home in Maryland, to Montpelier to receive their blessing. When their coach arrived James insisted on getting up from his bed and, leaning on the arm of Paul Jennings, stood on the portico to greet them. Though he was not well enough to join the family at dinner, he stood in the doorway between his bedroom and the dining room to drink a toast to the bridal couple. Dolley was charmed by their new niece. She exclaimed with delight over her wedding finery, mourned over the couple's departure, and cherished Ellen's letter of appreciation which, she noted, was "full of intelligence and amusement."

Guests continued to come—and go, the going sometimes too long delayed. Uninvited strangers, Madison confessed to a very welcome guest, fell like public finance into two categories; "some were taxes and others bounties."

One of the "bounties" came early in 1835, though a stranger, certainly not an uninvited one. When Sir Charles Vaughn, the British minister, informed them that Harriet Martineau, the eminent English sociologist who was touring America, was eager to visit Montpelier, Dolley willingly sent her an invitation. It had been a long cold winter, with little of interest to stimulate Jemmy intellectually except through the guests who came and the books Dolley read aloud to him when the weakness of her eyes permitted.

It was February 18, a "sweet day of early spring," Miss Martineau called it when she and her friend Miss Jeffries arrived at Orange Courthouse. Hiring a carriage for which they were grossly overcharged, the people at the inn not informing them that Madison had asked for a messenger to be sent over for his carriage as soon as they arrived ("the only occasion but one, in our journey of ten thousand miles in the United States, that we were overcharged!"), after the five mile ride through a slough of mud they arrived at Montpelier, where Dolley and Anna Payne greeted them warmly on the portico.

In her *Retrospect of Western Travel*, Miss Martineau gave an interesting description of her meeting with her famous host.

"He was in his chair, with a pillow behind him, when I first saw him; his little person wrapped in a black silk gown; a warm gray and white cap upon his head, which his lady took care should always sit becomingly; and gray worsted gloves, his hands having become rheumatic. His voice was clear and strong, and his manner of speaking particularly lively, often playful. Except that the face was smaller, and, of course, older, the likeness to the common engraving of him was perfect.

"His relish for conversation could never have been keener. I was in perpetual fear of his being exhausted, and at the end of every few hours I left my seat by the arm of his chair, and went to the sofa by Mrs. Madison; but he was sure to follow and sit down between us; so that, when I found the only effect of my moving was to deprive him of the comfort of his chair, I returned to my station, and never left it but for food and sleep, glad enough to make the most of my means of intercourse with one whose political philosophy I deeply venerated."

Dolley took little part in the conversation, but she listened and rejoiced in the rapport between them. Not for months had Jemmy been so alert, so sparklingly articulate. They talked of everything, it seemed, under the sun—education, literature, religion, government— with the guest eagerly absorbing comments which would later appear in her book.

"There is no need to add another to the many eulogies of Madison. I will only mention that the finest of his characteristics appeared to me to be his inexhaustible faith; faith that a well-founded commonwealth may be immortal, not only because the people in its constituency never die, but because the principles of justice in which such a commonwealth originates never die out of the people's heart and mind."

But on one subject his faith seemed to waver. Slavery. He expressed his hatred of it, his hopes for the Colonization Society, yet his almost despair. The Bible taught that it was a sin, but the clergy did not preach it, the people did not see it. It was a moral crime, a curse to society. It *must* be abolished. And it was not profitable. He had sold some of his best land to feed the increasing numbers of his own slaves, and had still been obliged to sell a dozen of them only the preceding week. Not against their will, however. And he had never separated members of a family. He still clung to hope. Somehow—sometime—in this democratic society the problem would be solved.

"During all our conversations," Miss Martineau noted, "one or another slave was perpetually coming to Mrs. Madison for the great bunch of keys; two or three more lounged about the room, leaning against the doorposts or the corner of the sofa." Certainly no discontent or mistreatment of human life here—except in the deprivation of freedom. But freedom, as Miss Martineau well knew, the right of self-determination and self-development, was for James Madison a prime essential for human beings in a democratic society.

Listening, saying little, performing her usual duties, Dolley would have been surprised had she known the celebrated guest's impressions of her hostess.

"Mrs. Madison is celebrated throughout the country for the grace and dignity with which she discharged the arduous duties which devolve upon the President's lady. For a term of eight years she administered the hospitalities of the White House with such discretion, impartiality, and kindliness, that it is believed she gratified every one and offended nobody. She is a strongminded woman, fully capable of entering into her husband's occupations and cares; and there is little doubt that he owed much to her intellectual companionship."

Intellectual! Dolley would have pooh-poohed the idea. She read to him, yes, discussed with him those subjects with which he was most concerned—slavery, tariffs, nullification, even that old bugbear, the national bank. And she had her own ideas about all of them. But as for being intellectual—!

"Miss Martineau was so interesting," she wrote one of her nieces after the guests had left, "that we hastened to buy her books, and are now reading her political economy so handsomely illustrated."

4

"Please!" begged Dolley. "No more dictating letters, not for a while, or working on the papers! It's too much for you."

But he would not listen. The letter to Ned Coles, he insisted, had already been postponed too long and must be answered. Then they spent the usual five hours going over more of the convention papers. They followed the usual procedure. She would read them to him, and if any letter, line, or word struck him as likely to injure the feelings of anyone or was wrong in itself, she would change it. Then, very likely, he would fall into an uneasy sleep.

He had become increasingly ill after the visit of Miss Martineau in February 1835. March had found him "feeble and indisposed." Spring was slow in coming.

"Once it really gets warm," he tried to boost Dolley's flagging spirits, "we'll be riding again. That mountain air is all I need to put life into this ailing old body."

"Yes," returned Dolley with valiant cheerfulness, "and when July comes we'll go to the Springs. The sulphur water will be a wonderful tonic."

But when April restored warmth to the heady mountain air they did not go riding, and in July they did not go to the Springs. The doctors did advise sulphur water, but James was drinking it at home. In the same month news came that Chief Justice Marshall who, in spite of their onetime sharp political differences, had given strong support to Madison's fight against nullification, had died. Now James was the only living American who had been a national figure during the Revolution. He was pleased to hear that he had been elected President of the Washington National Memorial Association. Of course it was an honorary appointment, but he accepted it, hoping that a monument worthy of the memory of Washington would commemorate "a virtue, a patriotism, and a gratitude truly national, with which the friends of liberty everywhere will sympathise, and of which our country may always be proud."

Monuments! Dolley did not like the sound of the word. In spite of the summer heat it made her shiver. And a letter from Thomas McKenny about plans for the Washington memorial was all too specific a reminder of her fears. "Mr. Madison," he wrote, "will leave monuments behind him, go when he may, as lasting as time."

Time. It seemed to stand still that summer of 1835, as if the world, locked in its prison of glaring sun and heat, waited for some disruption, as once Dolley had waited, in the same summer doldrums, with the sound of guns in the distance coming steadily nearer. But in spite of the knot of fear deep down in her subconscious, she went about her tasks as usual, entertaining guests, superintending the household, spending most of her time, as she wrote her "precious Dolché," "nursing and comforting her patient." He was plunged into illness again, able to walk only from the bed where he breakfasted to the little chamber at the rear of the dining room, where there was another bed, high-posted with a crimson damask canopy, brought from the Tuileries by Monroe, a desk where he could write, a couch, and a table where he took his meals. But mentally he was as virile as ever, insisting on greeting every guest and participating in each dinner party from his bed outside the entrance to the dining room. His sense of humor remained unimpaired.

"Oh!" he riposted once, his eyes gleaming, when one guest urged him not to try to talk in his recumbent position. "I always talk more easily when I lie."

It was not an unhappy summer. Payne was nearby, embarked on another pet scheme, putting up a strange concoction of buildings on his land at Toddsberth, one of them an octagonal "ballroom," as he called it, with benches around its walls for prospective dancers. It was to have "towers," he explained enthusiastically, on top. One of the buildings would be his home, with five rooms which he would add to as inclination developed, and there would be a separate kitchen, guesthouse, and servants' quarters. Where the money was coming from for this project he did not disclose. Dolley was so happy about his proximity and purposeful activity that Madison forbore to inquire too deeply into the project. At least he was not paying for it—yet.

Sometime, he thought uneasily, Payne would be master of Montpelier. He had revised his will the preceding March, leaving Dolley the land, houses, and slaves, his valuable papers, everything except a few legacies hopefully to be derived from the sale of his *Notes on the Debates in the Federal Convention,* the major part, of course, to be included in Dolley's inheritance. The *Notes,* he reckoned, should be worth at least fifty thousand dollars. The five small legacies to be deducted from it would go to the Colonization Society, the education of his fatherless grandnephews, Princeton University, a college named after him in Pennsylvania, and the University of Virginia. Dolley should have a choice of three hundred of his books, the rest to go to the university.

While he hated to think of the irresponsible Payne becoming in the end his chief heir, and he knew his brother William hotly opposed the idea, he was adamant in his decision. The boy had always been, *was,* like his son, and he must remain so. If only he could protect Dolley from the dangers of the leniency of which they had both been guilty! After much hesitation and with great reluctance, he made one further decision. He entrusted John Payne, Dolley's brother, with a packet containing vouchers for all the payments he had made on Payne's debts unknown to Dolley. It would be delivered to her after his death. Not that he wanted any credit for the dire sacrifices he had made for their son! And he knew the knowledge would cause her untold pain. But it might just put her on her guard and protect her from further unwise yielding to such importunities after his death.

Autumn brought welcome reprieve. Never had the grapes turned a richer purple, the sky a deeper blue, the oaks and maples a brighter bronze and crimson. The air became heady and blessedly cool. The ring of distant mountains cloaked the rolling hills like a gorgeous paisley shawl. Within Dolley's being the knot of fear seemed briefly to unwind, and all because Jemmy seemed so much improved. So supple were his fingers again that he could wield a pen and write some of his own letters, even work on his unfinished introduction to his notes on the Constitutional Convention. The house was merry with neighborhood friends and travelers returning from the White Sulphur Springs and stopping over for a day or night on the way home.

But it was a short reprieve. By November he was again scarcely able to walk across the room. He was once more dictating to Dolley, a few hours of work ending in feverish sleep. It was the beginning of six months of grueling worry and attendance when Dolley scarcely left his side. Fortunately she had competent helpers. Nelly Madison Willis, daughter of James's deceased brother Ambrose, and her own niece Anna Payne, brother John's daughter, were with her much of the time. And she could not have managed without the help of Paul Jennings, James's longtime devoted personal servant. She and Paul had been through many crises together, not the least of them those hours of waiting for the British before the burning of the capital. She could still see him calmly setting the table as usual for the guests who never came, then playing the "President's March" on his violin at the declaration of Peace! Peace! Now he faithfully, lovingly, performed the necessary services for his master, shaving him every other day as he had done for the last sixteen years, lifting him in his arms from bed to chair or bed to bed when he was unable to walk. Again and again Madison had tried to give this devoted slave his freedom, but Paul Jennings had refused. This was all the freedom he wanted, to serve his master as long as he was needed.

Weakness did not prevent the work of revision on the precious Convention papers. Dolley knew with a terrible foreboding that he was trying to finish the revision while there was still time. He begrudged the hours that must be spent dictating necessary letters or talking with the guests that, even in winter, persisted in coming. The papers, he impressed on Dolley, were sacred, more important than any other of their possessions. They were the only living record of perhaps the most important event in human history, certainly in the history of their nation. Also, he might have added, they were for herself his most valuable legacy, her assurance of future security.

"Yes—oh yes!" agreed Dolley. She took his dictation until her fingers were cramped, her weak eyes watered and filmed so she could hardly see. Then, when their reading time came, she chose passages in the Bible she knew almost by heart so he would not realize how overburdened she had been. But they were sections they both loved best, which answered her own deep need for eternal verities.

"I will lift up mine eyes unto the hills, from whence cometh my help." How often they had repeated the words, sitting on the portico and looking away to the encircling mountains!

Spring came, beautiful as usual, but somehow without the promise of renewed life. She brought armfuls of blossoms from the first flowering trees into the house, filling his room with their fragrance. Paul Jennings lifted him into a chair by the window so he could look out at the little Greek temple he so loved, see the greening of the broad lawns, watch the changing lights and shadows on the distant hills.

On May 2 there was a welcome guest, Charles J. Ingersoll, the man first to officially give James the title "Father of the Constitution."

"He was extremely feeble," the guest wrote later. "But he raised his almost exanimate body from the couch . . . and, infirm as his body is, his understanding is as bright as ever, his intelligence, recollections, discriminations and philosophy, all delightfully instructive."

"You do the talking," Dolley advised worriedly. "Don't let him say too much, for he has difficulty in breathing."

But James had much to say and refused to listen instead of talking. He "spoke often and anxiously of slave property as the worst possible for profit." Two thirds of his own slaves, he said, were either too young or too old to work much, and it took nearly all he made to feed, clothe, and keep them comfortable. "I'll wager," he asserted, "that Richard Rush's ten-acre farm near Philadelphia is more profitable than my own with 2,000 acres!"

But after the guest had gone, there was reaction from these stimulating talks. James was "unable to write, or even to exert his thoughts without oppressive fatigue." Later in the month Dr. Dunglison came from Baltimore, but he had no remedies to offer. Rest was the only antidote he could suggest for the weakness and fatigue. There was no remedy for the basic cause of his ailments, old age.

June came. But its burgeoning life, its roses climbing over the trellises, its bursts of glorious color in the gardens, meant nothing to Dolley. The tight knot of worry had become a hard core of despair. She could no longer hide her grief. "Uncle Madison," wrote Anna Payne, "kept begging her to be composed if not cheerful." And she tried. Unable to dissuade him from answering letters, she managed to keep writing at his dictation, on June 22 accepting for him honorary membership in the Erodelphian Society of Miami University in Ohio," on June 27, when it seemed he was too weak to utter a single word, acknowledging George Tucker's dedicatory inscription to James in his Jefferson biography.

"It's—ten days old already. It—must be answered," James insisted. The dictation, slow because of his difficulty in speaking, not because of any impairment of intellect, took several hours. His reply was as sound and clear as any he had ever composed. Dolley wrote automatically, keeping her face carefully averted. This time it was tears, not weakness, that blurred her vision.

"It could not escape me that a feeling of personal friendship has mingled itself greatly with the credit you allow to my public services. I am at the same time justified by my consciousness in saying that an ardent zeal was always felt to make up for deficiencies in them by a sincere and steadfast cooperation in promoting such a reconstruction of our political system as would provide for the permanent liberty and happiness of the United States." He signed his name, but his hand was so trembling that the "James Madison" was barely legible.

They were the last words he was to compose. The next morning, June 28, Paul Jennings came early, about six, to attend him. His wife, Sukey, brought him his breakfast. But he was unable to swallow.

"What's the matter, Uncle James?" asked Nelly Willis in alarm.

He smiled up at her, a hint of the old mischief in his eyes. "Nothing more than a change of *mind*, my dear."

As Paul Jennings later described it, "his head instantly dropped, and he ceased breathing as quietly as the snuff of a candle goes out."

There was no time for tears, even if the hard core at the center of her being had permitted their release. With mechanical but meticulous planning Dolley arranged for the necessary ceremonies—the funeral, the burial in the family cemetery half a mile south of the house with their neighbors James and Philip Barbour, Charles Howard, and Reuben Conway acting as bearers. At a memorial service in Orange County a month later ex-Governor James Barbour described the scene.

"Many of you were at his funeral, you must have seen his slaves decently attired in attendance, and their orderly deportment; the profound silence was now and then broken by their sobs. . . . It was not only the personal servant Paul Jennings, who wept, standing directly by me, but the hundred slaves gave vent to their lamentations in one violent burst that rent the air."

The whole nation grieved at its loss, not only of a revered ex-President but of this last of its founding fathers. Congress hastened to pass condolatory resolutions which came to Dolley in a personal letter from President Jackson. As with the hundreds of other letters that poured in, all acknowledged in her own handwriting, she sent back an appropriate answer.

"I received, sir, in due time, your letter conveying to me the resolutions Congress were pleased to adopt on the occasion of the death of my beloved husband, a communication made the more grateful by the kind expression of your sympathy which it contained.

"The high and just estimation of my husband by my countrymen and friends, and their generous participation in the sorrow occasioned by our irretrievable loss . . . are the only solace of which my heart is susceptible on the departure of him, who had never lost sight of that consistency, symmetry and beauty of character in all its parts, which secured to him the love and admiration of his country, and which must ever be the subject of peculiar and tender reverence to one whose happiness was derived from their daily and constant exercise.

"The best return I can make for the sympathy of my country is to fulfill the sacred trust his confidence reposed in me, that of placing before it and the world what his pen prepared for their use,—a legacy the importance of which is deeply impressed on my mind. With great respect, D. P. Madison.

"To the President of the United States."

The papers. Her sacred trust. Already, before the summer was over, she was attempting to find a reputable publisher for his *Notes on the Debates of the Constitutional Convention.* She could not rest, could not even take time to grieve, until she had fulfilled this obligation. But summer passed . . . autumn . . . and still no offer had been made. In July, Payne had taken two copies of the revised papers to New York to submit them to publishers, without success. In November she wrote to Henry Clay explaining her delay in answering his letter of August 18 because of "a very severe affliction of my eyes."

"The sources of consolation in my bereavement which you suggest, are those which my heart can most truly appreciate. The reflected rays of his virtues still linger around me, and my mind now dwells with calmer feelings on their mellowed tints. He left me, too, a charge, dear and sacred, and deeply impressed with its value to his fame and its usefulness to his country. The important trust sustained me under the heavy pressure of recent loss, and formed an oasis to the desert it created in my feelings."

She begged him to help in offering the papers to the patronage of Congress, the three volumes of *Debates* (near six hundred pages each) now ready for the press. The same month she placed the matter before the President, who on December 6 presented it for action to Congress. And once more, as she had done so often throughout life, she waited . . . and waited. It was three long months later, the day before another President was to enter the White House, that Congress finally took action, appropriating thirty thousand dollars, not the fifty thousand that Madison had assessed as their worth, for the first three volumes of the papers. When the bequests of Madison's will were taken care of, it would leave her only about nine thousand dollars.

There! It was done. Now, suddenly, the weeks, months, years of worry, nursing, endless writing, took their toll. She became desperately ill. Her eyes were so weak that she could barely use them to sign her name. She spent weeks in bed, its curtains drawn to shut out the light, while Anna and Nelly and Sukey and others tended her with the faithful solicitude she herself had so long devoted to her patient.

But this too passed. Doctors persuaded her to take some weeks at the White Sulphur Springs, and she returned able to resume neglected duties.

"Accept a thousand thanks, dear friend," she was writing Anthony Morris on September 2, "for your two unanswered letters, containing the best advice in the world, and which I have followed as far as I could on my visit to the White Sulphur Springs, a new world to me, who have never left Montpelier for nearly six years, even for a day. . . . I passed two weeks at the Springs, drinking moderately of the waters and bathing my poor eyes a dozen times a day. The effect was excellent. My health was strengthened to its former standing, and my eyes grew white again. . . ."

It was well that she was feeling stronger on the day that brother John placed in her hands the packet that James had asked him to give her after his death. She opened it with trembling fingers. What—? It was as if he were there by her side, comforting, bringing some message of assurance. Wondering, she drew out the thick sheaf of papers, began reading them one by one. As she read her eyes widened, her cheeks flushed, she drew quick convulsive breaths. Vouchers. Payments for debts, her son's debts, debts and payments she had never known about. Hastily she reckoned the amounts. More than twenty thousand dollars! A sum equal to all the amounts she had known of his paying! At least forty thousand in all, the price of so many fields he had lost, so many worries over unpaid bills! How much he had loved her, tried to spare her—yes, and had loved her—*their* son!

Suddenly the tears came, and she was weeping, freely, healingly, as she had not been able to do since his death. The hard core that had so tightly imprisoned her grief at last dissolved. As if such love as they had known could separate them, even by death!

Tears. And, being Dolley, she soon found them giving way to laughter. It came with a letter from her friend Margaret Smith in Washington, bubbling, of course, with all the latest news and gossip. Dolley would never believe this. It had happened this year, back in February, on Washington's Birthday. Remember that GREAT CHEESE back in Jefferson's time, when the President's House had been turned into a shambles? Well, history had repeated itself. A year before, a man named Colonel Meecham of New York had decided to send his hero Jackson a cheese that would vie in size with the fabled monstrosity presented to Jefferson. It had arrived in 1836 at the White House, decked with roses, tipping the scales at fourteen hundred pounds! Jefferson's, it was reported, had weighed only twelve hundred. The President had put it away to ripen, and just this year he had sent out an official announcement that it would be cut on February 22, and all were invited to come to the Palace from one to three to sample it. Excitement! Abolition agitation, the squabble over Texas—all were insignificant beside the CHEESE!

If Dolley could have seen it! It began early in the morning, people crowding into the city. Even the Senate had adjourned for the occasion. And the White House! The halls were slippery with cheese, it was ground into the furniture. For hours people trooped in and slashed at the huge creation, carrying away huge hunks, leaving only fragments to be trampled under foot. Even worse than the Jefferson melee, this one had taken the cake—or should one say, the *cheese!* It was said that Van Buren was so disgusted that he had decided refreshments on a big scale would be abandoned during his administration. "And, believe it or not, my dear, if you go to the White House now, you can still smell it! If only you had been here!"

Dolley laughed. The sound brought nieces and servants running, for it had not been heard like that in months—her old gay, rippling, rollicking laughter. She read them the letter, then laughed again until she cried. And they laughed with her, less for the ridiculous picture the letter conjured, for they could not share her memories, but for the knowledge that Dolley was herself again, had come back to them.

If only you had been here! For the first time in twenty years Dolley felt a twinge of homesickness. The winter months loomed ahead, indescribably lonely and dreary. With James there she had welcomed them, rejoicing in the infrequency of guests, their increased intimacy and togetherness in the warmth of the great open fires. Somehow this did not seem like home anymore without him, this big echoing mansion so full of memories.

She felt a slow stirring of excitement as the idea took shape. Why not? The house was there, it was part of her inheritance. Richard was no longer using it, he had left Washington. There were so many old friends . . . just for the winter, of course, unless . . . She could leave Payne in charge of the plantation. It would be good for him, perhaps his salvation, away from city temptations. He had shown more responsibility of late, helping brother John make extra copies of the papers to send to England, and taking them himself to New York. After all, Montpelier would be his some day.

Then suddenly it was not just an idea, but a firm decision. Almost running in her eagerness, she went to find Anna, the niece who had taken the other Anna Payne's place not only in name but in Dolley's affections. The girl looked up from her task of cutting garments for the slaves' winter clothing, surprised at the excitement, a hint of the old sparkle in the other's eyes.

"My dear!" said Dolley, smiling. "I have news for you, wonderful, exciting news. We're going to Washington!"

PART SEVEN

Lafayette Square
1837 – 1849

1

Strange! It was almost as if she had never been away, as if the twenty years of her absence from the city had been a dream. She felt like the man in that story which their friend Washington Irving had written in his *Sketch Book* that had made him famous, the one who had gone to sleep—what was his name? Rip something. Oh yes, Rip Van Winkle— who had suddenly awakened to resume life where he had left it twenty years ago.

Washington, of course, had changed. Houses had sprung up like mushrooms where before there had been only marshland and woods. Country lanes had turned into decently paved streets. Jefferson's rows of poplars, what was left of them, had become tapering giants. The population had nearly doubled, reaching more than fifty thousand. Candles and oil lamps were being replaced by chandeliers with gaslight fixtures. Furnaces, with hot air registers, were appearing in many houses to supplant the old roaring hearth fires. Not in Dolley's house, however. Richard had been unable to afford such modern gadgets. Here all was blessedly familiar. Life could be pursued in almost the same manner as in the Octagon or the Seven Buildings twenty years before. Not that any life, of course, could really be considered living without Jemmy!

Dolley liked the house, small and simple compared with the Montpelier mansion, and, since there was nothing to remind her of Jemmy's onetime presence, less haunted by memories and echoes. Situated at the northeast corner of what L'Enfant's original plans had designated as President's Square but which had been renamed Lafayette Square after the famous Frenchman's visit, it was a cosy, two-story-and-attic building of gray stucco with a gable roof and dormer windows which looked out on the park, attractive with its fine trees, shrubbery, and statuary, once the old apple orchard of the early settler, David Burns. It was so small she could get along very well with a minimum of servants. Strict economy, she knew, must now be an essential rule of her life.

Almost across the street, at the corner of F Street and Sixteenth, was St. John's Episcopal Church, completed in 1816, Jemmy's last year in the presidency, a beautiful building designed by Benjamin Latrobe, the famous architect of the Capitol. Dolley could look out from her bedroom window and see its dome surmounted by Latrobe's famous "lantern," and Sundays she and Anna could cross the street and worship under that soaring dome in the magic of its stained-glass windows. Though she could no longer sit in the President's pew, attending services here brought her a touch of nostalgia, but a healing one, for she could almost imagine Jemmy sitting there beside her.

But it was relatives and friends who made the place seem like home. Her beloved nieces, Mary and Dolley, who were living nearby on Fourteenth Street and had made the house ready, were there to greet her. And, to her amazement, her coming was greeted all over the city as an event of social and political importance.

"Her return to Washington," Mary was to write later, "was hailed by all, by those who had formerly known her and those who desired to know this 'First Lady of the Land.' Her house was filled both morning and evening with the most distinguished of all parties, each claiming her as their champion. While she, with her gracious smile and warm heart, made friends with all, and with infinite tact took no decided part, except by giving preference to her friends of the longest standing."

Among the first visitors were ex-President John Quincy Adams, now a Congressman, and his wife, Louisa. It was Adams who had announced the death of Madison to Congress, emphasizing his service to the country as the "Father of the Constitution." Dolley had read his speech and was grateful. "Is it not transcendentally," he had demanded, "by his exertions that we address each other here by the endearing appellations of countrymen and fellow citizens?"

Though she had never known her well, Dolley had always admired his wife, the cultured English-born First Lady who had accompanied her husband on his diplomatic mission to Russia in Madison's second term, leaving her two oldest children in the New England where she had never really felt at home, encountering "unspeakable terrors" in a forty-day journey with her little son Charles Francis across war-ravaged Europe to rejoin her husband at Ghent. Shared memories of those tumultuous days united the two former First Ladies in a bond even closer than intimate friendship.

"This morning," Adams wrote in his diary on October 24, "I visited Mrs. Madison, who had come to take up her residence in this city. I had not seen her since March, 1809. The depredations of time are not so perceptible in her personal appearance as might be expected. She is a woman of placid appearance, equable temperament, and less susceptible of laceration of the scourges of the world abroad than most others."

Twenty years? The astounding welcome she received swept them away. She was encompassed by old friends. Just around the corner on H Street was Betsy Schuyler Hamilton, widow of Alexander. Dolley had known her well in Philadelphia. The political differences that had separated their husbands now long forgotten, the two could view even tragic events involving them both with equanimity—the fateful epidemic that had meant survival for one, death for another; the duel in which the friend of one had taken the life of the other's husband. Though nearly eighty, Betsy was still as slender and active, her eyes as bright, as when, the debutante daughter of the wealthy General Philip Schuyler, she had captured the heart of the dapper impetuous young secretary of General Washington.

An even closer friend through the years was Mrs. Tobias Lear, known to many as "Aunt Fanny," whose husband had occupied many official posts during both Jefferson's and Madison's administrations. Then there was Mrs. William Thornton, who had been her next-door neighbor during the first Washington years. There were the Henry Clays, the Daniel Websters, the William Prestons, Mrs. Stephen Decatur, and, of course, Margaret Smith. All, with other friends both old and new, welcomed her back with the same warmth and deference she had been accorded twenty years before. Soon she was using a Congressional directory to check her debts for calls, the names covering not only Washington but its suburbs for miles around. She could not afford a carriage of her own, but she was swamped with offers of private carriages in which to make her journeys.

"Of course all these visits to me are for Jemmy's sake, not mine," she said to Fanny Lear, who was urging her not to expend so much strength in returning calls. Her friend only smiled.

The first invitation to the White House came soon after her arrival.

The PRESIDENT
Requests the honor of
Mrs. Madison's
Company at dinner Friday the 24th Nov.
at 5 o'clock
The favor of an answer is desired.

Dolley was both eager and apprehensive. To revive memories of the house where she had spent such triumphant and tragic years? To see a stranger occupying Jemmy's place at the dinner table? How would it make her feel? But she had more mundane worries. What would she wear? She had trunkfuls of gowns, many of the finest fabrics, but all hopelessly outdated. Women were not wearing the Empire styles any more, and the turbans she had made so fashionable were quite out of style. But—she tossed her black curls defiantly—what matter? She had never let others set her styles of living. Then suddenly she had an idea. There was the crimson velvet gown she had made out of the curtains salvaged on that fateful day from the windows of the oval drawing room. It was faded, yes, heavier than more delicate velvets, probably too small by now, but there was plenty of material and she could let it out. Why not? It would be a bit of droll irony, which Jemmy would have appreciated, taking it back incognito to the place from which it had made such an abrupt and ignominious departure.

"You look—regal," breathed Anna rapturously when her aunt appeared, ready to leave, the crimson velvet with its long severe lines adjusted to fit the increasingly buxom figure, "just like a queen."

Queen Dolley! She smiled wryly. Nobody had called her that for years, and probably never would again. She hoped not. Somehow the words never seemed appropriate for the wife of the democrat James Madison, even if the still more obdurate republican Jefferson had indulgently interpreted them to mean "queen of hearts!"

She need not have worried about the revival of memories. Mounting the steps of the new imposing twelve-columned North Portico, finished by Jackson after Latrobe's design in 1830, she might have been entering a completely foreign building. The interior also seemed strangely new. In spite of his populist credo resulting in such forays as the cheese debacle, Jackson had been an epicure, and Van Buren had added many luxurious features. Dolley marveled at the new cut-glass chandeliers, each one holding eighteen candles, the Brussels carpets, the rich draperies, the marble-topped tables, the splendid china and glassware and French silver service on the dining table. And, she learned, most remarkable of all, running water had been piped into the house. No more sending servants to carry it from Franklin Park half a mile away!

The new President also was no reminder of the past, for Martin Van Buren had come to Washington as senator from New York in 1821, three years after she had left. Since then he had been Secretary of State, Minister to England, and Vice President. Seated as guest of honor around the end of the table at his right, Dolley could covertly appraise her host. Little Magician, he was dubbed, the "little" because of his short compact figure, the "magician" because of his almost uncanny ability to manipulate events to suit his purposes. Was John Quincy Adams justified in his not too flattering comparison between him and her husband?

"There are many features in the character of Mr. Van Buren strongly resembling that of Mr. Madison—his calmness, his gentleness of manner, his discretion, his easy and conciliatory temper. But Madison had none of his obsequiousness, his sycophancy, his profound dissimulation and duplicity."

Dolley suspected that this estimate by a political opponent was prejudiced. Always prone to think the best of people, she felt only admiration and sympathy, shrewdly sensing that the suave ease of manner masked a profound uneasiness. The wave of prosperity that had swept Van Buren into office was ebbing. Banks were suspending payment of gold and silver. Already the economic crisis which would be known as the Panic of 1837 was sweeping the country. "Magician" wiles might have won him his high office, but the magic was fading. And well Dolley knew how blame for all ills soon focused on the President! In 1812 it had been "Mr. Madison's War." In 1837 it would be "Mr. Van Buren's Panic."

"You have made this house a place of real beauty," she said with a warm smile. "I had heard that you are a connoisseur of things of fine taste, and now I can well believe it."

"And I, my dear lady," he returned promptly, his Dutch accent, heritage of his Holland ancestry and his youth in the old Dutch community of Tenderhook, New York, giving the words a courtly European flavor, "have heard that you were the most amiable and beloved hostess ever to grace this house, and now I can well believe it."

Dolley was not surprised at the slight wistfulness she detected in his voice. And no wonder. For now the White House had no hostess. Like

Jefferson, Van Buren was a longtime widower, and his four sons were unmarried. The void was apparent. The house was lacking in those small amenities that only the touch of a woman could provide. Even the gold and silver plates which were proving the last straw to the Jacksonian "plain people" did not make up for the ill-chosen menu and the poor service.

Dolley's gaze roamed the table, rested on the President's oldest son, Abraham, his secretary, a handsome young man who was already the target of every predatory young female eye in Washington, and into her own eyes came a sudden gleam which Jemmy would have recognized, had called "that matchmaking glint." And why not? Didn't she have three nieces who would fit the role of hostess to perfection? Dolley, perhaps, at twenty-six, was a bit too old for the youthful Abraham and not too robust in health. Mary Estelle at twenty-three was a better possibility. But best of all there was her own Anna.

As had always been her custom in Washington she prepared for guests on New Year's Day, making ready refreshments for far more than she expected. In fact, she wondered if anyone would come. Again she was amazed—and humbled. Almost everyone who visited the White House—and that was nearly all of Washington—came across the square to the little gray house on the far corner. She met them at the front door, Anna beside her. Then her other nieces conducted them to the refreshment tables, saw that they were engaged in entertaining conversation, and ushered them out the back door. When Abraham Van Buren arrived with his brothers, Dolley was glad that she had insisted on purchasing Anna a new rose-colored velvet cut in the latest style, with high waist, low square neck, and short puffed sleeves, and given her some of her own gold and pearl jewelry with drop earrings to wear. Anna was not beautiful. Her features were irregular. Her charm was in her lively, loving nature, which unfortunately revealed itself only in intimate associations. At a time like this she was reserved and tongue-tied.

"What did you think of the President's son, the handsomest one—Abraham, I believe his name is?" Dolley questioned her casually in succeeding weeks, after several attempts to arouse their interest in each other. "It must be hard for all those boys, alone without a mother in the White House. Should we invite them to dinner, perhaps?"

Anna gave her a sly, knowing smile. "Don't try," she said bluntly. "He isn't a bit interested in me or I in him. And anyway," she gave her aunt an affectionate hug, "everything I want in life is right here with you."

Dolley's sigh was one of relief as well as disappointment. She could not bear the thought of even brief separations from this dear adopted daughter. Not Anna. Who, then? She did not easily relinquish a project. There came a letter from one of her cousins in South Carolina, Angelica Singleton, great-granddaughter of Uncle John Coles, who had married her great-aunt, Mary Winston. Angelica was coming to Washington and hoped she could call on Dolley while she was there. Dolley hastened to write and invite her to be her guest. Angelica happily accepted.

The minute she saw the girl Dolley knew: this was the one. She could see her greeting ambassadors and congressmen in the East Room, presiding at a faultlessly arranged table, conversing as knowledgeably about politics with men as about food and fashions with women. Angelica had attended Madame Greland's fashionable seminary in Philadelphia, had been to Europe. And she was beautiful. But —how to proceed? The President had dispensed with all levees and morning receptions. The public was admitted to the house only on New Year's Day and July Fourth or by formal invitation. Shades of the cheese devastation, perhaps! But Dolley was seldom at a loss for ways to implement her purposes. She wrote a note begging a favor of the President. A relative visiting her was humbly desirous not only of meeting the chief executive but of seeing the magic he had wrought in the house where her cousin had once lived. If it would not be asking too great a favor . . . An invitation to take informal tea with the President and his sons came by return messenger.

Again Dolley knew the moment she saw them together, and in the following weeks she had the satisfaction of seeing the courtship progress. But the wedding of Abraham and Angelica solemnized near the end of the year came for her in a season of sorrow, not rejoicing. In the fall her sister Anna's second son, Thomas, had died, and in December death came unexpectedly to Anna's fifth child, Dolley Payne Madison Cutts, her namesake, her beloved Dolché, whose birth twenty-seven years before had almost filled the void in her own childless marriage. It was all she could do that winter to pursue the usual round of entertainment, calling, and social engagements in her usual outwardly cheerful and enlivening manner.

As if the burdens of grief were not enough, anxieties multiplied. There were many more papers in addition to the three volumes of the

Debates purchased by Congress—writings and letters on Constitutional subjects, selections from James's early correspondence which might form a volume on the legislative proceedings of Virginia, historical letters on the period from 1780 up to the formation of the new government. These should be committed to the press as soon as possible after the publication of the *Debates,* though Congress seemed in no hurry to perform the latter. She had had correspondence with Harper's about the publication of these additional volumes, but they also were slow in responding, due no doubt to the furor of panic sweeping the country. It was a matter of constant worry, since she considered this obligation her prime purpose in living.

There were other anxieties. In spite of her rigid attempts at economy the nine thousand dollars remaining of the amount paid by Congress was vanishing at an appalling rate. Expenses for entertaining were an enormous drain, yet what could she do? Guests were continually presenting themselves, foreign visitors, diplomats, government officials, all, of course, bent on doing honor to Jemmy, not to her. And she was constantly receiving invitations for which returns must be made. Hospitality had always been a prime tenet of their household. She could not bring disgrace on Jemmy's memory by being niggardly or reclusive.

Even the incredible success of her bout at matchmaking was not without its flaws. True, Angelica was an impeccable First Lady, presiding over the White House with a skill and elegance Dolley knew she herself had never achieved. A honeymoon in Europe following her marriage had given her additional social polish—possibly a little too much. She was criticized—probably by the same Washington cliques that had cast innuendos on Rachel Jackson and Mrs. Eaton—for attempting to install European court airs and customs. Gossip scored her for wearing three large feathers in her hair, for receiving guests seated in an armchair on a raised dais, for wearing a long-trained purple velvet gown at some of her levees.

But most of Dolley's worries were more personal. The farms were not prospering. Montpelier was costing far more than it produced. She did not blame Payne. It was a time of economic depression, and all Virginia plantations were struggling for survival. Brother-in-law Richard and his son James Madison Cutts, who acted as her financial advisers, were urging her to sell Montpelier. But the thought was horrifying. So much had it been a part of Jemmy's being that it would seem almost like dismembering his dead body. But something must be done. In the summer of 1839 she came to a decision. She would return to Montpelier and try to manage the estate herself. Swiftly she made her plans. Her old friend "French John" Sióussat was still in Washington, working for the Bank of the Metropolis. Once more, as in salvaging the Washington portrait and the red velvet curtains, he was her willing assistant. Yes, he would be glad to take care of her Washington house while she was away. He would keep it in repair, rent it if she chose, pay her bills. And, yes, he would see that her cow, a thoroughbred brought from Montpelier, a far more necessary appendage to her Washington regime than a carriage, was either rented or happily attached to his own household.

Montpelier again. At first it was heaven to be back. Jemmy's spirit seemed far more pervasive there than in Washington. The house was a challenge of unsightliness and neglect. Under Payne's haphazard management much had been stolen—quilts, blankets, sheets, linens, silverware. Dolley plunged happily into its rejuvenation, and soon the old atmosphere of warmth and cheer and hospitality prevailed. Neighbors came to visit. Anna became involved in the old round of young people's activities. Lucy, twice-widowed now and looking older than her years, older than Dolley's seventy-one, came to stay for an extended period.

But Dolley's efforts to restore the plantation's prosperity were less successful. Though in her letters to Margaret Smith she hopefully dubbed herself a "Farmeress," it was an unhappy misnomer. She knew nothing about farming. James, who had been an expert agriculturist, had imparted to her nothing of his expertise. And Payne, she had to admit, though with her usual excuses, was of no help. He was more concerned with his continued building at Toddsberth than with the humdrum round of duties on a plantation. Though his exile from city life had curbed his gambling propensities, it had only aggravated his penchant for liquor. Still Dolley did not despair of his eventual reform.

"He means well." Sturdily, at times defiantly, she repeated the old refrain.

Lucy was still sure that it would take only a good marriage to redeem Payne from his weaknesses, and she was more ardent in the pursuit of prospects than Dolley had ever been. Dolley had long since relinquished the hope of ever becoming a grandmother.

Lucy, who had never adjusted to life in Kentucky and was still unsettled after the death of her husband, remained with her for about a year, drawing renewed vigor from Dolley's outflowing vitality and the constant liveliness of Montpelier's social ménage. As Dolley wrote Margaret Smith in August 1841, "I have been much confined for the last year, though most agreeably so, in adding comfort to my sister, whose health and spirits are better than on her arrival."

But with Lucy gone back to her own home at Harewood, she was forced to more decision making. Her attempts to make the plantation pay were futile. Her capital was nearly gone. The small amounts Sióussat was able to send her from rental of the Washington house, first to her old friend and relative William C. Preston, then for a brief time to Attorney General John J. Crittenden, were barely enough to pay for its upkeep. Even that precious asset, her cow, had wandered off, much to the apologetic dismay of the faithful Sióussat. She hastened to reassure him.

"I am truly sorry, my good friend, that the cow should behave so badly, but still hope that she will return to the kind protection of your family—If she has failed however to do so until this time and you think it best you will advertise for her (as your own). I enclose $10 to reconcile the little ones for their fatigue in hunting her as well as for the honor you may do the wanderer by announcing her in a newspaper."

There had been more disasters in Washington than the loss of a cow. Fortunately Dolley had been absent during the bitter and tempestuous presidential campaign of 1840. Van Buren's stigma from association with the panic had indeed brought about his downfall, and the popular hero of wartime fame, William Henry Harrison, had been swept into office on boisterous waves of parades, banners, floats bearing the log cabins and barrels of cider typifying the rustic Westerner, slogans, especially the stirring and rhythmic "Tippecanoe and Tyler too." After forty years of democratic-republicanism starting with Jefferson, the opposition, once styled Federalists but now Whigs, were again in power. But Harrison had lived only a month, succumbing to pneumonia, possibly contracted from delivering his two-hour inaugural address while standing in a freezing northeast wind. John Tyler, a Virginia planter chosen chiefly to attract the Southern vote, was now President.

Dolley was torn between choices.

Montpelier? Stay here in a further effort to save it from greater deterioration which might well result in bankruptcy? Save it, perhaps, Jemmy's beloved patrimony, from going, like Jefferson's Monticello, into strangers' hands? Yet she had struggled for two years, gone into the fields herself to inspire courage in dispirited laborers, bent over bewildering accounts by candlelight until her weak eyes streamed and the figures blurred into even more hopeless confusion.

Washington? Return to the social rounds that could not be avoided and inevitably meant more expense besides loss of the meager rental from the house? It was empty now, for with the change in administrations Attorney General Crittenden had been removed from office. But Washington offered far better opportunities for pursuing her prime purpose, the preservation of Jemmy's papers. Congress had finally published the three volumes of the Constitutional Convention *Debates*. But there were more volumes equally important, five of them. She *must* get them published. That they constituted her own sole source of financial security she scarcely considered. All that mattered was their preservation.

Washington? Montpelier? Her head swam. A choice perhaps between saving Montpelier, Jemmy's past, or his papers, his legacy to the future. There could be only one answer. Payne must take over the administration of the estate, at least temporarily. She would return to Washington.

2

She was accomplishing nothing—of importance, that is. Oh, she was pursuing the usual sequence of activities prescribed by her inescapable popularity in Washington society. Holding her receptions on New Year's Day and the Fourth of July, wearing her outmoded gowns with the same dignity and poise as when they had been Parisian imports in the height of fashion, the name of each guest as glib on her lips at age seventy-five as at forty. Extending her dainty lava and platinum or cloisonné snuffbox to Henry Clay and Daniel Webster and John Quincy Adams as once she had offered it to Alexander Hamilton or Patrick Henry. Skimping on needed supplies for the household in order to serve decent dinners and wines and cakes to the ubiquitous guests. Making calls in borrowed or rented carriages, at least once as many as thirty recorded in the course of two weeks. Giving eagerly sought advice to Patricia Cooper Tyler, wife of the President's son Robert and to Letitia Tyler Semple, his daughter, after the latter became White House hostess following the death of her invalid mother Letitia in September of 1842.

"The greatest trouble I anticipate," confessed young Mrs. Robert after taking over her duties as hostess, "is paying visits. There was a doubt at first whether I must visit in person or send cards; but I asked Mrs. Madison's advice on the subject, and she says, return all my visits by all means. So three days in the week I am to spend three hours a day driving from one street to another in this city of magnificent distances. . . ."

Dolley soon became an intimate friend of the whole Tyler family, and informal notes and invitations were constantly being carried by servants between the two houses. In January 1842, when Elizabeth, the nineteen-year-old daughter of the Tylers had a quiet wedding in the East Room, Dolley was among the honored guests. And, what pleased her even more, one of the small Tyler grandchildren selected her to sit opposite her and share the festivities of her fifth birthday. A child's affection pleased her far more than an honor paid by a great official.

But her important task was far from fulfillment, Jemmy's papers were no nearer publication. In April of 1842 she made a hurried trip to New York, the first time she had ever ridden on a train, that marvelous invention propelled by steam instead of horses. Though Harper's had agreed to publish the remaining volumes and had even stereotyped some of them back in 1840, nothing more had been done. The trip resulted in no further agreement.

More successful but equally distressing was her interview with her old friend John Jacob Astor, who, after satisfying himself as to the worth of her property, agreed to take a mortgage on her Washington house for a loan of three thousand dollars, to be paid in at least seven years at 6 percent interest, all of which was soon exhausted to pay her mounting debts. The only happy feature of the trip was her stopover in Philadelphia, grown astoundingly in the half century since she had left it, but still containing old friends, many of them Quakers, some of them among those attending a ball given in her honor. How had the old inhibitions fallen!

It was with relief that at Payne's urging she turned the handling of the papers over to him. Doubtless, as he explained, a man would be better able to secure favorable results in such complex matters of business.

"I am to confer with the Harpers," he wrote her in March 1843, "as soon as I can see him about a difference in balance in your favor and an advance on books and money. Your writing would not be understood, and might embarrass my obtaining any for you." Or "for myself," had he neglected to add?

She waited hopefully for results. Nothing. Then the following winter she was urged to offer the papers once more to Congress. Lucy suggested that it would be a favorable time, "Congress being at this time engaged in nothing of importance—tho' the feeling of retrenchment and economy may operate somewhat against you." She wrote to Payne immediately. Still nothing.

"If you love me, my dear son," she wrote in January 1844, "write me—tell me when you will come to offer the papers to Congress and to do something with the 4th volume—We are without funds and those we owe are impatient. . . . Oh, my son! I am too unhappy not to have you with me, and not to have even your opinion and directions, what to do myself, or what individual to engage and at what

time! Do not let this often repeated regret offend or hurt you my son
. . . but reflect on the miseries of your mother when she sees that
nothing but a happy and early result of this duty will give her bread or
continue to her what is better, a respectable standing before the world.
But I will say little more—as it is not good for me to write."

No one seeing her would have known that she was getting desperate
over her financial straits. In February she was invited by President
Tyler to take a cruise down the Potomac on the new steam-powered
ship *Princeton*. It was a gala celebration, marking the maiden voyage
and exhibition of the ship's new marvel weapon, a cannon so powerful
in its destructibility that it was dubbed "The Peacemaker." Tyler had
assembled a host of notables to witness the first salute of this tremendous servant of progress, among them his cabinet, members of the
Congress, and foreign dignitaries.

Among the guests was the family of David Gardiner, scion of a
prominent and wealthy New York family, who with his daughters
Julia and Margaret, was spending the winter in Washington. Dolley
was charmed with the beautiful and accomplished Julia, who had
become the acknowledged darling of the capital. Already famous as
"the Rose of Long Island," the lovely Julia had most of the eligible
males of Washington at her feet, not the least among them, Dolley
noted with good-humored appreciation, the President himself.

On the way down the river the great gun was fired, the men of the
party open-eyed with admiration, the women, eyes closed and with
fingers in their ears, uttering little squeals of simulated terror. After
dinner, served faultlessly and sumptuously in the ship's cabin, some
professed a desire for the great gun to be fired again. The men went up
on deck, the women remaining below in the cabin, also the President,
who appeared loath to part company with the fair Julia.

Suddenly there was a tremendous explosion. The ship rocked cra-
zily, timbers strained. Dolley was flung from her chair. Furniture in
the cabin was overturned. Picking herself up, she found herself unhurt
except for a few bruises, but moans from others proved them far less
fortunate. Agonizing screams were issuing from the deck above. Julia
Gardiner, also apparently unhurt and equal to the occasion, was
busily ministering to some of the women, uttering words of assurance,
easing the fallen into more comfortable positions, trying to quiet their
fears.

"I'm going up on deck," Dolley told her tersely. "You stay here and
help. I'll see what I can do there. Those screams!"

There was no cessation of them. As she climbed the steep narrow stairs they grew louder, and she stepped out into pandemonium. The deck was a shambles, for the great gun had exploded, sending its deadly metal shafts in all directions. Bodies were lying everywhere, in all stages of injury, mutilation—death. The floors were slippery with blood. With those less injured of the party Dolley did what she could. With quick presence of mind she tore off her long muslin petticoat, used it to wipe bleeding faces, tore it into strips to bind wounds— skillfully, as she had sometimes done for slaves on the plantation— even took a piece of it to cover an unrecognizable dead face.

Time had no meaning. The horror seemed to go on forever. She knew the ship was moving, though slowly. She herself moved, almost unconsciously, like an automaton, comforting, trying to ease pain but not succeeding, until someone touched her shoulder.

"Come. We're back on shore. There are carriages waiting."

She obeyed, almost without volition. Standing on land again, feet surprisingly steady, she felt like someone awakened from a nightmare, restored suddenly to reality. The confusion resolved itself into clear but disconnected shapes, like patterns in a kaleidoscope—the battered ship, its proud "Peacemaker" so ill-named—a line of stretchers moving endlessly, it seemed—the face of a friend, the wife of a well-known senator, dissolved in tears . . . President Tyler, bending over a wildly weeping Julia Gardiner, obviously trying to comfort her . . .

Then, after an interminable succession of jolting travel, clattering of hooves, streets lined with shocked faces, she was at home, being helped from the carriage, finding her drawing room filled with anxious friends and relatives. Though the terrific blast had been heard as far away as the city, news had not reached it for over an hour, and then with no specific information about the victims. She entered quietly, bowed with her usual graciousness to greet them, tried to smile.

"Aunty, you're safe! We were so frightened when we heard—!"

"What a terrible experience! The whole city is in shock. And to think you were there!"

"Why, you might have been killed!"

"No wonder you're so pale and trembling!"

Dolley could not speak. They fussed over her, made her lie down, covered her with a rug, uttered soothing sounds. "There, there, dear, you're all right now. You're safe. Try to forget—" Forget! As if she could ever forget! They did not understand. The silence, the pallor, the trembling, they were not for herself. *She* had not suffered. They were all for those others.

Shock from the disaster rocked the city. Nearly forty were either dead or wounded, the dead including two members of the President's cabinet, a naval captain, ex-Senator Gardiner, a foreign deputy, and many crew members. Had the President not remained below in the cabin with the ladies, he might well have been one of the victims.

Dolley could never trust herself to speak of that terrible afternoon and never heard it mentioned without turning pale and trembling. For many weeks she spent her spare time ministering to the needs of the bereaved families.

One happy event may have stemmed from the tragedy. The President's comforting of the bereaved Julia Gardiner had not been inspired by fatherly solicitude. Four months later he and the beautiful Julia were married, and the White House had a new charming and capable First Lady. In spite of the thirty years' difference in their ages, the Tylers' was a remarkably happy and congenial marriage. Though her reign as First Lady was to last only eight months, she filled it with the utmost grace and vivacity, a perfect hostess, her white satin and black lace gowns worn in deference to the prescribed period of mourning complementing her vivid brunette beauty. "The most beautiful woman of the age," President Tyler called his new bride, "and most accomplished." She and Dolley reigned over Washington society in complete harmony, one in her black-and-white finery augmented by ostrich plumes and accompanied by maids of honor dressed all in white, the other appearing just as queenly in her outmoded black velvet and turban.

The far happier celebration of another invention than the ill-named "Peacemaker" soon followed the *Princeton* tragedy. On May 24 Dolley was invited by Samuel F. B. Morse to witness a test of his newly invented electric telegraph, a connection for which had been set up between Baltimore and Washington. In spite of the incredulous hootings of many of its members, the House had voted to expend twenty-five thousand dollars for Morse's experiment. Inconceivable, many scoffed, that words could be transmitted for forty miles over a little wire!

Dolley went to the demonstration with a mixture of emotions—doubt, hope, anticipation. Only a select few had been invited to attend the tryout, which at the Washington end was to be held in the old Supreme Court room in the basement of the Capitol. With sixteen other people Dolley stood gazing at the strange instrument, waiting with breathless suspense to see the experiment either succeed or fail. With amazing calmness and confidence Morse sent his message, dictated by Annie Ellsworth, daughter of the commissioner of patents, Henry L. Ellsworth.

"What hath God wrought!"

Followed moments of tense waiting, then the message was tapped back from forty miles away in Baltimore, loud and clear. "What hath God wrought!"

Silence, as poignantly electric as the impulse that brought the speeding message! Then the little company burst into cheers. Morse turned to Dolley.

"Mrs. Madison, would you like to send a message?"

Dolley gasped. It was like being asked to give a cue to the Angel Gabriel! What could she possibly say that would be worthy of this historic occasion? She looked helplessly up at Henry Clay, who was standing beside her, but he only smiled encouragement. Finally common sense came to her rescue. After all, this was just another kind of communication, like greeting a guest or inquiring after the health of a friend. And she had a cousin in Baltimore, wife of Congressman John Wethered.

"Message from Mrs. Madison," she said clearly. "She sends her love to Mrs. Wethered."

Not a bad message, certainly, one of love between persons, to follow that first tribute to divine power sent over the scientific miracle of which the *Baltimore Patriot* would write the following day, "This is indeed the annihilation of space."

Personally, Dolley had little of achievement to celebrate. Though in January of that year, 1844, the House had voted to give her a seat in the hall whenever she chose to visit, instead of in the gallery where ladies attending had to sit, the highest compliment it had ever paid a woman, it had made no move to buy James's papers, an act far more necessary to the attainment of her major goal, and, increasingly, to her own survival. In February she had written Payne asking if he knew where she could borrow two hundred dollars. He had made no reply except to tell her that he was enlarging his cluster of buildings at Toddsberth, was even putting rooms on one floor just for her, on the ground floor because he knew she disliked stairways, with wide large steps leading from her apartment into the dining room. In the round towerlike room which he called the Ballroom she would be able to do the grand entertaining to which she was accustomed. Where he was obtaining funds for these projects he never revealed.

"The residence of her eccentric son," her grand-niece was to describe this building monstrosity in her *Memoirs* of Dolley.

Dolley agreed, but could not chide him too much for such evidences of his love and concern for her. When Anna, Mary, and others were harshly outspoken in their criticism, she made the reply which had become almost a byword through the years.

"My poor boy, forgive his eccentricities. His heart is right."

Her problems multiplied. Worst of all was news that came in a letter from her trusted slave Sarah in July. It was Sarah who kept her informed about happenings at Montpelier.

"My mistress: I don't like to send you bad news but the condition of all of us, your servants, is very bad. . . . The sheriff has taken all of us and says he will sell us at next court unless something is done before to prevent it. We are afraid we shall be bought by what are called negro buyers and sent away from our husbands and wives. If we are obliged to be sold, perhaps you could get neighbors to buy us that have husbands and wives, so as to save us from misery which will in a greater or less degree be sure to fall on us at being separated from you as well as from one another . . . The sale is only a fortnight from next Monday, but perhaps you could make some bargain with somebody by which we could be kept together."

Well did Dolley know who was responsible for this situation. James's brother William, who had always been intensely jealous of Payne's status as the eventual heir of Montpelier and who had recently brought suit against the estate for a sum he claimed was due him from his father's will, must be behind this tragic move. In her confusion following James's death Dolley had hastily and unwisely signed a note promising to pay the sum at some future time if the debt should be proved genuine. William was also refusing to relinquish some of James's letters which it was necessary to obtain before she could include them in any sale to Congress. William had threatened to have the slaves seized as surety in his lawsuit.

That Payne had known of this development and had not told her was indicated by a notation he had made in his diary on June 4.

"I have promised to meet Mr. Fraser to give him a list of Negroes belonging to Mrs Madison on Thursday, the 20th of June, for the purpose of a levy in the case of Madison vs. Madison."

Dolley was appalled. See her beloved servants put on the auction block, husbands separated from wives, mothers from children, children she herself had helped bring into the world, visited when they were sick, cut and sewed their clothes, seen their faces light up over Christmas gifts, arranged their marriages! She felt sick with horror. Sarah . . . Sukey . . . Betty . . . perhaps even Paul Jennings . . . she could mention a dozen who were as dear to her as her own relatives! But—what could she do? She felt so helpless without Jemmy to advise her, and Payne—could she really depend on Payne? Suddenly she knew what she must do—not for herself. She would rather starve first. But for them, these her "people," who had served so faithfully, for whose welfare she was responsible—yes, and for Jemmy. She could almost hear what he would say. "Persons, my dear. They are always more important than things." But—was there time? Two weeks, Sarah had said, and letters did not carry swiftly.

She sat down immediately and wrote to Henry Moncure of Richmond, to whom she had sold a small portion of the Montpelier property some years ago and who had offered to purchase the whole estate. Yes, she would sell it, and for the low price he had offered, provided that all slaves could be included without breaking up their families or abandoning the aged ones. She sent the letter off by special messenger, commissioned to make utmost haste and to wait for an answer. He arrived in time. By July 19, when the two weeks were up, the deal had been consummated. Dolley sent Moncure a deed to the estate on August 12, but he noted a keen regret in her letter. "No one I think can appreciate my feeling of grief and dismay at the necessity of transferring to another a beloved home."

Bothered by this note of reluctance, Moncure wrote that he would cancel the sale if she wished, even suggesting that he might make arrangements with her creditors so she could retain some part of Montpelier. But she refused. All she asked was the privilege of choosing some of the furniture, a few of the slaves, and the ownership of the family burial ground. There. It was done. The slaves were safe in their cabins. True, Payne would never inherit Montpelier, her dearest wish, but she had become reconciled to this eventuality. He had never succeeded with the plantation, and now his interests were confined to Toddsberth, where he had removed himself permanently.

It was Payne, given the power of attorney, who handled the transfer of the property. He moved most of the valuable furniture to Toddsberth, all of Dolley's books and papers, and the treasured works of art of which he was a true connoisseur, having purchased many of them for Madison in Europe. His building operations proceeded at an even more grandiose scale, undoubtedly encouraged by the possible new source of income, which, knowing his mother, he would have largely at his disposal. However, Moncure kept postponing payments, due to his dissatisfaction with certain statements in the deed.

"The sale to Moncure I consider a most unfortunate one," Payne was writing his mother in September, "and would certainly wish it done away with for he is a source of more difficulty than could have been apprehended." Unfortunate, he might have added, because the delay in payment retarded some of his own most urgent plans.

It was Dolley who suffered most from the delay. Knowing that the sale had been made and expecting her to be flush with funds, creditors closed in. The Bank of the Metropolis urgently demanded the payment of a loan. Since there was already a lien on her house, she offered to mortgage her furniture and personal effects. Never had she felt more destitute. And Payne took this occasion to increase her embarrassment. He had heard of a vacancy in the consulship at Liverpool. Would his mother kindly request President Tyler to give him this appointment? It would mean that he could give her at least five thousand dollars a year out of his salary and make them both financially independent.

Dolley was in a quandary. Even as the President's wife she had consistently refused to solicit preference for friends who were continually requesting her help. But—for her beloved Payne? Dutifully, reluctantly, she wrote to the President suggesting that her son, now a mature fifty-two, a former attaché to the peace legation in her husband's administration and experienced in European politics, might fill the position of consul with competence and distinction.

The answer came back, polite but firm. "Mr. Todd is not fitted for the office." Payne's reputation for dissolute and prodigal living extended far beyond his immediate circles. Dolley's chagrin was oddly tinctured with relief. Payne, she knew, was far safer in the partial seclusion of Toddsberth than if subjected to the tempting diversions of European society.

She was more fortunate in another instance of family intervention, this time in her favorite role of matchmaker. Her young nephew Richard Dominicus Cutts, Anna's youngest son, was in love with Martha Hackley, Thomas Jefferson's granddaughter. But they had no money, no prospects. Just as he had taken his childish problems to his loving and understanding aunt, so now he wrote asking her for advice. What should he do? His beloved Martha had promised him her hand, but, as Dolley well knew, neither of them had anything but devotion to offer each other. Should they marry—or wait, perhaps for years, until he could provide for her as he would like to? Please! He had no mother to help him.

This was a commission after Dolley's own heart. Just as once she had run races with him on the portico, got down on her knees beside him to help weed his tiny garden patch, so now, joyfully and with a bit of bravado, she proceeded to give advice which would have even further shocked her tradition-bound peers.

"I have just received yours my very dear Richard," she wrote boldly, "and I hasten to give you freely that which you ask of me 'the advice of a mother.' It is that you immediately secure for your life and even after, the lonely one who has promised you her hand—she who I am persuaded would be a prize to any man. Why then should delay obstruct your happiness, when your father's house tho small would be a pleasant abode for a few months at the end of which you could take one more ample and suited to your mutual taste? This is my opinion and counsel dear Richard and may Heaven's blessing follow the pursuance of it & strengthen that judgment and pure spirit which I know lives in your soul. Your aunt and constant friend."

Others' problems, it seemed, were easier to solve than her own. But when late in that year of 1844 the Senate authorized the purchase of the remainder of James's papers, her spirits soared. Surely now her worries were over. She would have fulfilled her commission from Jemmy, and, significant but of less importance, her worrying financial embarrassment would be relieved. She could pay her debts and have enough left over to carry on her public and domestic life on a decent scale.

"My anxiety to have all these writings before the public is intense," she wrote her brother-in-law, Richard Cutts, "and has been for the last two years, but disappointing impediments have occurred and seem augmenting in my sad way."

Now, please God, the waiting would soon be over. But time passed, and the House of Representatives failed to follow the leadership of the Senate. She was now almost at the end of her resources. It was well she did not know that she would wait another four whole years before action would finally be taken.

3

"This is where I came in!" she might have told herself as she dressed for the inaugural ceremonies marking the end of one administration and the beginning of another. How many Presidents had there been? Ten, this retiring one would make, and she had known them all. Washington and his Martha had encouraged and blessed her marriage, in fact had been family relations. John Adams, Vice President when Jemmy was in Congress, had been their friend in spite of political differences. She had been hostess for Jefferson, First Lady for Madison, close friend of fellow-Virginian Monroe. John Quincy Adams had been first to call on her after her return to Washington and was still in Congress. She had welcomed Jackson back from his victory at New Orleans, found a glamorous First Lady for the son of Van Buren. She had seen Harrison commissioned for the command that had made him the hero of Tippecanoe, and for four years John Tyler had been her neighbor, guest, and friend.

But this new President was less known, not just to her, to all of Washington, indeed, to most of the nation. "Who is James K. Polk?" had been the satiric campaign slogan of the Whigs, for, though he had been a Congressman, Speaker of the House, and Governor of Tennessee, as a presidential candidate he was what was to be known as a "dark horse," winning the election over the Whig Henry Clay because of Andrew Jackson's support and the Democrats' popular platform plank, "Annexation of Texas and Oregon!" For the country was in an expansionist mood, all eyes except those of the industrial Northeast focused on the West. The election had been close, however, with only the volatile New York vote squeaking Polk into office.

It was a hopelessly rainy day, and Dolley was almost glad she was still unable to afford new clothes for such an occasion. As John Quincy Adams remarked, the new President delivered his address "to a large assemblage of umbrellas." Though his expansionist views were well known, he did not mention that he was not only planning to fulfill his campaign promises by taking Texas, but also adding the acquisition of New Mexico and California.

Dolley was under one of the umbrellas, attending the ceremony with old and distinguished friends, Mrs. George M. Dallas, whose husband had been Jemmy's Secretary of the Treasury, and Richard Rush, well known in politics. But, though they had a place of honor there, she was amazed when, after the inauguration, the new President walked across the square and appeared among her assembled guests. He had paid her a signal honor. She would have been even more surprised could she have heard an exchange between him and an acquaintance at the White House reception that day.

"I see Mrs. Madison is here," remarked a guest. "She has certainly become a Washington institution."

"Sir," replied the President, "let me correct you. As President Jackson once said of her, she is a *national* institution."

At the ball that evening at the National Theatre, Dolley renewed her friendship with Sarah Childress Polk, whom she had known briefly during the first years of her return to Washington. Mrs. Polk was a handsome and accomplished woman. Healy's portrait of her the following year would show a comely brunette, dark curls framing a high intellectual forehead, wide dark eyes whimsically sparkling beneath heavy brows, a low-cut but modest black gown accentuating the whiteness of neck and shoulders. She was dressed so tonight, her easy and cordial manner commanding both admiration and respect. Like Dolley, she did not dance but not because of deference to the former First Lady. She and her husband were strict Methodists, as rigidly opposed to dancing, card playing, and the theater as Dolley's early Quakerism. Her reign as First Lady would be noted for its sedateness and sobriety. At least, Dolley would remind herself humorously as once more she donned her outmoded black velvet for some state occasion, she would not be outblazoned in color by the First Lady, for Sarah Polk always wore black.

There was one small casualty at the ball that affected Dolley. A young officer, Commodore Elliott, lost his wallet. He regretted most, he told someone, and it was repeated to Dolley, the loss of a letter she had written him and a lock of hair of Mr. Madison which was in company with similar locks of Washington, Franklin, and Jackson.

She could compensate him for the loss of the letter, and did so immediately. She could even enclose in it a few strands from her precious memento of Jemmy's hair, though the relics of the other three dignitaries were beyond her power to replace. She could well understand how he would treasure such a memorial of her famous husband, but why he should think a letter from her worth saving was beyond her comprehension. She was always surprised, humbled, a little embarrassed when people kept asking for her autograph, women waiting for her outside the doors of the Senate chamber or the court-rooms, even boys and girls proffering their autograph books with an unmistakable look of hero worship in their eyes. As if her increasingly shaky scrawl was worth saving! She never wrote personal statements but always tried to write some little helpful thought, perhaps a poem of her own, more often a quotation.

One such request once came from a Miss Dahlgren, sister of a well-known admiral. "I have a new autograph album," she said eagerly, "and I must have you write in it before anyone else."

Dolley threw her arms about the girl. "Well, you darling little flat-terer," she returned. "If you will get me a good quill, I will do it. I cannot write with these newfangled steel pens."

After much thought she wrote painstakingly:

> Deliberate on all things with thy friend;
> But since friends grow not thick on every bough,
> First on thy friend, deliberate with thyself!
> Pense, ponder, not eager in the choice
> Nor jealous of the chooser; fixing, fix
> Judge before friendship, then confide till death.

More and more she chose for such requests quotations from her Quaker childhood, words which, long half-forgotten, suddenly re-turned with more poignant memory than many more recently learned. She could almost feel the hard bench and the cramps in her dangling legs, hear Teacher John's confident voice repeating them.

"Listen to that of God within thee."

"Take heed, dear friend, to the promptings of love and truth in thy heart, which are the leadings of God."

"Wait on God, in his Light to receive his counsel."

Was it such nostalgic reminders of her Quaker heritage that brought the conviction that something was lacking in her spiritual life? Or did the death of Richard Cutts that April, one of the last of her generation of family, suddenly impress on her the uncertainty of everything in the world? She was seventy-seven on her birthday in May, many years more than the proverbial three score and ten. It was not enough, she decided, to cross the street to St. John's Episcopal Church and sit in a pew each Sunday, as once she had sat there with Jemmy, even to feel the sun shining through the glorious stained-glass windows flood her spirit with the Inner Light. It was time to make a more personal commitment—to *belong*.

The rector, Reverend Smith Pyne, was gladly receptive to her suggestion. On June 2 she was baptized, and on July 15 she was confirmed. Did Mr. Pyne have any counsel for her, she asked in a note sent him on that day.

"My dearest friend," he replied, "I have no counsel to give, but to go on as you have begun. God bless and keep you in His Holy Favor."

Now that young Richard's father was gone, Dolley felt even closer to his namesake. She wanted to share with her nephew this meaningful experience.

"And now, my dear Richard," she wrote, "I must tell you on what our thoughts have dwelt a great deal—and that is to become worthy of membership in the church which I have attended for the last forty years, and which Anna has attended all her life. Yesterday this long-wished-for confirmation took place. Bishop Whittingham performed the ceremony, and we had an excellent sermon from the Bishop of New Jersey—a fine preacher and beautiful champion for Charity, which 'suspects and thinks no evil.' "

At last, long prevented by his father's death, Richard Dominicus was able to fulfill Dolley's hopes. His marriage to his sweetheart, Martha Hackley, took place at Norfolk on December 16, 1845. Dolley was delighted when he brought his bride to visit, and she gave them a big reception. She could not afford it, but friends and relatives must be served well even if she herself went hungry. Just this once, though, she would have liked a new stylish gown for the occasion.

"What must people think of me!" she exclaimed, smiling ruefully as Anna fastened about her neck the necklace of medallions which had been Jemmy's wedding gift. "Wearing clothes that are are least twenty years old and as out of date as candles for lighting houses! I can just hear what they must be calling me—a frump, a laughingstock!"

Standing back, Anna gazed appreciatively at the gown which was to go down in history as worn on this occasion. Dolley had long worn it at all state affairs and would many times more, black velvet with leg of mutton sleeves, short waisted, the skirt in full gathers, its low neckline filled with white tulle rising to a ruff about her face. On her head was the inevitable turban, this time of white satin covered with layers of more tulle. Thrown about her shoulders was her favorite scarf of rich stripes in Roman colors.

"No," said Anna. "People don't expect you, want you to change. They like you just the way you are. You're like a loved portrait, timeless, ageless. Even young people who aren't used to such styles wish they dared to imitate them. I know. I've heard them talking."

Dolley gave her niece a quick suspicious glance, half-expecting to see the familiar sign of droll mischief in the girl's eyes. Anna loved her bit of fun, like the time one spring day when she had announced with blithe innocence that she had invited the President and his wife to dinner that night. Dolley had been driven into a flurry of frantic planning until Anna had amended impishly, "Oh! I forgot! I really didn't ask them. April fool!" Her eyes held no mischief now. They were clear and honest.

"Nonsense!" Dolley returned cheerfully. "You're prejudiced, darling. But of course it's really unimportant what people think or say."

Smiling roguishly at her reflection in the pier glass, she drew herself up to her full height—not five feet five now, for age was shrinking in its effect, not in bulk but in stature. She would not have had to wear low heels now to keep below Jemmy's level—and with dignity and confidence went down to greet her guests. It was one of the biggest social events of the year, for both bride and groom were favorites in Washington society, and all through the evening the crowds pressed in through the front door, greeted the couple, partook of the lavish refreshments, and went out at the back. It might have been a presidential levee.

The couple stayed with her for six months, little realizing that they were sending her even further into debt. With the sale of Montpelier she should have been in comfortable circumstances by now, with her obligations met and enough to live on frugally. But she could not find out from Payne just what was delaying Moncure's payments for the estate. And when any money did come, it was barely enough to pay the interest on her debts. She refused to harbor suspicion, as Anna did, that Payne's lavish building enterprise was progressing partly via funds received from Moncure as her agent. Her worries were all for his health, his drinking habits frankly revealed in his letters, and even his whereabouts.

"Will my good friend Mr. Hume have the kindness to write me a line," she penned a letter to the Orange postmaster in July 1845, "in which to inform me whether my son is in the neighborhood, or in

Richmond, as I am anxious for the acknowledgment of several letters which have been written by me to him lately."

All her letters, the postmaster wrote back, had been received and delivered personally and promptly.

Finances were the lesser of her problems. Brother-in-law William was not only pressing his lawsuit, but refusing to hand over that group of important papers that James had loaned him and that were necessary if the sale of his remaining papers to Congress could ever be consummated.

Life would have been even harder during these increasingly difficult days, months, years, without her nieces and nephews. She reveled in their nearness, their presence partially atoning for Payne's delinquencies. Especially she was fond of James Madison Cutts's little son, the only boy in the family as yet, another James Madison, who lived close by and was a constant recipient of her lavish attention—and indulgence.

"I was accustomed to stand by her side at her receptions," he would recall long afterward, "often holding her hand, and was introduced to her friends as 'her little Madison,' and well remember one of those occasions when I saw around her Webster, Clay and Calhoun, and ever after was accustomed to call the Kentucky statesman 'Cousin Henry.'"

The child returned her love with implicit faith. When at the sly Anna's instigation he came to Dolley on several of her successive birthdays asking, "Aunty, how old are you?" and received the same answer year after year, he believed for a long time that she could never grow older. Dolley could tease also, as well as Anna.

"You know that statue of Jefferson in front of the White House?" she once queried. The child nodded gravely. "Well, did you know that that statue always gets down and goes to dinner whenever it hears the bell ring?"

He took her at her word, sat for hours watching the statue, waiting for the White House dinner bell to ring and when it did, wondering why the statue did not move; until one day he came to Dolley with the dawn of reasoning logic in his child eyes.

"I thought you were fooling me, Aunty," he said wisely. "But you weren't. The statue can't get down and go to dinner, because statues can't hear bells ring."

"So!" Dolley's eyes, still as bright a blue as when they had sparkled at some droll remark of his father, widened in admiration. "Good!

Thee is a discerning fellow. I am proud of thee." Sometimes under stress of emotion she still reverted to the old Quaker forms of speech, just as she donned the gray habit and kerchief on most mornings.

Equally dear to her was her grandniece, little Rose Adele Cutts, who, like young Madison, returned her affection with both love and admiration.

"The earliest recollections I have of Aunt Madison," Rose Adele was to write, "are associated with a lovely day in May or June when arrayed in our best, my brother and I accompanied our mother across the ragged little square opposite the White House. We were ushered in by Ralph, the young negro, who had succeeded Paul so well known as Mr. Madison's body-servant in old times. We were announced as 'young Master and Miss.' This was called Mrs. Madison's Levee-Day, and everybody came. . . . Aunt stood near a window. I was a curious little girl only eight or nine years of age, and my wide-open eyes saw a very sweet-looking lady, tall and very erect. . . . Aunt Madison wore a purple velvet dress, with plain straight skirt amply gathered to a tight waist—cut low and filled in with soft tulle. Her pretty white throat was encircled by a lace cravatte, such as the old-fashioned gentlemen used to wear, tied twice around and fastened with an amethyst pin. . . . I thought her turban very wonderful, as I never saw any one else wear such a head-dress. It was made of some soft silky material and became her rarely. There were two little bunches of very black curls on either side of the smooth white brow; her eyes were blue and laughed when she smiled and greeted the friends who seemed so glad to see her. . . . This levee was over at four o'clock, when only we of the family remained with Aunt who was still fresh and smiling."

"Why do you wear all that white stuff around your neck?" little Rose Adele had asked curiously.

"Because," explained Dolley, smiling, "after seventy your throat becomes a little scraggy, and you need something fluffy to make your face look softer."

"After seventy." Dolley was always a bit vague about her age, and little Madison was not the only one who noticed certain inconsistencies. William W. Corcoran, founder of what was to become the Corcoran Gallery of Art, was a good friend of Dolley and sometimes provided her with the small loans she was continually seeking. At one time when she came to him he was bold enough to inquire, "Mrs. Madison, would you mind telling me how old you are?"

"Certainly, I'll be glad to tell you," replied Dolley, smiling. "I am seventy-two, Mr. Corcoran."

The next year she came to him again, and he made the same request. "How old are you, Mrs. Madison?"

And she made the same answer. "I am seventy-two, Mr. Corcoran."

No wonder at least one of her future biographers, trying to pinpoint the date of her birth, recorded it as four years later than it really was!

4

The country was in turmoil following President Polk's inauguration in 1845. Once more Dolley might have told herself, "This is where I came in," for it was the War of 1812 all over again. There were the same flag wavings, the same drumbeats, the same uniformed lines halting outside her windows saluting her with bugles, the same hot arguments between pros and cons. But the names overheard in her drawing room were different—Mexico, Rio Grande, Santa Ana, Oregon, California, Generals Zachary Taylor and Winfield Scott. The opponents whom she tried tactfully to conciliate called themselves, not Federalists and Democratic-Republicans, but Whigs and Democrats.

She was never quite clear what the fighting was all about. Democrats talked grandly about "manifest destiny," "making the new state of Texas safe for Texans," punishing Mexico's "act of aggression." Even England became a possible enemy with her title to much of the great northwest, and the slogan "54° 40′ or Fight" was bandied about. Whigs hinted darkly of the Southern attempt to extend slavery, of "a diabolical plot to get bigger pens to cram with slaves." Their newspapers declared that "every heart worthy of American liberty had an impulse to join the Mexicans." Again, as in 1812, it seemed to be a case of the North and East in head-on conflict with the South and West.

Dolley remained friends with both parties. She became even closer to Sarah Polk because she had endured the same calumnies. Now it was "Mr. Polk's War," its perpetrator Polk the Mendacious! Yet she was equally friendly with her near neighbor Daniel Webster, an obdurate Whig, rode often in his carriage, accepted his invitations to dinner. Her old friend William C. Preston, also a Whig, remained her ardent admirer, preserving a rather remarkable portrait of her for history.

"When I knew her in after life, widowed, poor and without prestige of station, I found her the same good-natured, kind-hearted, considerate, stately person that she had been in the hey-day of her fortunes. Many of her minor habits, formed in early life, continued upon her in old age and poverty. Her manner was urbane, gracious, with an almost imperceptible touch of Quakerism. She continued to the last to wear around her shoulders a magnificent shawl of a green color. She always wore a lofty turban and took snuff from a snuffbox of lava or platina, never from gold. Two years before her death I was in a whist party with her, when Mr. John Quincy Adams was her partner and Lord Ashburton mine. Each of the three was over seventy years of age."

The war fortunately did not concern Dolley personally. Mexico seemed even farther away than had England in 1812, and she had more than enough to concern her with her own problems. Her debts were tremendous. The deed to Montpelier, it seemed, was still in question. She had exhausted all possibilities for loans. She was literally struggling for survival.

One day in 1847 she was surprised when Paul Jennings, Jemmy's faithful personal servant, turned up in Washington. He had been living at Toddsberth, presumably performing the same services for Payne that he had for James. Dolley was puzzled by his presence but delighted. He could give her news of her son! But Paul was stubbornly close-mouthed on the subject. Yes, Payne was well. His buildings were growing. He was making a house ready for her. He hoped she would come and live there. It was only by persistent prodding that she got him to admit the truth. Paul had come to her because he did not like the way things were going at Toddsberth, especially the selling of so many slaves. Perhaps—how did he know?—he might be next.

Dolley gasped. "You—you mean—Payne has been selling—"

Oh yes, didn't she know? He had sold as many as three groups, getting probably as much as six thousand dollars for them all. She must have known, for they were her slaves. His eyes became probing.

Dolley could find no words. Payne had sent her no reports, certainly no money from such sales. She sat down immediately and wrote him, knowing, however, that she would probably receive no answer.

It was soon afterward that Daniel Webster came to her with a startling request. He wanted to buy Paul Jennings. He had seen in the past what a faithful servant he was. He would not treat him as a slave, but pay him each month for his services, so that in a short time he could purchase his freedom.

"I—I—" Dolley was so surprised, so disconcerted, that at first she could find no words. "I—shall have to consult with Paul—"

"He and I have already talked about the matter," said Webster, "and he finds it quite agreeable. In fact, it was he who—" He stopped, embarrassed.

And suddenly Dolley knew. He and Paul had devised this scheme to help relieve her dire financial stress. She had tried not to let people know, but this kindly discerning neighbor with the stern, uncompromising lips and keen probing eyes had been long cognizant of the truth. He had tried, with other Congressmen, to get certain of his wealthy friends to club together and provide her with an annuity, but she had indignantly quashed that idea in the bud. The wife of James Madison accepting charity was anathema enough—but to accept it from New England Whigs!

Paul Jennings became Webster's property, serving him faithfully as once he had cared for his beloved Madison . . . serving Dolley, too, in ways he could not possibly have done as a part of her household. While the amount Webster had paid for him was infinitesimal compared with her needs (only $120), he was now in a position to observe conditions in the neighboring house and report them to his new master and mistress. Sometimes, when he was sure Dolley and her household were actually in need of food, a basket of groceries would pass between the two kitchens, many times without Dolley's knowledge. His mistress, Leroy Webster, besides entertaining Dolley and Anna at frequent dinners, would send special gifts, like some West India preserves she had just received from her nephews in Cuba. It was a way the neighbors could help without seeming to give charity.

In spite of his delinquencies—"poor boy, he means well!"—Dolley's letters to Payne expressed confidence in his ability to solve their mutual problems.

"My Dearest—It has been too long since I was cheered with a line from you—What are you about that prevents your communicating with your mother? You are taking care of our mutual property of every sort, I trust—and my confidence in you to restore it to me is not diminished by the sad and tedious time in which I have been deprived of its use. . . . Anxious—Mother."

On September 24, 1847, she was writing, "My beloved—I am too sensible to all the troubles you encounter but I trust in Our Heavenly Father who has in His Mercy supported us to this day—let your faith

in Him, with prayers for his continued goodness, to us, who are nothing without Him . . .

"I have borrowed as you must *know* to live since and before we
parted last, but I am now at a stand, until supplies come from you.
. . . I have nothing to convey away nor with which to benefit myself.
My eye rebels. Adieu for this time."

Waiting . . . but, being Dolley, not in idleness. Soon after coming
to Washington she had been asked, with Mrs. Hamilton and Mrs.
John Quincy Adams, to organize women in raising funds for the pro-
jected Washington Monument. James had been an early President of
the National Monument Society, and she felt happy in continuing his
labors. This year of 1847 was one of furious activity, holding fairs,
sales, concerts, teas, levees. She was ashamed because she had so little
to contribute to the project. She ransacked her belongings, managed to
find a few articles on her almost bare shelves to add to the sales booths
—a black silk scarf which could perhaps bring five dollars, a copy of
Dickens's *"Pickwick Papers"*, two volumes of *Tales of the Grotesque
and Arabesque.*

Then suddenly, with the coming of the New Year . . . hope. Congress was considering again the purchase of Jemmy's remaining papers. Not that the possible financial benefits were of much importance!
All she wanted was to fulfill the commission Jemmy had left her.

Then, just when success seemed to be in reach, suddenly the papers
themselves were thrust into jeopardy. Someone—an enemy, critic, perhaps just a chance vandal, or could it be someone who did not want
the papers published?—pushed burning refuse between the shutters of
the hall window and the staircase of her house. It was very early in the
morning, no later than three, and none of the household was up. A
neighbor saw the issuing smoke and aroused one of the servants.
Flames were already mounting the stairs when the servant, Ralph,
broke down Dolley's door. He found her quietly sleeping in the midst
of dense clouds of smoke.

"Mistress!" he cried. "Here I am, come to save you!"

Dolley roused, slowly became aware of the danger. Coughing, her
tender eyes blinded by the smoke, she sprang out of bed. He tried to
drag her toward the door. "Come, hurry, mistress! The stairs are
burning already. Quick, or it may be too late!"

Dolley pushed him away. The papers! The most precious things she
owned, she kept them in boxes here in her own room. Nothing else

mattered, not her scant store of money, not her jewels, not even her own life.

"Here!" As other servants appeared, Anna with them, she began thrusting the boxes into their hands. "Take them! Carry them somewhere to safety. You, Anna, see that it's done. No, I tell you I won't leave until I'm sure they are safe. You go with them, Anna. I insist."

It was Ralph who came back after her, seizing her in his arms, rushing her down the burning stairs, out of a side door, placing her in safety in a far corner of the garden. While neighbors and servants were putting out the fire, he rushed upstairs again, took the black velvet dress which she had worn the night before, and threw it out the window. The mistress must not be seen in just her nightclothes! The fire was soon extinguished. There had been more smoke than flames.

Once she was assured of the papers' safety, Dolley was restored to her usual good-natured competence. She was laughing at herself when, as calmly self-assured as if bare feet and nightcap were the proper accoutrements of a velvet gown, she thanked the neighbors and went back into the house. The damage was dismaying but unimportant. Her relatives and friends did not think so. They came rushing up as soon as they heard—Mary and her brother James Madison Cutts with his excited children, the Websters, the Prestons, the Decaturs—and in spite of the devastation she insisted on serving them tea.

"If the neighbors hadn't seen it, you might have burned to death!"

"Weren't you frightened, Aunty? I'd like to have seen the fire!"

"You shouldn't have waited so long." This sternly from the nephew who bore her husband's name. "Even valuable papers are not that important."

No? Dolley only smiled.

The arsonist was never discovered, for Dolley refused to press the investigation. She wrote Payne, "It has been supposed to be the work of an incendiary, and the watch is nightly around the city."

On May 20, 1848, her eightieth birthday, James Madison Cutts, age eleven, ran into the house, radiant, out of breath. "It—passed!" he gasped. "The motion. Father sent me—from Senate—to tell you. He said you'd want to know— quick. It's good news, isn't it? And—happy birthday, Aunty!"

She hugged him to her tightly, tears streaming down her cheeks. "My dear, thank you! You can't know what good news it is!" Twelve years she had waited for it, longer than this shining-eyed boy so dear to her had lived!

Later she learned that her friend, Congressman Alexander H. Stephens, had been influential in getting the motion passed. He had urged the appropriateness of this honor being paid her husband on her eightieth birthday. There had been a heated debate, Andrew Johnson of Tennessee strongly opposing the bill's passage. An unwarranted expenditure, he shouted, of public funds. He was also to oppose the acceptance of the funds offered to build the Smithsonian Institution.

Dolley had agreed to the terms of the bill some time before. Congress would pay her twenty-five thousand dollars for the documents. They would not purchase them outright but would set up a trust giving her an annual income. But, learning of the mortgage on her house, her many debts, the pawned silver, the committee that waited on her had agreed that five thousand dollars of the sum would be released to discharge her obligations. She had confirmed the agreement in writing before the bill had been brought to the floor of the house.

It was a gala day, that May 20, with the house crowded with visitors. Congratulations began to pour in from all over the country. One that pleased her most was from her nephew Richard Cutts in Maryland.

"I have just heard by way of New York of your Bill being passed. I shall expect to find you ten years younger than when I left you."

As previously agreed, most of the twenty-five thousand dollars voted to purchase the papers was put in a trust for her, the interest to be available as long as she lived. (It was a device, of course, derived by her friends, to keep it safe from the hands of her notoriously greedy son.) But the five thousand dollars promised was made immediately available. First, of course, she paid her outstanding bills. Then seventy dollars of it went to redeem the silver forks and spoons on which she had borrowed money. Twenty more were spent to reclaim a gold chain she treasured. She even took enough from the five thousand to pay one of her nephews for postage on his letters to her, an account she had requested him to keep. And, oh, the relief in being able to face the world, knowing that she owed no one a penny!

Payne was not pleased with the arrangement, and to Dolley's amazement and dismay she learned that he was planning to sue the trustees. She hastened to write him, expressing shock that he should even consider the idea.

"I say all this *for you* because I do not believe even *yourself* if you declared such an intention, which would at once ruin your fair fame—

your mother would have no wish to live after her son issued such threats which would deprive her of her friends, who had no other view of taking the charge but pure friendship."

Of course she was somewhat disappointed herself. Could the full amount have been made available to her, she could have lived more at ease, free from financial worries. But it did not really matter. Her debts were paid. The papers, Jemmy's bequest to future generations, would be preserved.

A fitting climax to her celebration came on July 4 when she stood with Mrs. Alexander Hamilton to see the laying of the cornerstone for the Washington Monument. It was a beautiful sunny afternoon after a dismally rainy morning. Mrs. John Quincy Adams, wife of another of the founding fathers, had been invited, but since her husband, who was to have delivered the address, had died in February, she sent regrets.

Dolley rode to the celebration in an open barouche, escorted by General Walter Jones, a former Congressman from Virginia and old friend. She had made her own contribution to the occasion three months before, writing a poem in honor of Lafayette, the gallant Frenchman to whom, as well as to Washington, America owed her freedom. He also should be honored, she felt, in this hour of remembrance. With her best goose quill and her most careful script she had transcribed it to be placed with other mementos of this special day.

This was Jemmy's hour of triumph as well as Washington's, thought Dolley, one the Father of his Country, the other the Father of the Constitution. As the great cornerstone was swung into place, she did not look down but up into the clear blue, unclouded now, and saw in her mind's eye the finished monument already planned. A stately obelisk, simple, majestic, towering, a slender pyramid rising, like a pointing finger, to a peak. A pyramid. It reminded her of something, something Jemmy had said not long before his death. He had been talking about the federal system as created by the Constitution, a government deriving all its powers from the great body of the people, with such division of powers that society would be guarded both against oppression by its rulers and the injustice of oppressive combinations among the citizens themselves.

"But the federal principle," he had said, "can be modified to indefinite extents of space, resulting in a pyramid of federal systems. Nothing but time and space could control its practical extension over the globe."

Lafayette

"Born nurtured, wedded, prized within the pale
  Of peers and princes, high in camp — at court
He hears in joyous youth, a wild report,
Swelling the murmure of the Western gale
Of a young people struggling to be free
  Straight quitting all across the wave he flies,
  Aids with his sword, wealth, blood, the high empize!
And shares the glories of its victory.
  Then comes for fifty years, a high romance
Of toils, reverses, sufferings, in the cause
    Of man and justice, liberty and France
Crowned at the last with hope and wide applause
Champion of Freedom! Well thy race was run!
All time shall hail thee, Europe's noblest Son!"

D.P. Madison

Washington April 25th 1848.

Poem to Lafayette. With a goose quill pen, Mrs. James Madison in her eightieth year paid tribute to her esteemed friend, General Lafayette. Courtesy of the Mrs. D. Madison Cutts III Collection—L.C.

That Constitutional Convention of 1787 when he had played such a leading role in uniting thirteen jealous, squabbling colonies! Always, she knew, it had seemed to him a preview of what might, *must* evolve on a larger and larger scale, involving not just colonies, or states—but nations, a world federation.

James might have helped frame the ideal form of government, thought Dolley during the following weeks and months, but its processes of change were sometimes slow and cumbersome. The founding fathers had not counted on the emergence of political parties. It was election year. Though the Whigs had professed moral outrage at "Mr. Polk's War," they took advantage of its success by nominating its hero, General Zachary Taylor, for the presidency. Polk, either from choice or from expediency, was not a candidate for reelection. The Democratic convention nominated Governor Lewis Cass of Michigan, an ardent expansionist and supporter of the Mexican War, a Northerner who defended Southern principles. But the Democrats were so divided that Taylor was elected.

If the year's end brought political strife and confusion to the country, for Dolley there was suddenly more ease and freedom from worry than she had known for years. At last the problem of the deed that had held up the settlement with Moncure was resolved. Payments began to come regularly, though it was uncertain, decided Anna, how much Payne was withholding for himself. Dolley accepted his statements without question. An agreement had also been made to satisfy William Madison's claim, and he had turned over Madison's letters and other papers. The worries that had beset her for many years had at last been laid to rest.

At President Polk's last reception on February 7, 1849, Dolley, at eighty, looked as young and far more animated than the fifty-three-year-old President. Polk had literally burned himself out in securing the "peace, plenty and contentment" he boasted of attaining during his administration, as well as the acquisition of territories that made the country nearly as great as the whole of Europe, excepting only Russia. Already these achievements were inspiring a vast western migration toward an "abundance of gold" just discovered in California which would make the year renowned in history.

Dolley did not wear her black velvet on this occasion. Perhaps her freedom from dire poverty inspired a burst of extravagance, or perhaps she sensed that the event marked for her the end of an era. Eleven Presidents she had known well and had played in many of their administrations a woman's role which would remain unique in American history. This twelfth President soon to come was a stranger, an unknown quantity. Not that she expected, or wanted, the official recognitions that she had so long been accorded. She welcomed the prospect of less social involvement. Indeed, she was feeling a little tired some of the time these days. But tonight's gala was certainly a climax for the Polks, and she wanted to do justice to it. She wore a white satin gown, its draping of sheerest tulle, cut very low, which displayed her arms and shoulders, as white and beautiful as ever. Her turban was of white satin with a fringe of the same shade twined about her head. She sat on a raised platform with Mrs. Polk, receiving the same admiration and looking far more at ease than the First Lady, who, Dolley knew, wanted nothing so much as to get her harassed husband away to their home in Tennessee.

That night President Polk recorded the evening's activities in his diary.

"Wednesday, 7th February, 1849. . . . General notice had been given in the City papers that the President's Mansion would be open for the reception of visitors this evening. All the parlours including the East Room were lighted up. The Marine band of musicians occupied the outer hall. Many hundreds of persons, ladies and gentlemen, attended. It was what would be called in the Society of Washington a very fashionable levee. Foreign ministers, their families and suites, Judges, members of both houses of Congress, and many citizens and strangers were of the company present. I stood and shook hands with them for over three hours. Towards the close of the evening I passed through the crowded rooms with the venerable Mrs. Madison on my arm. It was near 12 o'clock when the company retired. . . ."

The "peace, plenty and contentment" of which Polk had boasted was wishful thinking. The new President came to office in a country racked with conflict. *Slavery.* It had become a white-hot issue. There was something called the Wilmot Proviso, which the Northerners wanted passed, to keep slavery out of the new territories. Southerners were resolved on "determined resistance at all hazards." In April a toast to "a Southern confederacy" was hailed with cheers in South Carolina. It was nullification rearing its head all over again.

Dolley remained aloof from the political melee until her nephew James Madison Cutts told her with deep concern that some Southerners were reviving the old misrepresentation of the Virginia Resolutions and claiming that Madison had claimed for states the right of secession.

"But they can't!" protested Dolley. "Jemmy would—would turn over in his grave!"

She had to do something. Suddenly she remembered one of the last statements he had written. It was among his papers, but it might be a long time before it was published. She had a copy of it and brought it now to Richard.

"Take it," she said. "Use it if—*when* it becomes necessary. I know he sent a copy of it to Ned Coles, but you should have it too."

As Madison Cutts read the two short paragraphs, his eyes lighted. As some of the shocked would-be secessionists were to remark later after its publication the following year in the *National Intelligencer,* it was like a calm authoritative voice from the tomb.

ADVICE TO MY COUNTRY

"As this advice, if it ever see the light will not do it till I am no more, it may be considered as issuing from the tomb, where truth alone can be respected and the happiness of man alone consulted. It will be entitled therefore to whatever weight can be derived from good intentions, and from the experience of one who has served his country in various stations through a period of forty years, who espoused in his youth and adhered through his life to the cause of its liberty, and who has borne a part in most of the great transactions which will constitute epochs of its destiny.

"The advice nearest to my heart and deepest in my convictions is that the Union of the States be cherished and perpetuated. Let the open enemy to it be regarded as a Pandora with her box opened, and the disguised one, as the Serpent creeping with his deadly wiles into Paradise."

There! Dolley was satisfied. Surely she had done all she could to ensure that Jemmy's unswerving loyalty to his country's unity remained unquestioned. And the papers that were his greatest legacy to the future, the fruit of his unending struggle to secure the rights and privileges of her people through democratic processes—they also were safely preserved for generations to come. As long as those rights and liberties remained intact, were not forfeited by force or political intrigue or any other manipulation, he would remain alive in both memory and human aspiration.

5

"Are you sure you are well, Aunty dear?" Anna was definitely worried. "You don't seem like yourself."

"It must be the heat, darling. Everybody is saying we are having an especially hot and humid July."

"But the heat has never bothered you before. Last year you were out in the garden digging when it was no worse than this."

"Don't worry, dear. Perhaps I am just a little tired. We all get that way sometimes."

But not Dolley, Anna told herself. She had never seen her ceaselessly active and ebullient aunt like this before. She consulted Mary Cutts. Perhaps they should get her away from the city. It was unbearably hot. That trip she had taken down the Potomac in the spring had seemed to give her new life.

Dolley appeared to have something on her mind, something that worried her. "Oh, for my counselor!" she mourned more than once. Did it have some relation to Payne's visit in June, wondered Anna, when they had been closeted for such a long time? He had been urging her, persuading her, Anna suspected, to make a will, possibly at the behest of some of his ubiquitous creditors who wanted to make sure of a profit through his probable inheritance. Whether he had succeeded or not, Anna had no idea. But she felt it did not really matter. He should know that, will or no will, he was his mother's legal heir. Certainly she herself, though considered an adopted daughter, had no claim and desired none.

Dolley had no wish to share the details of that June encounter with anyone, least of all her beloved Anna. In fact, it was largely because of Anna that she now felt so disturbed. What had she done! But Payne, as always, had been so reasonable, so persistent, and—yes, so lovable. Just so he had been able to wheedle her into yielding to his childish desires when their object had been a sweet or a toy or a request to drop her work and run with him in the garden. The engaging smile, the persuasive voice, the merry blue eyes so like her own!

"You remember that at Father's request I helped him make a will," he had come at last after many pleasant, even gay banalities to the obvious purpose of his visit. "Everyone should do it, you know, even people as young as I am."

Dolley sighed. "I—know, dear. Madison Cutts has been—suggesting—"

"There! You see? It's considered the proper thing, even though a person may have years to live, as we all hope—trust—you have." He drew a sheet of paper from his pocket. "It just happens that I jotted down a few notes which you might just like to check and see if they agree with what you would like. I made it very simple."

Dolley took the paper. Her eyes did not seem to focus. The shutters in the parlor where they sat were closed, but bright sunlight would have made it even harder for her to see. "Perhaps—you had better read it, dear. These weak eyes of mine—"

He did so. He had made it simple indeed. Everything of which she was possessed, including all claim to the trust set up by Congress, was to go to her son.

"I knew of course that was what you would want," he said, smiling, his voice beguilingly affectionate. "Now why don't you let me rustle up some witnesses, and we can finish it here and now. Then you will have no further worries."

"But—" Dolley was confused. There was something that did not seem quite right. "Anna—"

"Of course." He was gently reassuring. "Anna will be taken care of. I understand your concern. But, after all, she is only a niece. I promise you, however, that she won't be forgotten when—if anything happens, which we hope will not be for years and years."

Dolley was scarcely aware of what happened next. It all seemed vague, like a scene in some kind of story. Payne had rounded up a couple of witnesses, a Mr. Addison and a Mr. Van Tyne, who seemed perfect strangers, and obediently, almost without her volition, she had taken the pen Payne put in her hand and written her name where he had indicated. So pleasant were the hours that followed, like the old times when his presence had brought gaiety to the house and set her feet dancing, that she had almost forgotten the uncertainty and worry that had accompanied his visit. Perhaps she had merely dreamed . . .

But as days passed the knowledge grew that it had not been a dream, and Anna was right. Payne's visit, not the July heat, was the cause of her worry. Anna's obvious concern only made her more moody and distraught because it aroused feelings of guilt. But what could she do? "Oh, for my counselor!" Then suddenly she could almost hear his voice, quiet, sane, gently reassuring. "A mistake, my dear, I have found, can often be corrected."

Of course. How simple! Her eyes brightened with purpose. "Bring me some paper, dear," she told Anna, "a good piece of foolscap, and a good quill, not one of those steel things, I can't bear them."

Relieved, Anna brought the writing utensils. "Shall I do it for you, Aunty? Write a letter to someone?" Because of the weakness of Dolley's eyes, her niece had learned to imitate her handwriting so successfully that she had often written letters at her dictation without the recipients' realizing the difference.

"No, dear, it's not a letter, and perhaps I should try to do it myself."

But Dolley had written only a few words when she relinquished the quill. "You do it, dear. My hands and eyes don't seem to get together."

Anna regarded with dismay the few shaky lines on the paper. Just three months ago Dolley's handwriting had been almost as firm and even as a calligrapher's script. And when the dictation began she was even more confused and dismayed.

"In the name of God. Amen. I think that's the way it's supposed to begin. I, Dolley Madison, widow of the late James Madison, being of sound mind and disposing mind and memory but feeble in body, in view of the uncertainty of life and the rapid approach of death do make publish and declare the following . . ."

"But, Aunty, you—you're making your will!"

"Yes, dear, and it's time. I should have done it long ago. Everybody should make a will. It doesn't mean I'm going to die right away."

Dutifully, but with her own vision blurred and her fingers a bit unsteady, Anna wrote down the provisions. Ten thousand dollars of the twenty thousand appropriated by Congress and still remaining was to go to her adopted daughter Anna Payne; another ten thousand to John Payne Todd; in the event of either one surviving the other, the sums so devised should be held by the trustees for the survivor, free from all conditions. Everything else—the Washington house, furniture, valuable paintings, slaves—was to go to her son.

"There!" Dolley leaned back, satisfied. For weeks she had been regretting the document she had signed under Payne's persuasion a month before. It had not been fair to leave her dear Anna nothing. "Now it must be made legal. Get your cousin Madison to arrange it, dear, and bring it here for me to sign."

It was well she could not know that one of the two beneficiaries would attempt to break the will after her death, hoping to secure both bequests for himself.

On July 9 the will was properly executed and signed by Dolley and three witnesses, Sally B. L. Thomas, the wife of her physician, J. Madison Cutts, and, to Dolley's delight, Elizabeth Collins Lee (her old friend Eliza) who was in Washington. The two friends spent hours together talking of old times, reverting naturally to the "thees" and "thous" of their Quaker youth. To Anna's relief Dolley acted quite like her old self, except that all the rest of that day she seemed to be living in the past, recalling events of her childhood, still using the Quaker forms of address. When Anna read to her, she asked not only for favorite passages from the Bible but for selections from the writings of George Fox, Stephen Crisp, John Woolman.

"Did I ever tell thee, Anna, about how I lost the first piece of jewelry I ever owned, a pin shaped like a butterfly? My grandmother, who was not of the Society of Friends, gave it to me. It was only a cheap little bauble, but oh, how I loved it! I found another almost like it one day years afterward, and I bought it. It's in my jewel case, I think. If thee will go and find it, dear, I would like to show thee."

Anna returned empty-handed, frustrated, almost angry at herself. There were so few things her aunt wanted these days, not to be able to satisfy her, and with such a small request!

"My dear," Dolley smiled, "do not trouble thyself about it. There is really nothing in *this* world worth caring for. Yes," she said thoughtfully, "that is what my mother once told me. I can remember almost her exact words. Yes," she repeated, "there is nothing—no *thing*, that is—in this world worth caring about."

The next morning, Tuesday, Dolley was too weak and ill to get up and dress. "I—I think I'll just lie here for—a little. Nothing to worry about, dear."

But of course they did worry, all of her relatives and friends. Many came to her bedside during the next two days. She slept a great deal, but sometimes she would awaken, and, as one of her nieces would remember, she would "smile her long smile, put out her arms to embrace those whom she loved and were near her, then gently relapse into the rest which was peace." That she was conscious of one missing face was evident from her searching eyes and her occasional murmurs, "My poor boy! . . . My poor boy!" Anna had sent a messenger post-haste to Toddsberth, but so swiftly did the illness progress that she had no hope of his arriving in time.

Dolley had never been one to postpone any commitment that seemed necessary or prolong the preparation for it. She did not now. Presently, while Anna was reading to her from her favorite book of St. John, she fell into an even deeper sleep and never regained consciousness. On Thursday, July 12, 1849, just two days after taking to her bed, she was gone. Apoplexy, the doctors pronounced it. More likely, felt Anna, it was just that she had lived her life to the full, had accomplished all her most desired goals, and was ready to go.

Guests crowded the little house all the rest of the week, as they had done so many times during the last twelve years. It was only a few steps across the street to St. John's Church, the "Church of the Presidents," and never had she traveled the short distance as slowly or accompanied by such a throng of people. Hundreds came to the church on Monday morning as she lay before the chancel, and at the services at four that afternoon the church was filled. All of the noted men and women of the city were there, come to do honor, not only to the wife of a former President but to "Queen Dolley," their beloved friend.

In one pew just behind the family sat Elizabeth Collins Lee, who perhaps had known her longer and more intimately than any other person present. During the service she found herself studying the profile of an elderly man next to her, whose face, she thought, looked very familiar. "Anthony," she breathed. "Anthony Morris." Their eyes locked in swift recognition and remembrance. Strange but fitting that these two who had been Dolley's attendants at her wedding almost sixty years before should be here together at this last, most solemn ritual!

No President or general could have been followed by a more imposing cortège than accompanied her on the journey toward the vault in the Congressional Cemetery where Payne Todd, arriving in time to complete the arrangements, had requested that her body be placed temporarily, until it could be removed to the family lot where James was buried. The procession, it was noted, was the largest yet seen in the city. Its order was impressive. The reverend clergy, attending physicians, ten pallbearers, the family, the President and his cabinet, the Diplomatic Corps, members of the Senate and House of Representatives, judges of the Supreme Court and courts of the District, officers of the Army and Navy, Mayor and Corporation of Washington, and, last but by no means least in numbers, citizens and strangers.

It was over, this life that had spanned over eighty years, compassed the terms of twelve Presidents, made an indelible impress on the manners and culture of an emerging nation, influenced its political history as few other women would ever do, saved some of its most precious treasures for future generations. Of course there were many eulogies, most of them extravagant and flowery after the literary style of the period.

"With saddened hearts . . . beloved of all who personally knew her, the venerable Lady closed her long and well-spent life with the calm resignation which goodness of heart combined with piety only can impart. . . . spirit of benignity and gentleness, united to all the attributes of feminine loveliness . . . All of our own country and thousands in other lands will need no language of Eulogy to inspire a deep and sincere regret . . . touched all hearts by her goodness and won the admiration of all by the charm of dignity and grace."

But no words could have expressed the love and admiration of the country better than the simple statement of its twelfth President, who had known her for only such a short time.

"What an extraordinary, great lady she was!" said Zachary Taylor. "America will never know another like Mrs. Madison."

Selected List of Sources

BOOKS

Aikman, Lonnelle. *We the People: The Story of the United States Capitol.* Washington, D.C.: U.S. Capitol Historical Society, 1966.

America: Great Crises in Our History. Told by Its Makers. A Library of Original Sources. Vol. V. *1812: Before and After, 1803–1820.* Chicago,: Veterans of Foreign Wars, Americanization Department, 1925.

Anthony, Katharine. *Dolly Madison: Her Life and Times.* Garden City, N.Y.: Doubleday & Company, Inc., 1949.

Arnett, Ethel Stephens. *Mrs. James Madison, The Incomparable Dolley.* Greensboro, N.C.: Piedmont Press, 1972.

Barnard, Ella Kent. *Dorothy Payne, Quakeress.* Philadelphia: Ferris and Leach, 1909.

Beeman, Richard R. *Patrick Henry: A Biography.* New York: McGraw-Hill Book Company, 1974.

Bivins, Caroline Holmes. *Study of Dolley Payne Todd Madison Through Bibliographical Sources.* Brevard, N.C.: Privately printed by Blue Ridge Quick Print, 1982.

Boller, Paul F. *Presidential Anecdotes.* New York: Penguin Books, 1981.

Book of Discipline of the Religious Society of Friends. Adopted by the Philadelphia Yearly Meeting. Philadelphia, 1927.

Bradford, Gamaliel. *Wives.* New York and London: Harper and Brothers, 1925.

Brant, Irving. *James Madison.* Vol. I. *The Virginia Revolutionist;* Vol. II. *The Nationalist;* Vol. III. *Father of the Constitution, 1787–1800;* Vol. IV. *Secretary of State, 1800 to 1809;* Vol. V. *The President, 1809–1812;* Vol. VI. *Commander in Chief, 1812–1836.* Indianapolis: The Bobbs-Merrill Company, 1941, 1948, 1950, 1953, 1956, 1961.

Burt, Struthers. *Philadelphia: Holy Experiment.* Garden City, N.Y.: Doubleday, Doran and Company, 1945.

Busey, Samuel C. *City of Washington in the Past.* Washington, D.C.: William Ballantyne and Sons, 1898.

Christian Life, Faith, and Thought in the Society of Friends. London: The Friends Bookshop, 1921.

Clark, Allen C. *Life and Letters of Dolly Madison*. Washington, D.C.: W. F. Roberts Company, 1914.

Colman, Edna M. *Seventy-five Years of White House Gossip*. New York: Doubleday, Page and Co., 1925.

Cutts, James Madison. *Dolly Madison*. A paper read before the Columbia Historical Society, May 2, 1898. Washington, D.C.: Published by the Society, January 1900.

Dean, Elizabeth Lippincott. *Dolly Madison: The Nation's Hostess*. Boston: Lothrop, Lee and Shepard Co., 1928.

De Angeli, Marguerite. *Thee, Hannah*. New York: Doubleday, Doran and Co., 1940.

De Hartog, Jan. *The Peaceable Kingdom*. New York: Atheneum, 1971.

Donovan, Frank. *The Women in Their Lives*. New York: Dodd, Mead and Company, 1966.

Eames, E. Ashley, and Stone, Nancy H. *Case Studies in American History*. Case 4, "The Election of 1800." Case 5, "Mr. Madison, Why the War of 1812?" Cambridge, Mass.: Educators Publishing Service, Inc., 1964.

Fleming, Thomas. *The Man from Monticello: An Intimate Life of Thomas Jefferson*. New York: William Morrow and Co., 1969.

Frost, J. William. *The Quaker Family in Colonial America*. New York: St. Martin's Press, 1973.

Furman, Bess. *White House Profile: A Social History of the White House, Its Occupants and Festivities*. Indianapolis and New York: The Bobbs-Merrill Company, Inc., 1951.

Gerson, Noel B. *The Velvet Glove: A Life of Dolly Madison*. Nashville and New York: Thomas Nelson, Inc., 1975.

Goettel, Elinor. *America's Wars: Why?* Chapter II, "The War of 1812." New York: Julian Messner, 1972.

Goodwin, Maud Wilder. *Dolly Madison*. New York: Charles Scribner's Sons, 1896.

Gordon, Lydia L. *From Lady Washington to Mrs. Cleveland*. Boston: Lee and Shepard, 1889, pp. 87–103.

Hunt, Gaillard. *The Life of James Madison*. New York: Doubleday, Page and Co., 1902.

Hunt-Jones, Conover. *Dolley and the "Great Little Madison"*. Washington, D.C.: American Institute of Architects Foundation, 1977.

Jeffries, Ona Griffin. *In and Out of the White House*. New York: Wilfred Funk, Inc., 1960.

Jennings, Paul. *A Colored Man's Reminiscences of James Madison*. Brooklyn, 1865.

Jensen, Amy La Follette. *The White House and Its Thirty-two Families*. New York: McGraw-Hill Book Company, 1958.

Kane, Harnett T. *The Amazing Mrs. Bonaparte*. Garden City, N.Y.: Doubleday & Company, Inc., 1963.

Ketcham, Ralph. *James Madison: A Biography*. New York: The Macmillan Company, 1971.

Klapthor, Margaret Brown. *The First Ladies*. Washington, D.C.: The National Geographical Society, 1975, 1983.

Koch, Adrienne. *Jefferson and Madison. The Great Collaboration.* New York: Oxford University Press, 1950.

Langford, Laura Carter Holloway. *The Ladies of the White House.* Philadelphia: A. Gorton and Co., 1882.

Martineau, Harriet. *Retrospect of Western Travel.* Vol I. New York: Harper and Brothers, 1838.

Means, Marianne. *The Woman in the White House.* New York: Random House, 1963.

Memoirs and Letters of Dolly Madison, Wife of James Madison, President of the United States. Edited by her grand-niece. Boston and New York: Houghton, Mifflin and Company, 1887.

Miller, John C. *The Federalist Era.* New York: Harper and Row, Harper Torchbooks, 1960.

Moore, Virginia. *The Madisons: A Biography.* New York: McGraw-Hill Book Company, 1979.

Muzzey, David S. and Link, Arthur S. *Our American Republic.* New York: Ginn and Company, 1963.

Muzzey, David Saville. *The United States of America.* Vol. I. *Through the Civil War.* Boston and New York: Ginn and Company, 1922.

Orange County Bicentennial Series. Six pamphlets. Orange, Va., 1975. Copyright by William H. B. Thomas.

Palmer, Kenneth T., and Horan, James F. *Studies in American Politics: Samples of the Federalist Papers by James Madison,* No. 10, No. 39. New York: MSS Information Corporation, 1974.

Parton, James. *Life of Andrew Jackson,* Boston: Field, Osgood, and Co., 1870.

Peterson, Merrill D., editor. *James Madison: A Biography in his Own Words.* New York: Newsweek, 1974. Two vols.

Prindeville, Kathleen. *First Ladies.* New York: The Macmillan Company, 1954.

Smelser, Marshall. *The Democratic Republic, 1801-1815.* The New American Nation Series. New York: Harper & Row, 1968.

Smith, Margaret Bayard. *The First Forty Years of Washington Society.* New York: Frederick Ungar Publishing Co., 1965. First edition, 1906.

Taylor, Tim. *The Book of Presidents.* New York: Arno Press, 1972.

Thruston, Minna. *Dolly Madison.* From Madison College Library, Harrisonburg, Va.

Upton, Harriett Taylor. *Our Early Presidents, Their Wives and Children: Washington to Jackson.* Boston: D. Lothrop Company, 1890.

Van Doren, Carl. *The Great Rehearsal: The Story of the Making and Ratifying of the Constitution of the United States.* New York: The Viking Press, 1948.

Virginia: A Guide to the Old Dominion. Compiled by the workers in the Writers' Program of the Work Projects Administration in the State of Virginia. New York: Oxford University Press, 1940.

Wharton, Anne Hollingsworth. *Social Life in the Early Republic.* New York and London: Benjamin Blom, 1902, 1969.

The White House. Washington, D.C.: The White House Historical Association, 1963.

Whitney, David C. *The American Presidents.* Garden City, N.Y.: Doubleday & Company, Inc., 1968.

Williams, J. Paul. *What Americans Believe and How They Worship.* Chapter IX, "The Quakers—Practicing Mystics." New York: Harper and Brothers, 1952.

Willison, George F. *Patrick Henry and His World.* Garden City, N.Y.: Doubleday & Company, Inc., 1969.

PERIODICALS

Aikman, Lonelle. "The Living White House." *National Geographic,* Vol. 130, November 1966, pp. 593–653.

Brant, Irving. "Timid President, Futile War?" *American Heritage,* October 1959, pp. 46–47.

Briceland, Alan V. "Virginia's Ratification of the Constitution." *News Letter,* University of Virginia, Institute of Government, October 1984.

Butterfield, Roger. "The Camera Comes to the White House." *American Heritage,* August 1964, pp. 33–47.

Campbell, Charles. "A Slave's Memory of Mr. Jefferson." *American Heritage,* October 1959, p. 112.

Cannon, Mark W., editor. "Toward the Bicentennial of the Constitution." National Forum, Fall 1984.

Carson, Gerald. "Hair Today, Gone Tomorrow." *American Heritage,* February 1966, pp. 42–47.

Catton, Bruce. "The Moment of Decision: Jefferson and the Louisiana Purchase." *American Heritage,* August 1964, pp. 49–50.

Commager, Henry Steele. "The Constitution: Is it an Economic Document?" *American Heritage,* December 1958, pp. 59–62, 100–3.

———, "Jefferson and the Book Burners." *American Heritage,* August 1958, pp. 65–68.

Dahl, Curtis. "Mr. Smith's American Acropolis." *American Heritage,* June 1956, pp. 38–43, 104, 105.

Dangerfield, George. "If Only Mr. Madison Had Waited." *American Heritage,* April 1956, pp. 8–10, 92–94.

Dos Passos, John. "The Conspiracy and Trial of Aaron Burr." *American Heritage,* February 1966, pp. 4–9, 69–84.

Eaton, Clement. "Everybody Liked Henry Clay." *American Heritage,* October 1956, pp. 26–29, 108–9.

Farmer, Laurence, M.D. "Moschetoes Were Uncommonly Numerous." *American Heritage,* April 1956, pp. 54–57, 99.

Fast, Howard. "The President's Wife." *The Ladies' Home Journal,* Vol. 56, August 1939, pp. 16–17.

Forester, C. S. "Bloodshed at Dawn." Duel in Jefferson's administration. *American Heritage,* October 1964, pp. 41–45, 73–76.

Halliday, E. M. "Nature's God and the Founding Fathers." *American Heritage,* October 1963. Idea of separation of church and state.

————, "The Man on Horseback: The Hero of New Orleans." *American Heritage,* August 1964, pp. 12–13.

Hazelton, Jean Harvey. "Thomas Jefferson, Gourmet." *American Heritage,* October 1964, pp. 20, 21, 102–5.

Howard, Clifford. "When Dolly Madison Saved the Declaration of Independence." *The Ladies' Home Journal,* Vol. 14, July 1897.

Hunt, Gaillard. "Mrs. Madison's First Drawing Room." *Harper's Monthly,* Vol. 121, June 1910, pp. 141–48.

Jensen, Amy La Follette. "The President's Lady." *American Heritage,* August 1964, pp. 55–60.

Jensen, Oliver. "The Peales." *American Heritage,* April 1955, pp. 40–51, 97–101.

Ketchum, Richard M. "Faces From the Past—XIX." *American Heritage,* February 1966, pp. 24, 25. Old daguerreotype of Dolley.

Livingston, Robert. "The Letter That Bought an Empire." *American Heritage,* April 1955, pp. 26–29.

Lunny, Robert M. "The Great Sea War." *American Heritage,* April 1956.

Minnegerode, Meade. "Dolley Madison, An Informal Biography." *Saturday Evening Post,* Vol. 197, November 29, 1924, pp. 72–74, 76–80.

Nichols, Roy F. "It Happens Every Four Years." *American Heritage,* June 1956, pp. 20–23. Rise of political parties.

Sifton, Paul G. "What a Dread Prospect . . . Dolley Madison's Plague Year." *Pennsylvania Magazine of History,* Vol. 87, April 1963, pp. 182–88.

Thornton, Willis. "The Day They Burned the Capitol." *American Heritage,* December 1954, pp. 49–53.

Wamsley, James S. "At Home with Tom Jefferson." *Reader's Digest,* August 1984, pp. 161–68.

Webster, Donald B., Jr. "The Day Jefferson Got Plastered." *American Heritage,* June 1963, pp. 25–27.

CHRISTIAN HERALD ASSOCIATION AND ITS MINISTRIES

CHRISTIAN HERALD ASSOCIATION, founded in 1878, publishes The Christian Herald Magazine, one of the leading interdenominational religious monthlies in America. Through its wide circulation, it brings inspiring articles and the latest news of religious developments to many families. From the magazine's pages came the initiative for CHRISTIAN HERALD CHILDREN and THE BOWERY MISSION, two individually supported not-for-profit corporations.

CHRISTIAN HERALD CHILDREN, established in 1894, is the name for a unique and dynamic ministry to disadvantaged children, offering hope and opportunities which would not otherwise be available for reasons of poverty and neglect. The goal is to develop each child's potential and to demonstrate Christian compassion and understanding to children in need.

Mont Lawn is a permanent camp located in Bushkill, Pennsylvania. It is the focal point of a ministry which provides a healthful "vacation with a purpose" to children who without it would be confined to the streets of the city. Up to 1000 children between the age of 7 and 11 come to Mont Lawn each year.

Christian Herald Children maintains year-round contact with children by means of a *City Youth Ministry.* Central to its philosophy is the belief that only through sustained relationships and demonstrated concern can individual lives be truly enriched. Special emphasis is on individual guidance, spiritual and family counseling and tutoring. This follow-up ministry to inner-city children culminates for many in financial assistance toward higher education and career counseling.

THE BOWERY MISSION, located at 227 Bowery, New York City, has since 1879 been reaching out to the lost men on the Bowery, offering them what could be their last chance to rebuild their lives. Every man is fed, clothed and ministered to. Countless numbers have entered the 90-day residential rehabilitation program at the Bowery Mission. A concentrated ministry of counseling, medical care, nutrition therapy, Bible study and Gospel services awakens a man to spiritual renewal within himself.

These ministries are supported solely by the voluntary contributions of individuals and by legacies and bequests. Contributions are tax deductible. Checks should be made out either to CHRISTIAN HERALD CHILDREN or to THE BOWERY MISSION.

Administrative Office: 40 Overlook Drive, Chappaqua, New York 10514
Telephone: (914) 769-9000